Juvenile Justice Systems
International Perspectives

edited by

John A. Winterdyk

Canadian Scholars' Press   Toronto   1997

Juvenile Justice Systems: International Perspectives
Edited by John A. Winterdyk

First published in 1997 by
Canadian Scholars' Press Inc.
180 Bloor Street West, Ste. 402
Toronto, Ontario
M5S 2V6

Visit our Web site at **http://www.interlog.com/~cspi/cspi.html**

Canadian Cataloguing in Publication Data

Main entry under title:
Juvenile justice systems: international perspectives

Includes bibliographical references and index.
ISBN 1-55130-122-9

1. Juvenile delinquency. 2. Juvenile justice, Administration of.
I. Winterdyk, John.

HV9061.J89 1997   364.36   C97-930280-3

Page layout and cover design by Brad Horning

Table of Contents

Acknowledgments

Acknowledgments

I would like to first acknowledge my parents who in their philanthropic lifestyle exposed me to many different cultures at a very early age. I quickly developed a love for travel and a curiosity for learning about other cultures, languages, and ways of life. I have since carried this passion over into my academic career. Since joining Mount Royal College in 1988 (the year Calgary hosted the Winter Olympics), I have conducted accredited criminology study tours to various European countries on a biannual basis. In response to rising costs and supportive feedback from students and colleagues, the inception of this book was spawned.

Not feeling knowledgeable enough to produce a comparative textbook on my own and wanting a global perspective, I sought out leading experts from ten other countries. To all the contributors I am indebted for their support and commitment to this project. In particular, I am indebted to Drs. Hans-Jörg Albrecht, Lynn Atkinson, and Harold Traver who contributed short descriptions on their respective countries for my edited textbook entitled *Young Offenders in Canada* (Toronto: Harcourt-Brace, 1996). Collectively, they provided names and encouraged me to follow through with the idea of this book. All the contributors, in-spite of language barriers, distances, and their other commitments, were all exceptionally accommodating. To work in such company and under such a supportive environment is both heart-warming and exciting. And while a number of colleagues encouraged me to pursue the compilation of such a project, publishers were considerably more cautious in wanting to embrace the project. I am deeply grateful to Canadian Scholars' Press for believing in this project and supporting me through its gestation period. In particular, I would like to acknowledge Brad Lambertus, the Managing Editor of Canadian Scholars' Press, for his support, dedication, and diligence in bringing this project to print form.

To my wife Karen, I am blessed by her patience and enduring optimism in me. When things looked grim, as I looked for contributors, surfed the Net for the most current information, and a publisher, she reminded me that I should not lose sight of my conviction and commitment to the concept.

Thank you to my fellow colleagues, especially Sandie McBrien who read several chapters for me, and students who gave of their time and patience and feedback. To Roland LaHaye, our chairperson, who gave me breathing room to work on this project and to Brenda Laing without whom our department would not function as well as it does. In addition, she found time to do those 'little extra things' to ensure I could complete this book. A special thank you is extended to Kim Visser, the college's graphic artist who provided invaluable assistance in coordinating and compiling the chapters into manuscript form. Finally I would like to acknowledge the internet Kootnet (www.libby.org) server located in Libby, Montana. Their service enabled me to stay in touch with the contributors over the summer months while working on this project in this beautiful part of 'Big Sky' country.

Introduction

A national crisis is seldom merely national anymore.
Oyen, 1992:2.

At the Eighth (United Nations, 1990) and Ninth United Nations National Congress on the Prevention of Crime and the Treatment of Offenders (*CJ International*, 1995), crime and managing criminal justice were recognized as a growing problem worldwide. Be it drugs, violence, hate crime, gang activity, organized crime, or youth crime; there are few places in the world that are not currently dealing with one or more of these issues.

At the Ninth United Nations Congress it was also reported that youth crime is increasing around the world—especially in countries in transition (see Table 1). It was also noted that the average age of onset was dropping. The fact "that by the year 2000 more than 50 percent of the world population will be under the age of 15," serves to further "highlight the seriousness of the problem of juvenile delinquency and youth crime" (United Nations, 1995a:17).

We live in a world of great social unrest and instability, and such conditions can create opportunity for crime and delinquency to thrive. Thus a very practical issue that most countries must face is how to manage youth crime.

Rational for Comparative Studies

There is no reason to believe there exists an easy and straightforward entry in comparative research. Oyen, 1992:1.

While the vast majority of criminological and sociological literature on crime has been based on a unilinear model—"focussed within countries and without pretense to being general"—this has begun to change in recent years (Teune, 1992:35). The interest in comparative research would seem closely aligned to macro global changes as well as advances in technology. For example, as a result of the Great Depression many researchers turned their focus inwards, while in the aftermath of World War II it became necessary to do comparative research as a necessary part of decentralizing world order (see Nelken, 1994; Teune, 1992). The process, as Marsh (1967) observed, emerged rather slowly, especially with respect to the phenomena of crime. But in recent years there has been a dramatic shift.

The United Nations (UN) at the Seventh UN Congress on the Prevention of Crime and Treatment of Offenders, held in Beijing, China from 14 to 18 May 1984, endorsed the "Standard Minimum Rules for the Administration of Juvenile Justice." These standards are commonly referred to as "the Beijing Rules" (see Box 1).

Box 1: Highlights of "the Beijing Rules" (1984)

<u>Fundamental perspectives</u>: 1.1 To further the well-being of the juvenile and her or his family; 1.2 To develop conditions that will ensure a meaningful life in the community for the juvenile; 1.4 Administration of juvenile justice should represent an integral part of the natural development process of each country.

<u>Age of responsibility</u>: 4.1 The beginning age shall not be fixed at too low an age level, bearing in mind the facts of emotional, mental, and intellectual maturity.

<u>Aim of juvenile justice</u>: 5.1 Emphasize the well-being of the juvenile and shall ensure that any reaction to juvenile offenders shall always be in proportion to the circumstance of both the offender and the offence.

<u>Scope of discretion</u>: 6.2 Efforts made to ensure sufficient accountability at all stages and levels in the exercise of any such discretion.

<u>Protection of privacy</u>: 8.1 Right to privacy shall be respected at all stages in order to avoid harm being caused by undue publicity or by the process of labelling. 8.2 No information that may lead to the identification of a juvenile offender shall be published (UN, 1986).

As can be seen in Table 1 and Figure 1, the level of attention different systems and societies pay to the 'age of responsibility' reflects major practical and theoretical differences between systems and countries. Also in Figure 1, it can been seen how countries vary in their definition of what legally constitutes a *juvenile* or *young offender*. The variations reflect different cultural, historical, political, and social differences than can make comparisons challenging.

Not only are there variations between countries but even within counties. In Canada, for example, the Young Offenders Act defines the minimum age of responsibility as twelve and the upper limit at eighteen (see Box 2). However, because the provinces are responsible for administering the act, there is considerable variation between the provinces in their sentencing and transfer to adult court practices and their respective interpretation of the act (see Ch. 6).

Box 2: Justice in Singapore

Although Singapore's judicial system is modeled after the British judicial system, Islamic law sets the age of accountability at PUBERTY, not a fixed year. It recognizes differences in children and their differing maturation periods. Following a **welfare** type model of juvenile justice, male offenders are sent to approval schools while female delinquents are sent to approval homes. In spite of its harsh penal code, juvenile crime increased 30 percent from 1988 to 1993 (Wiechman, 1994).

By contrast, countries like Norway and Sweden (Box 3) have no special act regarding juvenile delinquency. However, the General Civil Penal Code (section 46) of Norway states that criminal responsibility begins at age fifteen and section 55 makes special provisions for the sentencing of young offenders (Askim and Berg, 1996). Their neighbour to the east, Sweden, has no direct equivalent in their language for the English concept of "juvenile delinquent." Rather, they speak of juvenile criminality that does not include status offences (i.e., acts declared by statute to be an offence but only when committed by a juvenile). In Sweden criminal responsibility begins at age fifteen and the upper limit is twenty (Sarnecki, 1996). However, like Norway, Sweden has special provisions for young criminals between the ages of fifteen and seventeen.

Box 3: Youth Justice in Sweden

In Sweden the responsibility for handling young people is shared by the social authorities and the judicial system. In the Swedish language there is no equivalent concept for "juvenile delinquent." Instead they speak of juvenile criminality. This system does not formally recognize status offenses. Such behaviors are dealt with through social welfare measures. All juvenile crime falls under the Swedish Penal Code of 1990. By law juveniles receive special consideration when found committing a crime. Youth under the age of 15 are handled by social authorities rather than the police. Criminal responsibility begins at age 15. Over 80 percent of all juvenile crimes are not prosecuted but dealt with informally. Nearly 50 percent are resolved through the use of day fines (approx. $30 CDN) without a trial procedure being used. Fewer than 10 percent of delinquent youth are placed on probation. The Swedish model is more treatment oriented than most Western countries. But, in recent years the model has been subjected to substantial criticism as youth crime in Sweden has been on the increase and there does not appear to be any empirical support for the treatment oriented programs (Sarnecki, 1996).

Another qualm to conducting comparisons stems from the fact that just because most countries have legally prescribed lower and upper limits of criminal responsibility for youth, there are, in many instances, situational factors that enable exceptions to the law. For example, Reichel (1994) found that in China and Romania while sixteen is the preferred lower limit it can be dropped to fourteen if the offence is very serious (China) or if the youth is capable of understanding right from wrong (Romania). In a number of the contributions (e.g., Canada and the United States) we will see that the limits of criminal responsibility may also involve transfer conditions to the adult system.

Aside from these categorical differences, six different juvenile justice models can be defined to describe the handling of juveniles. The models are based on research by Corrado (1992) and Reichel (1994). The models are summarized in Figure 1 and are used as the primary criteria for the order in which the countries are presented. The variation in these models can serve as visible indicators of how different nations view the same phenomena (i.e., juvenile delinquency) and form different perspectives. Yet, as Reichel (1994) notes, the models are not mutually exclusive. In fact, the reader will find that the distinctions between certain countries, despite their allocation in the book, are not as dissimilar as might be implied. Furthermore, because such countries as Australia and Canada allow a degree of state or provincial autonomy in administering their respective juvenile justice systems, one can identify different justice models within individual countries. This had been especially evident in Australia (see Ch. 2).

At the time this book was being compiled there were several textbooks on comparative criminal justice (see suggested readings). While they all take a different approach to examining criminal justice systems, a number of common themes run throughout the books. First, they each suggest that examining crime trends and reactions to crime may provide insight into how one can better address the crime situation in one's own country. Comparative information, after all, provides a practical window of opportunity to gain new insights and adopt, adapt, and develop new responses. For example, why is it that juvenile crime rates not only differ between northern and southern European countries but the importance of socio-demographic factors, in some instances, also vary between these countries (see Junger-Tas, 1994).

A second theme is that cross-cultural comparisons allow for the comparison of (current) criminological theories and/or philosophies and criminal justice practices. For example, researchers at the Research Centre for Criminology and Youth Criminology of the State University of Groningen (Holland) embrace a sociological model to explain and respond to youth crime.

Figure 1

Continuum of Juvenile Justice Models

	Participatory	Welfare	Corporatism	Modified Justice	Justice	Crime Control
General Features	Informality	Informality	Administrative decision-making	Due Process informality	Due Process	Due process/discretion
	Minimal formal intervention	Generic referrals	Offending	Criminal offences	Criminal offences	Offending/status offences
	Resocialization	Individualized sentencing	Diversion from court/custody programs	Bifurcation: soft offenders diverted, hard offenders punished	Least restrictive alternative	Punishment
		Indeterminate sentencing			Determinate sentences	Determinate sentences
Key Personnel	Educators	Childcare experts	Juvenile justice specialists	Lawyers/childcare experts	Lawyers	Lawyers/criminal justice actors
Key Agency	Community agencies/citizens	Social work	Intragency structure	Law/social work	Law	Law
	School and community agencies					
Tasks	Help and education team	Diagnosis	Systems intervention	Diagnosis/punishment	Punishment	Incarceration/punishment

	Participatory	Welfare	Corporatism	Modified Justice	Justice	Crime Control
Understanding of Client Behaviour	People basically good	Pathology/ environmentally determined	Unsocialized	Diminished individual responsibility	Individual responsibility	Responsibility/ accountability
Purpose of Intervention	Re-education	Provide treatment (*Parens Patriae*)	Retrain	Sanction behaviour/ provice treatment	Sanction behaviour	Protection of society/retribution deterrence
Objectives	Intervention . . . . . through education	Respond to individual needs/ rehabilitation	Implementation of Policy	Respect individual rights/respond to "special" needs	Respect individual rights/punish	Order maintenance
Countries	Japan	Australia The Netherlands	England/Wales Hong Kong	Canada	Italy The Netherlands Russia	USA Hungary

Source: adapted from Corrado, 1992; Reichel, 1994.

The primary model being tested entails four major concepts: delinquency, feeling of societal injustice, personal bonds, and societal position as an explanatory model of youth crime (see Dijksterhuis and Nijboer, 1986; Ferwerda, 1992; Ploeg, 1991). Ferwerda (1992:236) notes a proactive "interdisciplinary approach involving school, police, justice authorities, parents and assistance organizations" for preventing delinquency is usually advocated. By contrast, other parts of Europe, such as France, prefer a less scientific approach to access the guilt or innocence of a youth in lieu of a philosophical examination of youth crime. French judges are well informed about their cases and effectively apply their inquisitorial model to constructively assess the circumstances surrounding the youths' behaviour (Hackler, 1994).

For policy-makers the choice between empirical information or philosophical and even moralistic principles can result in a delicate balance between morality and social science. And until the emergence of comparative studies, ethnocentric practices limited juvenile justice (and criminal justice, in general) from breaking traditional modes of operations. Such limited perspectives can, and have, left their mark on society. For example, countries like Canada and the United States, which are provincial in their approach, continue to be plagued by increasing rates in youth crime. Their "get-tough" mentality has been both unimaginative and counter-productive in addressing crime (see chs. 6 and 11). Fortunately, however, some politicians and criminologists in Canada, the United States, and elsewhere around the world have begun to break ground in this arena.

Increasingly, provincial thinking has given way to an openness toward cooperation of alternative measures and testing different ideas under different conditions. Several years ago in Calgary, for example, the police used the Los Angeles Police Department's (LAPD) model and definition of youth gangs to better address a growing youth gang problem in the city. In the early 1990s Calgary's CRASH (Community Response Against Street Hoodlums) program for youth gangs was based on a LAPD program for dealing with gangs. (The program was terminated in 1993 due to a organizational concerns and was not replaced in spite of the continued presence of youth gangs). Australia has recently adapted the New Zealand model of family group conference mechanism as well as elements of the 'boot camp' programs currently popular in the United States (see Ch. 11).

As the world gets smaller, euphemistically, it becomes more imperative that we seek universal laws. Marvin Wolfgang (1991:v) illustrates this need in the foreword to a German book on crime and crime control:

the gap, between what empirical criminology in Germany has produced and what English and American scholars know, has been unfortunate.... This collection is probably the most sophisticated, theoretically and empirically, that has appeared during the past quarter century in Germany.

The idea that different social and political views can be brought into alignment has been expressed by the United Nations Crime Prevention and Justice Branch in Vienna, Austria. Under Rule 5.1 of the Standard Minimum Rules for the Administration of Juvenile Justice (see Box 1), the UN advocates the use of the **welfare model**. The UN takes the position that the well-being of young offenders should always come first. They cite South and Western Australia (see Ch. 2) and Scotland (see Box 4) as contemporary examples of the welfare model in action.

Box 4: Juvenile Justice in Scotland

Children under sixteen who break the law are reported by the police to the Reporter to the Children's Panel. The Reporter who is usually well versed in law has a particular interest in the welfare of young people. For trivial and ordinary offences, young offenders are usually referred to the social work department for guidance by a social worker. Similarly, for cases where a child shows a likelihood of becoming delinquent or needs help the youth is, again, likely to be referred to a social work. Only for serious offences such as murder or assault are juvenile offenders directed through the legal system. If the Reporter recommends some type of care, the offender and his/her guardian must attend a Hearing of the Children's Panel. The panel is made up of three volunteer citizens who are trained to decide what may be in the best interest of the child (The Scottish Police, n.d.).

A third theme found in comparative criminal justice text books, as noted earlier, comparisons allow us to understand and appreciate the significance of different cultural, economic, moral, political, and social values. India, for example, which did not pass its first national Children's Act until 1986, set uniform age limits for criminal culpability at sixteen for boys and eighteen for girls (Hartjen, 1991). Hartjen notes that while criminal conduct among Indian youth is not a serious national problem the trend is changing as Western influences invade the Indian economy and culture (see Box 5). Similarly, since Romania's accelerated transition to a free market economy, the country has begun to experience an increasing problem with juvenile delinquents: the increase in youth crime has been attributed to the "removal of old structures, without rapid replacement by newer, more efficient structures" (Nistoreanu, 1992:4). Ogburn (1952) refers to this concept as *culture lag*. He argued that crime increases because the non-material culture does not evolve as rapidly as the material culture. On the other hand, in response to their rapid economic growth, the Japanese government introduced major crime prevention measures for an escalating delinquency problem during the early 1960s to counterbalance the temporary material and non-material gap. One of the unexpected benefits was a drop in the number of rape offences (Yokoyama, 1995; also see Ch. 1).

Finally, in New Zealand married (or formally married) persons aged fourteen and over but under seventeen are subject to the formal process of trial and conviction for all offences. In New Zealand it would appear that if you feel you are old enough to be married then you are old enough to bear full responsibility (Mclellan, 1996). This is a concept that does appear to be widely embraced (see Box 6).

By examining countries which use different juvenile justice models as well as countries which are undergoing major social or political change, we move into a position of being better able to understand how and why different models may work in some countries and not others. As well, such comparisons may help to illuminate what kind of factors appear universal in their effect.

Box 5: Juvenile Justice in India

In 1980 the Juvenile Justice Act (JJA) was uniformly adopted by all but two states—Jammu and Kashmir. These states still use the Jammu & Kashmir Children Act of 1970. The JJA classifies children into two typologies—delinquent and neglected and has variable ages of responsibility (see Figure 1). Delinquents are dealt with by stipendiary magistrates of the Juvenile Court while neglected youth come under the care of the juvenile welfare board. The overall delinquency rate has dropped from 3.1/1,000 in 1988 to 1.1/1,000 in 1993. The delinquency rate may be somewhat misleading as the chances of a case coming to trial is very low and the number of cases awaiting trial is very lengthy. This is further compounded by the fact that recidivism rates continue to climb. Youth between the ages of 1-16 comprise 80 percent of all delinquent cases. The majority of offences are related to theft and burglary. The primary attributes of juvenile offender is low education and poor economic background. The juvenile justice system in India can be described as loosely representing a combination of the Welfare and Justice model (Kumari, 1996).

Hackler (1994:343), for example, argues that "Canada, perhaps less than the United States, has developed an inferior criminal justice system." He suggests that this is largely due to the self-righteous attitudes that many

Box 6: Juvenile Justice in New Zealand

In 1989 New Zealand introduced new legislation for the handling of juveniles: The Children, Young Persons and Their Families Act. Under the Act, criminal responsibility begins at age 10 but under section 22 of the Crimes Act (1961), youth between ages 10-14 cannot be convicted unless 'mens rea' has been proven. However, under the 1989 Act, youth between the ages 10-13 can be prosecuted for murder and manslaughter. Initial preliminary hearings take place in Youth Court, but should the case go to trial then the process involves a jury trial in the High Court. Youths aged 14-17 can be charged with criminal offences—summary (less serious) are handled in Youth Court. The New Zealand model can best be described as a **Welfare Model** (Saxon, 1996). As in Australia, Canada, and the United States the indigenous people of New Zealand, the Maori, are over-represented in the criminal justice system and suffer from many of the same ailments—socially oppressed, high-unemployment, and limited access to quality education. A recent admission of injustice and a 133 year old land claim settlement may bear promise for the Maori (Louisan, 1996).

countries have about their legal systems. Hackler (1994) also point out that, unlike France, Canadian youth court judges have no mandatory specialized training to serve as youth court judges; that the system is out of touch with societal needs, and that Canada's "get tough on young criminals" policy not only lacks imagination but serves to avoid "facing issues that might make a difference" (p. 346). And while it may be that decision-makers and legislatures try to make informed decisions, it seems apparent that such perceptions can be both limiting and naive. Hackler refers to the differences between the Swiss legal model and the common-law-based model of England to illustrate the strengths and weaknesses of each. In Switzerland "the guilty were more likely to be convicted and the innocent never brought to trial" while the slower, drawn-out process in common-law in countries like England and Canada "favoured guilty persons with resources" (p.344).

A fourth theme is that cross-cultural comparisons put different crime phenomena and societal reactions into perspective (see Box 7). For example, while North Americans are preoccupied with punishing young offenders, Europeans and several other countries covered in this book are more open to a wide variety of alternatives (see Figure 1). Boers and Sesser (1991), for example, found that Germans see restitution as a more constructive form of conflict resolution than fines or imprisonment. An understanding of their respective social, cultural, and political history helps to put trends and practices into perspective. In Germany the deterrence principle had been somewhat suspect given the negative experiences during the Nazi regime. However, Schumann and Kaulitzki (1991:18) argue that "positive" general deterrence

---

Box 7: Cuba: Children with Conduct Problems

According to a UNICEF report (n.d.), Cuba's experience with juvenile offenders is more evolved than most Latin American and Caribbean countries. Cuba emphasises education as a preventative measure. From 1953 to 1988, the percent of youth between 6 and 14 years of age who were enrolled at school rose from 55.6% to 98.5%. Prior to the Cuban revolution in 1959 problem youth received minimal treatment. Instead, many were used as a cheap labour source. The Castro regime did away with corporal punishment and inhumane treatment of youth and replaced it with resocialization programs through special school and social integration programs. The legal principles were formally drawn up in Decree 64, dated September 30, 1982.

The decree is directed to youth "with conduct problems" from ages 6 through 16. The causes of their anti-social behavior is seen to be muti-faceted and multi variable in nature with an emphasis on home life, living conditions, and mental capacity (p. 60). Anti-social youth are categorized into one of three classification based on the gravity of their problem and conduct. In addition to re-education through schooling, treatment also involves family programs and social and other popular organizations. The UNICEF report sites that the problem of anti-social youth is very low with only 0.4% of youth between ages 6-16 being so classified. Petty theft and robbery are the most prevalent crimes, although blackmarketering is also a problem. Conceptual Decree 64 could be described as promoting a **welfare model** of juvenile justice, however given limited resources and qualified staff, its implementation and actualization is an area of concern.

(e.g., perceived certainty of being caught) with juveniles has gained acceptance as a leading principle to legitimize penal law (see Ch. 10 for further discussion).

Understanding social and political differences and history may also help to identify means by which to initiate constructive change (see, for example, Yokoyama's excellent article on prostitution in Japan, 1995 and Ch. 1). Fortunately, thanks in large part to some of the macro global changes and better methodologies, there is a growing acceptance of comparative research. It is an acceptance that would seem long overdue.

Gaining Popularity

The growing awareness of the importance of comparative criminal justice studies is further supported by the growing number of schools which offer courses on comparative criminal justice. Today several universities offer comparative criminology/criminal justice courses and international comparative excursions for undergraduate and graduate students. The OICJ (Office of International Criminal Justice), located in Chicago, Illinois, has an extensive international program and it produces three publications in the area of international criminal justice. The Max Plank Institute in Freiburg, Germany, specializes in foreign and international penal law. There are a number of similar institutes around the world. I have simply identified two with which I am quite familiar. Finally, Freda Adler (1996), in her 1995 presidential address to the American Society of Criminology, stressed the importance of comparative criminology and the need to develop a macro level model of the relationship between social change and crime.

Since the early 1980s we have also witnessed a growing number of books (see suggested readings), articles, and international conferences. The interest and ease of doing comparative research has been further facilitated by the advances in electronic data processing and telecommunications technologies. Speaking at the Ninth UN Congress on Crime, Coldren (1995:7) noted that the "possibilities for international co-operation and technical assistance have never been more obtainable." Unfortunately one area that has received comparatively little attention in this regard has been juvenile justice and juvenile delinquency. A number of years ago, however, Malcolm Klein (1984) compiled such a reader after participating in an international symposium on delinquency at the University of Wuppertal in Germany (see suggested readings). Since then, however, there has been a dearth of similar collections. One recent exception is the comprehensive European self-report study on youth crime (Junger-Tas, Terlouw, and Klein (Eds.) (1994)). This project involved an international self-report survey on youth crime in thirteen different countries—mostly European. Since the study is ongoing, the authors cautiously offer only some key findings. Several of these include (p. 379):

- A great similarity in rates of delinquency behaviour in the countries that participated.
- The use of drugs is more prevalent in the United States and Western Europe than Southern Europe.
- The lower the educational level, the more violent behaviour is reported.
- Parental supervision appears to be a strong predictor of delinquent behaviour.
- 'Ever' prevalence rates are generally quite high, which may mean that some delinquent behaviour forms part of the growing-up process of Western children.

Therefore, it seems timely that another reader be prepared which can offer a cross-sectional view of juvenile justice from around the world.

A Truly International Phenomena
Delinquency, or youth crime, is perhaps of greater concern in the West than elsewhere (Reichel, 1994). But, as reflected in Table 1, few societies appear to

have escaped this growing phenomenon. As we will see, the rates and patterns of delinquency can vary dramatically from one country to another.

By comparing procedural and statistical similarities and differences between the countries and juvenile justice models, readers will hopefully be able to draw some conclusions which will further help them to understand the strengths and weaknesses of each system as well as identify possible responses which may not be practised in their respective countries. For example, as mentioned earlier, in Canada none of the legal actors in the juvenile justice system receive any special training in the handling of young offenders. While this fact may reflect the nature of juvenile justice administration it is not in keeping with the Beijing Rule 1.2 (see Box 1).

Other questions or concerns which might be explored include: How do different countries view the causes of delinquency? How do they respond to youth crime? What are their respective concerns? What measures are being undertaken or being considered? What kind of current or future actions are being taken to ensure that the Beijing Rules, designed to protect youth from exploitation, are being addressed? Can these issues be realistically compared?

Problems with Comparative Studies

Until recently, a number of researchers believed that comparative studies have generally resulted in fragmented knowledge since the comparisons tend to use "temporal and/or spatial logic" (Teune, 1992:38). Newman (1977) identified several other key obstacles, some of which include:

- **Language barriers**: An obvious limitation if you do not have access to an interpreter.
- **Definition barriers**: Known offenses vary from country to country. For example, in the United States the *Uniform Crime Reports* provide compilations of known offenses for eight categories of crime, called Index offenses (Part 1). Yet, in England and Wales *Criminal Statistics* include 64 known crimes which are further divided into 8 major categories. As for Canada, *Crime and Traffic Enforcement Statistics* lists 25 known offenses which are divided into several subcategories. The United Nations reports that some countries do not even have formal legislation for juvenile offenders.
- **Reporting and recording practices**: In Canada, for example, official reporting agencies utilize different reporting and recording practices

than are employed in different countries. This is sometimes due to political agendas, or financial and/or manpower available. In Greece, officials keep separate statistics on convicted, recorded, and suspected youth crimes. In Oman there is only data available on male juvenile offenders (UN, 1990).

• **Administrative variations**: There are numerous factors such as law enforcement, the judicial system, corrections or public support which can effect how justice is administered. This will become evident as you read the different contributions.

Yet, in spite of these apparent hurdles, the academic and technological study of criminology has become increasingly international and comparative. In recognizing the hurdles, non-equivalent concepts, and array of other possible unknown intervening factors, it is possible, if not necessary, to engage in objective analysis that may provide new insights into a complex problem. This book, through its varied collection of contributions and standardized format (see below), represents an effort to allow the reader to engage in comparative analysis.

Critical Lessons

When there is crime in society there is no justice. (Plato)

In recognizing the limitations identified above, our technological and theoretical advances can now enable us to engage in comparative research. As already noted, the doors have been opened and the growing volume of literature in the area would suggest that the movement is gaining credibility and is indeed necessary (see Beirne and Hill (1991) for a comprehensive annotated bibliography on comparative criminology). In fact, one of the major "requests" made of the Commission on Crime Prevention and Criminal Justice at the Ninth UN Congress (UN, 1995b) was that it not only acknowledge resolutions being explored by member states but also engage in "comparing national crime and criminal justice databases." This process has been facilitated as the methodological techniques for conducting comparative research have evolved from basic description (see Nelken, 1994; Stewart, 1982) to functional analysis which transcends national boundaries (see Hackler, 1984; 1994). This volume present a conceptual framework for a constructive functional comparative analysis.

Rather than attempt to impose a strict set of criteria to be covered, each author was asked to provide an overview of their juvenile justice system with the following key points in mind:

- Social and legal definition of delinquency.
- Nature and status of delinquency.
- Identify and describe the model of juvenile justice, as presented (see Figure 1), which best describes the country's administrative policies.
- Role of law enforcement, juvenile courts, corrections, and the broader community in administering juvenile justice.
- General philosophy and practice of juvenile justice.
- Current theoretical 'bias' used to explain and justify responding to young offenders.
- Current issues, legally and socially, confronting young offenders.

The format will enable the reader to accomplish several tasks. First, countries can be examined on an individual basis. Second, two or more countries can be compared based on a variety of criteria ranging from descriptive information to comparing juvenile justice models. And thirdly, a transnational approach can be adopted in which all countries are examined in light of the larger international phenomena of delinquency. And as Kohn (1989) has noted, each approach may produce different practical and theoretical outcomes.

Since this book is intended to serve a wide international audience, the contributors were asked not to make any direct comparisons to any specific country(ies) other than those they might feel comfortable discussing. In this way the reader is free to compare and contrast as they deem relevant. Any direct reference to other chapters in this collection have been made by the editor. Possible considerations might involve using the major factors listed in Figure 1 to formulate comparisons, or one can compare countries based on their different juvenile justice models, whether their laws are based on civil or common law principles, or against the Standard Minimum Rules for the Administration of Juvenile Justice as defined by the United Nations (see Box 1). Finally, readers of countries not profiled in this book can even examine and compare specific issues that may be unique to their country.

In an attempt to facilitate comparisons the countries were divided according to their general model of juvenile justice (see Table 1). However, as noted earlier, the classifications in some instances may appear arbitrary as new legislation or current practices do not necessarily enable strict classification.

Limitations of this Book

While I attempted to solicit a respectable list of international contributors, it is apparent that there is no detailed representation from Africa or South America. Similarly, Asian and Middle Eastern representation is limited. This void is in-part due to the difficulty in locating contributors in these areas as well as the fact that many of their juvenile justice systems are not be seen to be very progressive and/or the information is quite limited. I did however attempt, through contacting their Canadian embassies/high commissions, to contact the relevant juvenile justice administrative departments. An eclectic and incomplete summary is presented in Table 1.

Since the intent of this book was to offer a cross-section of original contributions from countries whose juvenile justice systems represent one of the six models identified (see Figure 1), it is considered less critical to have equal global representation. However, as can be seen from the countries represented, there is a strong international flavour, and Table 1 along with the various box inserts provide additional international coverage. Finally, in a reader of this nature, one has to establish parameters which limit the extent to which ambitious goals can be realistically actualized. There is a limit to which anyone can assimilate such a diverse range of coverage and parameters and remain within their publisher's guidelines.

Organization and Strengths of this Book

As noted above, there are a variety of ways in which this book could have been produced. In developing the concept I felt that rather than attempt to offer a one-sided interpretation, or solicit North American experts who would likely be more comfortable writing in English, I sought to solicit original contributions from contributors who are recognized experts on the subject in their respective country. The list was compiled in two ways. Most of the contributors were solicited on others' recommendations while several of the contributors were identified after reading some of their published works. The chapters are divided into six parts. Each part includes a contribution(s) from a country which matches (to a varying extent) one of the six juvenile justice models described in Figure 1.

Any significant grammatical difficulties, I have tried to correct without detracting from their style of writing or their perspective. In inviting each contributor to submit an original article I only asked that they each address, as best as possible, the list of common subject areas identified above. Hence, each chapter is somewhat similar in its layout and format. And rather than having to deal with possible limited contextual comparative interpretations, the reader can utilize their own criteria in conducting comparative analysis. In this way it is hoped that the book will have a wider international appeal. Again, by not drawing direct comparisons to any one country or any one model of juvenile justice, it is hoped that the book will generate more discussion than answer questions. The reader (and instructor) is encouraged to use the material to draw comparisons as best suits your respective interests. To this end I hope that the contributions are both general enough to gain a good overview and specific enough to allow for a deeper level of analysis where appropriate. Naturally, any limitations in this regard are the sole fault of the editor as I defined the chapter format and pedagogy for the contributors.

Finally, should you have any comments or suggestions for a future edition, I would appreciate hearing from you. I can be reached in a number of ways:

John Winterdyk
Department of Criminology
Mount Royal College
Calgary, AB., CANADA T3E—6K6
Tel.: (403) 240-6992
Fax: (403) 240-6201
E-mail: jwinterdyk@mtroyal.ab.ca

In the meantime, thank you for selecting this book and I hope you find it as informative and useful to read as I found it interesting and challenging to produce.

Table 1

Juvenile Delinquency: Country Profiles*

Country	Minimum[1]— Maximum Age	Conditions/Justice Model[2]
Egypt	? -18...	Juvenile Law No. 31 (1974). Youth are segregated by age: 12 & under, 12-15, & 15-18. Under 15 required to attend school & over receive vocational skills. Judge aided in deliberation by 2 (appointed) experts—one must be female. /**Corporatism**
Singapore	?-12...	Islamic law set the minimum age of criminal responsibility at puberty. **Welfare-Justice** model (see Box 2)
Cuba	6-16...	The Castro regime in 1959 introduced a progressive **Welfare** based model for "children with conduct problems." (see Box 7)
United States	7-15+..	The upper limit can range up to Age 20 in some States; for most it is 17/**Crime Control** (see Ch. 10)
India	7-16...	for boys and 18 for girls./**Welfare-Justice** (see Box 5)
Cayman Islands	8-17...	8-14 classified as young persons, 14-17 classified as juveniles/**Welfare**
Philippines	9-15...	youth offenders, 15-18 suspended sentences. 18-20 criminally responsible but entitled to leniency/**Welfare-Justice Model**
Australia	10-16/17..	two jurisdictions have lower minimum age/**Welfare** (see Ch. 2)
Canada	12-18...	/**Modified justice** (see Ch. 6)
England	12-18...	/**Corporatist** (see Ch. 4)
The Netherlands	12-18...	/**Modified Justice** (see Ch. 3)
France	13-18...	Problem youth are addressed under the Ordinance No. 45-174 of Feb. 2, 1945. Modified 1958 and 1970. Specially trained 'children's judges/magistrates and social services for educational help used. Compared to most western European countries rate of increase among the lowest (2% from 1992 thru 1993./**Welfare** (social defense system) Lorenz, (1996).

Israel	13-16...	for boys and 18 for girls. In 1977 boys max. age also raised to 18. Juvenile Offenders Section(JSO), 1959. The ethical code of JSO personnel goes beyond the limits established by the Youth Act stressing protection./**Corporatist**
Poland	13-17...	responsibility based on mental and moral ability. 16-17 yr. olds' can be held criminally responsible/**Justice**
New Zealand	14-17...	Criminal responsibility begins at age ten but unless 'mens rea' can be proven, till age 14 they are not convicted. Exception to the rule is murder or manslaughter/**Welfare** (seeBox 6)
Germany	14-17...	18-20 may be transferred to juvenile Court/**Justice** (see Ch. 9)
Hungary	14-18...	no separate juvenile legislation/**Crime control** (see Ch. 11)
China	14-25...	partially responsible officially till 18. Law requires limited punishment. Between 1977 and 1991 steady increase and proportionate amount are young offenders./**Participatory**
Italy	14-18...	/**Legalistic** (see Ch. 7)
Japan	14-20...	/**Participatory** (see Ch. 1)
Norway	14-18...	In 1990 the minimum age was raised to 15. 18 yr. olds are the most frequently represented, recidivism rate continue to climb—41% among young offenders/**Welfare-Modified Justice**
Russia	14-18...	/**Justice Model** (see Ch. 8)
Austria	14-19...	Juvenile Justice Act 1988, amended 1993/**Modified Justice Model**. Between 1981-91 youth rates dropped—1799 to 763.
Sweden	15-20...	Known as "Juvenile criminals". Youth between ages 15-17 given special consideration./**Justice Model**(see Box 3)
Finland	15-21...	Have three important age limits: 15, 18, & 21. Under 15 not liable. Under the Penal Code, those under 18 recommended lighter sentences—"child", under 21 "juvenile". 1991 proposal to lower limit to 14—response to increase in youth crime./**Justice Model**
Switzerland	15-18...	7-15 are considered children, 15-18 are considered adolescent, & 18-25 are young adults—treated less severely.

Argentina	16-18...	their legal system for juveniles was described as being similar to that of Italy (Devoto, 1996). Youth regulated under the Penal Regulations for Youth Law 22.778, 1980. Very little work on youth crime. Only one study in 1994. Robbery and theft most common crimes and approx. 68% of crimes committed in "groups"/**Legalistic**
Scotland	- 16...	or 18 if already under supervision./**Welfare** (see Box 4)
Hong Kong	16-20...	juveniles (7-15)/**Corporatist Model** (see Ch. 5).

* Information for this Table has been obtained primarily through contacting foreign embassies and/or relevant juvenile departments.

[1] A 1985 United Nations report noted that some countries do not recognize a minimum age of criminal responsibility. Hence for some countries no age is given. The Napoleonic Code in 1804 in France was among the first codes to prescribe limited responsibility to youth under the age of 16.

Five countries still practice capital punishment of juvenile offenders—Bangladesh, Barbados, Iran, Pakistan, and the United States (Souryal, 1992).

[2] Models are only provided for countries in which sufficient information was available to attempt a description of their juvenile justice practices.

References

Adler, F. (1996). 1995 Presidential Address: Our American Society of Criminology, the World, and the State of the Art. *Criminology*, 34(1): 1-9.

Askim, B., & Berg, J. (1996, July 1). (Personal communication). The Royal Ministry of Justice and Police. Oslo, Norway.

Beirne, P. & Hill, J. (1991). *Comparative criminology: An annotated bibliography*. NY: Greenwood Press.

Boers, K., & Sesser, K. (1991). Do people really want punishment? In K. Sessar & Hans-Jurgen Kerner (Eds.). *Developments in crime and crime control research*. New York: Springer-Verlag. (Ch. 7).

CJ International. (1995). United Nations: Crime congress targets terrorist crimes, firearms regulations, and transnational crime. 11(4): 1,4-6.

Coldren, J.D. (1995). Change at the speed of light: Doing justice in the information age. *CJ International*, 11(4): 7-12.

Corrado, R. (1992). Introduction. In R.R. Corrado, N. Bala, R. Linden, & M. LeBlanc (Eds.). *Juvenile justice in Canada*. Toronto: Butterworths.

Devoto, G.E. (March 6, 1996). (Personal communication). Second Secretary, Embassy of Argentina, Ottawa.

Dijksterhuis, F.P.H., & Nijboer, J.A. (1986). *LBO—Onderwijs en delinquentie*. Den Haag: CIP-Gevens Koninklijke Bibliotheek.

Ferwerda, H. (1992). *Watjes en ratjes*. Grongingen: Wolters-Noordhoff B.V.

Hackler, J.C. (1984). Implications of variability in juvenile justice. In M.W. Klein (Ed.). *Western systems of juvenile justice.* Beverly Hills, CA: Sage.

Hackler, J.C. (1994). *Crime and Canadian public policy.* Scarborough, ON: Prentice-Hall.

Hartjen, C.A. (1991). Delinquency in India. *CJ International,* 7(1): 5-6, 10.

Junger-Tas, J. (1994). Delinquency in thirteen western countries: Some preliminary conclusions. In Junger-Tas, J., Terlouw, G-J., & Klein, M.W. (Eds.). *Delinquent behavior among young people in the western world.* New York, NY: Kugler. pp.370-380.

Junger-Tas, J., Terlouw, G-J., & Klein, M.W. (Eds.). (1994). *Delinquent behavior among young people in the western world.* New York: Kugler.

Klein, M. (Ed.). (1984). *Western systems of juvenile justice.* Beverly Hills, CA: Sage.

Kohn, M. L. (1989). *Cross-national research in sociology.* Newbury Park, CA: Sage.

Kumari, V. (1996, March 25). (Personal communication). Law Faculty, University of Delhi, India.

Lorenz, O. (January, 10, 1996). (Personal communication). Information Officer, French Embassy, Ottawa.

Louisan, S. (1996, June 15). 133-year-old Maori injustice admitted. *Calgary Herald,* J12.

Marsh, R.M. (1967). *Comparative sociology: A codification of cross-societal analysis.* N.Y.: Harcourt Brace and World.

Mclellan, A. (Jan. 24, 1996). (Personal communication). Justice Government of New Zealand, Wellington.

Nelken, D. (Ed.). (1994). *The futures of criminology.* London, England: Sage. (Ch. 10).

Newman, G.R. (1977). Problems of method in comparative criminology. *International J. of Comparative & Applied Criminal Justice,* 1(1): 17-31.

Nistoreanu, G. (1992). Juvenile delinquency: Realities and prospects. (Translated by Stefan Nimara). *CJ International,* 2(3): 4.

Ogburn, W.F. (1952). *Social change* (2nd ed.). NY: Viking Press.

Oyen, E. (1992). Comparative research as a sociological strategy. In E. Oyen (Ed.). *Comparative Methodology.* Newbury Park, CA: Sage. (Ch. 1).

Ploeg, G.J. (1991). *Maatschappelijke positie en criminaliteit.* Grongingen: Wolters-Noordhoff B.V.

Reichel, P.L. (1994). *Comparative criminal justice systems.* Englewood Cliffs, NJ: Prentice-Hall. (Ch. 9).

Sarnecki, J. (1996). Juvenile criminality in Sweden. In J. Winterdyk, *Issues and perspectives on young offenders in Canada.* Toronto, ON: Harcourt-Brace. (Appendix, pp. 301-311).

Saxon, T. (1996, Jan. 31). (Personal communication). Children and Young Persons Service: National Office. Wellington, New Zealand.

Schumann, K.F., & Kaulitzki, R. (1991). Limits of general deterrence: The case of juvenile delinquency. In K. Sessar & Hans-Jurgen Kerner (Eds.). *Developments in crime and crime control research.* New York: Springer-Verlag. (Ch. 1).

Souryal, S.S. (1996). Juvenile delinquency in the cross-cultural context: The Egyptian Experience. In C.B. Fields & R.H. Moore, Jr. (Eds.). *Comparative criminal justice.* Prospect Heights, Ill: Waveland. (Ch. 31).

Stewart, V.L. (1982). *Justice and troubled children around the world* (Vol. 1-5). NY: New York University Press.

Teune, H. (1992). Comparing countries: Lessons learned. In E. Oyen (Ed.). *Comparative methodology.* Newbury Park, CA: Sage. (Ch. 3).

The Scottish Police (n.d.). [Brochure]. Compliments of the Falkirk Police Department.

UNICEF (n.d.). Care for children with conduct problems in Cuba. Information Series Regional Programme No. 7.

United Nations (1986). *United Nations standard minimum rules for the administration of juvenile justice.* New York: Dept. of Information.

United Nations (1990). *Prevention of delinquency, juvenile justice and the protection of the young: Policy approaches and directions* (A/CONF.144/16). Vienna, Austria. UN Crime Prevention and Criminal Justice Branch.

United Nations (1995a). *Ninth United Nations congress on the prevention of crime and the treatment of offenders* (A/CONF.167/7 24 January 1995). Vienna, Austria. UN Crime Prevention and Criminal Justice Branch.

United Nations (1995b). *Ninth United Nations congress on the prevention of crime and the treatment of offenders* (A/CONF.169/Rev.1). Vienna, Austria. UN Crime Prevention and Criminal Justice Branch.

Wiechman, D. (Sept./Oct., 1994). Caning and corporal punishment: Viewpoint. *CJ International*, 13-19.

Wolfgang, M. (1991). Foreword. In K. Sessar & Hans-Jurgen Kerner (Eds.). *Developments in crime and crime control research.* New York: Springer-Verlag.

Wolfgang, M. (1996, May). Delinquency in China: Study of a birth cohort. *National Institute of Justice.* Rockville, MD: US Dept. of Justice.

Yokoyama, M. (1995). Analysis of prostitution in Japan. *Int. J. of Comparative and Applied Criminal Justice*, 19(1): 47-60.

Suggested Readings

CJ Europe & CJ International: Two criminal justice newsletters published bi-monthly by the Office of International Criminal Justice (OICJ) out of the University of Illinois at Chicago. These publications provide a broad range of information on current events and issues in Europe and internationally. In addition to providing general coverage of criminal justice events, the newsletters regularly include comparative or detailed information on various aspects of criminal justice. Furthermore, the newsletters serve as an excellent source for listing other publications dealing with comparative issues.

Fairchild, E. (1993). *Comparative criminal justice systems.* Belmont, CA: Wadsworth. Although not a comparative text on juvenile justice, it serves as an excellent text for the value and need for comparative research. Fairchild provides a comprehensive overview of six model nations (England, France, Germany, the former Soviet Union, Japan, and Saudi Arabia). Fairchild systematically covers each element of the criminal justice system; from the development of criminal justice systems to modern dilemmas of the criminal law as well as future developments in the field.

Fields, C.B., & Moore, Jr., R.H. (1996). *Comparative criminal justice*. Prospect Heights, Ill.: Waveland. The authors have collected thirty-three diverse articles (both original and previously published) in an attempt to offer a wide range of comparative views across five major subject areas. The articles have been written primarily by American scholars rather than contributors from the country being addressed. The sections range from a comparative view of 'crime and criminality' to 'corrections and punishment', with the final section entailing five articles on comparative juvenile justice. Two of the articles examine various aspects within Japan, while the other chapters cover Finland, Egypt, and Australia. Although an ambitious effort, this section lacks any standardization making it somewhat difficult to draw comparative analysis.

Heiner, R. (Ed.). (1996). *Criminology: A cross-cultural perspective*. St. Paul, MN: West. While this book does not focus on comparative juvenile justice, it does offer a fine review of comparative criminal justice issues. The book consists of a collection of twenty-seven published articles which are divided into four major subject areas. Heiner begins each contribution with a brief article summary, highlighting their significance as they might pertain to American criminologists. Part I consists of ten articles dealing with the subject of crime from different perspectives. Part II includes five articles which address policing issues in several different countries ranging from Canada to Germany. Part III contains six contributions on "Conceptions of Justice and Societal Responses". The articles cover topics ranging from Maori criminal justice to the legal system in Iran and the capital punishment controversy in the United States. The final part includes six articles covering correctional system issues. A summary of this book can be found on the Internet.

Junger-Tas, J., Terlouw, G-J., & Klein, M.W. (Eds.). (1994). *Delinquent behavior among young people in the western world*. NY: Kugler. Part of an on-going international self-report delinquency study involving twelve countries (mostly European); this report offers a comprehensive account of delinquency trends and socio-economic as well as demographic characteristics of young offenders. Even though the results are preliminary, the volume of information is worth examining and the tentative observations drawn strongly suggest that not only are delinquency rates similar between countries but that juveniles in the Western world share many similar characteristics.

Klein, M.W. (Ed.). (1984). *Western systems of juvenile justice*. Beverly Hills, CA: Sage. This book might well mark the first concerted effort to provide a comparative review of juvenile justice systems. While other authors have compiled descriptive accounts of different countries, the contributions in Klein's book begin with a diagram depicting the structure of their national system. This allows for easy comparisons between countries. In addition each chapter covers seven common categories (e.g., age, status offences, discretion, other systems, diversion, demographic bias, and trends). This further enables comparisons on common categories and the opportunity to examine differences. The final contribution from the Canadian criminologist James Hackler was solicited "as an illustration of the third stage of development, a conceptual analysis based upon comparative descriptions" (p. 14). For a retrospective look on juvenile justice, this is an excellent source.

Reichel, P.L. (1994). *Comparative criminal justice systems*. Englewood Cliffs, NJ: Prentice-Hall. A well written and organized book. In addition to its ten chapters covering everything from "Taking an International Perspective" to "Legal Traditions", policing, courts, corrections, delinquency, and a 'case study' of Japan, the author includes an appendix which is an "Almanac Information for Countries Referenced". Each chapter begins with a list of the key topics to be covered, key terms, and a list of the countries referenced. Chapter 9, "International Perspective on Juvenile Justice", provides an excellent overview of four of the models covered in this book. They include the welfare, legalistic, corporatist, and participatory juvenile justice models.

Terrill, R.J. (1997). *World criminal justice systems: A survey* (3rd ed.). Cincinnati, OH: Anderson. The fact that this book is in its third edition speaks to the need for comparative work. Drawing on five different types of legal systems, Terrill discusses the various aspects of their criminal justice systems including the juvenile justice system of each legal system/country. In his Introduction, Terrill notes that comparisons are made to the United States throughout the book. This rather voluminous and ambitious textbook provides a fine general legalistic survey of the respective juvenile systems covered.

United Nations Standard Minimum Rules for the Administration of Juvenile Justice. (1986). NY: Dept. of Public Information. In addition to providing a list of the minimum rules the publication provides commentary for each section offering the rational for setting the standards. The recommendations cover everything from "General principles" to "Institutional treatment" and "research, planning, policy formulation and evaluation." Since the rules were adopted by the Member States in 1984 in Beijing, subsequent Congress meetings on the Prevention of Crime and Treatment of Offenders have updated the progress of Member States' adoption of these rules. As some of the information can be accessed through the Internet, it should become more commonly referenced by anyone interested in learning more about international efforts.

chapter 1

Juvenile Justice: An Overview of Japan

Minoru Yokoyama
Faculty of Law, Kokgakuin University

Facts on Japan

Area: 377,812 sq. km. Japan is composed of five main islands from north to south; Hokkaido, Honshu, Shikoku, Kushu, and Okinawa. It is located from latitude 24° N to 45° N. It has one time zone. **Population**: approx. 125,879,000 in 1995 (pop. density 333 per sq. km), of which 99.2% were Japanese -pop. growth .32% per year. Koreans make up 51.7% of the non-Japanese population followed by the Chinese (15.9%). As of 1990, 77.4% of the population lived in urban settings. Thirteen major cities institute a ward system, of which Tokyo is not only the largest but is also the nation's capital (pop. 11.4 million). Persons between birth and fourteen years of age decreased from 29,798,000 in 1955 to 20,841,000 in 1993, while those sixty-five and over has increased from 4.7 to 16.9 million over the same time period. **Climate**: Although mostly temperate, the climate varies from north to south. For Tokyo the average monthly temperature is 5.2° C in January and 27.1° C in August. Heavy snowfall is common along the Japanese Sea in winter. **Economy**: Since World War II Japan has evolved from an agricultural and primary industry oriented nation to an industrialized and manufacturing nation. More recently, as Japan has become more developed, many people work in the tertiary industries. In 1993, 23.7% of the workforce was employed in the construction and manufacturing sectors while only 5.4% remained in some agricultural setting. **Government**: Under the Constitution enacted in 1946 the Emperor is a symbol of the state—a hereditary title. The sovereign power rests with the people, who elect both a member of the House of Representatives and that of the House of Councillors. The members of the Diet designate a prime minister, who organizes a cabinet. Between 1955 and 1993 the government was ruled by the Liberal Democratic Party (LDP). In 1993 a political scandal brought down the LDP. Since then a coalition cabinet has been in power. The autonomy of local governments remains limited.

There is no school equal to a decent home and no teachers equal to honest virtuous parents.

Mohandas (Mahatma) Gandhi

Japan's History

According to the ancient Chinese literature, the Japanese state existed at the latter half of the third century AD. Since the end of the sixth century, emperors ruled our country. In 604 the first Japanese constitution with seventeen articles was proclaimed. Its maxims were influenced by Buddhism. At the beginning of the eighth century, a legal system was established in imitation of that in Tang China. Some of the key periods include:

1. **Nara** period (710-793 AD): saw the widespread influence of Buddhism under the reign of powerful emperors, although many Japanese remained believers of Shinto, the core of which is the worship of nature and ancestors without a creator or bible like other main religions.

2. **Heian** period (794-1191): witnessed the emperor being deprived of political power, which resulted from the internal fights between the court nobilities. Then, as a result of this internal fighting, warriors gained political power.

3. **Kamakura** period (1192-1333): two legal systems co-existed; one for the court of the emperor and another for the military government of warriors that was founded by the Minamoto Shogun.

4. For over one hundred years from 1467, many wars occurred with the decline of the manor system. In 1543 the Portuguese were the first Europeans to come to Japan and introduced Christianity and guns.

5. **Edo** period (1603-1867): saw the establishment of rigid caste system under the feudal lords. To eradicate believers in Christianity, the government of Tokugawa Shogunate banned any further contact with Spain or Portugal. Only the Dutch and the Chinese were allowed to trade at an artificial island in Nagasaki Harbour. In 1742 the Tokugawa Shogunate compiled the Criminal Code of One Hundred Articles. Ordinary people had to comply with a sentence without knowing the laws. In the middle of the nineteenth century Japan was pressured by England, Russia, and the United States to abandon its isolation policy. This led to considerable internal squabbling over how to best address the response to the pressures. Consequently, the low-ranking warriors succeeded in overthrowing the Tokugawa Shogunate and restored the court of the emperor.

6. After the **Meiji Restoration** in 1868, Japan began introducing a Western legal system. In 1873 Gustave Boissonade, an agrege of the University of Paris, was invited to help with the transition of the legal system. He succeeded in enacting the Penal Code and the Code of Criminal Procedures. The short lived French model of the Penal Code was replaced by a new Penal Code in 1907 after the positivist model used in Germany.

7. With the defeat of Japan in the World War II (1945), the emperor's regime collapsed, Japan was stripped of its empire, and the criminal justice

system was democratized at the direction of the Allied Powers. Following the enactment of a new constitution in 1946 and the revisions of the Penal Code in 1947, a new Code of Criminal Procedures was enacted in 1948. The code was modelled after the American system to guarantee due process while its fundamental framework remained under the legal models found in most of Western Europe.

Development of Juvenile Justice

Criminal Responsibility

Since the eighth century the criminal laws for the court of the emperor had some prescriptions to exempt juveniles from penalty or to reduce sentences. It was the case even in the criminal laws for the court of warriors. For example, the Criminal Code of One Hundred Articles of 1742 allowed for the mitigation of criminal punishment for juveniles fifteen and under.

After the Meiji Restoration, Western systems for juveniles were introduced. In 1872 compulsory education was instituted. In 1880 the Penal Code was enacted, which included several provisions for juvenile offenders. For example, Article 79 defined the minimum age of culpability as twelve.

Emergence of Juvenile Facilities

The Prison Rules and its illustration of 1872 provided for the establishment of prison dormitory facilities. They were modelled after the English-style prison system used in Hong Kong and Singapore. Although the intention was to provide educational programs, limited resources restricted such provisions.

Around 1880, after learning more about the use of reformatory schools in Western countries, some volunteers introduced a reformatory school (Tsujimoto, 1990). The school was founded by a priest in a sector of Shinto in 1883. The priests of conventional religions such as Shinto and Buddhism played an important role in establishing these reformatory schools. In this movement we saw the start of the participatory nature of our juvenile justice system.

Enactment of the Reformatory Law and Juvenile Law

Given the strong support for the private reformatory schools, in 1900 the Reformatory Law was proclaimed to endorse their activities. Although the law encouraged the establishment of public reformatory schools, by 1908 only five prefectural reformatory schools were opened.

In 1907 the current Penal Code was promulgated. Article 41 prescribes that anyone under the age of fourteen can not be held criminally responsible. Confinement to the reformatory system was abolished. In 1908 the Reformatory Law was amended to treat juveniles who had been confined in the reformatories.

After nine years of debate, in 1919 the first drafts of the Juvenile Law and the Correctional School Law were completed. However, Shigejiro Ogawa, who had contributed to drafting the Reformatory Law, pointed out that in Japan there was not the same urgent need for a juvenile law as in the United States. Ogawa further suggested that offenders under the age of fourteen should not be adjudicated under the juvenile law, and that a correctional school similar to a juvenile prison should not be instituted in place of the well-functioning reformatory school.

In spite of such opposition, both acts were passed in 1922. However, owing to budgetary restraints between 1922 and 1942, the Juvenile Law was only enforced in five prefectures covering such large cities as Tokyo and Osaka. In 1933 the Juvenile Training and Education Law was enacted in place of the Reformatory Law to coordinate with the system under the Juvenile Law.

Box 1.1: Family Schools established by Kosuke Tomeoka

In 1873 the national government removed the ban on Christianity. Kosuke Tomeoka, a Christian, became a chaplain at Sorachi Penitentiary on the northern island of Hokkaido in order to improve the prison system (Correctional Association, 1984). He later went to the United States to learn about the Elmira Reformatory system and upon returning set up a reformatory school in Tokyo in 1899.

His reformatory was called a family school—Katei Gakko. A teacher and his family lived together with about ten juveniles in an independent house. The setting was very positive and nurturing under the influence of Christian beliefs. The basic model of this family school still operates at many child education and training homes (Kyogoin Homes) under the Child Welfare Law, although strict religious activities are not present in the public homes (see Hattori, 1996, for further discussion on the history and development of family schools).

Juvenile Justice Post WW II

Shortly after World War II there was a sharp increase in juvenile crime in Japan. This prompted discussions of enacting a new Juvenile Law. Being heavily influenced by the Allied Powers, Japan was expected to place greater emphasis on child welfare. Japan was also required to switch from the juvenile tribunals to juvenile courts in order to guarantee juvenile rights. The new

Juvenile Law, passed in 1948, reflected the principle of *parens patriae*. With the passing of the new Juvenile Law, family courts were founded.

Article 24 of the law prescribed three protective educative measures: putting juveniles under probation; committing them to a home for dependent children, or the child education and training home; and committing them to juvenile training school. The latter option required the passing of the Juvenile Training School Law in 1948. Under the new Child Welfare Law of 1947 many reformatory schools remained as child education and training homes.

Character of the Current Juvenile Law of 1948

With the proclamation of the Code of Criminal Procedure in 1948 we saw a switch from an approach similar to that in European countries to an American model which emphasized procedures to guarantee due process. The new classicists stressing human rights insisted that criminal policy shall be carried out under the principle of legality (Yokoyama, 1994). Since 1922 the Juvenile Law has been interpreted as following the **welfare model** because of the emphasis on rehabilitation and the doctrine of *parens patriae* (Yokoyama, 1992a). Under the current principle of *parens patriae*, Japanese Juvenile law is designed to provide educative measures for juvenile delinquents that will enable them to develop their individual ability. However, under the current format, there are no provisions for formally recognizing those cases in which youth are found to be innocent. Since 1966 the Ministry of Justice, the Supreme Court and the Japan Federation of Bar Association have met periodically to address this 'defect' in the procedure.

Recently, some lawyers have severely criticized practitioners in the juvenile justice system for laying false charges, reflecting that juvenile rights are not sufficiently guaranteed. However, as they also respect the welfare model and the rehabilitation one, they are reluctant to advocate the introduction of all criminal procedures that guarantee the same rights as those afforded adult defendants. Sawanobori (1994) insists that the Juvenile Law is a welfare law because of its paternalistic orientation, while guaranteeing due process as a procedural law. In addition, referring to Figure 1 (see Introduction), the Japanese model might also be described as representative of the **participatory model**, as many citizens have participated as volunteers in activities to realize the purpose of the Juvenile Law.

The most important provisions of the Juvenile Law include:

- The purpose of the law is to help ensure that juveniles are raised soundly. To this end, the law provides for protective educative measures.
- "Juveniles" are legally defined as those under the age of twenty, which was raised from eighteen years of age.
- The family court has jurisdiction over three kinds of juveniles: 1) juvenile offenders between the ages of fourteen and nineteen; 2) lawbreaking children under the age of fourteen; and 3) pre-offence juveniles under the age of twenty who are prone to commit some criminal offence. The later category is justified by paternalism, though it is contradictory to the principle of legality.
- Chapter 2 of the law prescribes procedures and dispositions for the protection of juveniles. They stress informality and the absence of a confrontation between the defendant and the prosecutor, as in the adult cases.
- All cases must be referred to the family court. However, the family court judge has the discretion to refer a case back to the public prosecutor. The youths who are referred for a criminal charge must be at least sixteen years of age. This would be analogous to transferring a youth to adult court in Western countries.
- Chapter 4 pertains to procedures and punishment in juvenile criminal cases. The procedures are more protective than for adult offenders. In addition, the criminal punishment imposed on juveniles can be mitigated.

The Dimensions of Delinquency

The national government has strong executive power and is able to collect various data uniformly from all over the country. Notwithstanding the obvious limitations of official statistics, the government's statistics are considered more reliable than those in de-centralized countries. Because of the government's stable bureaucratic system they are rarely influenced by the results of elections. Consequently, self-report and victimization surveys, unlike in Europe and North America, are not well funded and are carried out only sporadically (see Fujimoto, 1994).

We have three primary sources of formal criminal justice statistics: the National Police Agency compiles crime statistics; the Ministry of Justice produces annual data on prosecution, correction, and rehabilitation; and the Supreme Court publishes judicial statistics on an annual basis. In addition to these reports, the National Police Agency, the Ministry of Justice and the Administrative Affairs Agency publish white papers on police, crime, and juveniles respectively.

Delinquency Trends after World War II
There have been three major peaks of juvenile delinquency since World War II (Yokoyama, 1986a). The first occurred in 1951 when the rate of juvenile Penal Code offenders was 9.5 per 1,000 population of between ten and twenty years of age. Given that the police had been decentralized under the decree of the Allied Powers, it is suspected that the figure was quite high. The highest rate of juvenile delinquency probably occured in the chaos immediately after World War II when there were many poor and orphaned children. These youth often committed thefts because of absolute poverty (Yokayama, 1985).

The second peak happened in 1964 when the rate rose to 11.9 per 1,000. The early 1960s saw violent offences being committed by juveniles born during the baby boom after World War II.

The third peak occurred in 1983 when the rate climbed up to 17.1 per 1,000. Although there were a large number of investigations, most of them were for minor offences. The rise may in part reflect the net widening of guidance activities of the police (Yokoyama, 1989).

To understand the current situation I would like to compare some crime statistics from 1964, 1983 with those of 1993 when the rate dropped to 12.4 per 1,000.

Delinquency Trends and Patterns
The main characteristics of juvenile delinquency may be described as follows:

As indicated in Table 1.1, the increase in the number of thefts contributed to forming the third peak in 1983; it represented a 55% increase between 1964 and 1983. In 1993 the percentage of shoplifting, motorcycle theft, bicycle theft and other theft was 32.9%, 27.2%, 19.1%, and 20.8% respectively. Unlike many Western countries, break-and-enters and pickpocketing are infrequent. Also, perhaps unique to Japanese youth culture, motorcycle theft is more common than motor vehicle theft. *The White Paper on Crime in 1994* notes that only 0.5% of the thefts were motivated by poverty while 67.6% were motivated by greed and 25.9% for 'play'.

- Since 1964 there has been a sharp increase in the number of embezzlements (see Table 1.1). In Japan, this refers to crimes involving the taking of a lost or deserted thing, such as riding a lost or deserted bicycle, without the owner's permission. The increase might have been brought by police net widening.

Table 1.1: Juvenile Penal Code Offenders* Investigated by the Police

	1964	1983		1993	
	Number	Number	Index (1964=100)	Number	Index (1964=100)
Total	190,442	252,587	—	186,208	—
Theft	95,129	147,484	155	85,627	90
Fraud	1,636	561	34	677	41
Embezzlement	856	15,760	1,840	27,189	3,175
Robbery	1,909	720	38	713	37
Extortion	14,388	6,715	47	4,674	32
Intimidation	1,168	148	13	71	6
Minor Violence	13,097	6,735	51	1,929	15
Injury	16,125	10,520	65	8,071	50
Rape	4,181	723	17	272	7
Indecency	1,347	569	42	347	26
Murder	356	87	24	75	21
Arson	150	177	118	84	56
Professional negligence causing death or bodily injury	40,010	55,804	—	53,076	—
Others		6,594	—	3,403	—

*   Excludes the number of lawbreaking children

Sources: *White Paper on Crime* in 1965, p.253
          White Paper on Police in 1984, p.280
          White Paper on Police in 1994, pp.364-365

In addition, Table 1.1 indicates the dramatic decrease in murder and robbery as well as a reduction of violent crimes. The decline in all types of violent crime may be due to a very proactive campaign against violence which was initiated in the early 1960s.

Beginning in 1985 "bullying" activities in the schools drew national media attention. It is generally felt that bullying increased as a result of gloomy competition in the examination ordeal. However, I simply believe that bullying became a social concern because people's tolerance levels for violent crimes have declined. Bullying may not have increased in reality. For example, in 1993 there were only 234 juveniles charged with bullying *(White Paper on Police in 1994)*. However, it should be noted that most bullying incidents go unreported.

Sex crimes such as rape and indecency decreased drastically during the past three decades (see Table 1.1). Again, the campaign against violence seems to have had a positive impact on reducing the problem. Another explanation may be that with the development of the economy more persons have their own money—enough to buy the services of a prostitute, pornographic literature, and so on to satisfy their sexual appetite (Yokoyama, 1995).

"Hotrodders"* appeared in the late 1950s (Yokoyama, 1986b). Amendments towards criminalization were made to the criminal laws in order to address the problem (Yokoyama, 1990a). The criminalization against hotrodders has been carried out by practices within the juvenile justice agencies (Yokoyama, 1990b). However, their activities continue to be troublesome. In addition to the problems by hotrodders, over 50,000 juveniles killed or injured someone as a result of a traffic accident and were charged with professional negligence in causing death or bodily injury.

The use of hard drugs such as cocaine and heroin is not seen as a serious problem in Japan. Since the end of World War II, however, stimulant drugs composed of methanephetamines have been prevalent. Despite efforts to suppress this contamination through criminalization (Yokoyama, 1991), the police have not succeeded in eradicating the drug abuse because the Boryokudan (Japanese organized crime gangs, known as Yakuza in foreign countries) dominate the black market for the stimulant drug (Tamura, 1992). (The recent drug trade problem in Russia is similarly controlled by organized gangs (see Ch. 9)). Owing to the high price, however, ordinary juveniles have limited access to the drugs. In 1993 the total number of juveniles investigated on a charge of the Stimulant Drug Control Law amounted to 980 *(White Paper on Crime in 1994)*; although, many juveniles are sniffing thinner. In 1993 the police charged 9499 juveniles with thinner abuse *(White Paper on Crime in 1994)*.

Profile of Juvenile Delinquents

Delinquents and Gender

During the third peak of 1983, female delinquency rates increased dramatically. The number of non-traffic, Penal Code offenders rose from 11,866 in 1966 to

---

*   Japanese youth like to alter stolen motorcycles and automobiles so that they make a loud noise while riding or driving. Unlike in North America, Japanese juveniles tend to steal motorcycles more than they do cars for "hotrodding"—"joyriding experiences."

Box 1.2: The "play-type" delinquency or the "incipient-type" delinquency?

In the late 1960s serious and violent crime rates began to drop. The police were then able to direct their resources to the less serious offences such as bicycle theft, embezzlement of a lost or deserted bicycle, and shoplifting (Yokoyama, 1992b). Most of these crimes were committed for fun or thrills. Therefore, after 1970 the police referred to them as the 'play-type' delinquency. Play-type delinquency was committed by ordinary juveniles from middle- or upper-class families. The net widening efforts by the police contributed to forming the third peak of juvenile delinquency.

A 1981 study carried out by the National Research Institute of Police Science, Kiyonoga (1983) observed that many of the minor offences were being committed by lawbreaking children and juveniles who were fourteen and fifteen years of age. He also pointed out that these children and juveniles were prone to develop their criminal tendency toward committing a conventional theft, a violent crime, or engaging in drug abuse. In response the police renamed the play-type delinquency to 'incipient-type' delinquency in the *White Paper on Police in 1982*. Shoplifting, motorcycle theft, bicycle theft and the embezzlement of a lost or deserted thing were categorized under this new label. However, these four offences seem to be committed by juveniles with different criminal tendencies. For example, motorcycle theft is committed by juveniles who admire hotrodders, while riding a bicycle temporarily without the owner's permission tends to be committed by 'play-type' delinquents.

By advocating the category of the incipient-type delinquency, the police succeeded in giving the public a warning against the increase in minor offences which was mainly brought on by the net widening activities of the police. Judging from the decrease in serious offences over the past decade (Table 1.1), early intervention seems to have suppressed the escalation of delinquency from a form of play to more serious habitual criminal behaviour. However, behind this success we must notice the negative effects of labelling brought on by the early intervention of the police.

54,459 in 1983 (*White Paper on Crime in 1975* and that in 1984). This increase can be partially attributed to the change in lifestyle of young girls in Japan as well as to the declining tolerance levels towards minor offences by female juveniles by the police.

Of all female juvenile Penal Code offenders in 1993, 78.2% were caught on a charge of theft *(White Paper on Crime in 1994)*. Most of the thefts involved shoplifting. The increase coincided with a growth in large-scale department stores and supermarkets with the self-service system (*White Paper on Police in 1976*).

The use of illegal drugs has also increased among female delinquents in recent years. The percentage of juvenile females caught for sniffing thinner amounted to 34.4%, while the correspondent percentage for those abusing stimulant drugs was 50.4% (*White Paper on Crime in 1994*). The higher percentage of those abusing stimulant drugs corresponds to the increased number of young females working at night. Their increased income enables them to buy stimulant drugs and they are often exposed to risk of contact with members of Boryokudan (Yokoyama, 1991).

Juvenile Delinquents by Age

As indicated in Table 1.2, the highest rate of juvenile, non-traffic, Penal Code offences was for those youths between the ages of fourteen and fifteen years. In the third peak this rate climbed up to 29.5 per 1,000. The *White Paper on Police in 1994* reports that junior high school students are more likely to commit minor offences such as theft and the embezzlement of a lost or deserted thing (68.8% and 15.2% respectively). For juveniles who were employed, the corresponding percentages were marginally lower (63.6% and 12.4%) (*White*

Table 1.2: Rate of Juvenile Non-traffic Penal Code Offenders Guided and Investigated by the Police per 1,000 Population

	All Juvenile Offenders	Under 14*	14-15	16-17	18-19
1966	9.0	5.0	12.1	11.6	9.7
1983	14.1	801	29.5	18.0	7.7
1993	9.3	4.1	17.2	13.8	6.5

*   Rates of offenders under 14 years old per 1,000 population between 10 and 13 years old.

Source:*White Paper on Crime in 1994*, p.380

Paper on Police in 1994).

The delinquency rate among junior high school students may be explained by the heated competition for higher education opportunities (Tokuoka & Cohen, 1987). However, Harada (1995) found that students' maladjustment is short-term in nature. The rate of delinquency in the age group between sixteen and seventeen years drops because many juveniles are liberated from the stress of severe competition after graduation from junior high school.

After 1983, the rate of juvenile delinquency among lawbreaking children dropped by half. The decline may be explained by the fact that after the second baby boom in the early 1970s Japan entered the stage of a population decline with low birth rates and low death rates (Riesman, 1961), and that juveniles

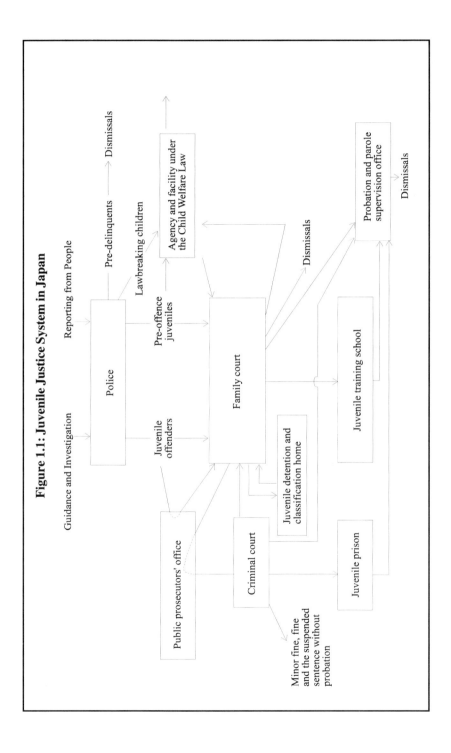

Figure 1.1: Juvenile Justice System in Japan

have recently been more protected or perhaps overprotected by adults. Recall that Gottfredson and Hirschi (1990) emphasize parental concern for the welfare or behaviour of the child as a necessary condition for successful child-rearing.

In summary, as the social and cultural factors of Japan continue to change so have the general characteristics of its juveniles. Japanese delinquency rates are still amongst the lowest in the world.

Administration of Juvenile Justice System

The judiciary is separate from and independent of the central and local governments. As can be seen from Figure 1.1, the flow of the juvenile justice administrative process involves many steps. This section concentrates on some of the major elements in Japan's juvenile justice system.

Preventive Activities in the Community

The participatory nature of our juvenile justice system is conspicuous in the preventive measures taken in the community. Rural areas have historically relied on a strong informal control in the family and in the neighbourhood, which prevents juvenile delinquency. And even though a majority of the population now live in urban settings, informal control still remains even in large Japanese cities, contrary to many Western countries. For example, we see town associations in cities throughout Japan, which almost all residents are expected to join. The town associations carry out many activities: festivals, athletic meetings, measures for traffic safety, recreational activities for the elderly and children, and so on. These activities create the close ties of a traditional neighbourhood within a city, which helps to prevent juvenile delinquency (Yokoyama, 1981).

In addition to the village and town associations, many civil groups participate in the movement to raise juveniles soundly. For example, in many communities organizations such as the mothers' associations are involved with juveniles (*White Paper on Juveniles in 1994)*. The informal, preventive activities by these organizations are usually encouraged by local government, law enforcement agencies, and juvenile justice agencies (Murai, 1979). These activities supplement formal social control.

Juvenile Guidance Centres

The first juvenile guidance centres for delinquents were established in Kyoto and Osaka in 1952. By 1963 there were 118 juvenile guidance centres. However, the national government did not subsidize them until 1964, during the second peak of delinquent activities. The guidance centres carry out three main activities: patrolling streets in the amusement quarters to guide juveniles, counselling juveniles and their parents, and improving the social environment for rearing juveniles soundly.

By the end of 1993 there were 693 juvenile guidance centres, with approximately 73,000 juvenile guidance volunteers (*White Paper on Juveniles in 1994*). In 1993 approximately 400,000 juveniles were assisted by juvenile guidance officers and volunteers. The total number of individual cases amounted to approximately 126,000. In small-sized or medium-sized cities many juvenile guidance centres are managed by the education department of the municipal government, in large cities they are administered by the department coping with the youth problem. Several juvenile guidance centres in larger cities are administered by police departments. In these cases the juvenile guidance centre resembles a law enforcement agency.

Preventive Activities by the Police

The police have developed organizations for the prevention of delinquency such as the crime prevention association, the company-police conference, and the school-police conference. Numerous organizations have collaborated with the police in efforts to prevent crime. For example, at the end of 1993 the total number of the liaison houses for crime prevention affiliated with the crime prevention associations amounted to 682,471 (*White Paper on Juveniles*, 1994).

During the second peak of juvenile delinquency in 1964, a growing number of the youths were committing delinquent offences. This was especially true for those coming from rural areas after graduation from a junior high school. They were the main target of the newly established company-police conference. Today, we still have approximately 700 company-police conferences in spite of the fact that more teenagers are entering the workforce than was the case in the mid 1920s (*White Paper on Police in 1994*).

After recovery from the economic difficulties in the aftermath of World War II, Japan began to focus on the growing amount of physical violence in junior high schools (Hiyama and Katsumi, 1974). In order to cope with the increase in delinquency of high school students, the school-police conference was organized. By 1969 every junior high school was required to have a teacher in charge of guiding students (Yokoyama, 1981) and by 1993 about 90% of all elementary, junior high, and senior high schools joined in the school-police conference (*White Paper on Police in 1994*).

Another proactive police organization included police boxes (Koban) in the urban areas and police houses (Chuzaisho) in rural areas. In 1993 there were about 6500 Kobans and about 8700 Chuzaishos (*White Paper on Police in 1994*). The police officers working at a police box or a police house carry out many crime prevention activities in their territory. One of these activities involves patrolling on foot, when police officers often guide and catch juvenile delinquents. In the police station there is a department in charge of maintaining a sense of harmony in the community. The police officers belonging to this department and the guidance volunteers patrol the amusement quarters to guide juveniles who are prone to deviant behaviour.

Finally, the police have also established three voluntary systems: the guidance volunteer, the police helper for juveniles, and the instructor for juveniles (Yokoyama, 1989). In 1993 the total number of guidance volunteers was approximately 55,000. In addition, about 1100 citizens, many of whom are retired police officers, work as police helpers in charge of dispersing the groups of juvenile delinquents, while approximately 5000 juvenile instructors authorized by the Law on Regulation of Business Affecting Public Morals of 1985 work to protect juveniles from unsound environments (*White Paper on Police in 1994*).

Under the Juvenile Law the police are not qualified to supervise juveniles. However, some juveniles, guided by the police, are given the after-care treatment at juvenile guidance centres, especially those affiliated with the police. The police also invite the juveniles to join some event and some sport such as Judo or baseball, which police officers supervise on a voluntary base.

Before the third peak, the police emphasized the necessity of early intervention and early treatment for delinquents. In 1982 the National Police Agency issued a general principle enabling the police to widen their activities to control juveniles under the name of rearing them soundly (Ayukawa, 1994). In 1993 the police held approximately 10,000 meetings for the prevention of delinquency, which were attended by a total of 1,170,000 elementary or junior high school students (*White Paper on Police in 1994*). The police also provide counselling for juveniles and their parents (Yokoyama, 1992a). In 1993 the total number of those counselled was 88,935 (*White Paper on Police in 1994*).

Fukuda (1988) suggests that the police have moved towards placing juveniles under total control and surveillance. The activities of the police for rearing juveniles soundly may prevent them from committing deviant behaviour. However, it would be more desirable if most of these activities were carried out by schools or child welfare agencies. The government should assign more resources to child welfare agencies such as the juvenile guidance centres.

In contrast, the police have earnestly campaigned for increasing the fixed number of police officers and reinforcing their resources. In addition, every time some heinous crime occurs the media point to some defects in the activities of the police. Then, the police succeed in getting more financial resources for improving these defects. As a result, the fixed number of police officers increased from 181,768 in 1972 to 259,098 in 1994 *(White Paper on Police in 1973* and that in *1994).* This increase has contributed to the net widening activities.

Disposition of Cases by the Police and Public Prosecutors

Under the Police Activity Rules of 1960, the police handle juveniles committing 'bad conduct' as pre-delinquents. If the police officer or the volunteer patrolling on foot find a pre-delinquent, they simply issue a warning and provide basic counselling. In 1993 there were 643,706 such warnings, of which 47.4% and 27.9% concerned smoking and loitering after midnight respectively (*White Paper on Police in 1994*).

According to the Juvenile Law, the category of pre-offence juveniles is defined under the principle of *parens patriae.* Since this category has been subject to criticism by a number of legal professionals, the police are careful when classifying a juvenile as a pre-offence delinquent.

Also under the law, police must refer all cases of pre-offence juveniles to the family court or the child guidance centre. In 1993 the family court disposed of 1008 pre-offence cases, of which 56.5% were for females *(Annual Report of Judicial Statistics for 1993).* Typically, girls who run away from home and associate with members of Boryokudan are treated as pre-offence juveniles for protective purposes.

Cases of law-breaking by children are reported to the child guidance centre. If the case worker in the centre feels that there is a need to impose protective measures under the Juvenile Law, the prefectural governor or the chief of the centre refers the child to the family court. In 1993 there were only 195 such referrals.

The police must refer all cases of juvenile offenders directly or via public prosecutors to the family court. Only a small number of cases of minor offences, for which the imprisonment is not prescribed by the law, are directly referred to the family court. The public prosecutors do not have discretion in screening cases. Therefore, after an investigation they must refer all cases to the family court. At the referral they can write their opinion; however, they cannot attend the hearing to state their opinion. The disposition adjudicated by the family court judge is usually milder than the one which public prosecutors wish to impose from the viewpoint of maintaining social order.

Imposition of Criminal Punishment

If the family court judges find that a youth between the ages of sixteen to nineteen should be punished, they can refer him/her back to the public

Box 1.3: Controversy about Restoration of Public Prosecutors' Authority

Under the initiative of the Ministry of Justice, of which senior positions are monopolized by public prosecutors, several drafts for the revision of the Juvenile Law had been put forth (Saito, 1986). The main purpose of the revisions was the restoration of public prosecutors' authority, which had been lost by the enactment of the Juvenile Law in 1948. For example, in the draft of the revised Juvenile Law of 1976 a special procedure for offenders between eighteen and nineteen years of age was proposed. The revision was designed to allow public prosecutors to take a more active part. But, many other legal professionals and the opposition parties have emphasized treating delinquents under the welfare model (see Figure 1, Introduction) as opposed to being crime control oriented.

The views for the crime control model are subject to further debate every time the media report a heinous crime committed by a juvenile. But, if we want to impose criminal punishment on juvenile offenders, it is not really necessary to amend the law toward tougher policy; rather, we only need to refer the appropriate cases back to the public prosecutor.

prosecutor. In 1994 public prosecutors prosecuted 16,727 juveniles, of which 98.2% were for offences of the Road Traffic Law or professional negligence causing death or bodily injury (*White Paper on Crime in 1994*). Most of the offenders of the Road Traffic Law are given a fine.

The total number of non-traffic cases referred to public prosecutors dropped from 3119 in 1965 to 407 in 1993 (see Table 1.3). The trend is similar to that for heinous offences by juveniles and offences by older juveniles (see tables 1.1 and 1.2). Unlike other countries, Japan is experiencing a trend towards milder punishments in juvenile criminal cases, with many youths receiving a suspended sentence. For example, in 1993 only fifty youths were sent to juvenile prisons.

Owing to the low number of juveniles receiving prison terms, young adults up to the age of twenty-six are also being placed in one of the eight juvenile prisons throughout the country (Yokoyama, 1982). These facilities are designed to offer many programs for vocational training and, as is the practice in many Western countries, inmates are usually granted parole before their term has been served. These elements reflect the welfare and participatory flavour evident in Japan's juvenile justice system.

Family Court Probation Officers and Tentative Probation

Since 1950 family courts have used probation officers who are trained in the behavioural sciences. Again, as in many Western countries, probation officers

Table 1.3: Final Dispositions of Juvenile Non-traffic Offenders at Family Courts

	Total	Dismissal		Referral to		Probation	Commitment to	
		without Hearing	after Hearing	Public Prosecutors*	Child Guidance Centers		Juvenile Training Schools	Facilities under the Child Welfare Law
1965	158,475	88,364	39,862	3,119	561	19,262	7,079	228
	(100.0)	(55.7)	(25.1)	(2.0)	(0.4)	(12.2)	(4.5)	(0.1)
1983	198,729	139,368	38,049	1,008	183	15,171	4,758	192
	(100.0)	(70.1)	(19.2)	(0.5)	(0.1)	(7.6)	(2.4)	(0.1)
1993	133,046	97,000	21,187	407	139	10,846	3,632	195
	(100.0)	(72.8)	(15.9)	(0.3)	(0.1)	(8.1)	(2.7)	(0.1)

*   Excludes cases referred to public prosecutors because of reaching majority.

Sources: *White Paper on Crime in 1984*, p.285.
White Paper on Crime in 1985, p.213.
White Paper on Crime in 1995, p.431.

are responsible for processing the case, conducting background research, and providing services while the youth is under supervision.

Before adjudication family court judges can place a juvenile delinquent under tentative probation. In some cases these youths are guided by volunteers, or accommodated in private houses. In 1993, 21,622 young persons were placed under tentative probation; of which 2693, 9984, and 8945 were charged with non-traffic offences, professional negligence causing death or bodily injury, and the offences of the Road Traffic Law respectively (*Annual Report of Judicial Statistics for 1993*). Although a popular option, the number of tentative probationary cases have declined since 1984. The number of those who were committed to some private house or facility also dropped from 840 in 1984 to 422 in 1993.

After completing their tentative probation, the youths must appear before the family court for their hearings. Usually the Family Court judges sentence them to dismissal so as to avoid a double penalty (Yoyokama, 1984). In 1993 the family courts heard 12,898 juvenile tentative probationers cases excluding those charged under the Road Traffic Law. Of these probationers, 88.5% were adjudicated dismissal, 6.4% were placed on probation, while 2.0% were committed to juvenile training schools (*Annual Report of Judicial Statistics for 1993*).

Juvenile Detention and Classification Homes

If crisis intervention is deemed necessary, the family court judges can decide to place the youth in a juvenile detention and classification home administered by the Ministry of Justice. In 1993 there were fifty-two juvenile detention and classification homes. The total number of juveniles admitted to the detention and classification homes changed from 35,341 in 1964, to 10,410 in 1974, to 21,854 in 1983, and to 14,964 in 1993 (*White Paper on Crime in 1994*). Under the Juvenile Law the maximum term of custody is four weeks. In the juvenile detention and classification homes specialists in behavioural sciences carry out many kinds of tests on inmates while observing their behaviour.

Adjudication by Family Court Judges

All judges in lower-class courts are professional. They are appointed by Cabinet, which follows the recommendation of the Supreme Court. Therefore, the family court judges are independent of any public image. They are expected to decide the disposition in the best interests of the juvenile.

For non-serious cases the Family Court judges decide the dismissal without hearing from the youth after screening by the family court probation officer. In other cases the judge may hear from the youth. Then, in consideration of reports from the probation officer and a specialist from a juvenile detention and classification home, they decide whether or not to impose the protective educative measures. Based on the total number of final dispositions of juvenile non-traffic offenders, the percentage of dismissal without hearing amounted to 72.8% in 1993 (see Table 1.3). This percentage increased from 55.7% in 1965. It seems to reflect a fact that juveniles having committed minor offences have been more frequently caught by the net widening of activities of the police.

Under the constitution we are guaranteed the right to a public trial. However, in juvenile cases the hearing is carried out in a closed court to prevent stigmatizing juveniles. Usually, the Family Court judge hears informally from youths as well as their parent(s) or guardian(s). Whenever necessary, the family court probation officer joins the hearing. Juveniles and their parent(s) or guardian(s) can employ a legal counsellor as an attendant at the hearing. In 1993 the total number of non-traffic juvenile offenders disposed of at the family courts amounted to 154,517, of which only 1.4% employed a legal counsellor *(Annual Report of Judicial Statistics for 1993)*. In almost all juvenile cases juveniles confess their offences rather than seek the legal counsel they are entitled to under Juvenile Law.

Recently, lawyers have participated in several activities to defend juveniles against a false charge. To get a confession, the police interrogators are apt to torture a suspect psychologically for long hours while confining the youth in a police station cell as a substitute for regular detention houses (Igarashi, 1989). The lawyers insist on the necessity of defending juveniles from a false charge brought by such interrogation and campaign for the importance of the legal counsellor as an attendant.

After the hearing the Family Court judge decides whether or not to impose protective educative measures. Many juveniles are dismissed after receiving a warning and advice at the hearing (see Table 1.3). Only a few are released because of their innocence. However, under the principle of *parens patriae*, 'innocence' is not formally sentenced under the Juvenile Law. Lawyers have pointed out that from the viewpoint of the principle of legality this is a serious defect of the law.

If the family court judges admit the necessity of protecting a juvenile delinquent, they will impose protective educative measures. While the old Juvenile Law of 1922 prescribed nine protective educative measures, the current

Juvenile Law provides (as mentioned earlier) for only three protective educative measures under Article 24: probation, commitment to juvenile training schools, and commitment to facilities for children of up to eighteen years old under the Child Welfare Law.

Facilities under the Child Welfare Law

The family court judge can place juvenile delinquents of younger ages in a home for dependent children or a child education and training home. In 1993, 195 delinquent children were placed in such facilities (see Table 1.3). Almost all of them were treated in one of the fifty-seven child education and training homes around the country.

In addition to the compulsory commitment by the family court, the majority of the children are accommodated in the child education and training homes by order of prefectural governor with the consent of their parent(s) or guardian. In recent years, however, the percentage of the total number of inmates in the homes per maximum occupancy rate has decreased from 58.7% in 1987 to 44.5% in 1991 (Hattori, 1992).

Local governments have been assigning ordinary officers as case workers at the child guidance centre. Unfortunately, their knowledge and understanding of the facilities for child welfare is limited and they often fail to obtain the consent necessary to commit the child to a child education and training home (Hattori, 1992). This is one reason why the number of inmates in the child education and training homes have decreased. Another reason may be that parents of smaller families wish to take care of their deviant child themselves.

Following the family school established by Kosuke Tomeoka (see Box 1.1), many child education and training homes maintained a system of treatment by a married couple in an independent house without any equipment to prevent possible escapes. This system has greatly contributed to the rehabilitation of troublesome children who are starving for affection. However, it becomes difficult to maintain this system owing to changes in the social structure of Japan (Hattori, 1996).

Juvenile Training Schools

Until the early 1960s juvenile training schools were overcrowded. This problem contributed to the difficulty of the facilities being able to offer educational treatment programs. Subsequently, judges and probation officers at the family court distrusted the treatment in these schools and referred fewer cases. In addition, serious offences by juveniles decreased after the second peak of juvenile delinquency (see Table 1.1). Therefore, the total number of juveniles admitted for the first time to juvenile training schools dropped from 8065 in 1966 to 1969 in 1974 (*White Paper on Crime in 1994*).

In response to the decreasing numbers, the Ministry of Justice began to reform the system of juvenile training schools (Yokoyama, 1992a). In 1977 the ministry introduced a system of short-term schools for juveniles of advanced criminal tendency and for juvenile serious traffic offenders. In response to the reform by the ministry, the Family Court judges began to place more juveniles in short-term school facilities. Therefore, the total number of juveniles sent to juvenile training schools increased to 4758 in 1983 (see Table 1.3). However, after the third peak of juvenile delinquency the numbers began to decline once again. To accommodate more juvenile delinquents, short-term schools with special training courses were introduced in 1991 in place of ones for juvenile traffic offenders. The average daily percentage of inmates in short-term schools increased from 34.5% in 1983 to 41.8% in 1993 *(White Paper on Crime in 1994)*. For the past decade juvenile training schools have widened their net over juveniles who have committed less serious offences.

With the decrease in number of inmates, staff in training schools have oriented themselves to education rather than control. In addition to better training, the schools have been upgraded to provide rehabilitation services.

The maximum term of consignment in the long-term juvenile training schools is two years, while inmates in the general short-term schools and those in the schools with the special training courses, are treated within six and four months respectively. The schools offer a variety of programs including academic education, vocational training, and guidance on living skills.

Probation and Parole

One of the protective educative measures under the Juvenile Law is probation. Juvenile probationers may be placed on probation, in principle, until they are twenty years of age. From 1965 to 1983 the adjudication of probation decreased (see Table 1.3), even though the short-term (three to four months) probation for juvenile traffic offenders was introduced in 1977. One of the reasons for this decrease may have been the net widening of juvenile training schools since 1977. However, we also saw net widening in the area of probation. For example, in 1994 the Ministry of Justice adopted a new system of the short-term probation of six or seven months to accept more juvenile probationers.

Under the law professional probation-parole officers are expected to work as specialist social workers. Most of them have to pass a special examination for employment. There are about 900 in number, which is too few for them to treat all cases as case workers. Usually the professional officers work only as distributors of cases and supervisors for the volunteer officers. And since specialists spend much of their time doing administrative work, they tend not to develop their abilities as social workers.

In addition to the professional officers, the minister of justice commissions a leader in the community to work as a volunteer probation-parole officer. This is another example of the participatory nature of our juvenile justice system. In 1993 there were 48,695 such volunteer officers (*White Paper on Crime in 1994*). The volunteers guide, supervise, and assist almost all probationers and parolees through their experiences. They may also utilize resources in the community more effectively than the professional officers who are transferred to another office every two or three years.

The average age of volunteer probation-parole officers rose from 53.2 in 1953 to 62.3 in 1994 (Ministry of Justice, 1994). Therefore, we may see a wider generation gap between volunteer officers and juveniles. Recently more females have become volunteer officers. The percentage of female volunteer officers rose from 7% in 1953 to 21.6% in 1994. Female volunteer officers are expected to have a good influence on juveniles in a different way from that of male officers. The volunteer officers occasionally attend meetings for study and training purposes.

Summary

After the Meiji Restoration, Japan developed its juvenile justice system. It was modelled after the system introduced in many Western countries. The general objective of following the modern juvenile justice system was that it offered specialized treatment and rehabilitation for juvenile delinquents. In keeping with Japanese tradition and culture, volunteers played an important role—hence the participatory nature of our juvenile justice system. In 1922 the Juvenile Law was enacted. However, owing to a poor budget, the juvenile justice system under this law was not established completely until 1942.

After World War II our justice system was democratized. A new Juvenile Law under the principle of *parens patriae* was promulgated in 1948. But owing to limited resources, the juvenile agencies had a difficult time meeting the needs of the growing number of poor juvenile delinquents. However, with the economic recovery in the early 1950s we succeeded in stopping the spread of juvenile delinquency.

With the growth of the baby boomers after the war, we saw the second peak of juvenile delinquency in 1964. This was marked by an increase in violent crimes. As a result, many resources were assigned to delinquency prevention activities. The police were very aggressive with their initiatives. These activities appear to have had an impact since the number of delinquencies declined in the early 1970s.

Until the late 1970s the police were well equipped to guide and investigate virtually any type of delinquent behaviour. As a result of the net widening activities of the police, we saw the third peak in 1983 of juvenile delinquency, which was committed by the young generation born during the second baby boom. For the past decade we have, once again, seen a decrease in official delinquency rates. This may be partially due to the fact that young people have come to be excessively protected, guided, and supervised by the surrounding adults in the aging society.

After the second peak, heinous and violent crimes committed by juveniles decreased. Therefore, the number of juveniles placed on probation or admitted to juvenile training schools declined. In response, the Ministry of Justice introduced the system of short-term juvenile training schools and short-term probation. This seemed to be another net widening phenomenon.

Recently, lawyers have been drawing attention to defects in the current juvenile justice system. Their criticisms have focused on the difficulty of guaranteeing due process. However, their challenges fall short of advocating a **just deserts** model. The current model, while being primarily a **welfare/participatory** model with an emphasis upon rehabilitation, has undergone partial improvement in guaranteeing due process. In many respects the juvenile justice practices complement the recommendations put for in the Beijing Rules (see Box 1—Introduction). However, we must continue to examine the prescriptions of our Juvenile Law and the practice of our juvenile justice agencies in consideration of the recommendations sited in the Beijing Rules and those declared at the Ninth UN Congress on Prevention and Treatment.

It is anticipated that the population of juveniles will decrease as the nation's birth rate continues to decline. If the current social structures in Japan do not change drastically, the total number of juvenile delinquents will continue to decline. If the juvenile justice agencies do not adapt to such a situation, they will not be able to maintain their current resources because the Ministry of Finance will have to curtail their budgets. In order to prevent the process towards reduction, the juvenile justice agencies are likely to carry out additional net widening strategies.

Net widening ventures have produced advantages and disadvantages. These ventures have likely contributed to the reduction in juvenile delinquency. Early intervention by the police has helped to prevent many juvenile delinquents from developing criminal tendencies. The net widening of the treatment programs in juvenile training schools and for those on probation has given them the opportunity to receive the educative protective services that are deemed in their best interests.

On the other hand, the aforementioned net widening may more seriously invade juveniles' liberties. By proceeding to the further stage in the juvenile justice system, juvenile delinquents may be stigmatized more infamously. They may receive negative effects, as labelling theorists point out.

Soon after World War II many democratic systems were introduced. They were mostly modelled after those initiated by the Allied Powers. As a result of the revolution in the economic structure, the distance between the rich and the poor was narrowed. The newly developed industries offered juveniles more chances to receive a good education and to get a good job. Though Japanese juveniles are under the influence of Western cultures, they do not yet suffer from the adverse effects of extreme individualism and isolation. Intimate human ties in families, neighbourhoods, schools, and places of work still remain even in the urban areas—a critical element for the participatory model to work effectively. In addition we have seen the success in formal social control (Yokoyama, 1986a).

Finally, as the proportion of young people continues to decline, we will likely see juveniles being excessively protected, guided, and supervised by adults. According to Merton's (1968) typology of the modes of individual adaptation, juveniles of the retreatism-type may increase over those of innovation-type, whom we often saw before the second peak of juvenile delinquency. If most of the juveniles become too comfortable with conventional norms, and if the juveniles of the retreatism persuasion increase in numbers, then Japan's current rate development would likely be compromised. From this viewpoint, too, we must examine functions of the juvenile justice system in Japan.

References

Administrative Affairs Agency. (1994). White paper on juveniles in 1994 (written in Japanese). Tokyo: Printing Bureau of the Ministry of Finance.

Ayukawa, J. (1994). *Sociology of juvenile delinquency* (written in Japanese). Kyoto: Sekai Shiso-sha.

Correctional Association. (1984). *Modern development of juvenile correction* (written in Japanese). Tokyo: Correctional Association.

Fujimoto, T. (1994). *Crime problems in Japan*. Tokyo: Chuo University Press.

Fukuda, M. (1988). *A critical analysis of juvenile justice system in Japan*. Paper presented at the 40th Annual Meeting of American Society of Criminology, Chicago, U.S.A.

Gottfredson, M.R., & Hirschi, T. (1990). *A general theory of crime*. Stanford, CA: Stanford University Press.

Harada, Y. (1995). Adjustment to school, life course transitions, and changing in delinquent behavior in Japan. *Current Perspectives on Aging and the Life Cycle*, 4:35-60.

Hattori, A. (1992). Future of the child education and training homes (written in Japanese). *Juvenile Problems* (Japan),198:31-44.

_____ (1996). Kyogoin Home in Japan. In C. B. Fields and R. H. Moore, Jr. (Eds.). *Comparative criminal justice*. Prospect Height, Ill: Waveland Press: 573-582.

Hiyama, S., & Katsumi H. (1974). *History of juvenile crimes after the war* (written in Japanese). Tokyo: Sakai Shoten.

Igarashi, F. (1989). *Coerced confessions and pretrial detention in Japan*. Paper presented at the 41st Annual Meeting of American Society of Criminology, Reno, Nevada.

Kiyonaga, K. (1983). Younger juvenile delinquents—Prediction from 1983 (written in Japanese). *Crime and Delinquency* (Japan), 56:104-129.

Merton, R. (1968). *Social theory and social structure* (Enlarged edition). New York: The Free Press.

Murai, T. (1979). Juvenile delinquency and community. *Hitotsubashi J. of Law and Politics* (Japan), 8:31-46.

National Police Agency. (1973). White Paper on police in 1973 (written in Japanese). Tokyo: Printing Bureau of the Ministry of Finance.

_____. (1976). White Paper on police in 1976 (written in Japanese). Tokyo: Printing Bureau of the Ministry of Finance.

_____. (1984). White Paper on police in 1984 (written in Japanese). Tokyo: Printing Bureau of the Ministry of Finance.

_____. (1994). White Paper on police in 1994 (written in Japanese). Tokyo: Printing Bureau of the Ministry of Finance.

Research and Training Institute of the Ministry of Justice. (1965). White paper on crime in 1965 (written in Japanese). Tokyo: Printing Bureau of the Ministry of Finance.

_____. (1975). White Paper on crime in 1975 (written in Japanese). Tokyo: Printing Bureau of the Ministry of Finance.

_____. (1984). White Paper on crime in 1984 (written in Japanese). Tokyo: Printing Bureau of the Ministry of Finance.

_____. (1985). White Paper on crime in 1985 (written in Japanese). Tokyo: Printing Bureau of the Ministry of Finance.

_____. (1994). White Paper on crime in 1994 (written in Japanese). Tokyo: Printing Bureau of the Ministry of Finance.

_____. (1995). White Paper on crime in 1995 (written in Japanese). Tokyo: Printing Bureau of the Ministry of Finance.

Riesman, D. (1961). *The lonely crowd.* New Haven, Conn: Yale Un. Press.

Saito, T. (1986). The Japanese Juvenile Law and amendment issues. *Konan Hogaku* (Japan), 26(2 & 3):267-285.

Sawanobori, T. (1994). *Introduction to Juvenile Law* (written in Japanese). Tokyo: Yuhikaku.

Supreme Court. (1994). Annual report of judicial statistics for 1993 (written in Japanese). Tokyo: Hoso-kai.

Tamura, M. (1992). The Yakuza and amphetamine abuse in Japan. In H. Tarver and M. Gaylord (Eds.). *Drugs, law and the state.* Hong Kong: Hong Kong Un. Press. pp.: 99-117.

Tokuoka, H., & Cohen, A.K. (1987). Japanese society and delinquency. *International J. of Comparative and Applied Criminal Justice,* 11(1 & 2):13-22.

Tsujimoto, Y. (1990). The historical development of child saving in Japan. *Bulletin of the Research Institute, Chuo-Gakuin University* (Japan), 8(1):5-27.

Yokoyama, M. (1981). Delinquency control programs in the community in Japan. *International J. of Comparative and Applied Criminal Justice,* 5(2):169-178.

_____. (1982). *How have prisons been used in Japan?* Paper presented at the World Congress of the International Sociological Assoc. Mexico City, Mexico.

_____. (1984). *Why doesn't Japan have diversion programs for juvenile delinquents?* Paper presented at the World Congress of the International Institute of Sociology. Seattle, Washington, USA.

_____. (1985). Criminal policy against thieves in Japan. *Kangweon Law Review* (Korea), 1:191-217.

_____. (1986a). The juvenile justice system in Japan. In M. Bursten, J. Graham, N. Herriger and P. Malinowski (Eds.). *Youth crime, social control and prevention.* Wuppertal: Centaurus-Verlagsgesellschaft-Pfaffenweiler, pp.: 102-113.

_____. (1986b). Social control and juvenile traffic offenders in Japan. *Kangweon Law Review* (Korea), 2,142-160.

_____. (1989). Net-widening of the juvenile justice system in Japan. *Criminal Justice Review,* 14(1):43-53.

_____. (1990a). Criminalization against traffic offenders in Japan. *International J. of Comparative and Applied Criminal Justice,* 14(1 & 2):65-71.

_____. (1990b). Criminalization against traffic offenders in Japanese criminal justice. *Kokugakuin J. of Law and Politics* (Japan), 27(4):1-27.

_____. (1991). Development of Japanese drug control laws towards criminalization.(Japan), 28(3):1-21.

_____. (1992a). Guarantee of human rights in juvenile justice system in Japan. *Kokugakuin J. of Law and Politics* (Japan), 30(2):1-30.

_____. (1992b). Net-widening in juvenile justice system [written in Japanese]. In the Committee for Celebrating the 70th Birthday of Prof. Kuniyuki Yagi (Ed.). *Modern development of criminal jurisprudence II.* Tokyo: Hogakushoin. Pp. 481-512.

_____. (1994). Treatment of prisoners under rehabilitation model in Japan. *Kokugakain Journal of Law and Politics* (Japan). 32(2):1-24.

_____. (1995). Analysis of prostitution in Japan. *International J. of Comparative and Applied Criminal Justice,* 19(1 & 2):47-60.

chapter 2

Juvenile Justice in Australia

Lynn Atkinson
Crime Research Centre, University of Western Perth

Facts on Australia

Geography: Australia, an island as well as a continent, occupies an area of 7,682,292 sq. km. It consists of six states and two territories. **Population:** As of July 1995 it had a population of approx. 18.3 million inhabitants—annual growth rate 1.41% (density: 2 persons/sq km). The capital is Sydney (pop. 3.5 million) while Melbourne is the second largest city (pop. 3.0 million). The majority of the pop. (about 85%) lives in urban areas located around the coastal rim. Australia is rapidly becoming a multicultural society. The freeing up of immigration policy in the 1970s has witnessed an expansion of immigration from non-English-speaking countries. People of Asiatic origin make up the largest influx of immigrants—now approx. 4.5% of the population. Australia's Indigenous people account for less than 2%. **Climate:** Generally arid to semiarid; temperate in the west and tropical in the north. There are vast, dry inland areas of Australia which are virtually unpopulated. **Economy:** Australia is a nation that lacks an abundance of fresh water but has many other natural and agricultural resources. Major exports are coal, gold, beef, and iron ore, and major imports are manufactured products (such as motor vehicles, computers, and aircraft), and crude petroleum (Australian Bureau of Statistics, 1994). Finance and services make up nearly 34% of the labour force. **Government:** The State and Territory and Commonwealth Parliamentary systems in Australia are based on the British Westminster system. The Commonwealth and most of the states have a bicameral parliamentary system—that is, the parliament consists of an upper and lower house. Members of both houses are elected to parliament. The Prime Minister of Australia and the premiers of the states are elected members of parliament and the leaders of the party in government. The two major parties are the Labour Party and the Liberal (conservative) Party. Local government provides the third tier to Australia's system of government.

During these last two decades, there were several key shifts in policy direction which underpinned a number of changes in juvenile justice. The first of these—the "back-to-justice" movement... the second... was the movement towards destructuring.

(C. Alder and J. Wundersitz, 1994:4)

Seminal Justice—An Historical Outline

The history of Australia from the beginnings of European settlement in 1788 to the middle of the nineteenth century is predominantly a penal history (Hughes, 1987; Shaw, 1966). The decision to establish a penal colony in what is now called Australia came about after the American Revolution halted transportation of British convicts to America. With overcrowded prisons and convict ships (hulks) back in their native land, the British were forced to seek alternatives (see Ch. 4).

The Australian Aboriginal people did not appear to pose a serious threat to penal settlement of the country: they were not war-like and they appeared to have no conception of private ownership. Their vast lands seemed to be there for the taking. It was not until 1992 that the convenient doctrine of Terra Nullius, which defined Australia as uninhabited prior to its colonization, was successfully challenged in the high court and the foundations were laid for Aboriginal land claims based on prior ownership.

The arrival in New South Wales of the first fleet in 1788 heralded policies and actions which ultimately were catastrophic for our Aboriginal people. From the beginning of colonization, the seeds of a process which dispossessed, disempowered, and criminalized Aborigines took root. Aboriginal people today are profoundly over-represented in the criminal justice system, young Aboriginal people in particular. As this chapter suggests, dealing with Aboriginal offenders and reducing their over-representation in the juvenile justice system presents one of the major challenges for our contemporary juvenile justice systems.

The human cargo on board the ships of the First Fleet is recorded by Hughes (1987). There were 736 convicts, including three boys and two girls under sixteen years of age, and a further 126 young prisoners aged between sixteen and twenty-five years. The average age of this first convict contingent was about twenty-seven years. Youthfulness was an important criterion for transportation, presumably because of the arduous tasks ahead in creating a self-sufficient colony from the harsh and resistant environment.

Other colonies eventually were carved from New South Wales, ultimately to become the eastern and southern Australian states of Queensland, Victoria and South Australia. In 1803 a convict colony was established on Van Diemen's Land (now the island state of Tasmania). A prison for child convicts was built there in the 1830s, on a barren promontory called, appropriately enough, Point Puer, from the Latin *puer*, meaning boy (Hughes, 1987; Seymour, 1988).

Western Australia, on the west coast and separated from the eastern colonies by extensive, desert-like regions, was the last colony to be established. In 1849 Western Australia made a controversial decision to introduce convict labour to alleviate its labour shortages after transportation was already drawing to a close in Van Diemen's Land and had long ceased in New South Wales (Hughes, 1987). Some remnants of a frontier response in Western Australia to its predicaments can be seen in some recent controversial juvenile justice policy decisions discussed below.

The colonies achieved statehood in the closing years of the nineteenth century. In 1901 the states united under a federal flag. However, the states and territories have always been reluctant to relinquish rights and responsibilities to the federal government. In the criminal justice arena, there are eight state and territory criminal justice systems. Some jurisdictions adhere to a codified criminal law, whereas the laws of others derive from British common law. Unlike a number of countries covered in this book, Australia's federal government has little involvement in criminal justice matters in general, and juvenile justice matters in particular.

Prototypes of Separate Treatment

The Juvenile Justice System

Many factors have influenced the development of juvenile justice systems in Australian jurisdictions. Economic issues, labour needs, key historical events, overseas movements and trends, and humanitarian concerns have all had an impact on the treatment of juvenile offenders since 1788. Seymour (1988) traces some important elements of juvenile justice in Australia in his seminal work on the nation's juvenile justice systems. He points out that the concept of separate treatment for juvenile offenders, which underpins juvenile justice legislation today, was at least embryonic in 1788. The death penalty was common in Georgian England and transportation the most frequent outcome for a commuted sentence. Children under capital sentence were more likely than their elders to be saved from the gallows. In some ways then, transportation might be considered to have been special treatment for juveniles.

New South Wales and Van Diemen's Land received many young convicts: for example, in the five years between 1833 and 1838, 991 boys were transported to New South Wales. Van Diemen's land received 200 convict boys in 1838 alone (Seymour, 1988). No special treatment was given to juvenile convicts at first, but after a time alternative methods were considered and tried.

In New South Wales in 1803, apprenticeships for juvenile convicts were introduced. Boys were apprenticed to learn trades, and girls became domestic servants. The system was not a great success, however, proving to be little different from the labour assignment systems that applied to adult prisoners.

By 1820 boy convicts under sixteen, in theory at least, were able to spend three years undertaking trade training before being assigned to labour in the colony. Moreover, for the first time separate accommodation, at Carters Barracks in Sydney, as well as a system of classification were established for this group of young prisoners. However, the system did not live up to expectations. It was phased out and finally terminated in about 1835. In 1837 the first Chief Justice of New South Wales attributed the failure of the system to "the association of a body of young criminals together, and the incorrigible effects of their example and communications upon each other" (quoted in Seymour, 1988:13).

In Van Diemen's Land convict boys had been taken to Point Puer at Port Arthur from 1834. It was intended that Point Puer be a place of rehabilitation and training for its young clientele, or "little depraved felons" as Governor Arthur called them (quoted in Hughes, 1987:408). Over 2000 boys passed through the institution in its fifteen years of existence. The regime was disciplinarian and harsh and corporal punishment was a central feature. However, in an effort to redeem the boys, equip them with skills which would be useful to them, and meet the labour needs of the colony, a system of trade training was instituted. The diversity of trades on offer was remarkable, but training places were limited.

The regime was also intended to provide the boys with religious instruction and basic literacy skills. Texts, however, were limited to the Bible and a handful of elementary readers and spelling books. Literacy education was thus essentially limited in its appeal, availability, and scope. Religious instruction failed to make a redeeming mark on the inmates. Given the context within which such instruction took place—the harshness of the regime and the pervasiveness of the inevitable prison culture—this is not surprising. The juvenile institution at Point Puer clearly failed to bridge the gap between its stated intention and philosophy and its accomplishments in practice. Point Puer was closed in 1849.

Although the institutions at Carters Barracks and Point Puer in Australia pre-dated the British prison for children at Parkhurst, it was nevertheless British models which informed the development in Australia in the second half of the nineteenth century of reformatory and industrial schools (Seymour, 1988). By this time the early Australian experiments in training and separate treatment for juvenile offenders seem to have sunk from official memory.

The Welfare System

Seymour (1988) traces the development of Australian child welfare systems to the early 1800s when the New South Wales government and a committee of private citizens established a home for orphans and destitute children, mostly of convict parents. Other colonies followed suit towards the middle of the nineteenth century.

While the establishment of special institutions was one response to child destitution, other official responses of the time resulted in these children being charged with vagrancy and imprisoned. Attempts were made in the second half of the nineteenth century to classify and separate "criminal" and "neglected" youth. Reform and industrial schools were intended to contain and serve two, apparently distinct, juvenile populations: delinquents and the merely destitute.

For practical as well as ideological reasons, the discrete labelling and the official responses attached to each group were never entirely successful. For the most part, the legislation of the various colonies (later states) allowed for flexibility in categorizing the young person, and for the considerable use of discretion by the court. Indeed, as Seymour illustrates, the assumptions which supported mutually exclusive categorizations of young people as "neglected" or "offenders" were questionable:

> The Council has learned by the experience gained in dealing with a large number of children that the so-called 'criminal' children are not the worst class. Many children convicted of stealing and sent to reformatories are found to be moral and well-behaved, while very often it has been proved that children committed to the Industrial School as neglected or destitute are vicious, immoral, and altogether unfit to mix with decent children (South Australian State Children's Council, quoted in Seymour, 1988:48).

Questions had also been raised towards the end of the nineteenth century about the merits of detaining children in large institutions. More community oriented alternatives, such as "boarding out" arrangements in foster homes, were introduced in some Australian states and, over time, the dual schools system was abandoned.

Juvenile Justice Systems in
Australian States

Welfare or Social Control?

The dual schools system reflected the dilemma about the relationship between "welfare" and "justice" in the response to juveniles coming to official attention. The dilemma did not diminish with the eventual demise of that system: it is still evident in the juvenile justice debate today. The dual schools system also highlighted the continuing difficulty of closing the gap between rhetoric and reality, theory and practice, in the juvenile justice arena.

By the early 1900s there was clear evidence that distinct juvenile justice systems were being established (Seymour, 1988). By this time most states had established special children's courts, the groundwork for this having been laid the previous century with the passing of legislation to enable a range of offences by children to be dealt with summarily. Although British legislation had provided models in many areas relating to juvenile justice and welfare, the Australian states took the idea for special children's courts from the United States. The most significant difference between legislation passed in many American states and acts applying in Australia was that Australian juveniles could be charged with specific offences, whereas American juveniles were dealt with on the basis that they were delinquent minors. In theory at least, delinquency in Australia was an act; in America it was a symptom. In practice, Australian jurisdictions tended to blur this distinction.

Australian juvenile justice systems in the twentieth century have continued to intertwine welfare and justice responses to juveniles who come within their ambit. The bias towards a "welfare" response was marked in the decades prior to the 1980s. The philosophy stated in section 4 of the extant and oddly phrased Tasmanian *Child Welfare Act* 1960 is typical of the era:

> ... as far as is practicable and expedient, each child suspected of having committed, charged with, or found guilty of an offense shall be treated, not as a criminal, but as a child who is, or may have been, misdirected or misguided, and that the care, custody, and discipline of each ward of the State shall approximate as nearly as may be to that which should be given to it by its parents.

During this time, 'treatment,' 'care,' and 'welfare' were concepts and terms which predominated in the official responses to delinquent juveniles. Under the guise of helping 'delinquents' who had been charged with status or criminal offences to reconstitute themselves as law-abiding citizens, the children's courts were able to make use of indeterminate sentences to detention. Incarceration of juveniles was not necessarily reserved for criminal offences. As part of an interdependent process, welfare authorities became responsible for rehabilitating youth in their custody and for determining when young detainees were ready to be released.

Young people could be kept in detention for long periods, particularly if their behaviour and general comportment signaled no evidence of reform. Rehabilitation was often seen to have been achieved when the young person demonstrated behaviour and skills consistent with the standards of the day. In setting those standards the values of the white, middle-class predominated. The system replicated and distilled prevailing gender and race biases and stereotypes, in determining both the clientele and the models of behaviour which the inmates were required to approximate. Girls were particularly vulnerable to detention for their care and protection, since any kind of rebellious behaviour was a transgression of stereotypical feminine norms. Boys had more leeway: the stereotype for this group allowed for the "sowing of wild oats." Aboriginal youth also were (and are) absorbed by the system in disproportionate numbers.

Although in Australian jurisdictions juvenile justice systems had always contained a mix of justice and welfare approaches and outcomes, the scope for abuse in the welfare-oriented systems at this time, particularly the use of indeterminate sentences, generated reviews of those systems and, in time, reforms.

A Change in Emphasis: Welfare to Due Process
In the second half of the 1960s in the United States, welfare-oriented juvenile justice systems came under attack. Two important decisions by the US Supreme Court, *Kent v. United States* (383 U.S. 541, 1966) and *Re Gault* (387 U.S. 1, 1967) exposed the shortcomings of a system which failed to protect the rights of the child. The *Gault* decision in particular was to have far-reaching and reverberating effects that influenced Australian law reforms in the 1970s. Seymour (1988:167) points out, however, that decisions in the United States were championed in Australia as a "matter of principle rather than as a response to identified deficiencies in this country's children's courts."

South Australia, with its Children's Protection and Young Offenders Act 1979 (since replaced by the Young Offenders Act 1993), was the first state to reform its legislation to give clear priority to due process of law rather than treatment of the offender. As of 1996 all jurisdictions except Tasmania have followed suit. Tasmania is currently reviewing its laws and procedures in relation to juveniles. Even so, the practice of juvenile justice in Tasmania clearly reflects the principles of due process.

Even though Australian children's courts operate according to the principles and practices of due process—justice model (see Figure 1, Introduction)— there are nevertheless important components of our juvenile justice systems that reflect a more forgiving and helpful approach to young offenders than is evident in the adult system. In most juvenile jurisdictions, for example, significant efforts are made to divert the majority of apprehended juveniles away from the courts altogether (i.e., the welfare model). For example, tariff sentencing (sentencing according to the seriousness of the offence) is one of the precepts of this model.

Juvenile clients range in age from ten years to sixteen or seventeen years (two jurisdictions have a lower minimum age). Juveniles apprehended by police can either be charged with an offence, in which case the matter is dealt with through the children's court; cautioned by police for a minor offence; or, referred to an alternative pre-court diversion scheme if such a scheme is available.

Due Process in Practice

The Children's Court and Formal Processing

Three juvenile jurisdictions in Australia are presided over by a judge of district court status. In Western Australia even the most serious indictable offence by a juvenile can be dealt with in the children's court; however the defendant can elect to have the matter heard before a judge and jury in the adult jurisdiction. Serious matters involving juvenile and adult co-offenders may also be dealt with in the adult jurisdiction. In Queensland the Juvenile Justice Act 1992 makes similar provision for even the most serious juvenile cases to be heard in the juvenile jurisdiction, unless the child elects to have the matter dealt with in the district or supreme courts. However, if a juvenile is found to have a case to answer on a serious (life) matter and is unrepresented, the case must be dealt with in the appropriate (adult) court.

In South Australia either the defendant, the director of public prosecutions, or a police prosecutor can apply for a serious matter to be heard in the adult jurisdiction, with homicide automatically being dealt with in the superior court. The South Australian Children's Court can also decide on the basis of a preliminary inquiry to commit a defendant for trial or sentence to the district or supreme court.

The remaining five jurisdictions are presided over by a magistrate. Leaving aside Tasmania, whose children's court still operates under welfare-oriented legislation, the jurisdiction of the children's courts in these states and territories extends to indictable offences, but there are mechanisms for transfer of serious indictable offences to the adult jurisdiction, either for hearing or sentencing. Both the New South Wales and the Victorian children's courts have jurisdiction to hear and determine indictable offences (but not 'serious indictable offences' in NSW or homicide in Victoria) and to undertake committal proceedings in relation to serious indictable offences.

In Australian children's courts the case is prosecuted by the police.

Victoria, which has an upper age limit of sixteen years for the juvenile jurisdiction, operates a unique system whereby young adults (seventeen to twenty-one years) can be sentenced in the adult jurisdiction to detention in a facility especially for that age group. No juvenile clients can be held in these facilities, yet they are administered by the juvenile authorities (who in this state come under the auspices of the Department of Health and Community Services) rather than by the adult correctional authorities.

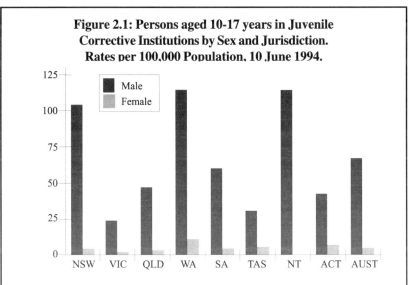

Figure 2.1: Persons aged 10-17 years in Juvenile Corrective Institutions by Sex and Jurisdiction. Rates per 100,000 Population, 10 June 1994.

NSW = New South Wales; VIC = Victoria; QLD = Queensland; WA = Western Australia; SA = South Australia; TAS = Tasmania; NT = Northern Territory; ACT = Australian Capital Territory; AUST = Australia.

In principle, detention for juveniles is used as a last resort. However, a state by state perusal of juvenile detention rates (see Figure 2.1) indicates that in some jurisdictions detention is less of a last resort than in others. Children's court sanctions, although proportional to the offence, are generally less harsh than they are for adults. Table 2.1 shows the proportional use of various dispositions available to the New South Wales Children's Court in 1993/94. The highest number of charges were disposed of by way of recognizance, or bond. Other jurisdictions employ similar sanctions, although the pattern of use differs across the jurisdictions.

Table 2.1: Outcomes of charges dealt with in New South Wales Children's Courts 1993/94

Outcome	Number of Charges	Percentage
Not determined	1437	10.3
No penalty*	1352	9.7
Dismissed and cautioned	1933	13.9
Rising of the court	—	—
Recognizance	2793	20.1
Probation	2190	15.7
Compensation	—	—
Fine	1862	13.4
Community Service order	779	5.6
Control (detention) order	870	6.3
Other	696	5.0
Total	13,912	100.0

Adapted from NSW Bureau of Crime Statistics and Research 1995, Table 2.3.

* This category includes some juveniles who were acquitted, some who were found guilty, and some whose charges were all dropped.

Questions are sometimes raised about how the ideals of due process actually operate in the juvenile jurisdiction. Most Australian jurisdictions now have specialist youth legal aid and legal representation services (O'Connor, 1992, O'Connor and Tilbury, 1986) and most Australian children's courts operate duty counsel schemes (O'Connor and Sweetapple, 1988). However, the quality and accessibility of specialist legal representation is variable between and within jurisdictions (O'Connor, 1992).

In theory, due process models of juvenile justice uphold the rights of young people in court. In practice, a high proportion of our young people plead guilty to charges against them in any case, so their cases are never tested in court. It is estimated that roughly 95% plead guilty to charges laid against them (Freiberg, Fox and Hogan 1988). For those young offenders offered the opportunity to avoid court by participating in a pre-court diversion program, an admission of guilt is an entry requirement.

Serious questions have been raised about the capacity of young people to participate effectively in court proceedings against them (O'Connor and Sweetapple, 1988). The court itself is an alien environment for young people, and Australian cultures and education systems are not supportive of young people speaking out. Genuine participation by a young person in court, or even a real understanding of the process, is rare.

Detention is used more sparingly under a due process model of juvenile justice. Tasmania is the only state whose legislation still sanctions detention for reasons of care and protection. Even so, it is rare for this to happen. In 1994/95 in Tasmania, only one admission to youth detention out of a total of 102 was for non-criminal reasons (Community and Health Services Tasmania, unpublished data). Hence with secure detention applying almost entirely to criminal rather than welfare cases, and with more community-based sentencing options available to the courts, the current rate at which juveniles are detained

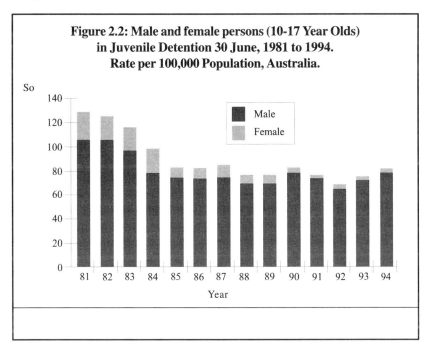

Figure 2.2: Male and female persons (10-17 Year Olds) in Juvenile Detention 30 June, 1981 to 1994. Rate per 100,000 Population, Australia.

in Australia is just over half that of 1981 (see Figure 2.2). With the shift from a welfare to a justice model, the drop has been proportionally greater for females. It is interesting to note, in light of the recent punitive responses to young offenders (see below), a slight increase in the rate of juvenile detention each year since 1992.

Informal Processing or Pre-court Diversion

While the juvenile court system has moved closer to the theory and practice underlying the adult court system, important philosophical and practical differences distinguish the two systems. The young, as part of their growing-up, are expected to make mistakes along the way, but in so doing most also "grow out" of crime. Our juvenile justice systems generally give some support for this line of thinking. For example, section 3 of the South Australian *Young Offenders Act 1993* states that

> the object of this Act is to secure for youths who offend against the criminal law the care, correction and guidance necessary for their development into responsible and useful members of the community, and the proper realization of their potential.

At a functional level, pre-court diversion schemes reflect a philosophy of second chances for juveniles. These schemes serve to divert minor offenders from the courts and thus minimize the negative consequences of court appearances and criminal records.

Until the early 1990s, formal pre-court diversion schemes either took the form of police cautioning or, in the case of Western Australia and South Australia, children's panels (in essence, admonishment by a small panel of social workers and police). In the past few years, pre-court diversion has altered significantly. There have been three major changes: the panel schemes have been abandoned, police cautioning programs have been extended, and restorative justice-based programs (known generically as "family group conferences" or FGCs) have taken root.

The seeds of change came with the shift from a welfare- to a due process-oriented juvenile justice system and accompanied the growth of the victims' movement and the political conservatism of the 1990s. Concerns about the efficacy of pre-court diversion schemes as they operated in the early 1990s were broadbased: where were the programs meant to assist young offenders to become more responsible and law abiding? If minimal intervention were justified on the grounds that most young offenders do not re-offend, what about those who do? Finally, if offenders' needs are to be addressed in the

Box 2.1: Youth Crime Shake-up: Victims Set to Confront Offenders

Victims may confront young criminals under rules of the new Youth Court which comes into effect in South Australia on Saturday... A Victims of Crime Service police representative, Senior Sergeant Elke Pfau, said the new approach would help crime prevention.... 'If a juvenile is confronted with the victim and told the effect of his actions, it gives the juvenile something to think about,' she said. 'It might stop them from doing it again'.... (Sylvia Kriven, *The Adelaide Advertiser*, 30 December 1993, p.3).

Youth Punishment Scheme Criticized

The director of the National Children's and Youth Law Centre, Mr. Robert Ludbrook, said there were serious problems in allowing police to take part in the whole process.

'They have the power to influence outcomes,' he said. 'They investigate crimes and prosecute crimes, and allowing the police to then mete out punishment breaches the whole concept of separation of powers'... (Elizabeth Jurman, *The Sydney Morning Herald*, 2 April 1994, p.3).

interests of crime prevention, what about the question of redress for the victims of crime (see Box 2.1)?

In addressing these issues, Australian states and territories have looked with interest at some New Zealand juvenile justice innovations (see Box 4, Introduction). New Zealand has a tiered model of justice for juveniles, with interventions increasing in intensity from police cautioning, through FGCs, and ultimately the children's court. In particular, it is the New Zealand system of family group conferences that has captured the imagination of most Australian juvenile justice authorities.

As an initial response to minor offending, jurisdictions have shifted away from children's panels to police cautioning programs. Such schemes are the most cost effective and minimally intrusive. Most police services currently operate formal juvenile cautioning schemes. There are different eligibility criteria for cautioning schemes across the jurisdictions, but an admission of guilt is required by all. Legal representation is not part of these diversionary procedures.

If a young person is formally cautioned by the police, a record is kept for administrative purposes. Evidence of previous cautions can also be submitted to the children's court should a cautioned juvenile subsequently appear there. Cautions, however, are not meant to constitute a formal criminal record. This means that a cautioned juvenile with no convictions can truthfully claim, when seeking employment for instance, to have no criminal record.

But what of those young offenders who need help and who need more than the shock of being apprehended and cautioned to curb law-breaking behaviour? And what about the victims' movement, the perceived program deficiencies since the shift to due process, and the law-and-order constituency? Currently all Australian juvenile jurisdictions except Victoria are adopting or trialling pre-court, restorative justice-based programs—family group conference schemes—to target these offenders and satisfy these multifaceted community interests.

The South Australian juvenile justice system conforms most closely to the New Zealand idea of a tiered model of juvenile justice. Recent South Australian legislation (the Young Offenders Act 1993) provides for a dual level approach to pre-court diversion and a three-tiered juvenile justice system: minor offenders are dealt with by police cautioning, more serious offenders

Box 2.2: Family Group Conferences

Family group conferences are convened according to specific guidelines operative in a particular jurisdiction, usually for offences involving a victim. A conference is convened only if the offender agrees to take this path. As well as the offender, the conference generally includes members of the offender's immediate or extended family, or relevant people from the local community. Ideally the victim will be present and a police officer also attends.

There is generally a dual focus to FGCs: **restoration** and **restitution** for the victim on the one hand and offender rehabilitation and reintegration on the other (Alder and Wundersitz, 1994). The balance between these foci varies, depending on the particular model in place. The process is interactive, with all parties having some level of participation. Possible outcomes include apologies, community work, and compensation to the victim.

Because the FGCs are more intrusive and more costly than police cautioning the schemes should be targeted to more serious, potentially entrenched offenders. This is the intent of the New Zealand legislation, and the rationale behind the South Australian three-tiered system. However, in some jurisdictions quite minor offences are dealt with in FGCs

The debate in Australia about FGCs centres largely on questions of control and tends to obscure other fundamental questions such as, who do FGCs benefit, at what point in the process might FGCs be most effective, and are they indeed the best response to problems within a particular juvenile justice system? The state of Victoria has the lowest juvenile detention rate of all Australian jurisdictions. Victoria stands alone in its current disinclination to introduce a pre-court FGC scheme. Instead, it is piloting a post court conferencing scheme to assist in the constructive sentencing of serious young offenders.

Family group conference schemes in Australia have not been operating long enough for their effectiveness to be known, particularly in relation to their impact on repeat offending. However, a review of the South Australian scheme conducted after FGCs had been running for some fourteen months, showed a high rate of compliance with the orders arising from FGCs (86%), and high levels of positive responses (93%) from victims whose views were sought in a pilot study (Wundersitz and Hetzel, 1996).

participate in FGCs (see Box 2.2), and only the most serious offenders proceed to court. Western Australia also combines police cautioning and FGCs in their pre-court diversion plan. Only South Australia and Western Australia currently provide for FGCs in their juvenile justice legislation.

Juvenile Crime and Justice—The Situation in the 1990s

In what appears to be an international trend, in the 1990s there has been a public backlash against young people in Australia. This has been fuelled by hard economic times and a climate of conservatism. The economic recession of the early 1990s and continuing economic restraints have impacted on education and training, employment, housing, and health and welfare systems. While young people are bearing the consequences, they have also become significant targets of public fear and disquiet.

The Nature and Extent of Juvenile Crime

As noted in most other contributions here, hard data on juvenile crime are limited in terms of their availability, reliability, and comparability across jurisdictions. However, bearing these caveats in mind, it is possible to make the following general comments about juvenile offenders and offending in Australia. We know that juvenile offenders in Australia commit mostly minor property offences (Wundersitz, 1993); that serious assaults tend to be committed not by juveniles but rather by young adult males just beyond the age range of the juvenile justice system (Walker, 1991); that a very small group of young offenders appears to be seriously recidivist (Youth Justice Coalition, 1990), and that the majority of young people apprehended once do not make a re-appearance in the juvenile justice system.

The youth crime problems facing the United States (see Chapter 10), of gang violence and violence in schools, are not entrenched problems in Australia (Australian Bureau of Criminal Intelligence, 1991; Challinger, 1987; Hickman, 1991). Furthermore, there is no particular issue in Australia concerning the use of firearms by juveniles.

The issue of teenage street gang activity in Australia is clouded by the tendency of the media to label young people in groups in public places pejoratively as gangs (compare with Chapter 8 on Russia). Youth gangs as depicted in the press tend to comprise young people of a common, often

Asian, ethnic or racial origin. Undercurrents of racial discrimination pervade media representations and public perceptions of so-called youth gangs (Victorian Community Council Against Violence, 1992). On the other hand, there is growing concern about the involvement of young people of Indo-Chinese origin in drug dealing, and some evidence of gang activity associated with this (Standing Committee on Social Issues 1995). Graham (1994) found that in New South Wales youth of Indo-Chinese origin are substantially over-represented in juvenile detention, particularly for the more serious drug offences.

Despite the concerns of the public, overall, juvenile crime rates do not appear to be increasing dramatically. Wundersitz's (1993) profile of juvenile offending across Australia throughout the 1980s (see Figure 2.3) indicated no significant increase in total recorded official rates of intervention against juvenile offenders during this period, except in Western Australia. However, Harding et al. (1995) confirmed Wundersitz's conjecture that the steep climb in offence rates in Western Australian to 1990, and the reversal after this period, were due to technical problems and legislative changes rather than to variations in levels of criminal activity. Unfortunately, upheavals in many juvenile justice systems since the early 1990s have led to gaps in the data being recorded.

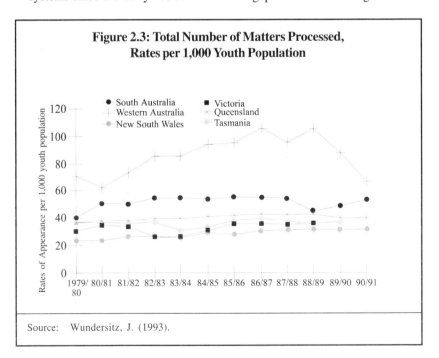

Figure 2.3: Total Number of Matters Processed, Rates per 1,000 Youth Population

Source: Wundersitz, J. (1993).

With pre-court diversion data now unavailable in most jurisdictions, it is not possible to assess and compare total juvenile interventions in the period from 1992.

Box 2.3: Aboriginal youth—The disadvantaged

In her seminal work on Aboriginal over-representation in the criminal justice system, Eggleston (1976) raised serious concerns about access to bail for Aboriginal people. Aboriginal people were vulnerable to being denied police bail, either as an outcome of the social disadvantage that they so often suffered, or because racist stereotypes prevailed. For example, Luke and Cunneen (1995) found that in New South Wales there appeared to be no significant differences between the rate of bail refusals for Aboriginal and non-Aboriginal youths. It is possible, as the authors suggest, that the establishment of the Royal Commission into Aboriginal Deaths in Custody in 1987, which generated an ethos of minimizing police custody for Aboriginal people, influenced this state of affairs. A recent Western Australian study found that similar proportions of Aboriginal and non-Aboriginal youth had been granted bail in the years 1990 to 1994 (Crime Research Centre, 1995).

Aboriginal Youth, Crime and Justice

Aboriginal youth are grossly over-represented in juvenile justice systems in Australia. In 1993 in Western Australia, for example, Aboriginal youth, who comprise about 4.1% of the state's juvenile population, were convicted of almost 38% of all juvenile offences (Harding et al., 1995). At a national level, the 1994 National Aboriginal and Torres Strait Islander Survey revealed that 14% of male Aboriginal youth aged between thirteen and seventeen years had been arrested at least once in the preceding five years (in most jurisdictions the five years includes a period where the thirteen and fourteen year olds were too young to be dealt with in the juvenile justice system, hence for the fifteen to seventeen year olds alone the percentage is probably higher) (unpublished data, Australian Bureau of Statistics). Aboriginal youth are progressively over-represented as they move through each stage of the juvenile justice system. Nationally, Aboriginal youth in Australia are twenty-one times more likely to be detained than non-Aboriginal youth, and in Western Australia they are thirty-two times more likely to be detained (figures for June 1994, Australian Institute of Criminology).

The police, who are at the threshold of this process of over-representation, have been slow to embrace the use of alternatives to arrest such as summonses and court attendance notices (Blagg and Wilkie, 1995), especially in relation to Aboriginal youth (see Box 2.3) (Gale, Bailey-Harris, and Wundersitz, 1990).

A study across four Australian states of perceptions of the treatment of young people in the juvenile justice system found that an extremely large proportion (80%) of young respondents had been stopped in the street and spoken to by police (Alder, O'Connor, Warner, and White, 1992). Despite the widespread intervention of police with young people generally, Aboriginal youth in the sample were more likely to have been stopped than other groups, more likely to have been taken to the police station, more likely to have been held in cells, and more likely to have been roughed up. In his study of police violence against Aboriginal youth, Cunneen (1991) found that, of the 171 Aboriginal juveniles interviewed in detention centres in New South Wales, Western Australia, and Queensland, 85% of them reported having been physically assaulted by police.

Aboriginal people officially became Australian citizens only after a constitutional referendum in 1967. It was not until the 1970s that the Commonwealth embarked on its fractured course to counter almost 200 years of dispossession and discrimination. As with the Native Indians of North America, Aboriginal people had lost their lands, much of their culture and their independence to the colonizers, and often their children to an assimilationist child welfare system. It is little wonder that Aboriginal young people were and are recruited into the juvenile justice system in disproportionate numbers, and little wonder that with the system's non-Aboriginal structures, values, personnel, and modus operandi, the legitimacy of the juvenile justice system appears to have been soundly rejected by them.

Getting Tough with Young Offenders

The 1990s have seen a toughening of attitudes to young offenders, particularly to serious repeat offenders. Aboriginal youth continue to be disproportionately represented in the group of serious (Harding et al., 1995) and repeat offenders (Cain, 1994). Western Australia, a state that has a relatively high proportion of Aboriginal youth, is one state that has produced some controversial policies targeted at the repeat offender group. In 1992 Western Australia produced a landmark piece of legislation, the *Crime (Serious and Repeat Offenders) Sentencing Act*, which was designed specifically to impact on recidivist young car thieves whose use of stolen vehicles led to police pursuits, serious crashes, and much social turbulence (see Box 2.4). Many of these offenders were Aboriginal (Broadhurst, Ferrante, and Susilo, 1991,1992). The act mandated a fixed minimum term in detention, to be followed by an indeterminate period of detention at the governor's pleasure for those fitting the criteria of serious, repeat offender.

Box 2.4: Justice Ministry Director-General David Grant said the Aboriginal imprisonment rate was WA's biggest social justice issue.

"The facts are that around 3 per cent of WA's population—the Aboriginal people—make up a third of the State's prison population at any given time', he said...." (Karen Brown & Jane Seymour, *West Australian*, 29 November, 1994, p.11).

"... all the broad social justice issues which deplete and harrow the daily lives of Aboriginal families also contribute to patterns of offending.

In a very real sense, to focus on [Aboriginal] juvenile criminal justice issues is to focus on the cart before the horse. In many ways our kids are drawn to court by collective forces and circumstances which they are born into and which are beyond their control. But for which they are judged and must take the consequences as individuals. And so generations of disadvantage are compounded in the present and lead to future disadvantage and further over-representation in the criminal justice system..."

Commissioner Mick Dodson, Aboriginal and Torres Strait Islander Social Justice Commissioner, 'Aboriginal Justice issues', paper presented to the Crime in Australia: *The First National Outlook Symposium*, Australian Institute of Criminology, 1995.

On the face of it, the act marked out all those defined as serious repeat offenders for harsh criminal justice system responses. The real target, however, was a particular, vexatious group of young, predominantly Aboriginal, chronic offenders. The Crime (Serious and Repeat Offenders) Sentencing Act , which contained a two-year sunset clause, has since expired; however, components of it have been re-shaped to avoid earlier criticisms that it breached a number of UN conventions (Broadhurst, Wilkie, and Susilo, 1992; Wilkie, 1992) and have been re-cast within more recent legislation. The highly controversial provision for detention at the governor's pleasure has been abandoned. Despite an initial national outcry about the act, the apparent electoral appeal of a tough posture on juvenile crime has not been lost on some other jurisdictions. Manifestations of a tougher posture include "truth in sentencing" legislation (which effectively maximizes the custodial component of a sentence), tighter conditions on juvenile access to bail, parental responsibility legislation, and a reluctance to expand the list of cautionable offences.

Boot Camps

A second significant move in Western Australia, with the potential for a disproportionate impact on Aboriginal offenders, has been the establishment of a juvenile work camp. Because of strong criticism of the military model, which informed the early plans for an American style boot camp, the work camp that ultimately evolved in 1995 emphasized structure and discipline but shied away from the military basic training model (Atkinson, 1995). As part of the sentencing process, young offenders fitting the eligibility criteria can agree to serve time in detention at the work camp in exchange for a shorter term of incarceration. The Western Australian work camp for juvenile and young adult offenders is located at a remote outpost, over 800 kilometres from the capital city of Perth. Very few offenders have passed through the work camp in the first year of its existence, suggesting that neither potential clients nor the magistracy is fully supportive of the program. Its operations are currently under review.

While there is no evidence to suggest that the military model impacts favourably on levels of offending, it appears that intense aftercare programs and programs which deal in a holistic way with the offender in the community hold promise. There is nothing to suggest that such programs require the framework of a boot camp as a springboard to their existence or success (Atkinson, 1995).

Aboriginal youth, because of their over-representation in the juvenile justice system, are particularly vulnerable to boot camp—or work camp—interventions. The processes of colonization have been invariably destructive to Aboriginal people and cultures. Seen in this light, the structures of work camps are unlikely to strike a positive chord amongst Aboriginal people concerned for the future of their youth. Although some interstate interest has been expressed in work camps, there has been no proliferation of the model so far.

Conclusion

Public disquiet about the youth of the day is nothing new. Often adult concerns about youth offending and delinquent behaviour are manifestations of the generation gap, rather than responses to a real growth in youth crime. In Australia in the 1990s, the media have helped generate and sustain images of a juvenile crime wave—hard evidence for which is questionable. However, notwithstanding the gap between public perceptions of the type and level of juvenile crime and any realities that can be constructed from the official data, the 1990s have highlighted concerns about juvenile crime and the juvenile justice system that cannot be dismissed simply as media hype or the recurring cycle of public hysteria.

In placing juvenile offending in a conservative context, it is nevertheless clear that there is a small group of young offenders—serious offenders who continue to offend—for which the state seems to have few answers. A disproportionate number of these young people are Aboriginal. Aboriginal youth are over-policed and over-represented at every stage of the criminal justice system. The process of criminalization began with the settlement of Australia as a penal colony and has been re-invented and re-enforced as successive generations of Aboriginal people have survived the policies and practices of the times.

The challenges for the second half of the 1990s are to address the issues associated with the small group of serious, repeat offenders and to tackle Aboriginal youth over-representation in the juvenile justice system. Neither issue can be addressed solely within the narrow framework of juvenile justice system reforms, but the juvenile justice system is clearly both the springboard and anchor point for ameliorative work in these areas. By dichotomizing 'justice' and 'welfare' in the past, the possibilities for reparative programs have either been too few, or the clientele has been too broad. Now that there are substantive moves away from this polarization of models in the juvenile justice system, there is still a reluctance to take on the hard issues and to direct reforms and resources to those crucial areas where they are most needed.

Australia has its own unique social and political history, and a particular racial and ethnic mix amongst its people. It has a scattered, predominantly urban population and systems of government that allow for a level of decentralized control over juvenile justice. These unique features contribute to some of the problems in relation to juvenile justice and should help to generate some of the solutions. However, for administrative and legislative models of juvenile justice, Australia has looked to other nations, traditionally Britain and the United States, but more recently to New Zealand. Policy-makers in Australian jurisdictions need to be careful when they import and impose overseas models on their constituents. To create a better fit between problems and solutions in juvenile justice, and to address the inequities between some sections of the youth population, particularly where Aboriginal young people are concerned, there needs to be a strong commitment in Australian jurisdictions to community consultation and to recognizing and valuing cultural difference.

References

Adey, K., Oswald, M., & Johnson, B. (1991, unpublished). *Discipline in schools: A survey of teachers, survey no. 1: Teachers in metropolitan Adelaide.* Salisbury, S.A.: University of South Australia.

Alder, C., O'Connor, I., Warner, K., & White, R. (1992). *Perceptions of the treatment of juveniles in the legal system.* A report to the National Youth Affairs Research Scheme. Hobart, Tas: National Clearinghouse for Youth Studies.

Alder, C., & Wundersitz, J. (Eds.). (1994). *Family conferencing and juvenile justice: The way forward or misplaced optimism?* Australian Studies in Law, Crime and Justice. Canberra: Australian Institute of Criminology.

Atkinson, L. (1995). Boot camps and justice: A contradiction in terms? *Trends and Issues No 46.* Canberra: Australian Institute of Criminology.

Australian Bureau of Criminal Intelligence (ABCI). (1991). *Australian youth gang assessment*, Report No. SD 913250. Canberra: Strategic Analysis Section, ABCI.

Australian Bureau of Statistics. (1994). *Year Book Australia 1995.* Canberra: Australian Bureau of Statistics, Commonwealth of Australia.

Blagg, H., & Wilkie, M. (1995). *Young people and police powers.* Sydney: The Australian Youth Foundation.

Broadhurst, R. G., Ferrante, A. M., & Susilo, N. P. (1991). *Crime and justice statistics for Western Australia: 1990.* Nedlands, W.A.: Crime Research Centre, University of Western Australia.

Broadhurst, R. G., Ferrante, A. M., & Susilo, N. P. (1992). *Crime and justice statistics for Western Australia: 1991.* Nedlands, W.A.: Crime Research Centre, University of Western Australia.

Broadhurst, R. G., Wilkie, M., & Susilo, N. (1992). *Crime (serious and repeat offenders) sentencing act: Crime control or political opportunism?* Nedlands, W.A.: Crime Research Centre, University of Western Australia.

Cain, M. (1994). *Juveniles in detention. Special needs groups: Young women, Aboriginal and Indo-Chinese detainees.* Sydney: NSW Department of Juvenile Justice.

Challinger, D. (Ed.). (1987). *Crime at school*, Seminar Proceedings No. 20. Canberra: Australian Institute of Criminology.

Crime Research Centre. (1995). *Aboriginal youth and the juvenile justice system of WA.* Royal Commission into Aboriginal Deaths in Custody, Vol. 3. Nedlands, W.A.: Crime Research Centre, University of Western Australia.

Cunneen, C. (1991). Aboriginal juveniles in custody. *Current Issues in Criminal Justice,* 3 (2): 204-219.

Dagger, D. (1996). *Persons in juvenile corrective institutions no 67.* Information Series. Canberra: Australian Institute of Criminology.

Eggleston, E. (1976). *Fear, favour, or affection. Aborigines and the criminal law in Victoria, South Australia and Western Australia.* Canberra: Australian National University Press.

Freiberg, A., Fox, R., & Hogan, M. (1988). *Sentencing young offenders.* The Law Reform Commission sentencing research paper no. 11. Sydney: Alken Press.

Gale, F., Bailey-Harris, R., & Wundersitz, F. (1990). *Aboriginal youth and the criminal justice system: The injustice of justice?* Melbourne: Cambridge University Press.

Graham, I. (1994). Managing cultural diversity—The NSW experience. Atkinson, L. & Gerull, S.A. (Eds.). *National Conference on Juvenile Detention. Conference Proceedings.* Canberra: Australian Institute of Criminology.

Harding, R., Broadhurst, R., Ferrante, A. & Loh, N. (1995). *Aboriginal contact with the criminal justice system and the impact of the Royal Commission into Aboriginal Deaths in Custody.* Sydney: The Hawkins Press.

Hickman, P. (1991). Street gangs or colour gangs? *Australian Police Journal*, 45, (2): 64-72.

Hughes, R. (1987). *The fatal shore.* London: Collins Harvill.

Jurman, E. (1994, April 2). Youth punishment scheme criticised. *The Sydney Morning Herald.* p. 3.

Kriven, S. (1993, Dec. 30). Youth crime shake-up: Urchins set to confront offenders. *The Adelaide Advertiser.* p. 3.

Luke, G. & Cunneen, C. (1995). *Aboriginal over-representation and discretionary decisions in the NSW juvenile justice system.* Sydney: Juvenile Justice Advisory Council of NSW.

NSW Bureau of Crime Statistics and Research. (1995). *New South Wales criminal courts statistics 1994.* Sydney: NSW Bureau of Crime Statistics and Research.

O'Connor, I. (1992). Lawyers, legal advocates & legal services. In a report to the National Youth Affairs Research Scheme *Perceptions of the treatment of juveniles in the legal system.* Hobart, Tas: National Clearinghouse for Youth Studies.

O'Connor, I., & Sweetapple, P. (1988). *Children in justice.* Melbourne: Longman Cheshire.

O'Connor, I., & Tilbury, C. (1986). *Legal aid needs of youth.* Canberra: Australian Government Printing Service.

Oswald, M., Johnson, B., & Adey, K. (1991, unpublished). *Discipline in schools: A survey of teachers, survey no. 2: teachers in South Australian country schools.* Salisbury, S.A.: University of South Australia.

Seymour, J. (1988). *Dealing with young offenders.* Sydney: The Law Book Company.

Shaw, A.G.L. (1966). *Convicts and the colonies.* London: Faber and Faber.

Standing Committee on Social Issues (1995). *A report into youth violence in New South Wales.* Standing Committee on Social Issues, Legislative Council, Parliament of New South Wales.

Victorian Community Council Against Violence (VCCAV). (1992). *Public violence in Victoria.* Melbourne: Author.

Walker, J. (1991) Understanding crime trends in Australia. *Trends and Issues*, 28. Canberra: Australian Institute of Criminology.

Wilkie, M. (1992). Crime (Serious and Repeat Offenders) Sentencing Act 1992: A human rights perspective. Statute Note. *University of Western Australia Law Review.* 22 (1): 187-196.

Wundersitz, J. (1993). Some statistics on youth offending: An interjurisdictional comparison. In F. Gale, N. Naffine & J. Wundersitz (Eds.). *Juvenile justice: Debating the issues.* Sydney: Allen & Unwin.

Wundersitz, J., & Hetzel, S. (1996). Family conferencing for young offenders: The South Australian experience. In J. Hudson, A. Morris, G. Maxwell & B. Galaway (Eds.). *Family group conferences: Perspectives on policy & practice.* The Federation Press, Annandale NSW, and Criminal Justice Press.

Youth Justice Coalition (NSW). (1990). *Kids in justice: A blueprint for the 90s.* Full
Report of the Youth Justice Project. Sydney: Author.

Epigraph:

too much

I went to court
all dressed up
in high heeled shoes
and a deadly suit
for the whole four days

Sitting in that court room
knowing I was guilty
and lying through my teeth
—only made it harder

The threat of their time
—too much to bare

I wish for death
but each morning
when I wake
I'm pleased
and stay pleased until night hits

But left alone I feel like
a beast that can't sleep
& bang my head against the wall
pacing up and down
like a tiger
Knowing I'm really
a cub
that's been deserted.

n.g.

from *Heroes and Villains* an anthology of poems by young people in detention, Via
Magenta, Adelaide, Australia, 1994.

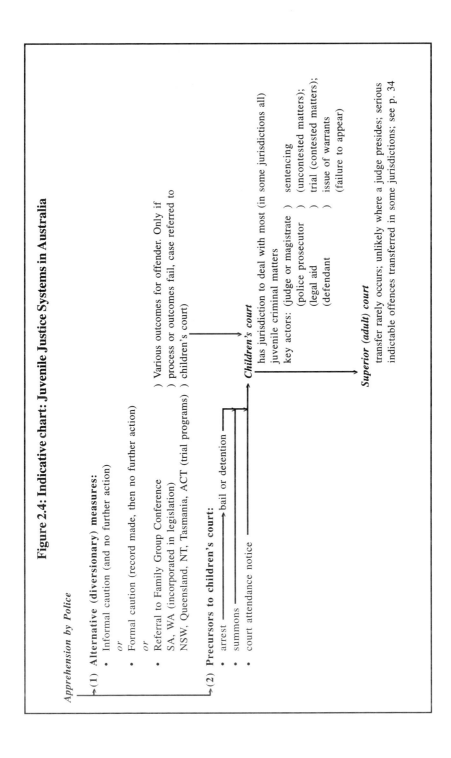

Figure 2.4: Indicative chart: Juvenile Justice Systems in Australia

Apprehension by Police

→ **(1) Alternative (diversionary) measures:**
- Informal caution (and no further action)
  or
- Formal caution (record made, then no further action)
  or
- Referral to Family Group Conference } Various outcomes for offender. Only if
  SA, WA (incorporated in legislation) } process or outcomes fail, case referred to
  NSW, Queensland, NT, Tasmania, ACT (trial programs) } children's court)

→ **(2) Precursors to children's court:**
- arrest ——→ bail or detention
- summons
- court attendance notice

Children's court
has jurisdiction to deal with most (in some jurisdictions all)
juvenile criminal matters
key actors: (judge or magistrate) sentencing
            (police prosecutor) (uncontested matters);
            (legal aid) trial (contested matters);
            (defendant) issue of warrants
            (failure to appear)

Superior (adult) court
transfer rarely occurs; unlikely where a judge presides; serious
indictable offences transferred in some jurisdictions; see p. 34

chapter 3

Juvenile Delinquency and Juvenile Justice in the Netherlands

Josine Junger-Tas
Ministry of Justice

Facts on the Netherlands

Area: The Netherlands is a small country of 37,330 sq. km. divided into twelve provinces. **Population:** Slightly over 15.4 million, of which 4 million are under the age of twenty. Population growth since 1965 amounts to approximately .25%—.52% per yr. The population density is approximately 462 people per sq. km., which is among the highest in the world. Amsterdam is the national capital (1.1 million pop.) and Den Haag (545,796 pop.) is the seat of government. Holland has increasingly become a multicultural nation. Over 4% of the population consists of foreigners, most of whom are of Turkish or Moroccan origin. In addition, there is a substantial number of Surinam people of Dutch nationality. A demographic point of note is that almost half of the houses in the Netherlands are rented rather than owned. **Climate:** Temperate, marine, cool summers and mild winters. **Economy**: Holland is a modern, industrialized, and affluent welfare state based on private enterprise. Trade and financial services contribute over 50% of the GDP. Unemployment is around 8.8% (Dec. '94). The comparatively low unemployment rate is in part due to the highly sophisticated social security system which absorbs about a third of the national income. The country is now facing a number of social and economic problems, mainly due to the recent economic recession, rising rates of unemployment, and a growing influx of immigrants. **Government**: The seat of government is situated in the Hague, which is also the site of the International Peace Palace. Dutch government is based on a parliamentary monarchy with the monarch being a hereditary title.

> Juvenile delinquency is purely a social disease.
> (Stephen Sondheim, 1963, from 'West Side Story')

Contextual Overview

Since the 1960s Dutch society has been revolutionized by increasing secularization and individualization. It has had a profound impact on many life aspects. For example, marriage instability has increased and a growing proportion of young adults form households without being married. Contraception and abortion were legalized, producing the lowest abortion figures in the world, and Holland has developed a rather pragmatic—though not everywhere applauded—policy with respect to soft drug use. The latter is essentially seen as a health problem instead of a moral problem.

The Netherlands has a reputation of liberalism and tolerance, probably related to its long-standing merchant marine and commercial tradition that flows from its geographical situation. Moreover, Holland has never had despotic rulers, nor has it known an aristocracy of any significance. Indeed, the country can best be characterized as a 'civil society', governed for long periods by a class of rich merchants, jealous of their autonomy and inclined to consensus by negotiation and democratic decision-making. During the 1980s Dutch tolerance began to show some flaws. This is partly related to a restricting economy, budgetary constraints in housing and education, and higher levels of unemployment. All this is partly due to wider changes and pressures experienced in the Western world. One negative consequence is that asylum seekers and immigrants from poor countries are blamed for the difficulties of the welfare state, leading to the rise of some small, extremist right-wing parties.

Although crime has never been of particular concern to Dutch citizens, since the 1970s it has become a political issue. It is true that—similar to what happened in other Western countries—crime rates substantially increased between the 1960s and the 1980s: recorded crime, in particular petty and property crime, increased almost tenfold and rates per 1000 rose from thirty-eight to seventy-five. Bi-annual victim surveys, which have been carried out since 1975, show that crimes such as burglary and destruction of private property have almost doubled (van Dijk and Junger-Tas, 1988). However, recent estimates show that only about 2% of minors in the Netherlands belong to a hard core of juvenile delinquents (Ferwerda, Jakobs, and Beke, 1996).

Background of the Dutch Juvenile Justice System

It was not until the sixteenth and seventeenth centuries that Dutch society slowly realized it had special responsibilities for orphans and abandoned children. All over Europe groups of children who had lost their parents because of wars or famines, and the plague roamed the countryside. At that time no distinction was made between neglected and abandoned children on one hand and delinquent children on the other. The children joined groups of tramps, thieves, and beggars and took over their lifestyle. One of the first childcare measures was established in Amsterdam in 1613. A special group, the Almoners, were to pick up roaming and begging children and, depending on their age, place them with wet nurses or foster parents, or with craftsmen to learn a trade. However, the number of roaming orphans and deserted children was increasing so rapidly that other solutions had to be sought. In 1666 a special courthouse was opened as well as two orphanages (ter Schegget, 1976). The problem of orphans joining groups of beggars and robbers continued well into the nineteenth century. One of the punishments, both in England and in Holland, was to send the boys to sea when the merchant navy was short of crew.

Although this could be considered harsh by today's standards, a report on criminal sentences in the sixteenth century showed that persons older than sixty and younger than fourteen years of age were not submitted to torture on the rack. Moreover, there was no trace of children under the age of twelve in the documents, which probably indicates that children under that age were not brought before the court but were disposed of unofficially. The punishment meted out to older children was generally whipping and sometimes expulsion from the city. In many sentences the young age of the offender was mentioned as well as the expression "because of his youth" (om sijne jonckheyt), which shows that the age of the offender was taken into account (Penders, 1980). During the eighteenth and nineteenth centuries there was a slow recognition that children form a separate category and that, as a consequence, care and punishment should be different from what is usual for adults. The nineteenth century was characterized by poverty and child labour, which led to several large health inquiries in the country. Dutch child labour was abolished in 1874 and the first children's institutions were founded in the second half of the nineteenth century. The philanthropic reform of the nineteenth century (see Platt, 1969; Rothman, 1971) led to an increase of social control, not only on juvenile delinquents but also on poor, begging, drinking, or truant children. In fact, there was hardly any distinction between children in need of care and delinquent children. On the other hand, the conviction that society has a responsibility to neglected, suffering, and misbehaving children, and that children should not be victims of the organization of society or of their environment, should be seen as positive. All this led to the creation of a separate juvenile jurisdiction in many Western countries at the turn of this century (see other contributions in this book). Many changes in the Netherlands, as elsewhere, have been influenced by the philanthropic movement in the United States.

The Dutch Criminal Code of 1809 distinguished three categories of juveniles. Children under the age of twelve could not be punished, children aged twelve to fifteen could have so-called children's punishments, and juveniles aged fifteen to eighteen received mitigated adult punishments. But in 1811 the Criminal Code was replaced by the Code Pénal, introduced by

Napoleon, which did not make any distinction between children and adults. The new Penal Code of 1886 merely added that children under the age of ten could not be prosecuted, but it did not elaborate a separate system of sanctions.

The first Dutch children's acts date from 1901 (Wever and Andriessen, 1983). The first (civil) law made it possible to encroach on parental authority in cases where the child is in need of protection. The second (juvenile penal law) abolished the requirement of 'discernment between right and wrong' as a criterion for guilt in children, and also abolished any distinction based on age. The law ruled that children could no longer be detained with adults but must be placed in separate youth institutions. The law also created three special youth sanctions: reprimands, fines and placement in a reformatory for a period of no less than one month and no more than twelve months. Juveniles aged sixteen to eighteen who had committed serious crimes may be sent to prison. Mentally disturbed juveniles may be placed 'at the disposal of the government' (T.B.S.) in a treatment institution until their majority at age twenty-one.

A separate juvenile judge competent in civil and in penal matters was introduced in 1922. The law also introduced the supervision order. A major revision took place after World War II and resulted in new legal dispositions in 1965. One might say that this law formally introduced the welfare system in juvenile justice. The age limit of twelve years for prosecution was reinstituted. Much emphasis was placed on informal proceedings: legal safeguards were considered against the interests of the child. The position of the juvenile judge was reinforced: prosecutors must ask the judge's advice when they wish to prosecute a case, and the juvenile judge plays a major role at every stage of the proceedings, including the execution of sanctions and measures. The juvenile justice system as a welfare system reached its peak in the 1960s and 1970s. Its characteristics were:

— large discretionary powers, especially for the juvenile judge, based on the concept of *parens patriae*, which presumes that the judge always acts in the best interests of the child;

— irrespective of the criminal act, the personality and the needs of the child are predominant and dictate the decision;

— the emphasis is on treatment and assistance to the family and child instead of on punishment;

— informality of the proceedings—court hearings are not open to the public, all proceedings are of a confidential nature; and

— there are hardly any procedural safeguards because in a welfare system these are deemed unnecessary.

New Legislation on Juvenile Justice

The old concept of juvenile justice was inspired by social optimism and was based on two assumptions: 1) that human nature is flexible, so that if one takes the 'right' measures people can be influenced and changed; and 2) that on the basis of scientific knowledge and rational processes, social problems can be solved. These conceptions formed the basis for the reform of the system at the beginning of this century. The child was not seen as a free agent consciously choosing evil acts and deserving punishment. Causes of crime were sought in the environment of the child. It was argued that the best way to combat crime would be to give adequate treatment to the child and the family. In this way the juvenile justice system would serve both the needs of the child and the demands of society.

As in other Western countries of the time, in practice the juvenile justice system contained a number of drawbacks that received mounting criticism. The most important one was the system's large discretionary powers: parents as well as children could not get themselves heard and had hardly any rights. Many institutions were more like warehouses than educative homes. Last but not least, children proved to be considerably less changeable than had been expected. Growing prosperity, more and higher education, secularization, and individualization led to emancipation movements of numerous groups, such as ethnic minorities, women, mental patients, homosexuals, and young people. This initiated a concern for more procedural safeguards for juveniles and an emphasis on the legal due process/crime control aspects of juvenile justice rather than on the welfare aspects.

However, in the 1980s and the 1990s, the juvenile justice system underwent drastic changes. This period meant the end of our post-war economic boom. Holland, as many other countries, experienced a recession, unemployment rose, immigration from trouble spots in the world increased, and the future looked insecure to many. The crime picture also changed. The spread of drugs and illegal immigration brought more street crime, such as robberies. Changes in lifestyle went together with more burglaries and all kinds of thefts. For the first time in our history crime became a political issue of importance: fear of crime had increased while tolerance for juvenile misbehaviour had diminished (see Box 3.1). There was a noticeable shift away from deterministic environmental causes of crime and a belief in education and treatment to a philosophy of free will in which juveniles are considered responsible for their actions. The emphasis shifted to the victim rather than the offender, which has led to forms of restorative justice—reparation to the victim. This has led to a renewed emphasis on punishment as well as on early detection of troublesome behaviour. The shift is quite contrary to the standards which have been put forth in the 1984 Beijing Rules (see Box 1, Introduction). The trend may reflect the social-political nature of reform and a growing sentiment of conservatism in the Netherlands.

Box 3.1: Special Needs

"Parent training, education, meaningful leisure occupations, social assistance and employment can give an important contribution to the prevention and reduction of factors that foster criminal and deviant behavior" Commission Juvenile Crime, March, 1994.
"Young people have the future, that is a fact! How this future will look is not sure: a criminal career is also a career. Investing in youth is not only the responsibility of society but also a professional responsibility of the police organization." M.E. Polman, Amsterdam police, Feb., 27, 1996.

New legislation in the Netherlands came into force in September 1995. The most important dispositions are the following.

The role of the juvenile judge as a kind of welfare actor has been greatly reduced in favour of a judicial role. Hence, the usual informal consultations between juvenile judge, prosecutor, and the child protection council has been abolished. Juveniles are entitled to legal assistance provided for by the state. They are obliged to appear at the trial, which generally remains closed to the public. The age limits of twelve to eighteen have not been changed, but it has become easier, as in Canada (see Chapter 6), to transfer sixteen to eighteen year olds to the adult system. The new law allows transfer in cases where only one of three conditions is fulfilled. The three conditions include: the criminal act was serious, the circumstances of the act were serious, and transfer is required because of the offender's personality. In cases warranting a sentence of more than six months or in cases of mental disturbance, the case can no longer be dealt with by the individual juvenile judge; the case must be tried in full court by three judges. This practice is more commonly found in European countries than in North America or Asia.

The use of reprimands and the supervision orders have been removed from juvenile justice (the latter continues to exist in the civil child care and protection legislation). A positive aspect of the new legislation is that police diversion for minor offences, such as vandalism, minor shoplifting, and minor

Figure 3.1: The Dutch Juvenile Justice System

The Police   –No Further Action
                      –Dismissal (after hearing parents)
                      –Juvenile sent to diversion project
                      –Report sent to prosecutor

Prosecutor   –Unconditional discharge
                      –Conditional discharge
                         • payment to special funds (max. f. 5000)[†]
                         • fine
                         • alternative sanction (max. 40 hr.; if
                           >20 hr. assistance by counsel)
                         • supervision by social worker for max. six
                           months
                      –Referral to juvenile judge

Juvenile Judge   –Pre-trial detention (in the capacity of judge of
                      instruction)
                      –Probation (maximum six months)
                      –Fine (max. f. 5000); may be substituted by custody
                      or alternative sanction
                      –Alternative sanction
                         • community service
                         • reparative work on behalf of the victim
                         • special training course
                      –Custody—only in case of crimes
                         • <16 years of age: max. 12 months
                         • 16-18 years of age: max. 24 months
                         • 16-18 years of age: transfer possible to adult
                           court
                      –Placement in institution: if serious crime, danger for others
                      or in need of special education (max. six years)

[†]   'f' represents the symbol for the Dutch Guilder = 100 cents

assaults, and alternative sanctions have now been given a legal basis (see Figure 3.1).

The most troublesome component of the new legislation pertains to the enlarged options for youth custody. Under the old legislation the maximum length of custody was six months. This has now been changed to twelve months for those aged twelve to sixteen and to twenty-four months for those aged sixteen to eighteen. Moreover, if the youth reaches the age of eighteen years while in custody, youth custody may be converted into an adult prison sentence. Together with the enlarged possibility of transfer to the adult penal system, punishment will become considerably harsher than it used to be. To date there has been limited discussion as to the financial impact of this legislative change.

Most of these changes have also been introduced in a number of other Western countries, such as England (Chapter 4), Canada (Chapter 6), and the United States (Chapter 10), the significance of which is a clear shift from a **welfare model** to a **justice model** (see Figure 1, Introduction).

Having reviewed the relevant legislation, let us now examine some of the Netherland's juvenile delinquency trends and patterns. We will draw on official crime data and self-report studies.

Trends in Delinquency

Police Statistics

In terms of juvenile delinquency, the Netherlands does not present a very different picture from most other Western European countries. Crime rates for those aged twelve to eighteen and eighteen to twenty, which had been rather low, started to rise in 1955, the year that is generally considered the starting point of the economic boom. This increase continued until about 1982 and was followed by a period of stability. In the 1990s the rates seem to be on the rise, but the latest statistics suggest the likelihood of some (normal) fluctuations.

In absolute figures there appeared to be a slight decline in the number of cases recorded by the police after 1980. However, when taking into account the demographic changes in which there was a decline of more than 25% among the youth population; in reality there has been a slight increase in delinquency rates. Between 1980 and 1994, the increase in recorded cases has been around 3.4% annually suggesting considerable stability over the fourteen year period. There has only been a slight increase in the 1990s.

Male criminality and female criminality follow different patterns. Since the late 1970s female delinquency has been increasing faster than rates for young males. For example, in 1994 the male delinquency rate was about 20% higher than in 1980, while among females the rate was about 50% higher. But even though the picture is changing, males still commit far more crimes than do young females. In the 1970s the ratio was about ten to one for males; during the 1990s the ratio dropped to seven to one for females. This means that on a yearly basis 6.5% of males and 1% of females of the same age population are charged by the police. As observed in other chapters in this book, this trends seems fairly widespread.

With respect to the nature of crime, it is important to emphasize that most juvenile delinquency is property crime, which helps determine the delinquency trends and rates. Table 3.1 shows the distribution of offences by gender in 1992 as recorded by the police.

Table 3.1: Juveniles heard by the police by offence type and gender: 1992

Offense category	Males N=36,240	Females N=5,126
Public order	9.5	5.0
Sex offences	1.5	—
Violence against persons	11.0	8.5
Property offences	63.5	82.0
Wilful damage	13.5	4.0
Other	1.0	0.5
Total	100	100

Source: *Central Bureau of Statistics*, 1992.The Hague: Central Bureau of Statistics.

What we see in Table 3.1 is that more than 80% of the female offences known to the police are property offences. Violence against persons is a distant second at 8.5%. Among males property crimes are also the largest category, making up about two-thirds of all crimes known to the police. Compared to females, males commit more varied offences—more vandalism and public order offences. However, the proportion of males and females committing violent offences does not differ much, they are respectively 11% and 8.5%. Since 1980 the proportion of violent offences has doubled for both sexes. Seen in perspective, however, it should be observed that only about one-tenth of all offenders become involved in a violent offence.

Assaults represent the largest category of violent offences. From 1980 to 1992 there was an increase of 80%; this was the case for both sexes. However, the largest increase was for theft with violence, which showed a fourfold increase. This trend was supported in a 1990 report from the ministry of justice. The trend is not, however, reflected in statistics on feelings of insecurity or fear among the population. In a 1983 victimization survey, 73% of those interviewed said they were never afraid when "home alone" at night, the number decreased to 64% in 1987 and increased to 73.3% in 1992. These fluctuations may have something to do with the growing deterioration of the urban structure, which is partly due to the economic recession mentioned earlier.

Although violence has been on the increase among both sexes (see Table 3.2), the increase is steeper for females than males. For example, since 1980 the number of assaults by females has increased fourfold, while for males the number has doubled. Contrary to the general trend in juvenile delinquency, which is reasonably stable, theft with violence among males started to rise in the early 1980s; among females the increase began around 1989. Theft with violence or robbery is an *instrumental* crime committed frequently by drug addicts and by (illegal) immigrants as a means of survival (de Haan, 1993). The data seem to suggest that male violence is more often instrumental in nature (one in which an offender gets some satisfaction from the product of the crime), while female violence is essentially of an *expressive* nature (one in which the act itself fulfils an emotional need for the offender).

Table 3.2: Juveniles aged twelve to eighteen heard by the police in 1992 by violent offense and gender

Violent offences	Males N=3,907	Females N=433
Theft with violence	29.5	17.0
Extortion	8.5	7.5
Threats	10.5	7.5
Offences against life	4.5	4.0
Assault	47.0	62.5
Other	0.5	1.5

Source: *Central Bureau of Statistics*. Junger-Tas and van der Laan, 1995.

Looking at the different offence types (see Table 3.3) one may note that the proportion of males recorded for simple theft, embezzlement, and forgery did not change much over the years—aggravated theft and fencing even declined. The only offence that shows an increase in the 1990s is burglary. Females show a different pattern: simple theft increased by 50% and burglary more than doubled. Moreover, the proportion of females recorded for property crime is much higher than that for violent crime: on the total number of juveniles heard by the police for a violent offence or a property crime in 1992, females were heard for 10% of the violent offences and 16% of the property offences.

The distribution between the genders for different types of property offences, however, shows that females still have a separate offence pattern.

Table 3.3: Juveniles aged twelve to eighteen heard by the police by property crime and gender

Property crimes	Males N=22,344	Females N=4,147
Simple theft	42.5	68.0
Burglary	42.5	18.0
Aggravated theft	10.0	11.0
Embezzlement/forgery	3.0	2.5
Fencing	4.5	1.0
Total	100	100

Source: *Central Bureau of Statistics*, 1992.

Females primarily commit simple thefts. The number of females committing burglaries, although on the rise, is still limited (18%). With respect to males it appears that 85% of all property crimes is either simple theft or burglary. They seldom commit any other property offences.

Property crime decreased between 1982 and 1990. There was some increase in 1990 and 1992, followed again by a decline. Thus in 1994 the level of property crime is hardly above the 1980 level. As property crime is really what juvenile delinquency is about, the result is that juvenile crime in the Netherlands has been fairly stable since 1980.

Self-report Measures

Since 1986 the Dutch Research and Documentation Centre, which is the research institute of the ministry of justice, has been conducting a bi-annual, self-report survey on the basis of a national random sample of youngsters aged twelve to eighteen. As of 1996 there have been five such surveys. The objective is to compare and eventually complement the police figures and obtain a better view of delinquency trends in the Netherlands. Because of changes in the questionnaire after the first trial, the results from 1986 are not comparable to the later surveys. Therefore, we will compare some of the results over the years 1988 to 1994 (see Table 3.4). Of course self-report studies cannot be directly compared with police data. Without going into methodological details about how both sources measure different types of offences, let us just say that each source has its strengths and weaknesses. If they show the same trends, we may have more confidence in the results.

Offences that were most frequently reported in 1992 were travelling in public transport without a ticket (34.5%), vandalism (29%), non-serious shoplifting (27%), carrying arms (25.5%), and involvement in fights (23.5%). Nijboer and Timmerman (1992) reported that an increasing percentage of youngsters go out equipped with knives, chains, sticks, and in some cases small firearms. Overall, however, these results have remained fairly stable over the years.

The stability in these results is rather striking as are the changes. Both essentially confirm the trends in police statistics. That is, while property crime and vandalism have hardly increased during the eight-year period, there have been some real increases of an aggressive nature. These trends are comparable with police data, although the self-report differences are not as pronounced as the police figures. It does seem to suggest that there is a trend towards more violent behaviour among young people. Again the findings are fairly consistent with juvenile delinquency trends experienced by most of the countries covered in this collection.

Another interesting trend is that comparisons over the years 1988, 1990, and 1992 show an increase in police contacts for a number of illegal acts, such as fare-dodging, graffiti, vandalism, shoplifting, arson, and assault (Junger-Tas and van der Laan, 1995). This seems to illustrate the tendency among authorities to intervene at an earlier stage and more frequently in the lives of children, which is in keeping with our new juvenile justice philosophy.

Although in self-report studies females report fewer offences than males, the gender difference is far smaller than is the case in police statistics: 30% of the females in the sample versus 50% of the males admitted to having committed one or more illegal act in 1992. However, in cases of fare-dodging, graffiti, and shoplifting, gender differences are slight. The more serious the offence the larger the gender difference.

Summary

If one considers the police picture of juvenile delinquency one must conclude that for most offences that picture did not change very much during the past fifteen years. Although there seems to be some increase in total figures, one should take into account two confusing elements. One is a certain shift in the definition of what constitutes a crime. For example, there are indications that the definition of offences such as purse snatching, which was defined as

Table 3.4: Self-reported offenses by year, 1988-1994

Offences	1988 N=994	1990 N=1006	1992 N=1038	1994 N=1096
no fare paid	13.5	16.5	21.0	15.5
graffiti	10.0	8.5	9.0	10.0
harassment	9.5	11.5	11.5	14.0
vandalism	8.5	9.5	10.5	9.0
shoplifting	5.0	7.5	7.0	7.0
arson	3.5	5.0	3.5	4.0
fencing	3.5	5.0	3.5	4.0
bicycle theft	2.0	3.0	3.0	2.5
assault	2.0	2.5	3.0	3.0
burglary	1.5	1.5	1.5	1.5
theft payphone	–	1.5	1.0	1.0
theft at school	–	6.5	8.0	7.0
riots/fights	–	6.5	9.0	11.5
injuring w. weapon	–	0.5	0.5	0.5
carrying weapon	–	–	13.0	20.5
threats for money	–	–	0.5	0.5
Total	34.5	38.0	38.0	38.0

simple theft, are now defined as theft with violence or robbery, a more serious offence (Freeling, 1993; Kester and Junger-Tas, 1994). A second element is the computerization of police information during the 1980s and 1990s: calculations made by the Central Bureau of Statistics showed that at least half of the rise in crime in the years 1980 to 1992 was due to registration effects related to the computerization of police information (Kester and Junger-Tas, 1994).

On the other hand it is an undeniable fact that, according to police figures and self-report figures, two types of violent offences have clearly increased:

assault and theft with violence. The former shows an increase from 1990, but the latter started to rise in the 1980s. Furthermore, delinquency among females has been slowly increasing since the end of the 1970s—most of it is property crime. Violence among females is first and foremost fighting. Theft with violence as well as burglary remain essentially male crimes. Why? Numerous theories abound, but one series of research projects suggests that social vulnerability may offer a viable explanation (see Box 3.2).

Finally, the latest self-report results suggest a growing tendency for the authorities to intervene in the case of juvenile misbehaviour.

We will now examine the elements and agents of the juvenile justice system in the Netherlands which have also undergone some changes in recent years.

Box 3.2: Explanation for Delinquency: Social Vulnerability

Ferwerda's publications (1992, 1993) form one of the most extensive recent theoretical excursions based upon empirical research on juvenile delinquents in the Netherlands. His findings on criminal careers among juveniles serve to identify many of the key problems of Dutch male young offenders. He based his findings on a sample of seventy-seven serious education and school problem youth with their classmates over a four-year period. Ferwerda viewed the problems experienced at the age of twelve as indicative of increased potential delinquency. He calls these youth 'socially vulnerable', a term coined by Vettenburg, Walgrave, and van Kerckvoorde in 1984 who gave the concept a marginally different meaning.

In accordance with an integrative approach, Ferwerda's ideas concerning the origin of delinquency focus on the interaction between the concepts of '**incentives**' and '**control-factors**'. He considers the socially vulnerable position of juveniles to be the most important source of criminal incentive. The only reason why not everyone in a socially vulnerable position commits a crime is because one also needs to take in account the youths' individual positions, attitudes, and perspectives. These are elements of the potential control factor. In short, criminal behaviour is a result of the interaction between incentives and control factors.

Ferwerda's 1993 findings support the official trends discussed in the main text. He further observed that the youth who commit serious property crimes increasingly tend to analyse their potential profits and losses; their main motive lies in the material gains of the crime. Statistically, Ferwerda found that socially vulnerable males (i.e., 68%) showed more criminal behaviour than those in non-vulnerable social positions (i.e., 47%).

With the increasing trend towards more serious delinquency, it is necessary for Dutch policy-makers to understand these trends and recognize which youths might best benefit from the programs available.

The Juvenile Justice System

The Dutch juvenile justice system is a well-articulated and flexible system. Interventions are possible at any level of the system, with the objective to stop further proceedings and deal with the juvenile, whenever possible, in an informal way (see Figure 3.1).

This is in part reflected in the definition of delinquency. In the Netherlands delinquent behaviour includes only those behaviours that are infractions of the criminal law and that would be punished if committed by an adult. This means that so-called 'status-offences', that is offences related to the status of a juvenile under age eighteen, such as truancy, running away, using alcohol or (soft) drugs, and dropping out of school, are not considered as delinquency but as problem behaviour. As such they can only lead to intervention of juvenile judges in their civil capacity, under the provision of child protection dispositions. Moreover, children under the age of twelve are not penally responsible. Legally they are considered unable to form *mens rea*. Of course a child under age twelve may—as the law states—"when a minor is threatened by physical or moral danger by his own behaviour or by the behaviour of those who should take care of him." In that case the juvenile judge may order a civil measure of protection, a supervision order which implies educational assistance for the family by a social worker. Under this civil law provision the child may be separated from their family and be placed in a home.

The Police

When juveniles come to the attention of the police different things may happen. If the offence is minor the police may drop the charges and simply send the juvenile home with a warning. In fact about 30% of all juvenile cases coming to their attention are informally dealt with. In cases specified by guidelines from the prosecutors general, the police may refer the juvenile to a diversion program called **HALT**, which means 'stop' in Dutch and is an acronym for *Het Alternatief* (see Box 3.3). In such cases the police make an informal summary report, which is not sent to the prosecutor. If the juvenile satisfactorily follows the diversion program, the charges are dropped and the case is dismissed; if not, the summary report is transformed into an official report and is sent to the prosecutor. In cases of serious offending the police will report directly to the prosecutor.

Box 3.3: HALT—An Alternative Sanction

HALT represents Holland's first experience with diversion. It was introduced in the 1970s in the city of Rotterdam and spread throughout the country. In 1996 there were more than sixty HALT programs financed by the municipalities and the ministry of justice. The objective of the program is to allow juvenile males (very few females are ever referred) to work, clean, or repair the damage done during a free Saturday (four to eight hours work) and imposes them, where appropriate, to pay damages. A study by Kruissinck (1990) revealed that the youth referred to HALT tended to be more delinquent than ordinary Dutch juveniles. The study found that considerably more males in the experimental group than in the control group stopped committing acts of wilful damage or decreased their destructive activities. This is impressive in light of the fact the HALT group tended to be more problematic than the control group.

It should also be kept in mind that the intervention is spread out in time: a first meeting with project staff takes place within weeks after the police contact, followed by a second meeting. In general it will take about eight weeks before work starts. This means that the intervention is more 'intense' than it would appear and certainly more interfering than a simple warning.

HALT has become very popular among the police. They now have a useful tool which allows them to interfere in a rather light manner. And in 1995 it was introduced in the new law as a form of police transaction. The police may now propose a maximum of twenty hours HALT activities as an alternative to prosecution and on a voluntary basis. Both the juvenile and his or her parents have to agree. The police may only do so in the case of a limited and specified number of offences: wanton destructiveness, vandalism, simple theft, hooliganism, and infractions of the fireworks regulation.

The Public Prosecutor

Under the old law there were compulsory tripartite consultations between the juvenile judge, the prosecutor, and the Council of Child Protection, a body that collects information for the court. The prosecutor could not take any decision without consulting the judge. The new law changed this and gave the prosecutor virtually the same autonomy as in adult criminal law.

Public prosecutors are key figures in Dutch law. Upon receiving the relevant information on the offender from the Council of Child Protection, they decide whether the case will be prosecuted. Like the police the prosecutor dismisses a great many cases: in 50% of all recorded cases (i.e., 70% of the cases submitted) the prosecutor drops the charges either by a written note or following an official reprimand. They may also decide to bring the case before the juvenile judge. Only about 20% of all recorded cases make it to trial. But the prosecutor can do a great deal more. In addition to imposing an alternative sanction (maximum length, forty hours) they may order a conditional dismissal to be accompanied by an order to pay a fine, to pay damages, or to accept supervision by a probation worker for a maximum of six months.

Alternative sanctions include community service, work done on behalf of the victim, or one of a series of special training courses, such as social skills training, sexual education, or vocational training. Where the prosecutor proposes a fine higher than f. 250 or an alternative sanction of more than twenty hours, juveniles should be assisted by counsel. The juveniles are not compelled to follow the proposal of the prosecutor, but if they do accept and fulfil the requirements, the charges will be dropped and there will be no criminal record. If they do not accept, they will have to stand trial.

The Juvenile Judge

The juvenile judge is a civil and a penal judge. When the offender is young and has committed their first offence, or when there is a problematic family background, the judge may divert the case from criminal proceedings. As a measure of child protection the judge may release or remove parental rights or impose a supervision order which includes educational guidance by a social worker. The first two options were created at the beginning of the century to make intervention possible in cases where parents were unable to give adequate care to their children (release of parents' rights) or where there was ill-treatment or abuse (removal of parents' rights). The supervision order as well as the specialized juvenile judge were introduced into law in 1922.

Under the old law the juvenile judges had considerable discretionary powers. In fact no decision concerning a juvenile could be taken without the judge's consent. They led the investigation and decided on the length of detention. The new law put an end to excessive discretionary power. It introduced the formal separation of powers as is the case in adult penal law. Moreover, in cases where custody of more than six months is imposed or in cases of a measure of placement in a treatment institution, the case will be tried by three judges, one of which is the juvenile judge.

Alternative sanction options: The main options are a fine, custody, an alternative sanction and placement in a treatment institution. The maximum fine is f. 5,000 (approximately $3500 US), but the fine can be replaced (partly) by custody or by an alternative sanction. Custody can be imposed for a maximum of twelve months for twelve to sixteen year olds and twenty-four months for those aged sixteen to eighteen. There are three types of alternative sanctions which may also be combined: community service, voluntary work to compensate the victim, both with a maximum of 200 hours, or specialized training courses, which may take more time depending on the nature of the training.

Alternative sanctions cannot be imposed without the express consent of the juvenile. In general, however, consent is readily given. The Council of Child Protection must advise the juvenile judge on the feasibility of an alternative sanction and is charged with its execution and control.

The juvenile judge can also impose a penal measure, of which placement in a treatment institution is the most severe. Not unlike many Western countries, this will be imposed when a crime is committed that requires pre-trial detention, that endangers general security or the safety of specific persons, or when the measure is in the interest of the favourable development of the juvenile. The measure does not necessarily end at the juvenile's majority and its maximum term is six years. It can only be imposed in cases of partly or completely diminished responsibility. It is clear that this measure is imposed only in rare cases. For example, in 1990 only twenty-five juveniles were placed in this regime.

With respect to sentencing there have been some changes since the introduction of alternative sanctions. Today more than one-half of all sentences are now alternative sanctions. However, alternative sanctions are not substitutes for custody: in most cases they are substitutes for probation or for a fine. Custody is imposed in about 20% of all sentences up to 1995. We do not yet know whether custody will increase under the new law, although many professionals expect this will be the case.

Current Problems in Delinquency and Juvenile Justice

There are a number of problems that cause concern both to the authorities and to the public at large (see Box 3.4). And as can be seen by reading the Australian (Chapter 2), Canadian (Chapter 6), and German (Chapter 9) contributions, our concerns are not necessarily unique.

Box 3.4: A European Issue

"The legal system for minors, which has to reach verdicts on individuals who are at a stage of physical, intellectual and psychological development, particularly important for shaping their personality, out to be an integral part of the overall social process of training and protection for committing offences and take their place in society" (*Council of Europe*, Recommendation No. R (88) 6).

A major concern is the increase in violence. Although some of the increase is due to better registration of offences by the police and by more frequent prosecution of aggressive offences, some of it is real. This is an unusual development since for a long period crime in the Netherlands had been non-violent. The possession of guns was only allowed in exceptional cases and death by gunfire hardly ever happened. So the increase of assaults, robberies, and theft with violence by young people is a cause of considerable alarm to the government. Moreover, authorities are not very sure of how to tackle this problem as there do not seem to be any easy solutions.

A second problem is the increase of delinquency among females. Since the 1970s delinquency among young females has been rising continuously, but it is not only the increasing number of females committing delinquent acts that is the worrying trend. What is causing more concern is the changing nature of that delinquency since the last couple of years. Females used to commit essentially minor property offences, their delinquency was both less serious and less frequent than that of males. However, there is now a clear tendency among young females to commit more violent acts. More females are committing assaults and are institutionalized for violent behaviour. Whether this trend will increase in the coming years is still too early to say, but the general feeling is that it will.

A third major concern refers to the crime problem among ethnic minorities. Some ethnic groups are seriously overrepresented in the child-care system, in the juvenile justice system, and in its institutions. Compared to Dutch juveniles these groups are more involved in criminal activities and although the majority of delinquent acts are property offences, they tend to use more violence.

The major ethnic groups in the Netherlands are the Surinamese (250,000) and Antilleans (82,000) from the Carribbean region; Turkish and Moroccan immigrants account for approximately 400,000 people. The youth of these ethnic groups are heavily overrepresented in the system. This is more so for the Surinamese juveniles than the Turkish youngsters.

The government is aware that this problem is related to the negative educational and economic situations these groups find themselves in and the number of measures have been taken to improve these conditions. However, the problem is a very tenacious one and will not be solved easily.

Summary

In this chapter we have presented an overview of the Dutch juvenile justice system and examined some of the delinquency trends based on official and self-report studies. The Dutch criminal justice system was characterized as one in which sanction and the seriousness of sanctions are not just based on the offence committed. They also depend on the individual and the circumstances surrounding the offence. It was noted that this is especially true in juvenile court.

Although tagged with the reputation of having low crime rates and a moderate justice system, in recent years this image has been tarnished as delinquency rates have fluctuated after a period of stability throughout the 1980s. However, female delinquency has been on the increase, but fortunately the degree of seriousness is not as attenuated as is the case in North America. Nevertheless, in 1991 new legislation was introduced. It was intended to simplify and modernize the criminal justice system. The new model is more representative of a due process or modified justice (see Figure 1, Introduction). While the maximum fine was raised from 500 guilders to one million, reprimands are no longer used as a form of sanctioning, and there has been a noticeable move towards the use of alternative sanctions such as work projects and learning projects.

In keeping with trends observed in several other countries, alternative sanctions have become very popular. Their use may be more for practical reasons than being based on theoretical evidence. Nevertheless, programs such as HALT have proven reasonably successful in dealing with youths committing minor offences. It was also observed that the criminal law system in the Netherlands, with its strong orientation towards the individual young offender, offers ample possibilities for the use of alternative sanctions.

Overall, by international standards, the delinquency problem in Holland is not as severe as in a number of the countries covered in this book. This may be accounted for by a previously strong and stable social economy as well as a greater sense of social and cultural bonding perhaps not found in other countries. However, as described, increased social vulnerability may partly account for the changes observed in the 1990s.

With respect to Europe in general, it should be observed that the changes in the Netherlands are not unique. Similar changes have taken place in England, Sweden, and Germany (Junger-Tas, 1996). Moreover, there seems to be a growing tendency to intervene officially; more offences that were dealt with in an informal way before are now officially processed. In fact, the Netherlands is part of Europe and Europe, as Canada and the United States, are part of the Western world. We all share a common culture, and changes in one of these countries inevitably spread to others. Therefore, it may be constructive when conducting comparative analysis to note that in spite of its somewhat more lenient stance, we too are experiencing more problems with our young offenders, and it may be helpful to not only pay closer attention to these changes but to work more closely with other countries and share our efforts.

References

Central Bureau of Statistics, 1992. (1992). Criminaliteit en strafrechtspleging. 's-Gravenhage: SDU.

Council of Europe, Rec. No. R (88)6. Social reactions to juvenile delinquency among young people coming from migrant families. European Committee on Crime Problems. Strasbourg, 1989.

Dijk, J.J.M van & Junger-Tas, J. (1988). Trends in Crime prevention in The Netherlands. In: T.Hope & M. Shaw (Eds.), *Communities and Crime Reduction*. London: Home Office Reseach and Planning Unit. Ch. 17.

Ferwerda, H.B. (1992). *Watjes en ratjes*. Groningen: Wolters-Noordhoff.

Ferwerda, H.B. (1993). Jeudcriminaliteit en maatschappelijke kwetsbarrheid. In R.W. Jognman, *De armen van vrouwe justitia*. Nijmegen: Ars Aequi Libri.

Ferwerda, H.B., Jakobs, J.P., & Beke, B.M.W.A. (1996). *Signalen voor toekomstig crimineel gedrag*. Den Haag, Ministry of Justice.

Freeling, W. (1993). *De straf op Tasjesroof -hoe het strafklimaat strenger werd"*. Proces. pp. 76-83.

Haan, W. de. (1993). *Beroving van voorbijgangers—Rapport van een onderzoek naar Straatroof in 1991 in Amsterdam en Utrecht*. The Hague, Ministry of Internal Affairs.

Junger-Tas, J. (1996). Youth and violence in Europe. *Studies on crime and crime prevention*, 5(1).

Junger-Tas, J. & van der Laan, P.H. (1995). Central Bureau Statistics, Arnhem: Gouda Quint, WODC.

Kester, J.G.C & Junger-Tas, J. (1994). *Criminaliteit en Strafrechtelijke reactie*.

Kruissink, M. (1990). The HALT program: diversion of juvenile offenders. *Dutch Penal Law and Policy*, 1. 's-Gravenhage: WODC. Arnhem: Gouda Quint, WODC and CBS.

Nijboer, J.A. & Timmerman, H. (1992). *Eenvals gevoel veiligheid: wapenbezit onder jongeren*. Groningen: Rijks Universitiet.

Penders, J. (1980). *Om sijne Jonckheyt*. Utrecht: Rijksuniversiteit Utrecht.

Platt, A. (1969). *The child savers*. Chicago: University of Chicago Press.

Polman, M.E. (February 27, 1996). Personal Communication.

Rothman, D.J. (1971). *The discovery of the asylum*. Boston: Little, Brown and Company.

Schegget, H. ter. (1976). *Het Kind van de Rekening—Schetsen uit de Voorgeschiedenis van de Kinderbescherming*. Alphen aan de Rijn: Samson.

Wever, J. & Andriessen, M.F. (1983). *De Strafrechtelijke procedure voor Jeugdigen*. Arnhem: Gouda Quint.

chapter 4

Comparative Juvenile Justice: England and Wales

Loraine Gelsthorpe
Institute of Criminology, University of Cambridge
Mark Fenwick
School of Law, University of East London

Facts on the United Kingdom

Area: 244,820 sq. km. Britain comprises Great Britain (England, Wales, and Scotland) and Northern Ireland. Its full name is the United Kingdom of Great Britain and Northern Ireland. It is one of the twelve member states of the European Union, which it joined in 1973. **Population**: Britain is densely populated with a population of 58.3 million—growth rate 0.29% per year. The vast majority (88%) of the population live in England. The capital, London, has a population of almost 6.9 million. Other major cities include Birmingham (1 million), Leeds (700,000), Sheffield (530,000), Liverpool (480,700), Bradford (475,400), Edinburgh (429,000), and Manchester (438,000). Although the population has remained relatively stable over the last decade, it has aged considerably. In 1991 nearly 19% of the population were over the normal retirement ages (sixty-five for men, sixty for women) compared with 15% in 1961. Between 1983 and 1993 the number of young people aged between ten and seventeen fell by 19%. **Ethnicity**: Over the centuries many people have settled in Britain. It is worth noting that since 1981 there has been a tightening of the immigration law, something which has made it more difficult for foreign nationals to settle in Britain. In the 1991 census, just over 3 million people (5.5%) described themselves as belonging to an ethnic group other than the white group. **Economy**: Britain became the world's first industrialised country in the late eighteenth century. In recent years service industries have become increasingly important and now account for over two-thirds of employees. Financial and other business services have also grown in significance, particularly during the 1980s. **Government**: Britain is a parliamentary democracy with a constitutional monarch—currently Queen Elizabeth II—as head of state. Unlike many other parliamentary democracies, it has no written constitution. Instead it is ruled according to laws passed by Parliament, decisions made in the higher judicial courts, and (perhaps most importantly) tradition. The political party system is an essential element in the working of the constitution. Although the parties are not registered or formally recognised in law, in practice most candidates in elections, and almost all winning candidates, belong to one of the main parties. However, the Liberal Democrats and a number of other smaller parties are also represented in Parliament.

In the little world in which children have their existence, whosoever brings them up, there is nothing so finely perceived and so finely felt, as injustice.

(Charles Dickens, 1812-1870)

Overview of the Juvenile Justice System in England and Wales

In order to provide a reference point for the discussion of our juvenile justice system we provide a flow chart that shows the main decision points.

One of the most striking features of the juvenile justice system in England and Wales is the range of agencies which are involved, and it may be described as an open system (Singer and Gelsthorpe, 1996). By this we mean a system which involves a series of separate, but related, decisions and wide discretion. As with so many aspects of British life, an historical approach is perhaps the best way of understanding the form of the contemporary system. It will also highlight another striking feature of juvenile justice, namely the range of competing approaches to the problem of youth crime within the system itself.

Historical Background

Under common law the age of criminal responsibility was seven years until 1933. In England and Wales, juveniles between seven and fourteen were presumed incapable of crime and it was for the prosecution to prove that they knew that their conduct was wrong.[1] Such proof, however, was usually forthcoming. It was felt that sparing the penalties of law merely on account of age would have weakened the deterrent force of law. Accordingly, in the eighteenth and early part of the nineteenth century, juveniles accused of crimes were treated as adults at both trial and disposition stages—they could be executed, transported, and imprisoned.

The need for special jurisdiction over juvenile offenders was first mooted in the early nineteenth century when a number of liberal-minded magistrates began to question the efficacy of sending juveniles under fourteen to the same prisons as adult defendants while awaiting trial for minor offences. As a consequence a number of parliamentary bills were drawn up in the 1840s with the aim of allowing magistrates to try and sentence juveniles under twelve immediately. These bills, however, never became law because they were

---

[1]   The age of criminal responsibility was raised to eight in 1933 and subsequently to ten in 1963. Though English law distinguishes between children, that is, those aged ten to thirteen, and young persons, that is those aged fourteen to sixteen, for ease of reading, the term 'juvenile' is used to apply to both unless the context demands such a distinction to be made.

considered unconstitutional. They denied juveniles the right to a jury trial. Thus attempts to achieve separate justice for juveniles were rejected on the grounds that they did not accord with standards of justice accorded to adults. It was not until the 1879 Summary Jurisdiction Act that the number of juveniles in prison was markedly reduced—through various measures designed to try most juveniles at magistrates' courts (Morris and McIsaac, 1978).

Reformatory and industrial schools established by voluntary effort in the 1850s contributed to an overall reduction in the use of prison for juveniles (Carlebach, 1970). As a general rule, however, juveniles were still subject to the rigours of the penal system because of the 'prior imprisonment' rule (juveniles had to serve fourteen days in prison in expiation of their crimes before moving on to these institutions). This continued to undermine beliefs in differences in cause and kind between adult and juvenile crime.

It was not until the 1908 Children Act that the principle of dealing with juvenile offenders separately from adult offenders finally took root. But the establishment of the juvenile court (initially special sittings of the magistrates' court from which the public were excluded) reflected a primarily symbolic change in attitudes towards the juvenile offender. In spite of the change, the juvenile courts remained criminal courts and the procedures were essentially the same as for adults.

Herbert Samuel, introducing the Children Bill, stated that it was founded upon three principles, which are often taken to mark the beginnings of a welfare perspective within British juvenile justice:

- Juvenile offenders should be kept *separate* from adult criminals and should receive *treatment* differentiated to suit their special needs.
- Parents should be made more responsible for the wrongdoing of their children.
- The imprisonment of juveniles should be abolished.

However, closer scrutiny of Samuel's words confirms that, far from being a simple reflection of humanitarian ideas and welfare principles, the act reflected ideas and principles derived from concerns about criminal justice and crime control. From its inception conflict and ambivalence were embedded in the concept of the juvenile court. Samuel argued that the "courts should be agencies for the rescue *as well* as the punishment of juveniles" (emphasis added; House of Commons Debate, Vol. 183: col. 1435-6). It was further noted that "imprisonment would destroy the deterrent value *if used too soon*" (emphasis added; House of Commons Debate, Vol. 183: col. 1435-6).

The juvenile courts retained their original character and structure until the Children and Young Persons Act 1933. This implemented the recommendations of the 1927 Molony Committee, namely that there be a specially selected panel of magistrates to deal with juveniles and that the age of criminal responsibility be raised from seven to eight. The act also dictated that magistrates were to have regard for 'the welfare of the child'. The juvenile court was to act in *loco parentis*, establishing itself as the forum capable of adjudicating on matters of family socialization and parental behaviour, even if no 'crime' as such had been committed (see Morris and McIsaac, 1978; Rutherford, 1986).

A combination of crime control and welfare perspectives thus informed juvenile justice. These competing considerations were reflected in other developments in the period prior to the Second World War. By the end of the 1930s, there was evidence of a revitalized emphasis on punishment. In particular, the Magistrates' Association seemed determined to keep alive their idea for a new sentence of 'young offenders detention,' which was intended to provide a sentence midway on the tariff between borstal and probation. Further support for this came from the departmental committee on corporal punishment (The Cadogan Committee), which could only conceive of abolishing corporal punishment if it were to be replaced with other measures to strengthen the authority of the courts.

Juvenile Justice 1945-1970

Between 1945 and 1970 Britain experienced both Labour (1945-51 and 1964-70) and Conservative (1951-64) administrations for roughly equal amounts of time. One might assume that this led to a radical shift from one set of policies to another. However, the closing years of the war saw the development of a broad political consensus. One feature of this consensus was the creation of a post-war "welfare state." This involved state intervention in the economy in order to maintain full employment, with supporting policies on housing, unemployment and sickness benefit, health and child care (Marshall, 1975). These policies were shared between the two main parties. The word '*Butskellism*' was coined to reflect these similarities (Taylor, 1981; Bottoms and Stevenson, 1992).[2]

---

[2]   The word refers to successive chancellors of the exchequer from different political parties: Hugh Gaitskill, Labour (Chancellor, 1950-51; subsequently leader of the Labour Party, 1955-63) and R. A. Butler, Conservative (Chancellor, 1951-55; subsequently home secretary, 1957-62, and foreign secretary, 1963-4).

It was a period marked by major social change ranging from the gross domestic product and personal incomes to low unemployment rates and increases in the number of married women working and young people entering higher education. At the same time the rate of births to teenage mothers rose; divorce became easier to obtain; church attendance declined; and cars and televisions increasingly became regular features of family life (Halsey, 1988; Marwick, 1982).

This then was the context for a new phase in juvenile justice. A broad political consensus provided a backdrop for consensus with regard to criminal and juvenile justice policy. Nevertheless, despite the emergence of a welfare perspective in general and a sympathetic, child-oriented perspective in particular (Rose, 1989), the war years had seen a new clamour for an unequivocally punitive perspective towards young offenders.

As Bottoms and Stevenson (1992) point out, the key events of the post-war history of juvenile justice can be traced back to a letter to *The Times* on the 16th of March 1955 signed by, among others, the wife of the Archbishop of Canterbury, an eminent child psychiatrist, a celebrated penal reformer, and a leading social work thinker. Their theme was the urgent need for re-orienting the social services towards the maintenance of the family, not least because they believed juvenile crime often resulted from family breakdown. They called for the setting up of a committee of enquiry whose terms would be broad enough to include all causes of family breakdown, with positive recommendations for their prevention and alleviation. Their letter was followed up by a delegation to the Home Office.

At the same time the Magistrates' Association pressed the Home Office for a review of the procedure in juvenile courts and the treatment of juveniles coming before them. The Home Office of the Conservative government responded by setting up in 1956 a departmental committee (the Ingleby Committee) to consider the issues posed by both groups. The *Ingleby Report* was one of four major reports which influenced the direction of juvenile justice in the post-war period. The culmination of this period of activity was the Children and Young Persons Act 1969.

- In one sense the *Ingleby Report* (Home Office, 1960) merely endorsed the existing structure of the juvenile court, though there were recommendations to strengthen the powers of the court by allowing magistrates to sentence young persons directly to Borstal. However, the committee also proposed that the age of criminal responsibility be raised from eight to twelve. In 1963, as a legislative compromise, the age of criminal responsibility was raised to ten in the Children and Young Persons Act. Left-wing critics focused primarily on the missed opportunity for creating a unified family service. Such criticisms led eventually to the publication of a Labour Party report.

- The publication of *Crime—A Challenge to Us All*, the report of a Labour Party study group, known as the *Longford Report*, was produced some months before the Labour Party came to power in 1964. A fundamental principle underlying the report was that "delinquents are to some extent a product of the society they live in and of the deficiencies in its provision for them" (1964: 28). It also argued that the machinery of the law was reserved for working class youth and that "no child in early adolescence should have to face criminal proceedings" (1964: 24), that criminal proceedings were "indefensible" where the offence was trivial (1964: 24) and that serious offences were themselves indicative of "the child's need for skilled help and guidance" (1964: 24). The report's aim, therefore, was to take juveniles out of the criminal courts and the penal system and to treat their problems in a family setting through the establishment of family advice centres, a family service, and, for a minority, a family court.
- The subsequent white paper *The Child, the Family and the Young Offender* (Home Office, 1965) proposed the abolition of the juvenile court and its replacement by a non-judicial family council, linked to a unified family service. But there was concerted opposition to these proposals (see Pitts, 1988; Harris and Webb, 1987; Rutherford, 1986).
- In response to this opposition, the Labour government produced a second white paper *Children in Trouble* (Home Office, 1968). In this second attempt to promote reforms, the government leaned heavily on the expertise of the Home Office Child Care Inspectorate (Pitts, 1988) and, as a result, the language used changed. The appropriate response was one which depended on 'observation and assessment', 'a variety of facilities for continuing treatment', 'increased flexibility' and 'further diagnosis'. And this white paper managed to produce proposals which were largely acceptable to political, administrative, and professional constituencies. The cost of this was the retention of the juvenile court.

The 1969 Children and Young Persons Act which ensued dictated that juveniles under fourteen were not to be referred to the juvenile court solely on the grounds that they had committed offences (thus bringing Britain in line with many other European countries). Rather it was proposed that 'care and protection' proceedings should be brought. Criminal proceedings were to be possible against juveniles aged fourteen to sixteen who had committed offences, but only after mandatory consultation had taken place between the police and social service departments. The expectation was that these juveniles would also be dealt with under care and protection proceedings.

Integral to these proposals was an increase in the role of the local authority social worker. Considerable power was to be placed in the hands of social workers to vary and implement the dispositions made by the magistrates. Magistrates were no longer to make detailed decisions about the kind of treatment appropriate for juveniles; instead, this task was to be given to social workers.

A second main thrust of the act was an attempt to curtail magistrates' power to make use of custodial sentences. Prior to the act, magistrates had been able to remit juveniles of fifteen and over to the Crown Court with a recommendation that the judge impose a sentence of Borstal training. The act sought to prevent all those under eighteen from being remitted to the Crown Court in this way. Further, detention centres and attendance centres were to be replaced by a new form of treatment—intermediate treatment—and the form which this would take was also to be determined by social services (Bottoms et al., 1990).

Overall, the general aim of the act was to make the commission of an offence no longer a sufficient ground for intervention—that is, to decriminalize the court's jurisdiction and to encourage deinstitutionalization. In this way the government sought to blur the distinction between the deprived and the depraved. Put very simply, the juvenile court was to become a welfare providing agency, but also an agency of last resort: referral to the juvenile court was to take place only where voluntary and informal agreement could not be reached between social workers, juveniles, and their parents (Morris and McIsaac, 1978).

Juvenile Justice in the 1970s: The Eclipse of Welfare?
Having witnessed the development of a consensus, albeit a fragile one, the 1969 act brought latent tensions to the surface. The breakdown of this issue-specific consensus reflected the breakdown in the broader political consensus and set the stage for a very different conception of social order and of the appropriate response to juvenile offenders. The writings of the Conservative Party (see, for example, Cooper and Nicholas, 1963 and 1964) depict the law

breaker as choosing to commit offences and as doing so from personal iniquity and from demands or desires exacerbated by the welfare state rather than from social inequality. Neither psychological nor social conditions were viewed as relevant to understanding criminal behaviour. Consequently, juvenile offenders were viewed as personally responsible for their actions although, depending on their age, parents might share in this responsibility in that they had failed both to discipline their young and to inculcate in them basic values. Thus family responsibility was given a different force and meaning to that found in comparable Labour Party writings. Deficiencies in the family were to be remedied through discipline and external controls not through support and services. Parents were to be held responsible for the offences of their children by making them pay, quite literally. The appropriate response to the delinquent was correction through discipline and punishment. The role of the courts was also viewed as important in preserving respect for the law, ensuring parental responsibility, and making juvenile offenders accountable for their actions. Academic criminologists had very little input into this law and order ideology (for a discussion of this, see Brake and Hale, 1992).

As a result, sections of the Conservative Party were always opposed to the philosophy underlying the Longford Report, the 1960s white papers, and the subsequent legislation. According to Durham (1989:50), Conservative ideology—conservatism—rests on a belief in 'human fallibility' and a need for government in which established customs and traditions are preferred to radical social change. In essence Conservatives prefer to limit state controls, to cut government spending, to expand free enterprise, and to privatize even essential services. Through these strategies societies are believed to be better off as they encourage competition and competition means progress. The government's responsibility is only to provide a framework which enables each person to achieve their best.

What is significant in this context is that these ideological struggles impinged on the practice and practitioners of juvenile justice too. On the right, alliances were drawn between the Conservative Party and the Magistrates' Association; and on the left, alliances were drawn between the Labour Party, social workers, and liberal reform groups. Ideological differences provided the ammunition: policies for equality of opportunity were posed against those for achieving equality of results, the responsibility of juvenile offenders was set against their need for help, measures of punishment were contrasted with measures for treatment. Under the banner of the best interests of the child these ideological and professional differences were provided with a public forum.

Thus the Children and Young Persons Act 1969 was a compromise in two fundamental ways. First, in design, it promoted both diversion from courts and the provision of welfare in courts. And second, by design, it perpetuated these competing conceptions (i.e., diversion from courts vs. welfare in courts) of juvenile offenders and of how best to deal with them. The full machinery of courtroom adjudication was retained for those who saw juvenile offenders as responsible and who believed in the symbolic and deterrent value of such appearances. At the same time, an emphasis on social welfare was retained for those who saw juvenile offenders as the product of social circumstances. The sphere of influence of these competing conceptions was not, however, mutually exclusive; nor were the people charged with operating the new act—social workers, magistrates, and the police—isolated actors with a single conception of offenders or of how best to deal with them. Thus these conceptions collided at key points in the process: prosecution, adjudication, determination of the disposition, and implementation of the disposition. The act was never fully implemented. Like many acts of Parliament, certain sections in the Children and Young Persons Act 1969 were to be implemented at some future date.

What is more a Conservative government replaced the Labour one in 1970 and the Conservatives made it clear that they would not fully implement the act. When the Labour Party was re-elected in 1974, it was no longer politically or popularly viable to implement the act in full. Thus new welfare measures were added onto but did not replace the old punitive ones. The consequence was that, on occasions, the two systems collided.

More broadly speaking two opposing trends—first an increase in punitive dispositions generally and in custodial dispositions in particular and second an increase in the use of diversion—occurred in the 1970s. Neither are overtly linked with welfare; the opposite in fact. For example, in the late 1960s intermediate treatment (IT) was introduced. This term was first mentioned in a 1968 white paper (Home Office, 1968) and subsequently came to mean any intervention through community-based programs of supervised activity, guidance, and counselling. The primary objective was to reduce the level of juvenile offending by addressing the needs of juvenile offenders or potential juvenile offenders. In design and in practice, IT was also 'expansionist' (for a description of practice then, see Thorpe et al., 1980). This was particularly so with respect to females who were more likely than males to be involved in IT schemes on a voluntary basis and for reasons other than the commission of offences.

A third and paradoxical trend also occurred—a decline in the use of welfare-oriented dispositions despite the intentions underlying the act. The government raised particular concerns as they pertained to *certain* juvenile offenders (House of Commons Expenditure Committee, 1975; Home Office, Welsh Office, DHSS and DES, 1976). In effect, the perspective underlying the 1969 act was deemed to have failed; in reality, it had never been tried. But its moment had gone. Indeed Smith (1984) argues thoughtfully that, in some senses and in retrospect, the 1969 act represented an end, not a beginning.

Juvenile Justice in the 1980s: The 'Moment' of Crime Control.
In the 1980s in England and Wales, as elsewhere, there was an explicit revival of traditional criminal justice values. The 'need to stand firm against crime' was especially apparent in the electoral campaigns of the Conservative Party in 1979. This was in sharp contrast to the Labour Party, which was presented as excusing crime and as sympathetic to offenders. For example, the political rhetoric of the Conservative Party referred to 'young thugs' who were to be sent to detention centres for a 'short, sharp shock', secure places for juveniles were to be increased, and the number of attendance centres expanded. And later that year, after they had won the election, the new home secretary made good some of the electoral promises: two detention centres were, on an experimental basis, to have tougher regimes. A few years later, a white paper—*Young Offenders* (Home Office, 1980)—was introduced which set the scene for further changes.

Both this white paper and the resulting legislation—the Criminal Justice Act 1982—hit at the root of the social welfare perspective underlying the 1969 act. Both documents represented a move away from treatment and lack of personal responsibility to notions of punishment and individual and parental responsibility. They also represented a move away from executive (social workers) to judicial decision-making and from the belief in the 'child in need' to the juvenile criminal, what Tutt (1981) called 'the rediscovery of the delinquent'.

Overall, they attempted to toughen and tighten up the provisions of the 1969 act. In brief, the 1982 Act made available to magistrates three new powers of disposal: youth custody, care orders with certain residential requirements, and community service. Further, there were three major changes to existing powers: shorter periods in detention centres, restrictions on activities as part of supervision orders, and it was to become normal practice to fine parents rather than the juvenile.

I. Limiting custody and residential care. Against the predictions of academic commentators (see, for example, Morris and Giller, 1979), the number of fourteen to sixteen year old males found guilty of indictable offences and sentenced to custody declined dramatically during the 1980s: from 6900 in 1979 and 7700 in 1981 to 1900 in 1989 and 1400 in 1990. Also the proportionate use of custody hardly changed until 1989—custodial penalties made up 12% of juvenile court dispositions in 1979 and remained at that figure until dropping to 11% in 1986. It remained at that level until 1988 and only fell to 9% in 1989 and to 7% in 1990.

Over this same period, the decline in the use of custody for fourteen to sixteen year old females is less clear cut: the number remained relatively stable at around one hundred. However, it dropped to less than fifty in 1981, 1982 and 1988. It returned to one hundred in 1989 but fell to less than fifty again in 1990. This means that, over this period, the proportionate use of custody for young females increased from 1% in 1979 to 2% in 1984. It remained at this level until 1989 when it again dropped to 1% where it remained in 1990.

Decreases in the number of care orders and in their proportionate use occurred more rapidly. How is this decline in the use of custody and care orders and the rate of decline to be explained? Early research on the impact of the criteria introduced in the 1982 Criminal Justice Act intended to restrict the use of custody showed that they were not very significant: magistrates failed to follow statutory procedures (Burney, 1985; Parker, 1981). The research also questioned the belief that legal representation increased the provision of justice for juveniles. Gradually, however, case law on what amounted to an offence sufficiently 'serious' to warrant custody emerged.

Changes in the 1982 Criminal Justice Act forced social workers and probation officers to re-consider the provision and content of social enquiry reports and to re-form the provision and content of intermediate treatment. Though the original form of IT continued to be available a new format was also introduced in the 1982 act—the 'supervised activity requirement'. The significance of this was that the control and content of the order shifted to magistrates. This was an explicit attempt to increase the magistrates' confidence in such orders as realistic alternatives to custody.

But despite all these efforts, and although the number in custody declined (at least for males), the proportionate use of custody remained remarkably stable until 1989, at least at a national level, though in some areas 'alternative to custody' packages were effective (NACRO, 1989). It is only when we look at the proportionate use of custody for the whole of the known juvenile offender population that we see a very marked reduction: from 8% in 1981 to 1% in 1990. This indicates that it was the impact of diversion (cautioning) practices rather than deinstitutionalization (IT) practices, the increased use of fines, compensation or community service, the introduction of criteria to restrict the use of custody or legal representation which reduced custody.

II. The continued expansion of diversion. Throughout the 1980s diversion was repeatedly affirmed in government documents (for example, Home Office, 1980), consultative documents (Home Office, 1984), circulars to the police (for example, Home Office circular 14/1985) and in the Code of Practice for prosecutors (Crown Prosecution Service, 1986). In these various documents, it was made clear that prosecution should not occur unless it was 'absolutely necessary' or as 'a last resort' and that the prosecution of first-time offenders where the offence was not serious was unlikely to be 'justifiable' unless there were 'exceptional circumstances'. Prosecution was to be regarded as 'a severe step'. This principle was echoed in local police force procedures. Thus the proportion of fourteen to sixteen year old males cautioned for indictable offences increased from 34% in 1980 to 69% in 1990. The comparable figures for ten to thirteen year old males were 65% and 90%.

The Home Office Circular (4/1985) explicitly referred of the dangers of 'net widening' and encouraged the use of 'no further action' or 'informal warnings' instead of formal cautions and, since then, the number of juveniles brought into the juvenile justice system has declined.

There are a number of reasons why net widening is not now occurring. First, there is a declining youth population. Second, there is evidence the police have been making considerable use of 'instant cautions'. These are given to minor and/or first offenders usually within seventy-two hours of the offence. Many areas have also now introduced inter-agency consultation as a forum for deciding what action is appropriate to take for particular juvenile offenders in their area. Most police areas also now say that they will give 'multiple cautions' if each new offence meets the criteria in the guidelines, though in practice multiple cautions are very rarely given (Evans and Wilkinson, 1990). Farrington (1992) argues that the reduction in recorded juvenile crime over this period is illusory and due to changes in police practices rather than changes in juvenile crime, though it is not clear how common this practice is. Wilkinson and Evans (1990) examined practice in fifteen police areas and found eleven areas gave informal warnings. Their expansion is clearly envisaged in the National Standards for Cautioning produced by the Home Office in 1990 (Annex B, Circular 59/1990).

We can sum up the 1980s in this way. In 1979 the Conservative Party made crime a major election issue. The emphasis was on re-establishing 'Victorian values' in opposition to the legacy of the supposed permissiveness of the 1960s and its 'soft' approach to crime. Indeed, as McClennon (1987) has argued, it was not merely that left-wing and liberal writers failed to see the problems inherent in 'soft' approaches to crime, discipline, education, and so on, but that those 'soft' approaches were seen as contributing to permissiveness and all its unwelcome, politically unpalatable effects (see also Taylor, 1981). In such a supposedly de-moralising culture, crime and violence were seen as 'out of control': hence the need for 'law and order' policies to reassert the virtue and necessity of authority, order, and discipline and attempts to realign relationships between the state and civil society as a whole.

Juvenile Justice in the 1990s: The Return to Consensus?

The first significant event of the 1990s was the implementation of the 1989 Children Act which came into force in October 1991. This represented a major structural alteration to the law concerning the welfare of juveniles and covers an enormous range of matters previously dealt with in different legislation. The law affecting juveniles who offend is only touched upon, but the resulting changes, together with the act's underlying sentiments about the nature of the relationship between the state, children, and their parents, have significant implications for juvenile offenders.

The most important of these is the cessation of the use of the care order as a disposal available to the court in criminal proceedings and the removal of the offence condition in proceedings justifying state intervention in the life of a family. New rules also provide for the transfer of care proceedings from the juvenile court. These are now heard in a renamed 'family proceedings' court; the newly named youth court deals only with criminal proceedings.

Since the beginning of the 1990s there have been a number of other new developments in youth justice. These include:

• An increase in the maximum age-limit of cases dealt with by special courts for young people—renamed as Youth Courts following the 1991 Criminal Justice Act.

• The deliberate creation of a so-called 'overlapping jurisdiction' of community orders for sixteen and seventeen year olds found guilty; it is intended that courts should choose the most appropriate orders for defendants on an individualized basis, taking into account the maturity of the individual offender. (Hence, probation orders are now available for sixteen year olds, supervision orders for seventeen year olds, and the maximum number of community service order hours that can be imposed for sixteen year olds is now 240—as opposed to 180, the previous limit).

- There has also been an attempt to strengthen parental responsibility for children's offending (especially those under the age of fifteen years). This has been done by making stronger the requirement for parents to attend the youth court whenever their children appear (1991 Criminal Justice Act s.56). In addition, it gives the court powers to bind over parents with regard to their children's future behaviour, if it is satisfied that this would be 'desirable in the interests of preventing the commission by him of further offences' (1991 Criminal Justice Act s.58). Consequently, if children continue to offend then the parents can be fined for not exercising proper control and for being in breach of the binding over condition.
- The 1991 Criminal Justice Act also increased the minimum age for detention in a Young Offender Institution for males from fourteen to fifteen (this was the minimum for females prior to the act).
- Since October 1992, the Juvenile Court has become the Youth Court.

The nature and form of youth justice has also been influenced by the Criminal Justice and Public Order Act 1994. There are four main provisions of this act affecting the sentencing of young offenders. They are:

- The introduction of the Secure Training Order—a new custodial sentence for persistent juvenile offenders aged twelve to fourteen inclusive. The order is for a minimum of six months and a maximum of two years; with one-half to be spent in detention and the other half on subsequent supervision. There are special criteria for eligibility which revolve round the fact that the young offender must have been twelve when the relevant (that is, serious and imprisonable if an adult) offence was committed; he or she must have previous convictions for three or more imprisonable offences, and he or she must have been subject to a supervision order, which he or she breached, or committed a further imprisonable offence while he or she was subject to it. A number of researchers, Hagell and Newburn (1994b) for example, have pointed out that the legal definition is so particular as to lead to minimum demand for such orders. It should also be pointed out that the establishment of such training centres has still to be resolved. There are no immediate plans for the introduction of the orders—though they now lay on the statute books.

- The Criminal Justice Public Order Act of 1994 also extends to ten to thirteen year olds the existing powers of long-term detention (under the Children Young Persons Act 1933, s.53) available in respect of fourteen to seventeen year olds (that is, if a young person commits an imprisonable offence with a maximum sentence, for an adult of fourteen years or more. Such orders were previously only available to ten to thirteen year olds if they had committed murder or manslaughter.

- The act further allows ten to fifteen year olds to receive long-term detention for offences of indecent assault against a female. This line of 'toughening up' penalties for young offenders is also reflected in the increase in the maximum length of a sentence of detention for an offender fifteen to seventeen inclusive, in a Young Offenders Institution from twelve months to two years.

- Finally, the Criminal Justice and Public Order Act 1994 makes further attempt to strengthen parental responsibility by making clear that in a parental bind-over the parent should ensure that the offender complies with the requirements of a community sentence. The concerns relate to the fact that coercive action against parents will not necessarily ensure cooperation and, may indeed, exacerbate problems between parents and their children. Strong doubts have been expressed as to whether a bind-over of parents will have the desired effect of ensuring the good behaviour of children.

These new measures appear to have had significant impact on court-room practices. We can see a decline in the use of fines, a switch to supervision orders from probation orders; a slight increase in the overall use of custody for the age-group fourteen to seventeen, and many fewer cases appear to be going to the Crown Court than before. The significance of these points is demonstrated in a study of six youth courts in England and Wales by O'Mahony and Haines (1995) which shows that sentencing in the youth court is generally more severe than in the juvenile court. At the same time however, there appears to be a tendency to assimilate seventeen year olds into the juvenile court 'ethos' (fine levels have decreased and rates of committal; to the Crown Court have lowered).

Three other points are worth noting in this brief review of developments in the 1990s. The first concerns the idea of 'Boots camps' for young offenders. The government is considering the introduction of a pilot project in one young offender institution based on the 'high impact incarceration programs'—more commonly referred to as 'Boot camps'—which operate in the USA (see Chapter 10).

The second point concerns the age of criminal responsibility. As a result of court cases in 1994 and 1995 (most notably the case of the two boys aged ten and eleven who were tried for killing two year old Jamie Bulger) the principles governing the criminal responsibility of children between the ages of ten and thirteen were reviewed. Children between ten and thirteen are presumed in law to be *doli incapax* (incapable of criminal intent) and this presumption must be rebutted by the prosecution before they can be convicted. In order to rebut the presumption, the prosecution must show beyond all reasonable doubt that the child appreciated that what he or she did was 'seriously wrong' as opposed to merely naughty or mischievous.

The final point to raise here concerns interest in family group conferences. Family group conferences were developed in New Zealand and are based on the tradition systems of conflict resolution in Maori culture (see Chapter 2). Family group conferences involve a professional coordinator inviting the young offender and their extended family to a 'network conference'. The victim of an offence committed by the young person may also be invited. The aim is to provide a forum to discuss all aspects of the problem caused by the young person and to propose a mutually acceptable plan which addresses the needs of both the young person and the wider community. In England and Wales the Family Rights Group (a national voluntary organization) has been responsible for promoting and supporting a number of pilot projects in family group conferencing that have been particularly concerned with the care, protection, and welfare of children. The New Zealand model of family group conferences is not readily transferable to the youth justice system in England and Wales and, given the present climate, it is unlikely that family group conferences will find their way into legislation. But a number of pressure groups involved in penal reform are urging agencies to see how elements of family group conferences might be incorporated into the existing system. While it is appropriate to end this review with a more optimistic note on developments in England and Wales, there is scepticism as to the likely participation of families.

The arguments are clearly no longer about welfare, crime control, or justice, and the new philosophies cannot be allied to the political right or left as they once could. Indeed, there is every indication that the 1990s begin with a return to the consensus on crime that marked the post-war era. The manifestos for the 1992 election revealed little difference in the political parties' respective responses to crime and conceptions of justice (Conservative Political Centre, 1992; Labour Party, 1992).

In both rhetoric and practice, the formal arrangements for juvenile or, more accurately, youth justice are increasingly becoming linked with other social institutions and processes and there is ostensible concern among politicians to make strong connections amongst these processes where preventative and healing resources are perceived ultimately to reside.

Box 4.1: Juvenile Justice in Scotland and Northern Ireland.

Juvenile justice in Scotland has taken a completely different direction from juvenile justice in England and Wales since the 1960s. While moves to abolish the juvenile court from England and Wales were fiercely resisted, similar ideas in Scotland were accepted, a remarkable achievement perhaps given the country's Calvinist traditions which stress individual responsibility and the punishment of wickedness (Gelsthorpe and Morris, 1994). Indeed, Scotland has managed to implement, at least in theory, a social welfare approach to juvenile offenders.

The system for dealing with young offenders is essentially a hearing system. The age of responsibility for juveniles is eight to sixteen. Young offenders are referred to a reporter (a legally trained official) whose initial function it is to decide on the basis of reports, whether or not the juvenile referred to them is in need of 'compulsory measures of care'. If the juvenile or parents deny the commission of an offence the case is referred by the reporter to the Sheriff Court for the offence to be proved.

The hearing system essentially involves the reporter and a lay panel of members of the public. The panel can either discharge the referral by the reporter or impose a supervision requirement (SR), which may include residential conditions. The hearing has continuing jurisdiction; cases are reviewed annually. In contrast to the system in England and Wales, the lay panel has no power to fine the juvenile or his/her parents, to impose a custodial penalty, or to remit the juvenile to the Sheriff Court for sentence (Kearney, 1987; Young and Young, 1994).

Juvenile justice in Northern Ireland is largely governed by the Children and Young Persons Act (Northern Ireland) 1968. The juvenile court remains the judicial forum in which any statutory intervention into the lives of children and young persons takes place, protection and control—(the age of criminal responsibility in Northern Ireland is ten, as it is in England). The court is presided over by a magistrate who has at least six years' experience as a practising lawyer, assisted by two members of a lay panel. Disposals available to the court are: fines, absolute and conditional discharges, committal to a training school, committal to the care of a fit person order, supervision or probation orders, attendance centre orders, committal to a remand home, a period in a young offenders' centre, and community service. A review of legislation and services relating to the care and treatment of young people (chaired by Sir Harold Black in 1979) made some radical suggestions including the separation of juvenile justice and welfare systems (as in England, see Gelsthorpe and Morris, 1994), determinate sentencing, and for a fixed number of custodial places (in a secure unit as opposed to training schools). But many of Black's recommendations appear to have failed to attract much attention, though a Children and Young Persons Order dealing with some aspects of child care may give effect to at least some of the proposals.

Juvenile Crime: Trends and Patterns

Having outlined the development of juvenile justice within England and Wales and indicated some of the differences in Scotland and Northern Ireland (see Box 4.1), it is worth pausing to consider the nature and extent of the problem which the system has set out to deal with. In this section we will therefore examine recent trends and patterns in juvenile crime. The following statistics are drawn from the Criminal Statistics, England and Wales, 1994, published by the Home Office. It is worth noting that the age categories changed in 1993, following the 1991 Criminal Justice Act. As we noted in the previous section, one consequence of this act is that seventeen year olds are now dealt with in the Youth Court and not the Magistrates' Court. The age groupings of the statistics have thus changed, from fourteen to sixteen to fourteen to seventeen and from seventeen to twenty to eighteen to twenty (the category ten to thirteen remains the same).

As has been noted in the Introduction, official crime statistics do not necessarily portray the full picture of crime. For a variety of reasons, many offences are not reported to the police. Of those that are reported, depending on the type and seriousness of the offenses some go unrecorded. Of all offences that were recorded in 1994, only 26% were cleared up, that is prosecuted or resolved in some other way.

Figure 4.1 offers some indication of the extent of the crime problem within England and Wales over the last twenty-five years.

Although absolute comparisons between criminal justice statistics in different countries are difficult, comparisons based on general trends suggest that nearly all countries in Western Europe, as well as the USA and Japan, have shown a sharp increase in recorded crime between 1987 and 1994. Interestingly, however, the increase in England and Wales was the highest (35%) of those countries covered (Home Office Criminal Statistics, 1994: 19). In recent years the trend towards rising crime has been reversed in many countries with falls in 1994 of the sixteen countries for which data is available. The drop of 5% in England and Wales was the second highest amongst these countries.

What is particularly significant in this context is that offending is particularly prevalent among young people. In a self-report survey produced by the Home Office one in two males (ages fourteen to twenty-five) and one in three females admitted that they had committed an offence at some time (Graham

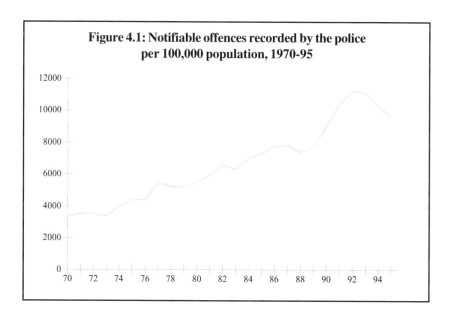

Figure 4.1: Notifiable offences recorded by the police per 100,000 population, 1970-95

and Bowling, 1995). The majority of offenders commit no more than one or two minor offences. Property offending was found to be more common than violent offending by a factor of about two for males and three for females (see Table 4.1).

One in four males and one in eight females admitted committing an offence in 1992; of these, about a quarter of male offenders and one in ten female offenders admitted committing more than five offences. According to Graham and Bowling, about 3% of offenders accounted for approximately a quarter of all offences.

Table 4.1: Percentage of males and females who said they had offended at some time

Offence	Males	Females
Property	49	28
Violence	28	10
Vandalism	25	16
All	55	31

It is important to note, however, that the number of young offenders aged ten to seventeen known to have committed an indictable offence (that is to say a more serious offence, which may be punishable by a custodial sentence) in England and Wales has fallen in recent years. In 1993, 129,500 young offenders aged ten to seventeen were found guilty of indictable offences, of these 100,200 were male and 29,300 were female. This compares with 204,600 young offenders aged ten to seventeen cautioned or found guilty in 1983, a fall of 37%. The fall in the number of known young offenders in the last ten years is only partly accounted by the decline of the juvenile population. As stated earlier, between 1983 and 1993, the number of young people aged between ten and seventeen in the population fell by 19%. For a more detailed breakdown of these figures see Figure 4.2 and 4.3.

In 1994 of all those male juveniles aged ten to fourteen found guilty or cautioned for indictable offences, 60% (13,600) had committed offences of theft or handling stolen goods; 18% (4100) had committed burglary; 10% (2200) had committed violence against the person; and 1% (300) had committed drugs offences. For males aged fourteen to seventeen, the figures were 47% (30,760) had committed theft; 17% (13,400) burglary; 13% (10,600) violence against the person; and 10% (8400) drug offences.

In 1994 of all those female juveniles aged ten to fourteen found guilty or cautioned for indictable offences, 85% (8000) had committed offences of theft or handling stolen goods; 3% (300) had committed burglary; 8% (700) had committed violence against the person; and 1% (100) had committed drug offences. For females aged fourteen to seventeen, the figures were 72% (1660) had committed theft; 3% (300) burglary; 14% (330), violence against the person; and 4% (900), drug offences.

Having considered the rate and nature of offending, lets now turn to an examination of what happens to offenders within the system.

As Table 4.2 shows a significant number of offenders are cautioned, which essentially means that they are given a formal warning by the police. There is no doubt that there has been an enormous expansion in the use of cautioning. The 1970s marked its first growth period. This trend continued into the 1980s and the 1990s.

Where children and young people are prosecuted and sentenced within the court there is a very wide range of sanctions available. The main ones appear in the table below. The least restrictive sanction involves an absolute or conditional discharge. Financial penalties are commonly used. For example, fines can be imposed on parents for their offsprings' criminal behaviour.

Figure 4.2: Persons found guilty or cautioned for indictable offences for 100,000 relevant population, 1970-95

a) Males

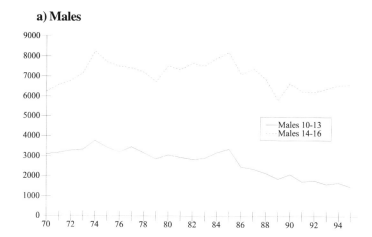

N.B.   1993-5 data for the older age group refers to age group 14-17 (not 14-16) following the intriduction of the Youth Court.

b) Females

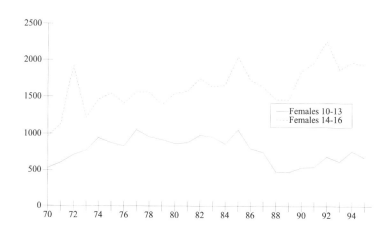

N.B.   1993-5 data for the older age group refers to age group 14-17 (not 14-16) following the intriduction of the Youth Court.

Figure 4.3: Statistics for reference

Year	Male 10-13	Male 14-16	Female 10-13	Female 14-16
1970	3123	6233	533	932
1971	3235	6561	655	1125
1972	3366	6871	736	1819
1973	3411	7072	775	1209
1974	3809	8191	922	1490
1975	3522	7861	894	1514
1976	3303	7567	819	1468
1977	3517	7519	1041	1570
1978	3187	7382	952	1572
1979	2923	6810	913	1457
1980	3075	7585	881	1539
1981	2993	7475	887	1566
1982	2919	7659	985	1721
1983	2926	7532	941	1659
1984	3090	7977	847	1666
1985	3231	8128	1048	2018
1986	2527	7048	761	1706
1987	2477	7385	676	1638
1988	2221	6949	492	1473
1989	1924	5926	492	1473
1990	2025	6759	523	1810
1991	1817	6378	535	1973
1992	1884	6333	689	2231
1993	1696	6406	621	1885
1994	1740	6461	756	1958
1995	1605	6468	687	1924

Supervision and probation orders place the offender under the supervision of a social worker or probation officer (depending on the age of the offender). Standard conditions such as reporting to supervising officer are normally attached to the order. Other conditions that may be attached for young offenders on supervision orders include intermediate treatment, which involves up to ninety days activity and instruction in social, community, domestic, and creative skills. Probation orders for the older age group might require residence in an

Table 4.2: Offenders cautioned as a percentage of offenders found guilty or cautioned by sex and age, 1984-95

Year	Total	Males All Ages	Males 10 to under 14	Males 14 to under 18	Females All Ages	Females 10 to under 14	Females 14 to under 18
1984	23	20	75	36	35	91	60
1985	26	23	79	40	41	93	68
1986	28	24	81	44	44	94	70
1987	30	26	86	49	45	96	73
1988	28	26	86	49	43	95	70
1989	29	26	88	52	44	95	72
1990	33	30	90	58	49	96	77
1991	36	32	90	59	54	97	80
1992	41	36	91	63	61	97	84
1993	41	37	90	63	60	97	84
1994	41	37	87	60	59	97	81
1995	41	37	86	58	59	96	79

approved hostel, or attendance at a probation centre for up to sixty days or evenings, for example. Community service orders (CSOs) can be made in respect of persons aged sixteen or over for between forty and 240 hours. Attendance centre orders available for ten to twenty year olds, though the centres dealing with ten to seventeen year olds are known as 'junior attendance centres'. The orders can be imposed for up to twenty-four hours for those aged ten to fifteen, and up to thirty-six hours for those aged sixteen to twenty (though those aged fifteen to seventeen will serve their hours in a junior attendance centre and those over this age in a senior attendance centre). Offenders are required to report to a centre on a weekly basis (often on a Saturday afternoon) for a range of activity including military drill, gym, social skills training, and creative skills (e.g., woodwork or metalwork). Combination orders involve a mixture of elements of a probation order and a community service order. The probation part of the mix must be for not less than twelve months and the community service part of the mix must be for not less than forty hours and not more than one hundred hours. Care orders were, until 1990, imposed on those young offenders who were deemed to be in need of residential care because of their welfare needs, as well as their offending behaviour. Only those aged twenty-one and above are sentenced to imprisonment, those between the ages of fifteen and twenty are detained in young offender institutions. There are limits on the period of detention according to age. Those under fourteen (and indeed, up to eighteen) may be detained under Section 53 (2) of the 1933 Children and Young Persons Act if they have committed an offence punishable with fourteen years' imprisonment or indecent assault on a woman. Under the 1994 Criminal Justice and Public Order Act a secure training order may be imposed on a juvenile if the offender was aged twelve on the day of the offence. A number of other sanctions are available, including hospital orders and guardianship orders. Between 1980 and 1995, the most common disposition for males (ages fourteen to sixteen), other than an absolute discharge or conditional discharge (29% in 1995 vs. 17% in 1980) was the use of supervision or probation order (14% in 1980 vs. 12% in 1995). The percentage of females (ages fourteen to sixteen) receiving an absolute or conditional discharge since 1980 has been consistently greater (27% in 1980 vs. 49% in 1995) than that for males. The percentage of supervision or probation orders has remained stable around 25%.

Contemporary Concerns re: Problem Youth

Having outlined the emergence and development of juvenile justice within England and Wales and pointed to trends and patterns in youth crime over the last twenty years, we now want to examine contemporary concerns about youth. It is arguable that specific aspects of youth crime have become the focus of a disproportionate amount of media and political attention. It is these specific anxieties about youth crime which have often fuelled policy changes, at least those changes which are initiated by the political system (as opposed to criminal justice practitioners). In this section we will examine a number of aspects of youth crime which have provoked, and continue to provoke, considerable anxiety, namely the murder of two year old Jamie Bulger, the emergence of a 'rave' sub-culture and problem of car crime amongst young offenders. Although discussion of these issues will be brief, we hope it will provide some kind of context for understanding the construction of problem youth within modern Britain.

The Bulger Case
The murder of two year old James Bulger by two ten year old boys on February 12, 1993 in Bootle, Merseyside, received massive national and international

media coverage and inspired an enormous amount of public and private debate. The event inspired a kind of national collective agony, evidenced both within the media and within individuals' discussions. The event was alternately seen in terms of being as symptomatic of social decay, the decline of morality, a cause of the swelling of parents' fears for their children and a spur to government policy relating to juvenile crime. Other media-inspired discussions revolved around the loss of innocence of childhood marked by the revealing of the 'evil' within two ten year old boys. More recently the case has generated extensive debate about the role of the executive (that is, the Home Secretary) in judicial decision-making following his handling of the sentence meted out by the judge and his pronouncements on the case that he would take into account public opinion into account when fixing the final tariff. Lord Justice Morland, dealing with the case, had ordered the boys to be detained at Her Majesty's Pleasure (the equivalent of a life sentence—though in effect, meaning that their release would be discretionary once a 'tariff' period had been served). In January 1994 it was discovered that the judge had recommended a 'tariff' of a minimum detention period of eight years for Venables and ten years for Thompson, with the overseeing Lord Chief Justice recommending a minimum period of ten years. Michael Howard, Home Secretary for the ruling Conservative Party, eventually ordered the two boys—Jon Venables and Robert Thompson—to serve a minimum of fifteen years (one and a half times their short lives), a decision which was criticized by some for making political capital out of the event. Interestingly, in May 1996, two judges in the High Court (a court of appeal) declared Howard's decision to fix a minimum sentence of fifteen years in custody for the two boys as unlawful—since he had treated them as 'adult murderers' rather than as children. Despite current moves to overturn this latest turn of events, there is obvious support from the European Court of Human Rights in Strasbourg for the criticism of the Home Secretary since the boys' general treatment is seen to have breached the European Human Rights Convention. We should add that the Bulger case was seemingly used by the government as a pretext for a number of criminal justice initiatives, including the building of 170 additional places in secure units for twelve to sixteen year olds, a point to which we have referred earlier.

There are two particular points that merit further attention here. The first revolves around the alleged influence of viewing videos depicting violence and horror on the boys' behaviour, and the increasing tendency for children to remain unsupervised. As Alison Young has put it:

> From the horror of the security videos, attention is shifted to the
> horror of the horror film. In addition to the comforting possibility
> that exposure to violent films might provide the answer to the question
> that the media had been asking for months (why did these boys do
> it?...), the focus on violent films is linked to the issue of parental care
> and the breach in the maternal relation. (1996:133)

After the jury had returned their verdict the judge presiding in the case
made a plea for a public debate on parenting and on the exposure of children
to violent films and videos:

> In my judgement the home background, upbringing, family
> circumstances, parental behaviour and relationships were needed in
> the public domain so that informed and worthwhile debate can take
> place for the public good in the case of grave crimes by young children.
> This could include exposure to violent video films, including possibly
> *Child's Play 3* , which has some striking similarities to the manner of
> the attack on James Bulger. (*The Guardian,* 27 November 1993)

A debate was thus sparked off, taking place between politicians, film critics
and theorists, and psychologists. Some twenty-five psychologists signed a
report entitled *Video Violence and the Protection of Children*, by Elizabeth
Newsom, Professor of Developmental Psychology at Nottingham University,
which pointed to direct effects on children's behaviour where they were
repeatedly "exposed to images of vicious cruelty in a context of entertainment
and amusement" (*The Guardian*, 1st April, 1994). The Newsom Report was
taken up with alacrity by all sections of Parliament and in April, 1994 the Home
Secretary stipulated that a new clause was to be inserted in the Criminal Justice
Bill 1994 (now an act) placing a duty on the British Board of Film Classification
in granting licences to take account of both the psychological impact of videos
on children and the possibility that they will show them 'inappropriate models
and techniques'. Video store owners who allow adult films to be rented by
under-age children will receive severe penalties: a minimum fine of £20,000 and
six months imprisonment, with a maximum of up to two years' imprisonment
and an unlimited fine. Underneath all this there is perhaps a sense in which the
Bulger case rocked, disturbed, and disquieted the public's notion of childhood
innocence, a notion which reflects the cultural and social investment in
childhood (Warner, 1994).

The second point concerns fears about children's *persistent* offending
behaviour. It is almost as if the Bulger case triggered alarm about the nature,
extent, and persistence of youth crime. Indeed, in the weeks following the

Bulger case there was a gradual transition in newspaper reports from a focus on the horror of a single event to the horror that hoards of young people were marauding the country—making a mockery of any attempts to control them on the part of schools or criminal justice agents. Hagell and Newburn (1994a) were quick off the mark to test out the proposition. Based on a sample of several hundred young people who had been arrested three or more times in one year, they considered the nature and extent of their offending and their experiences of the criminal justice system. Contrary to political and public discourse however, they did not find a distinct group of very frequent offenders. Moreover, the persistent offenders they did find were not disproportionately engaged in serious offending (see Box 4.2).

Box 4.2: Secure units for Juveniles

In 1993 the Home Secretary, Kenneth Clarke, came under fire after suggesting that youths between the ages of twelve to fifteen, convicted of three imprisonable offences, be placed in a secure training facility. However, several of his critics argued that such facilities would simply become "colleges of crime" and "penal pre-schools" . Most critics viewed the suggestion as a "retrograde step... repeating the mistakes of the 1960s and 1970s". Clarke did, however, find allies among the police who welcomed the idea. In the Home Office report Clarke points out that these facilities would focus on schooling first and provide a rich environment to teach responsibility and social skills often found lacking among persistent offenders. Clarke points out that the idea represents a balance between the public's demand for retributive measures and a more conciliatory approach that balances accountability with attempts to retrain youth (Brown, 1993).

Drugs and 'Rave Culture'

According to John Graham and Ben Bowling's study of juvenile crime, drug use is 'widespread' amongst young people today; every other male and every third female have used drugs at some time (1995: 2). This is mostly confined to cannabis, which is consumed regularly (at least once a week) by one in three male and one in five female users. 'Other drugs' are consumed less regularly, although 13% of male users and 19% of female users did so at least once a week.

What is interesting is that it is these 'other drugs' (particularly 3-4 methylenedioxymethaphtamine, otherwise known as 'Ecstasy') that have become the focal point of general cultural anxieties about drug use amongst young people in the 1990s. Ecstasy—approximately £15 for a non-addictive, energy-enhancing, rush—is the drug of choice amongst a generation of young people who attend raves. Since the late 1980s, 'rave culture' has emerged as the nadir of respectable society, a clandestine and highly dangerous world of teenage drug use and bacchic pleasures.

These kinds of fear first emerged in the late 1980s when raves first surfaced in the public consciousness. These fears culminated in legal action when in 1989 Conservative Party backbench MP Graham Bright placed raves on the statute books by introducing The Entertainments (Increased Penalties) Bill, a private members bill which strengthened penalties for unlicensed rave organisers. The new legislation closed this loophole as well as increasing fines for failing to obtain local authority permission from £2000 to £20,000 with a six-month prison sentence and confiscation of all equipment, i.e., sound systems. Bright's bill became law and was subsequently reinforced by provisions under the 1992 Crime and Public Order Act.

Tighter legal regulation of the event itself has meant that the focal point of public anxieties about the rave sub-culture have focused exclusively on the question of drug use, particularly 'mind-altering' drugs such as Ecstasy. A recent spate of 'high profile' deaths has served to exacerbate this fear. A particularly tragic case involved Leah Betts, the daughter of an Essex policeman who died at her own eighteenth birthday as a result of dropping a contaminated Ecstasy tablet.

What is interesting is that the popular imagination has historically seen drug use as a black problem. The image of drugs as an Afro-Caribbean issue has been consigned to history. According to a recent government report, drug use is substantially higher among younger whites than among blacks of the same age. An upsurge in drug-taking among whites in their late teens and twenties means the image of Afro-Caribbeans as having the highest drug use has been undermined (*The Guardian*, May 12, 1996). White, middle-class England no longer regards drugs as someone else's problem.

And yet, as anyone with familiar with post-war youth history would say, drug use in youth sub-cultures is nothing new. In fact, each generation appears to have its own favourite chemicals: mods used amphetamines, hippies LSD, and punks sniffed solvent. What is interesting, however, is that the rave scene seems to enjoy a much closer relationship to its chosen narcotic ('E') than previous generations. There is an unnerving sophistication in drug use amongst young people. Everyone has their own favourite cocktail, a post-modern collage of illegal pleasure:

> Mark 20: "Snowballs are best, they make you dance forever". Nick does Tangos: "Fifty per cent MDMA and fifty per cent Ketamine."
> (Huq, 1993: 12)

It is this kind of sophistication in drug use (see Box 4.3), not to mention the extent of drug use, which has made the rave sub-culture particularly threatening to respectable society.

Box 4.3: A drug problem among youth?
A major survey revealed that 93% of incarcerated young offenders were *regular* drug users. The authors of the report suggested that for the first time it has been demonstrated that there is a strong link between youth crime and drugs. The report showed that young offenders were spending 150 to 600 pounds on drugs. "Yet more than half of them were unemployed and nearly half had no financial support." The results were based on surveying youth fifteen to twenty-four in three penal institutions. Of those who admitted to being regular users, only 6% had ever been charged with a drug offence. At the conference, Kirby (1993) cites a comment from the Manchester police drug squad which points out that teenage gangs are increasingly competing for status with drugs and guns. A number of statistics were offered supporting this impression. The conference concluded with a call for more aggressive tactics in combating teen gangs. One suggestion was to copy the US 'Tactical Narcotics Teams', task forces comprising police, social workers, and local authority employees... to mount a clean-up operation and then move in to clear drug dealers and physically repair the streets (Kirby, 1993).

Joy-Riding and Urban Youth

Car crime, that is to say, theft from or of a motor vehicle, consistently accounts for around one-fifth of all recorded crime. The 1987 British Crime Survey, for example, found that theft of motor vehicles amounted to 21.8% of all crime. This is a remarkable figure when one considers the range of criminal offences. Curiously, however, it is a particular type of car crime—what is known as 'joy-riding'—which has come to dominate public discussion of this problem. The standard definition of joy-riding is a ride taken in a car, normally a stolen car, simply for fun and for the pleasure of reckless driving. According to a report in August 1991 by a chief superintendent working in the Oxford police force, David Lindley, in 1990 there were 2395 cars were stolen and 2924 were burgled. In the first half of 1991 car theft rose by 29%. Car theft in Oxford was running at about four thefts a day. In this context what is interesting is that joy-riding is almost always perceived as a youth problem, more specifically a problem of deprived, urban, male youth.

In a fascinating account of the joy-riding phenomenon, Beatrix Campbell (1993) links the upsurge in this kind of crime to the decline of the inner city within contemporary Britain. Long-term economic decline has meant that unemployment has become the norm amongst working-class youth. For the first time a generation of young people face the possibility of a lifetime without stable employment. Whereas men have historically lived their lives *working* in the public sphere, economic conditions now mean that such an option is no longer available. Men are thus banished to the family world in which women have always lived.

It is this celebration of masculinity, which, in Campbell's view, explains the attractions of crime. Other means of achieving recognition—of being a 'real men'—are denied to these young people. Violent and dangerous criminal activity becomes the only means of acquiring the mantle of manhood

Campbell describes how in the summer of 1990 car crime became theatre, with inner city estates providing the setting for a strange kind of performance:

> The displays united thieves, drivers and audiences in an alliance against the authorities. The performances were witnessed by people whose participation amounted only to watching, but whose gaze gave endorsement to the driver's audacity and, more than that, afforded protection . . . In the summer of 1990 the displays of 'auto acrobatics' were regularly being watched at 3 A.M. by an audience of thirty or forty people. (Campbell, 1993: 33)

Campbell argues that the police had no plan to deal with the joy-riding phenomenon itself, its addictive character, its pleasures, its public protection, and its dangerousness. The traditional response of pursuing joy-riders was stopped in 1990 when most police forces introduced a no-pursuit policy. Dangerous and sometimes deadly car chases through city streets had aroused great public criticism, not least because they had killed innocent pedestrians. However, the rather obvious consequence of discouraging the chase was that they were unable to catch the perpetrators.

So the police responded to the problem of the audience. There was a policing of the spectacle, with the police trying to stop young people hanging around. This, in turn, generated low-grade public order offences and a more general bad feeling. By the end of 1990, many people were seriously worried that nothing was being done to tackle the problem and that relations between the police and young people had reached a crisis point. Joy-riding was thus flung to the front of the public imagination, a symptom of a more general unease about deprived youth. Working-class youth were thus constructed as a pressing social problem and not just youth crime.

Summary and Conclusion

Having provided a schematic (Figure 4.4) overview of the juvenile justice system in England and Wales, this chapter presented an historical account of the emergence of this system. The main points of this narrative can be summarized as follows:

- The emergence of a distinct system of juvenile justice is a relatively recent phenomenon, dating from the early part of the twentieth century. A distinct system of juvenile justice was institutionalized by the 1908 Children Act, a legislative instrument which marked the introduction of a welfare approach to the problem of youth crime. The period between 1908 and the mid to late 1960s was marked by a broad political consensus in the treatment of juvenile offenders. A **welfare** approach combined with a more traditional **justice model** (see Figure 1— Introduction).

- While a welfare perspective blossomed in the 1960s, the 1970s saw the eclipse of such ideas within the courtroom with the reinstatement of the Conservative Party and a more punitive perspective which saw the use of custody rise. The idea of diversion persisted though so that the period of the 1970s reflected a curious mixture of increasing reliance on custodial sentences and on police cautions.

- The 1980s was a period which saw the explicit revival of traditional criminal justice values and policies and practices which hit at the root of the Labour Party social welfare perspective of the 1960s. It was a period of law and order and crime control, with policies that were designed to reassert the virtue and necessity of authority, order, and discipline.

- The 1990s have witnessed a number of developments which taken together seem to suggest that the arguments are clearly no longer about welfare, crime control or justice and that the new philosophies, where discernible amongst practitioners, cannot be allied to the political right or left as they once could. For example, the manifestos for the 1992 election revealed little difference in the political parties' respective responses to crime and the conception of justice. In the Introduction to this collection of readings, it is sugguested that the current model could be described as representing a **corporative model** (see Figure 1). For a comparison see the contribution from Hong Kong (Chapter 5).

Figure 4.3: Outline of the Youth Justice System in England and Wales

APPREHENSION & CHARGE

Parents are expected to attend the police station. If they do not, Social Workers may intervene following an arrest to act as an 'appropriate adult' during police interviews to protect the rights of young people.

The police apprehend or have reported to them young people suspected of committing criminal offences.

No national data is available on the numbers of such referrals or apprehensions.

BAIL

Social Workers or Probation Officers may intervene to try to secure the release of a young person on bail.

Intervention may include the provision of 'bail support' (i.e. temporary accommodation and/or short-term supervision)

Most young offenders who are arrested are bailed by the police (i.e. they return home)

Some young people are remanded in custody (national facilities: age 15+ only) or local authority accommodation, which may be secure accommodation (local facilities)

DIVERT

Most local areas have established multi-agency diversion panels to advise the police whether a formal prosecution is necessary.

Probation Officers, Social Workers and Education Welfare Officers (but not parents or victims) are commonly involved in multi-agency diversion panels

The police decide whether to prosecute or divert a young person from prosecution. Over 90% of known 10-13 year old offenders are formally cautioned by the police. Over 60% of known 14-17 year old offenders are formally cautioned.

Instead of a formal caution a young person may be given an 'informal warning' or 'no further action' may be taken. No national data is available on the use of these other disposals

PROSECUTE

Young people in need (including offenders) may be referred to Social Workers as welfare cases. Most such young people are dealt with under a voluntary agreement between the family and the SSD, but some cases may be taken to the family proceedings court

If (and only if) the police decide it would be right to prosecute, papers are passed to the Crown Prosection Service (CPS). Of those young people referred to the CPS by the police for prosecution over 25% are discontinued (on evidential insufficiency or public interest grounds)

YOUTH COURT

Parents are required to attend the youth court.

The probation service or the social services department may be asked to complete a Pre-sentence Report.

Legal representation is allowed, and is standard practice in more serious cases

Many young people appear in court on two or three occasions before sentence. Between court appearances the young person may be bailed, or remanded to local authority accommodation or custody (see above)

SENTENCE

CUSTODIAL SENTENCES	COMMUNITY SENTENCES			OTHER SENTENCES
	PROBATION SERVICE	SOCIAL SERVICES DEPARTMENT	OTHER BODIES	
Detention in a Young Offender Institution	Probation Orders* Supervision Orders* Community Service Orders	Supervision Orders*	Attendance Centres	Fine Absolute or conditional discharge Bind Over Compensation
15 years + only		10-17 years old	10-17 years	
Secure Training Orders	Combination Orders		Curfew Orders	10-17 years
12-14 years	16-17 year olds	* May contain additional specified requirements	16-17 years	

NOTE: This outline excludes allegations concerning very serious crimes, which if prosecuted are considered in the Crown Court and (for some crimes) can also attract a special sentence (long-term detention under s. 53 CYPA 1933)

Adapted from: Bottoms, A.E., Haines, K. & Mahony, D. (1977). "Youth Justice in England and Wales." In L. Walgrave and J. Mehlbye (Eds.). *Confronting European Youth*. Copenhagen: AKF. (Forthcoming).

The government's recently announced plans to introduce 'boot camps' signify that the alarm bells about youth crime are still echoing, but one key thing we can learn from history and the development of policy in relation to juvenile or youth crime is that it has to be understood in a social and political context; moral panics about youth crime also mask more general fears about modern society so that the evidence is sometimes tangential to the direction that policy takes (Pearson, 1983; Goode and Ben-Yehuda, 1994). Putting this another way, concerns about contemporary youth cannot be taken at face value for they may signify other concerns about social life and social order.

References

Allen, R. (1991). Out of jail: The reduction in the use of penal custody for male juveniles. *Howard Journal*, 30: 30-53.

Bottoms, A.E., Haines, K. & Mahoney, D. (1977). *Youth Justice in England and Wales*.

Bottoms, A.E., & Stephenson, S. (1992). What went wrong? Criminal justice policy in England and Wales, 1945-1970. In D. Downes (Ed.). *Unravelling criminal justice*. London: Macmillan.

Bottoms, A.E., Brown P., McWilliams, B., McWilliams, W., & Nellis, M. (1990). *Intermediate treatment and juvenile justice: Key findings and implications from a national survey of intermediate treatment policy and practice*. London: HMSO.

Bowden, J., & Stevens, M. (1988). Justice for juveniles: A corporate strategy in Northampton. *Justice of the Peace*, 24th May: 326-9.

Brake, M., & Hale, C. (1992). *Public order and private lives: The politics of law and order*. London: Routledge.

Brown, C. (1993, March 3). Secure units for juveniles. *The Independent*, p. 1.

Burney, E. (1958). *Sentencing young people*. Aldershot: Gower.

Campbell, B. (1993). *Goliath: Britain's dangerous places*. London: Methuen.

Carlebach, J. (1970). *Caring for children in trouble*. London: Routledge and Kegan Paul.

Cohen, S. (1979). Notes on the dispersal of social control. *Contemporary Crises*, 3: 339-63.

Conservative Political Centre. (1961). *Crime and punishment*. London: CPC.

Conservative Political Centre. (1965). *Putting Britain ahead*. London: CPC.

Conservative Political Centre. (1992). *The best future for Britain, Conservative Party manifesto*. London: CPC.

Cooper, B., & Nicholas, G. (1963). *Crime in the sixties*. London: Conservative Political Centre.

Cooper, B. & Nicholas, G. (1964). *Crime and the Labour Party*. London: The Bow Group.

Crown Prosecution Service. (1986). *Code of practice for prosecutors*. London: CPS.

Department of Health and Social Security. (1981). *Offending by young people: A survey of recent trends*. London: HMSO.

Ditchfield, J. (1976). *Police cautioning in England and Wales, Home Office research study no. 37*. London: HMSO.

Dodds, M. (1986). The restrictions on imposing youth custody and detention centre sentences. *Justice of the Peace*, 7th June: 359-62.

Dodds, M. (1987). The restrictions on imposing youth custody and detention centre sentences. *Justice of the Peace*, 19th September: 597-600.

Durham, M. (1989). The right: The Conservative Party and conservation. In L. Tivey and A. Wright (Eds.). *Party ideology in Britain*. London: Routledge.

Evans, R., & Wilkinson, C. (1990). Variations in police cautioning policy and practice in England and Wales. *Howard Journal*, 21: 123-35.

Farrington, D.P. (1992). Trends in English juvenile delinquency and their explanation. *International Journal of Comparative and Applied Criminal Justice*, 21: 151-68.

Farrington, D.P., & Bennett, T. (1981). Police cautioning of juveniles in London. *British Journal of Criminology*, 21: 123-35.

Fisher, C. & Mawby, R. (1982). Juvenile delinquency and police discretion in an inner city area. *British Journal of Criminology*, 22: 63-75.

Foucault, M. (1977). *Discipline and punish*. Harmondsworth: Penguin.

Gelsthorpe, L.R., & Morris, A. (1994). Juvenile justice. In M. Maguire, R. Morgan and R. Reiner (Eds.). *The Oxford handbook of criminology*. Oxford: Clarendon Press.

Goode, E., & Ben-Yehuda, N.B. (1994). *Moral panics*. Oxford: Blackwell.

Graham, J., & Bowling, B. (1995). *Young people and crime, Home Office research and statistics department, research findings no. 24*. London: HMSO.

Hagell, A., & Newburn, T. (1994a). *Young offenders and the media: Viewing habits and preferences*. London: Policy Studies Institute.

Hagell, A., & Newburn, T. (1994b). *Persistent young offenders*. London: Policy Studies Institute.

Halsey, A. (1988). *British social trends since 1900 (2nd ed.)*. London: Macmillan.

Harris, R. (1991). The life and death of the care order (criminal). *British Journal of Social Work*. 21: 1-17.

Harris, R., & Webb, D. (1987). *Welfare, power and juvenile justice*. London: Tavistock.

Home Office. (1960). *Report of the Committee on Children and Young Persons, chaired by R. Ingleby, Cmnd. 1191*. London: HMSO. (The Ingleby Report).

Home Office. (1965). *The child, the family and the young offender, cmnd. 2742*. London: HMSO.

Home Office. (1968). *Children in trouble, cmnd. 3601*. London: HMSO.

Home Office. (1980). *Young offenders, cmnd. 8405*. London: HMSO.

Home Office. (1984). *Cautioning by the police: A consultative document*. London: Home Office.

Home Office, Welsh Office, DHSS and DES Department of Health and Social Security, and Department of Education and Science. (1976). *Children and Young Persons Act 1969: Observations on the eleventh report from the Expenditure Committee*. London: HMSO.

Hood, R. (1965). *Borstal reassessed*. London: Heinemann.

House of Commons Expenditure Committee. (1975). *Eleventh report: The Children and Young Persons Act, 1969*. London: HMSO.

Huq, R. (1993). *'Hope I die before I get old': Raves place in deviant youth (sub)culture*. Cambridge: Unpublished Dissertation.

Kearny, B. (1987). *Children's hearings and the sheriff court*. London: Butterworths.

Kirby, T. (1993). Drugs at heart of crime wave among young. *The Independent*, p.10.

Labour Party. (1964). *Crime: A challenge to us all, report of a Labour Party study group chaired by F. Longford*. London: Labour Party. (The Longford Report).

Labour Party. (1992). *It's time to get Britain working again, Labour Party election manifesto*. London: Labour Party.

Landau, S. (1981). Juveniles and the police. *British Journal of Criminology*, 21: 27-46.

Mackenzie, D., & Souryal, C. (1994). Multi-site evaluation of shock incarceration. National Institute of Justice, Washington, D.C.

Marshall, T. (1975). *Social policy*. London: Heinemann.

Marwick, A. (1982). *British society since 1945*. Harmondsworth: Penguin.

Mayhew, P., Maung, N., & Mirrlees-Black, C. (1995). *The 1994 British crime survey*. London: HMSO.

McClennon, G. (1987). Sociological theories of crime: From disorganisation to class and abeyant. In Open University D3104 course booklet, *Thinking about crime: Theories of crime and justice*. Milton Keynes: Open University Press.

Morris, A. (1987). *Women, crime and criminal justice*. Oxford: Blackwell.

Morris, A., & Giller, H. (1979). *What justice for children?* London: Justice for Children.

Morris, A., & McIsaac, M. (1978). *Juvenile justice?* London: Heinemann.

National Association for the Care and Resettlement of Offenders. (1989). *The Children Act: Implications for juvenile justice*. London: NACRO.

O'Mahony, D., & Haines, K. (1995). *An evaluation of the introduction and operation of the youth court*. Unpublished Research Report Submitted to the Home Office.

Parker, H. (1981). *Receiving juvenile justice*. Oxford: Blackwell.

Pearson, G. (1983). *Hooligan: A history of respectable fears*. London: Macmillan.

Pitts, J. (1988). *The politics of juvenile justice*. London: Sage.

Pratt, J. (1989). The punishment of juveniles and commodification of time. In S. Jones (Ed.). *British criminology conference proceedings*. Bristol: Bristol and Bath Centre for Criminal Justice.

Reiner, R., & Cross, M. (1991). *Beyond law and order: Criminal justice policy in the 1990s*. London: Macmillan.

Rose, N. (1989). *Governing the soul: The shaping of the private self*. London: Routledge.

Rutherford, A. (1986). *Growing out of crime*. Harmondsworth: Penguin.

Rutherford, A. (1989). The mood and temper of penal policy: Curious happenings in England during the 1980s. *Youth and Policy*, 27: 27-31.

Singer, S., & Gelsthorpe, L. R. (1996). Criminalization and open contemporary systems of juvenile justice: The case of the United States and the United Kingdom. Paper presented to the Law and Society Meeting, Glasgow, Scotland, July 1996.

Smith, D. (1984). Law and order: Arguments for what? *Critical Social Policy*, 11: 33-45.

Stanley, C. (1988). Making statutory guidelines work. *Justice of the Peace*, 8th October: 648-50.

Taylor, I. (1981). Crime waves in post-war Britain. *Contemporary Crises*, 5: 43-62.

Thorpe, D., Smith D., Green, C., & Paley, J. (1980). *Out of care*. London: Allen and Unwin.

Tutt, N. (1981). A decade of policy. *British Journal of Criminology*, 21: 246-56.

Walgrave, L., & Mehlbye, J. (Eds.). (Forthcoming). *Confronting European Youth*. Copenhagen: AKF.

Warner, M. (1994). *Making monsters*. London: Vintage.

Wilkinson, C., & Evans, R. (1990). Police cautioning of juveniles: The impact of the Home Office circular 14/1985. *Criminal Law Review*, March: 165-76.

Young, A. (1996). *Imagining crime*. London: Sage.

Young, P., & Young, M. (1994). *Crime and criminal justice in Scotland*. Centre for Criminology and the Social and Philosophical Study of Law [now the Centre for Law and Society], University of Edinburgh.

chapter 5

Juvenile Delinquency in Hong Kong

Harold Traver
Department of Sociology, Hong Kong University

Facts about Hong Kong

Area: 1092 sq. kilometres. **Location and climate**: Hong Kong is located on the coast of southern China and directly adjoins Guangdong Province, which is part of the People's Republic of China. Hong Kong's climate is subtropical. **Population**: At the end of 1995 the total population of Hong Kong stood at 6,307,900 (5890 people per sq km). Hong Kong qualifies as one of the most densely populated places in the world. According to 1991 census data 97% of the population is Chinese. Canadians are the fastest growing expatriate group in Hong Kong. **Economy**: Because of a land shortage, Hong Kong imports much of its food supply. Its economy depends primarily on producing textiles, clothing, footwear, electronics, timepieces, etc. The country has several stock exchanges and is a major international financial centre. **Government**: Hong Kong has been a British colony since 1842 but is set become a Special Economic Region (SAR) of the People's Republic of China on July 1, 1997. As an SAR Hong Kong will have its own government and legislature and will be allowed a considerable degree of autonomy, expect in those areas that relate to foreign affairs and defence.

> Whilst thy father lives study his wishes; after he is dead study his life. He who for three years makes no change in his father's ways may be called a good son.
>
> Confucius[1]

Since the 1960s there have been a series of 'moral panics' in Hong Kong in regard to youthful misbehaviour and apparent dramatic increases in juvenile delinquency coming to the attention of the police (Gray, 1991). The facts, however, are not always what they appear to be. As with any other social problem our perception of delinquency is conditioned by prevailing social and cultural norms. In order to fully understand delinquency one must first understand the theory and practice of juvenile justice, and then be able to place this understanding within its proper historical and cultural context. Consequently, this chapter devotes considerable attention to examining the

---

[1] Lyall, L. (1925). *The sayings of Confucius.* London: Longmans, Green and Company, p. 2.

possible effects of Chinese cultural values on the development of juvenile justice in Hong Kong, the emergence of young people as a distinct segment within Hong Kong society, and the subsequent creation of youthful misbehaviour as a social problem.

Only by taking into account the cultural and historical forces that have shaped our conception of delinquency can one hope to arrive at some understanding of the nature and extent of delinquency in society. In the case of Hong Kong this means understanding why there has been continued public concern over increased involvement of young people in a variety of criminal offences ranging from serious assault and robbery to shop theft and other forms of petty theft. This chapter considers several possible explanations which may account for the apparent increase in delinquent behaviour. These explanations are as follows. First, that changing social and economic conditions in Hong Kong have helped to produce a real increase in crime and delinquency. In this case public concern merely reflects what is occurring in society. Second, the increase in delinquency is due to an increased willingness to report crime and delinquency. In actual fact, however, there may have been no significant change in crime or delinquency. Third, there is also the possibility that criminal justice policy may shift in such a way that an increasing number of people enter the criminal justice system. Once again, arrest and prosecution rates may change without there being any real change in the volume of crime or delinquency.

As the term is used here, juvenile delinquency refers to violations of the criminal law, or what could be called 'juvenile crime', and not to status offences such as truancy or running away from home. Status offences are unquestionably more common than 'juvenile crime' and since this chapter relies on official delinquency statistics, it will focus on 'juvenile crime' figures. Moreover, to a large extent the existence of the juvenile justice system is justified on the basis of the prevention and control of juvenile crime. Consequently, for these reasons this chapter devotes the bulk of its attention to juvenile crime.

Delinquency and Chinese Culture

In many respects juvenile delinquency in Hong Kong means very much the same thing as it means in the West. In Hong Kong delinquency essentially involves a failure on the part of the youth to conform to standards of behaviour laid down by adult institutions (e.g., family, school, police and the courts). Moreover, in line with most contemporary Western societies, Hong Kong has an extensive juvenile justice system which attempts to separate juveniles out from adults and places more emphasis on therapeutic programs than on punishment.

Despite its many similarities to the West, it should always be kept in mind that Hong Kong is still predominantly a Chinese society. Traditional Chinese society was organized on the Confucian principle that the perfect society was one in which individuals acted according to the duties imposed on them by their status in society (Lui, 1972). In Confucian society the family was the primary economic, social, and religious unit. The concept of filial piety, the obligation of children to show deference and respect towards their parents, represented the most fundamental social relationship in society and personified the correct attitude towards all forms of authority. Filial piety was seen to be the driving force for the maintenance of the stable hierarchal social order that lay at the very heart of Confucian society.

The concept of juvenile delinquency as a pervasive social problem suggests a degree of independence and separateness of children from adults that would be almost unthinkable in Confucian society. Therefore, when youthful misbehaviour was discovered it was treated as a family matter and as such was to be confined to the family rather than introducing juvenile justice authorities who were easily capable of administering arbitrary and harsh forms of punishment (Cohen, Edwards, and Chen, 1980; Ch'u, 1965).

Hong Kong, however, can hardly be characterized as a traditional Confucian society. Since World War II industrialization and urbanization has meant a rapid decline in informal family based systems of control. More parents are working away from the home and even more children spend most of the day in school in the company of their peers. Under such conditions it is reasonable to suppose that the family may not be fulfilling its socialization and control functions as effectively as it did in the past.

At the same time, some things have not changed that much. Filial piety continues to exercise a lingering hold over Hong Kong society. For instance, in 1986 a survey of 539 persons in the Kwun Tong District of Hong Kong over the age of eighteen found that 85% of the respondents were willing to financially support their aging parents. In the same survey, 86% of the respondents "agreed" or "strongly agreed" with the idea that the government should enact laws to force children to take care of their elderly parents, and 89% believed that filial piety was essential for a good society (Lau and Kuan, 1988: 59, 139).

Despite a Confucian stress on mediation and social harmony and a general de-emphasis on the role of law, the respondents were willing to use law to support filial piety, a central feature of Confucian philosophy. For example, according to a 1988 social indicator survey involving a sample of 1662 adults drawn from the general population 65% of the respondents stated that they trusted judges and lawyers, and 67% agreed that the "law was an efficient means of conflict resolution" (Kuan, Lau, and Wan, 1991:216, 218).

In the 1986 Kwun Tong survey, as well as in a larger 1988 social indicator survey, the 'youth problem' was ranked as the most serious of twelve different kinds of problems facing Hong Kong (Lau and Wan, 1991: 25-27). In both surveys a concern for the youth problem exceeded that shown for such problems as pollution, transportation and public order. The degree of concern shown for youthful misbehaviour suggests that while informal family based systems of control may have declined, conduct norms continue to demand a degree of conformity from juveniles that would be more characteristic of Confucian society than Western society.

What has changed is not so much the nature and extent of illegal behaviour among juveniles as the perceptions of parents and the authorities about the desirability of handing juveniles over to the juvenile justice system for formal processing. Whether or not a juvenile is judged to be delinquent depends less on the existence of a particular system of juvenile justice and more on how that system is perceived and used by the various sectors of adult society. The same observation also applies to specific forms of illegal behaviour. What may be taken as an indication of a serious act of delinquency in Hong Kong in another cultural context may be perceived merely as an example of normal youthful exuberance or experimentation.

The Creation of Juvenile Delinquency

In the West the notion that youthful misbehaviour is a specific type of socially undesirable behaviour emerged in the late nineteenth century as people increasingly came to view childhood and adolescence as relatively distinct and critical phases in the individual's transition to adulthood (see Hagan and Leon, 1977, Sutton, 1988). The final result of this evolutionary process was the creation of the concept of juvenile delinquency and the development of a juvenile justice system (see Figure 5.1).

Figure 5.1: Juvenile Justice System in Hong Kong

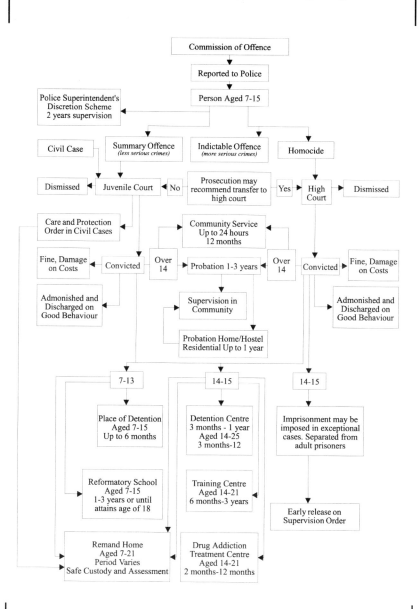

The Origins of Juvenile Justice in Hong Kong

The development of juvenile justice in Hong Kong was anything but the result of a gradual evolutionary process. Instead, Hong Kong's juvenile justice system emerged fully developed in 1932 when the Juvenile Offenders Ordinance was enacted establishing juvenile courts and probation officers to deal juvenile offenders. In the same year reformatories and industrial schools were established under the Industrial and Reformatories School Ordinance. Most of the laws which currently affect juvenile (aged seven to fifteen) and young offenders (aged sixteen to twenty), namely, the Juvenile Offenders, Probation of Offenders, Training Schools and the Industrial and Training Schools Ordinances, have been on the books in one form or another since at least the 1950s.

The motivation for the establishment of a system of juvenile justice came from the British colonial administration, which was legally obligated to see that laws in Hong Kong were more or less in line with English law. The 1932 Juvenile Offenders Ordinance was basically transferred from English law and 'grafted' into Hong Kong society and law with little or no thought about how well it might fit with local circumstances. More specifically, the Hong Kong Juvenile Offenders ordinance was based on English legislation, in particular the Children's Act of 1908 and the Probation of Offenders Act of 1908, and also took into account some of the recommendations of the Committee on the Treatment of Young Offenders 1927 that eventually were incorporated into the English Children and Young Persons Act 1933 (Allison and Giller, 1983).

The basic outline of Hong Kong's system of juvenile justice clearly predates any public or official concern with young people, or any evidence of a growing volume of delinquency in Hong Kong society (see Figure 5.1). In fact, in 1954/55 juvenile delinquency fell to an all time post-war low of 333 arrests, and while arrests and prosecutions tended to increase gradually after that date juvenile delinquency still continued to attract little attention.

The Discovery of the 'Youth Problem'

One of the earliest mentions of delinquency appears in the 1960 Hong Kong Report when, in the course of discussing the opening of two new magistracies during the year, it was observed that, "An increasing number of juveniles are now being remanded for at least a week so that probation officers may make inquiries (Hong Kong Government, 1961:176). The Social Welfare Department, which was, and continues to be, responsible for overseeing probation orders, also noted that in order to cope with the increased use of the remand home in Kowloon the maximum accommodation had been increased from fifty-four to seventy (Social Welfare Department, 1961). It should perhaps be mentioned here that even though adult probation has been on the books since 1956, probation continues to be largely confined to juveniles and young first offenders. Despite an increase in the number of juveniles on remand in the early 1960s, the authorities never raised the possibility that delinquency might represent an emerging social problem in Hong Kong. During this period when crime became the object of attention it was only to note that there had been a reduction in crime known to the police, which presumably included delinquency, and that this was "particularly impressive in the face of the steady growth of the population" (Hong Kong Government, 1961: 192-193).

Such apparent complacency was not destined to last for long. Events began to take shape during the 1960s that would profoundly affect the perception of delinquency in Hong Kong. The authorities, as well as the public, were just beginning to become aware of the fact that nearly 50% of the population in Hong Kong was under the age of twenty-one. The Hong Kong Report for 1961 for the first time called attention to the pressing problem of assessing the "interests and requirements of this segment of the population." The fact that the number of juveniles on probation had increased from less than 300 at the end of 1960 to about 500 at the end of 1961 is cited as evidence of declining standards of behaviour among young people. The report concludes its discussion of delinquency by noting that:

> [T]he experience of other Asian territories has shown that, where the energy and enthusiasm of youth are misdirected or not given constructive outlets, they will find expression in teenage violence and other anti-social behaviour. (Hong Kong Government, 1962:187)

In 1964 developments in Hong Kong added additional weight to the notion that young people posed a potential problem to the community. That year saw considerable publicity being given to the 'ah fei' (teddy boy) problem in the local press. As the term was used in Hong Kong, the 'ah fei' problem referred to young hooligans and criminals, usually under twenty-three years of age. A number of educational, religious, and Kaifong (charitable) associations demanded that the government adopt more stringent measures to control the problem.

Public concern over the 'ah fei' problem was sufficiently strong that the governor ordered the colonial secretary to set up a working party to examine "whether present legislation...enables the Courts to deal adequately with crimes of violence by young persons" (Hong Kong Government, 1965: 1). A few months later the working party produced the first official report dealing with juvenile delinquency in Hong Kong. The report concluded that, while the activities of youth gangs would need to be closely watched in the future, there was nothing to indicate an 'extraordinary upsurge' in juvenile crimes of violence. Even though the overall tone of the report was evenhanded and reassuring, for the first time juvenile delinquency was publicly identified as a social problem.

A year later in April 1966, a fare increase for the Star Ferry that transported passengers between Hong Kong Island and Kowloon sparked what came to be called the Star Ferry Riots. Young people were unquestionably involved in the leadership of the demonstrations against the fare increases as well in two nights of 'violence and looting' in Kowloon that month. Once again young people were in the news. The Kowloon Disturbances, as it was officially called, again produced an official Commission of Inquiry and an official report which give special attention to the prominence of young people aged fifteen to twenty-five in the disturbances. As a result of the 'ah fei' problem and the Star Ferry Riots, by the end of the 1960s delinquency and youthful misbehaviour were well on there way to becoming established social problems in Hong Kong.

During the 1960s several characteristic features of Hong Kong's conception of delinquency were beginning to take shape. First, there was tendency to discount the possible 'political' content of delinquency and view it instead as a manifestation of individual frustration over limited opportunities for achievement and youthful exuberance. In the absence of a radical overhaul of the existing economic system and the redistribution of economic rewards, there was very little that the authorities could hope to do about improving the availability of economic opportunities. An inability to control emotions and surplus energy, however, did not present the same problems. Here the authorities could safely come out in favour of more varied opportunities for recreation and leisure-time activities.

Second, as might be expected, there is a strong emphasis on prevention and diversion from being officially processed. The juvenile justice model is comparable to the corporatist model (see Figure 1—Introduction). The root causes of delinquency, and there are many, may be seen to be poverty, poor home environment, the influence of triads societies, or even compulsory education, but in all cases the solution is likely to be the same, namely, a better youth policy and more youth facilities (Fight Crime Committee, 1981; Fight Violent Crime Committee, 1973; Hong Kong Council of Social Service, 1981; Ng, 1975). In the past this was likely to mean more recreational facilities, although as professional social workers began to enter the juvenile justice system there has been a growing emphasis by juvenile justice specialists on responding to the developmental problems that young people face (Chow, 1987; Law, 1986). Third, in those cases where prevention has failed, the means advocated for dealing with delinquency and youth crime reflect the general view that it may be desirable to treat and rehabilitate (i.e., retrain) offenders rather than punish them. For instance in 1990/91 around 75% of those on probation in Hong Kong were below the age of twenty-one (Social Welfare Department, 1991). In Hong Kong the juvenile justice system continues to be firmly based in the doctrine of *parens patriae*, which sanctions the right of the state to assume the role of parent when a child's natural parents are unwilling or unable to act in the child's best interests (Jensen and Dean, 1992).

Finally, there is a conception of delinquency that can best be termed a reservoir theory of deviance. This refers to the idea that there is a large amount of potential juvenile delinquency just waiting to engulf the community if steps are not taken to stem the flow. The community, of course, is never engulfed, but the authorities and the public continue to maintain a vigilant and anxious eye for possible signs of impending trouble.

Delinquency and Social Organization

In sociological terms delinquency is related to society's social organization and its culture. A number of writers (Cohen, 1985; Ferdinand, 1989; Wilkins, 1965) contend that formal control efforts play a significant role in amplifying deviance in society. In so-called traditional societies, where formal attempts to control deviance are largely lacking, deviance has been observed to be relatively underdeveloped, spontaneous, and transitory. In contrast, modern industrial societies, which includes Hong Kong, are characterized by highly developed and elaborate formal systems of control and treatment. In such societies crime and delinquency are inclined to become established and intransigent social problems.

This may well be true, but if Hong Kong is anything to go by it would seem that formal control mechanisms in themselves do not automatically result in an amplification or intensification of deviance. In Hong Kong a juvenile justice system was in place for thirty years before there was any widespread concern either about the problem of delinquency or the possibility that a youth culture was developing whose values were contrary to those held by adult society.

As seems to have been the case in most of the countries covered in this volume, a growing feeling that young people might pose a threat to adult society accompanied social and economic changes. Unlike most other countries, these conditions emerged much later in Hong Kong—the 1960s. For instance, the government introduced compulsory universal primary education in 1971 and universal junior secondary education in 1978. From 1978 onward all children were required by law to be in full-time education from the ages of six to fifteen years. Today, most children now spend most of their day in school and in the company of their peers (see Box 5.1). The net result of all this was the creation of a distinct age segment of society that had not previously existed. It is probably no accident that during this period triad infiltration of schools starts to be seen as a serious social problem. What was once likely to be dismissed as merely 'gang bullying' or 'schoolyard intimidation' is now likely to be interpreted as an indication of triad activities.

Box 5.1: Juvenile Crime: An Educated Guess?

It is perhaps ironical that compulsory education is being cited for the surprising sudden surge in juvenile crime. Because one reason for launching compulsory schooling by stages to up to form three in 1978 was that it would "take the kids off the street." And hence reduce the risk of their becoming criminals.

Admittedly, the report of the working group formed by the Fight Crime Committee to probe the rise in juvenile delinquency stresses that the delayed effects of introducing compulsory education is only a contributing factor...

But it is convinced that we are paying the penalty for "inflicting" compulsory education without implementing any of the refinements. And it should have been obvious from the start that simply laying down the law that "you will go to school until 15" was not enough.

Of course there should be no suggestion of turning back the clock. Compulsory education to form three level must stay on the books. To think otherwise would be a ridiculously retrograde step...

But we must give serious consideration to the wisdom of extending compulsory education beyond form three. Youth at that age should be allowed to choose whether they remain at school or go out and seek a job. They must be given the option. It should not be forced on them.

One of the disturbing aspects of the surge in juvenile crime is that it has happened when recreational facilities are mushrooming. That is not to say that we provide sufficiently healthy outlets for a youngster's energies. But the quality of life in this area has improved dramatically in recent years. Yet more young people are turning to crime. (*South China Morning Post*, 4 April, 1981, p.2.)

In 1990 official concern with the 'youth problem' became a more or less permanent feature of government policy when the Commission on Youth was established. The stated objectives of the commission are to initiate research and promote cooperation and coordination of youth services in Hong Kong. Many of its recommendations are embodied in a Charter for Youth, which sets out important objectives and principles covering the protection, nurturing, and promotion of young people's interests (Commission on Youth, 1993). And while other social concerns in Hong Kong may demand a larger slice of the public purse, it would be safe to say that one would be hard put to find one that consistently attracts as much attention. However, one area that has drawn considerable attention in partial response to implications surrounding the transference of Hong Kong to the People's Republic of China is the abduction of children (see Box 5.2).

Box 5.2: Child Custody Treat—A Step toward International Protection

In April of 1997 Hong Kong is set to sign an international treaty that will ensure the swift return of children abducted and taken to foreign countries. The agreement is in reference to endorsing a proposal for the territory (Hong Kong) to sign The Hague Convention on the *Civil Aspects of International Child Abduction 1980*. The treaty would involve about thirty countries, including the UK, United States, Australia, New Zealand, Canada, and most European countries. China is not party to the convention. When signed the agreement would remove the current lengthy legal hurdles. The agreement is seen as a major step forward to protecting the interests of children as divorce rates are on the increase as are child abductions (Chan, 1996).

Delinquency and Youth Crime

For nearly the last thirty years the authorities and the public have been acting as if Hong Kong had a serious delinquency and youth crime problem on its hands. However, our perception of the nature and extent of delinquency and crime normally derive not from firsthand experience but instead from the official crime statistics. Unfortunately, the observation that these statistics are probably the "most unreliable and most difficult of all social statistics" (Sutherland and Cressey, 1966:27) is especially true for delinquency and youth crime statistics insofar as the age of the offender can only be determined when the offender has been arrested by the police or prosecuted by the courts.

Even though arrest and prosecution statistics may tell us something about the rate at which the police process offenders or the volume of traffic passing through the courts, the bulk of delinquency and crime goes either undetected or unreported. Furthermore, possible variations in police policies and court procedures upset any hope that these statistics will maintain even a constant ratio with the 'true rate' of delinquency and crime—whatever it is.

Legal Definition

Discussions of juvenile delinquency are further complicated by the fact that in Hong Kong there are a variety of legal definitions as to what constitutes a 'juvenile' as opposed to a 'child' or an 'adult' (Leung and Sihombing, 1997). For instance, under the Juvenile Offenders Ordinance a 'child' is defined as any person under the age of fourteen and a 'young person' is anyone fourteen years of age or upwards and under the age of sixteen years. The age of criminal responsibility begins at seven. No child may be imprisoned and detention is only possible for serious (indictable) offences such as attempted murder or manslaughter. For youths aged fourteen to sixteen imprisonment may only be ordered if there are no suitable alternatives, and in all such cases the young person is not allowed to associate with adult prisoners. The Criminal Procedures Ordinance also requires that before imposing a prison sentence on a person aged sixteen to twenty the court must obtain and consider all relevant information about the person and the circumstances of the case so as to be certain that there are no other suitable methods of dealing with the person. Official crime statistics are reported on the basis of the sixteen to twenty age criteria specified in the Crimes Procedure Ordinance. Consequently, in the official statistics a juvenile delinquent is anyone aged seven to fifteen and a young offender is any person aged sixteen to twenty. Primarily because it uses official statistics as its main source of data, this chapter adopts the 'statistical definition' of juvenile delinquency.

Observed Trends

Has there been a real or significant change in the volume of juvenile delinquency (aged seven to fifteen) and youth crime (aged sixteen to twenty)? Due to the limited availability of arrest rates (they only started to be published in 1989), we must rely primarily on prosecution rates as the main source of information for answering this question. Two sets of figures, arrest rates and prosecution rates, are likely to provide a reasonably similar impression of crime in Hong Kong, at least for young offenders and adult offenders.

In 1989 out of the 7437 juveniles arrested only 62% (4672) were prosecuted. However, over 95% of those juveniles not prosecuted (2647 out of 2765) were discharged under the Superintendent's Discretion Scheme, which in Hong Kong is the main means of diverting juveniles away from processing in the juvenile court. By way of contrast, just under 95% of all young offenders proceeded on to prosecution while the figure for adult offenders is nearly 100%.

Returning to the original question: Is there any reason to believe that Hong Kong is facing an increasingly serious delinquency problem?

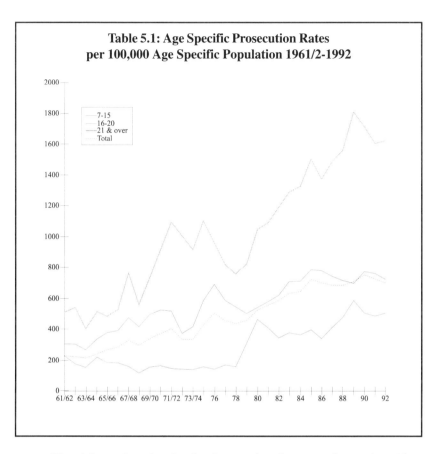

Table 5.1: Age Specific Prosecution Rates
per 100,000 Age Specific Population 1961/2-1992

First, it is worth noting that despite growing alarm over the youth problem in the 1960s, between 1961/62 and 1973/74 the prosecution rate for juveniles (aged seven to fifteen) declined from 236 per 100,000 to 158 per 100,000. However, during this same period the prosecution rate for young offenders (aged sixteen to twenty) increased from 512 per 100,000 to 1111 per 100,000. The juvenile prosecution rate only experiences significant increases after 1978. The prosecution rate for juveniles has always been well below that for young offenders. The gap between the two age groups has, however, narrowed over the years. In comparison with juveniles, in the mid-1970s young offenders were approximately six times as likely to be prosecuted, but by in the mid-1980s the margin between the two age groups had narrowed to around three times as likely.

Second, Figure 5.2, which includes rates for both the Police Superintendent's Discretion Scheme and prosecution, provides a somewhat

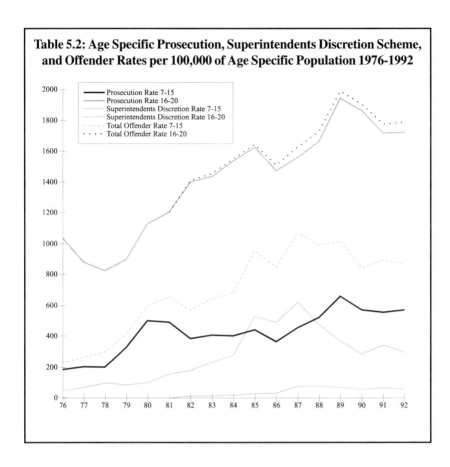

Table 5.2: Age Specific Prosecution, Superintendents Discretion Scheme, and Offender Rates per 100,000 of Age Specific Population 1976-1992

different picture. One thing that immediately stands out in this figure is that the use of supervision for juveniles increased dramatically between 1980 and 1987. As a result of this increase the offender rate for juveniles, the combined rates for prosecution and supervision, also increased significantly. This increase, however, was almost exclusively due to an increased use of supervision. In fact, between 1985 and 1987 more juveniles were being supervised than prosecuted. Few young offenders are eligible for supervision, but even this age group experienced an increase in the use of supervision. The increased use of supervision for juveniles means that more juveniles are being processed by the juvenile justice system, which in turn helps to foster the notion that there has been a rapid expansion in delinquency behaviour. Figure 5.2 also shows that while supervision rates have tended to decline since 1987 this has been accompanied by corresponding increases in the prosecution rate. This suggests that more juveniles are now being prosecuted where previously they would have been placed on supervision. Be this as it may, the net result is that the volume of delinquency has remained more or less constant since 1987.

Third, alarm over a possible increase in juvenile delinquency appears to find support in Table 5.1, which shows that, in comparison with young offenders, juvenile involvement in serious assault and robbery increased dramatically between 1976 and 1988. Even though the young offender rates for these offences have always been higher than the juvenile rates, juvenile involvement in these offences has supplied a reoccurring theme for many official discussions of delinquency in Hong Kong (see Fight Crime Committee, 1981). However, despite continued concern over juvenile involvement in violent crime, Table 5.1 shows that since 1989, when arrest rates first started to be published, juvenile involvement in serious assault and robbery has tended to level off or even decline.

The offence of 'unlawful society' which appears in Table 5.1 refers to membership in a triad society, which in Hong Kong is in itself illegal. This offence is included in Table 5.1 because recruitment into triad societies is widely viewed as a serious threat to young people. Given that there are periodic waves of public concern about the 'triad problem' and that it is relatively easy to arrest someone for 'unlawful society,' the prosecution rates for young offenders are highly variable (see Box 5.3). This probably has more to do with shifts in police policy than it does with any possible changes in triad membership.

What does all this tell us? First, the prosecution rate for young offenders (aged sixteen to twenty) is typically several times that of juveniles (aged seven to fifteen) and this observation holds true even when the rate is combined with the supervision rate (see Figure 5.1). Second, it should also be kept in mind that because the juvenile prosecution rate started out low any increase is likely to appear as quite dramatic. Third, since 1989, when arrest figures started to be reported, the juvenile rates for serious assault and robbery have tended to level off and in the case of serious assault actually decline. Fourth, despite any possible increases, juvenile serious assault and robbery rates typically account for only 10% and 15% of the overall rate of delinquency respectively. A similar observation applies to young offenders. It is still correct to say that in most cases the juvenile delinquency involves petty property offences such as shop theft and other relatively minor infractions of the law. Finally, there is a distinct possibility that even apparently serious offences as assault and

Table 5.1: Prosecution and Arrest Rates for Selected Offences per 100,000 Age Specific Population: 1976-1992

	Serious Assault		Robbery		Shop Theft		Other Theft		Unlawful Society	
	7-15	16-20	7-15	16-20	7-15	16-20	7-15	16-20	7-15	16-20
Prosecution Rates:										
1976	10.4	104.6	16.6	74.6	—	—	69.1	167.6	19.5	275.5
1977	10.5	109.2	18.3	55.7	—	—	92.6	194.8	10.7	146.8
1978	22.1	130.1	11.3	56.0	—	—	83.1	195.1	9.5	95.9
1979	23.6	128.8	26.4	75.9	—	—	145.6	211.9	12.3	52.9
1980	28.3	157.1	42.9	99.8	—	—	221.7	290.4	13.2	45.4
1981	29.9	156.8	56.0	98.9	—	—	204.2	318.9	15.6	38.2
1982	33.2	156.5	33.2	108.9	31.2	64.0	119.5	283.0	13.8	42.1
1983	37.6	166.4	40.9	92.7	53.6	110.0	98.4	263.4	12.5	25.3
1984	43.7	164.1	42.8	88.6	39.6	108.6	93.7	316.4	14.4	45.3
1985	40.1	173.0	55.4	104.6	59.4	156.3	77.8	280.0	23.5	68.4
1986	39.3	202.0	48.4	74.7	40.8	137.7	75.4	255.0	11.3	28.9
1987	39.4	160.2	69.5	103.3	64.3	126.9	81.9	238.3	17.8	30.2
1988	46.4	163.3	91.8	114.7	55.1	108.3	106.9	270.9	17.3	32.4
Arrest Rates:										
1989	58.9	180.0	127.0	169.7	330.0	153.9	249.1	348.3	26.3	43.1
1990	52.5	136.1	96.6	171.7	220.6	164.6	182.7	350.2	26.8	50.7
1991	59.6	152.5	127.3	185.6	228.8	144.2	201.5	321.3	31.3	61.1
1992	52.8	138.1	121.1	176.5	215.2	160.0	186.5	332.8	34.0	59.0

Box 5.3: "When only the Brave are Prepared to Speak Out"

Triads are preying on students and infiltrating schools, according to parents and teachers. But the authorities are anxious to dismiss such notions as exaggerated. Who is telling the truth?...

Kwok-wai, a Form One student, bumped into a gang of teenagers after school, was kicked a few times and then forced to hand over $10. He never reported the incident to the school authorities because he feared they belonged to the Sun Yee On triad society.

It is one of many incidents that go unreported in the territory's schools and highlights a problem that principals and teachers say is growing. Triads are becoming a worrying menace in the schools which are perfect recruitment grounds, according to school authorities. But there is little they can do...

Among the principals of 11 schools interviewed...,all had students claiming to be triad members. And all had reported incidents of triad intimidation during the past year.

"We can't say for sure whether the teenagers who hang around our school are really triads or not," said one school principal who asked not to be named. "They don't wear school uniforms and they don't go to work, yet they still have money to spend, what else can that be?"...

Tuen Mun is typical of the territory's bustling new towns. It also has one of the biggest juvenile populations in the territory. According to Deputy District Commander, Senior Superintendent Ian Seabourne, about 60 percent of the district's 330,000 population is under 16. That means two out of every three are youngsters and potential triad targets.

But according to Superintendent Seabourne, there is no evidence of triad infiltration in the schools. "There is no indication of a real effort by triads to recruit students here. I don't think the students are of any use to them. It is no use building up a gang of people who are too small to fight," he said.

But he admitted that the gangs that prey on the schools were ripe for triad membership. "Yes, it is fair to say that these loose gangs of 17 year olds may become triads one day. If kids think this is an easy way to earn a living and they want some money to spend, especially when most of the kids come from working class families, which make up the core of the population here, they may be attracted to it."

Pseudo-triads—as Superintendent Seabourne described the 17-year olds hanging around outside schools or video game centres—are involved in robbery, blackmail and intimidation of a smaller scale, and petty crimes. "They may bully other kids, threaten and take money from them, using the name of triads. We are receiving more and more reports but we rarely charge them of claiming to be triads. We don't believe them. They are just gangs," he said...

Most principals blame the problem on the nine-year compulsory schooling. "Children don't have to study hard to get promoted. Life is easier for them now than it was to us...And we are not allowed to expel any bad children, unless permitted by the head of the Education Department," he said.

Another principal...blamed the remote location and age range of his school. "We are a new town. There is nothing around us, expect construction sites. And the fact that we are new means we don't get the best students...And if these children are fed up with schooling because of their bad academic results, they will be easily led astray by these guys we see hanging outside of school," he said.

Superintendent Seabourne admitted that the number of complaints from schools was increasing, as were the number of juvenile crimes... (*South China Morning Post*, 1 April 1990, p. 13.)

robbery may in actual fact entail relatively minor degrees of violence normally associated with bullying or intimidation in schools and playgrounds.

Increased Reporting
One source of information that avoids some of the pitfalls associated with official statistics is a series of victimization surveys that have been conducted in Hong Kong. There have been five such surveys since the first one was conducted in 1978 (Census and Statistics Department, 1979, 1982, 1987, 1990, 1995). Two things stand from these surveys. First, the possibility that there may be an increased tendency to report crime finds clear support in the results of these surveys. The percentage of violent crime (assault and robbery) reported to the police increased steadily from 28.4% in 1978 to 44.6% in 1989, and then declined to 34.5% in 1994, which is more or less where it was at 1986. The reporting of household crimes (various theft offences) has shown a more consistent tendency to increase. Between 1978 and 1989 household crimes reported to the police increased from 18.7% to 24.2% and then declined slightly in 1994 to stand at 22.2% (Census and Statistics Department, 1995). Second, any increased tendency to report tends to be most marked for those offences most commonly associated with juvenile or young offenders, that is, relatively minor offences involving the theft of property. Between 1978 and 1989 the percentage of "personal crimes of theft" (e.g., snatching, pickpocketing, and other personal theft) reported to the police jumped from 9.5% to 41.3% while the figure for 1994 stood at 40.9%.

The survey reveals both an increase in delinquency and a wide range of criminal activity. In terms of crimes of violence where the victimizations involved single offenders, the figures for those offenders estimated to be under the age of twenty-one have fluctuated between a high of 25% in 1981 to a low of 15% in 1989 (Census and Statistics Department, 1979, 1982 and 1990). The figure in the latest victim survey was 23% under twenty-one years of age (Census and Statistics Department, 1995).

Victimizations involving multiple offenders tell a somewhat different story. Since 1981 the proportion of crimes of violence involving multiple versus single offenders has fluctuated from 46% to 53%. What has really changed is the proportion of personal crimes of violent victimizations involving multiple offenders under the age of twenty-one. In the 1978 and 1981 victim surveys, around 24% of all personal crimes of violence involving multiple offenders were committed by offenders estimated to be under twenty-one, while in 1994 this figure had increased to 56.4% (Census and Statistics Department, 1979, 1982, 1995).

This apparent increase may not be as serious as it might first appear. In 1994, 85.2% of all victimizations committed by multiple offenders under twenty-one involved victims between twelve and nineteen years of age. In other words the usual situation involves a group of young offenders victimizing members of their own age group, and the data suggest that many personal crimes of violence are likely to be relatively minor affairs involving local youths extorting lunch money and other similarly small sums of money from other less aggressive youths in the area. If this is the case, a great deal of 'serious' juvenile delinquency and youth crime may not be as serious as the official statistics would have us believe.

Amplification and Net Widening
Since the early 1960s labelling theorists have argued that the response of others serves to shape the individual's self image as deviant and thereby increases the commitment to a deviant career.

Concern about the amplification effects of crime control have tended to focus on the possible detrimental consequences of an expansion in diversion or community-based programs. This phenomenon is commonly referred as 'net widening'. For example, in Hong Kong an increase in the number of youths entering the official statistics as juvenile delinquents or young offenders may well have something to do with an increase in the services and resources available to criminal justice agencies.

In Hong Kong net widening can be clearly seen in the Superintendent's Discretion Scheme (see Gray, 1991). In effect the juvenile offender rate is as much subject to police discretion as it is to established rules of due process. Police supervision has been around since 1963 when a Juvenile Liaison Section in the police was set up to deal exclusively with the guidance of juvenile offenders. Its main goal was to supervise first offenders and improve parental control "rather than following the more drastic step of instituting criminal proceedings" (Hong Kong Government, 1964: 213). During the 1980s, when police supervision started to play an important role, nearly half of the juvenile offender rate (1984-1988) comes from the use of supervision and not prosecution (see Figure 5.2). A policy decision in 1985 to extend police supervision to youths up to the age of seventeen and include second and third time offenders in the scheme contributed to the significant increase in police supervision.

The fact that many offences committed by young people consist of relatively minor infractions of the law often means that they are more a matter of definition than fact in that they are more subject to changes in police policy or the public's willingness to report crime. As evidenced in the 1981 Fight

Youth Crime campaign, juvenile involvement in shop theft (shoplifting) is an example of such an offence.

Things started to change soon after the campaign. According to official statistics between 1982 (when shop theft cases started to be separately reported) and 1985 the number of juvenile (aged seven to fifteen) shop theft cases in which juveniles were prosecuted or placed under the Superintendent's Discretion Scheme had increased from 759 to 2926 (95.9 to 377.3 per 100,000). By 1985, 42% of the juvenile offender rate was attributable to shop theft as compared with only 18% in 1982. Shop theft peaked in 1987 when 2640 (342.6 per 100,000) juveniles were placed on supervision and another 498 (64.3 per 100,000) were prosecuted. During the same period similar increases were observed for young offenders (aged sixteen to twenty).

Why the dramatic increase in shop theft in the 1980s? The proliferation of shopping centres and supermarkets as well as the general increase in the use of open and enticing store displays are some of the explanations offered by the police (Royal Hong Kong Police Force, 1987, 1988). Improved security arrangements, an increased tendency to report shop theft to the police, or even an inexplicable decline in moral standards are other possible explanations. However, none of these explanations entirely accounts for the dramatic increase in juvenile shop theft. Another possibility is that many juveniles accused of minor first offences, which include most cases of shop theft, were being diverted into supervision whereas before they would have simply been released with a warning or not even brought to the attention of the police. If this actually occurred, the juvenile 'crime wave' of the 1980s may well have been at least partly a product of the increased use of police supervision for shop theft.

Summary

Which of the three possible explanations of delinquency best fits the facts? In trying to answer this it is worth pointing out that there are several things that make crime and delinquency in Hong Kong different from that found in many Western societies. For example, Hong Kong:

- Lacks racial or ethnic ghettos characteristic in many cities in the West.
- Is culturally and linguistically homogenous. With 96% of the population being Chinese, there are no minority groups in Hong Kong which are perceived to constitute a threat of law and order.

• Has experienced remarkable economic development which has been sufficiently widespread to preclude the development of an underclass. With respect to crime, these characteristics of Hong Kong society have meant that it has not been politicized in the way it has in many Western societies. In contrast to many Western societies, crime is normally seen to be committed by deviant individuals, not representative of oppressed and possibly dangerous racial or economic minorities. It may be for this reason that a **corporatist model** has remained in place since Hong Kong's juvenile justice system was first established. However, some of its parameters differ from those found in England and Wales (see Chapter 4). This is in part due to the possible effects of Chinese cultural values that preceded English influences.

The same is not necessarily true for delinquency. One of the most significant and clearly visible divisions in Hong Kong society is in terms of age. Throughout the 1960s and 1970s, just under half of the population was under the age of twenty-one. Since then the proportion has declined but it still stands at around 30% of the total population. As the only obvious major social division in Hong Kong society, juveniles become the focus for the community's concerns about order, stability, and continuity. These concerns may be especially strong in a society which still, to some degree, adheres to a Confucian view that children should be subservient to the will of their parents and serve their needs. Quite possibly a society may place relatively higher standards of behaviour on children if it believes, as Hong Kong appears to, that the maintenance of parental power is fundamental to the continued maintenance of social order.

The above refers to perceptions of juvenile delinquency. What about real changes in the volume of delinquent behaviour? Throughout this chapter evidence has been provided lending support to the notion that delinquency has increased over the last three decades. However, the official statistics also indicate that the situation is probably far less serious than is widely supposed and certainly far more complex than that presented in the media or by the authorities.

First, as mentioned above, the period under study has quite literally seen the creation of childhood as a distinct phase in the individual's development and the emergence of 'young people' as a separate segment of society.

Second, economic development and urbanization in Hong Kong has meant, among other things, that there is now quite simply more time, as well as opportunity, to get into trouble. In addition there are also likely to be fewer informal family based control mechanisms to keep the juvenile out of trouble.

Third, victim surveys also support the idea that there has been an increase in the tendency to report crime and delinquency. Whether the increased reporting patterns are the result of increased public confidence in the authorities' ability to maintain law and order or that it simply represents the fact that the police are becoming the only alternative available as parents progressively lose the power to control the lives of their children. In either case, the end result is more delinquent behaviour coming to the attention of the authorities. (Refer to other contributions in this textbook for similar observations).

Fourth, there is good reason to believe that in most cases delinquency involves relatively minor offences. This is obviously the case for petty offences such as shop theft, but the same observation may well apply to the apparently more serious offences such as assault or robbery. Fifth, this chapter has suggested that there is good reason to believe that an expansion of diversionary programs has contributed to recent increases in the official rates of delinquency. It is entirely possible that an increasing number of juveniles are being introduced into the juvenile justice system who previously either would have been merely released with a warning or would not have come into contact with the system in the first place.

Finally, it should be noted that the creation of a juvenile justice system preceded by several decades any widespread concern that juvenile delinquency might pose a threat to adult society. Such things as net widening and deviance amplification obviously have contributed to increases in the delinquency rate, but it is also obvious that any such effects do not automatically come into play. Instead the juvenile justice system only began to be utilized when certain social and economic conditions occurred that changed public and official perceptions of the position that young people occupy in society. Once again this is in line with the idea that there has been a decline in informal control mechanisms.

Epilogue

What about the future of juvenile justice in Hong Kong? At first glance it seems as if it is in for some major changes given that on July 1, 1997 the People's Republic of China resumed sovereignty over Hong Kong. However, contrary to what one might expect (see Gitting and Chan, 1996) this should not produce any significant changes in juvenile justice in Hong Kong. First, while Hong Kong is unquestionably an unalienable part of the People's Republic of China it is also a Special Administrative Region (SAR) within China. As an SAR Hong Kong continues to enjoy a high degree of autonomy. The only exception to this is in the areas of foreign affairs and defence. The various policies governing the transference of the territory are stipulated in the Sino-British Joint Declaration and in the Hong Kong Basic Law. Among other things, these two documents provide that the existing judicial system and all laws previously in force in Hong Kong shall be maintained for fifty years after China resumes sovereignty over Hong Kong. If all goes as planned the juvenile justice system of Hong Kong should continue to be firmly based on the rule of law and currently existing policies of treatment and rehabilitation.

Second, it should also be kept in mind that in terms of basic principles of juvenile justice, the People's Republic of China and the Hong Kong SAR share many things in common. In fact, there are more similarities than there are differences. Both systems emphasize treatment over punishment and both go to great lengths to see that children and young offenders avoid entry into the adult criminal justice system. Consequently, what the future has in store for the juvenile justice system in Hong Kong is more likely to be continuity rather than dramatic change.

References

Allison, M., & Giller, H. (Eds.).(1983). *Providing criminal justice for children.* London: Arnold.

Census and Statistics Department. (1979). *Crime and its victims in Hong Kong 1978.* Hong Kong: Government Printer.

___. (1982). *Crime and its victims in Hong Kong 1981.* Hong Kong: Government Printer.

___. (1987). *Crime and its victims in Hong Kong 1986.* Hong Kong: Government Printer.

___. (1990). *Crime and its victims in Hong Kong 1989.* Hong Hong: Goverment Printer.

___. (1995). *Crime and its victims in Hong Kong 1994.* Hong Kong: Government Printer.

Chan, Q. (1996, Oct. 16). Hong Kong to sign child custody treaty. *South Cina Morning Post. (Online).*

Chaney, D.C., & Podmore D.B.L. (1973). *Young adults in Hong Kong: Attitudes in a modernizing society.* Hong Kong: Centre of Asian Studies.

Chow, W.S.N. (1987). *A comparison of delinquent youth and non-delinquent youth on the aspects of parental supervision and schooling: A follow-up study on unruly youth in Tsuen Wan, Kwai Chung and Tsing Yi*. Hong Kong: Kwai Chung and Tsing Yi District Board.

Ch'u, T.S. (1965). *Law and society in traditional China*. Paris: Mouton and Company.

Cohen, J., Edwards, R.R., & Chen, F.M.C. (Eds.). (1980). *Essays in China's legal tradition*. Princeton, NJ: Princeton University Press.

Cohen, S. (1985). *Visions of control: Crime, punishment and classification*. New Brunswick, NJ: Transaction Books.

Commission on Youth. (1993). *Charter for youth*. Hong Kong: The Secretary, Commission on Youth.

Ferdinand, T.N. (1989). Juvenile delinquency or juvenile justice: Which came first? *Criminology*, 27(1): 79-106.

Fight Crime Committee. (1981). *Report of the working group on juvenile crime*. Hong Kong: Government Printer.

Fight Violent Crime Committee. (1973). *Interim progress report by the sub-committee on the social causes of crime*. Hong Kong: Government Printer.

Gitting, D.G., & Chan, Q. (1996, Oct. 2). Crime bill dropped in handover rush. *South China Morning Post*. (Online).

Gray, P. (1991). Juvenile crime and disciplinary welfare. In H. Traver & J. Vagg (Eds.). *Crime and justice in Hong Kong* (pp. 25-41). Hong Kong: Oxford University Press.

Hagan, J., & Leon, J. (1977). Rediscovering delinquency: Social history, political ideology and the sociology of law. *American Sociological Review*, 42(4): 587-598.

Hong Kong Council of Social Service. (1981). *Report on the prevention of delinquency by the ad hoc working group on the prevention of juvenile delinquency*. Hong Kong: Hong Kong Council of Social Service.

Hong Kong Government. (1961). *Hong Kong report for 1960*. Hong Kong: Government Printer.

___. (1962). *Hong Kong report for 1961*. Hong Kong: Government Printer.

___. (1964). *Hong Kong report for 1963*. Hong Kong: Government Printer.

___. (1965). *Report to governor in council by working party on the adequacy of the law in relation to crimes of violence committed by young persons*. Hong Kong: Government Printer.

Jensen, G.F., & Dean, G.R. (1992). *Delinquency and youth crime* (2nd ed.). Prospect Heights, ILL.: Waveland Press.

Kuan, H.C., Lau, S.K. & Wan, P.S. (1991). Legal attitudes. In S.K. Lau, M.K. Lee, P.S. Wan, & S.L. Wong (Eds.). *Indicators of social development: Hong Kong 1988* (pp. 207-223). Hong Kong: Hong Kong Institute of Asian-Pacific Studies, The Chinese University of Hong Kong.

Lau, S.K., & Kuan, H.C. (1988). *The ethos of the Hong Kong chinese*. Hong Kong: The Chinese University Press.

Lau, S.K., & Wan, P.S. (1991). Attitudes towards social problems. In S.K. Lau, M.K. Lee, P.S. Wan & S.L. Wong (Eds.). *Indicators of development: Hong Kong 1988* (pp. 25-40). Hong Kong: Hong Kong Institute of Asia-Pacific Studies, The Chinese University of Hong Kong.

Law, C.K. (1986). *A study on the behaviours and attitudes of youths in Kwun Tong.* Hong Kong: Working Group on Problem Youth, Kwun Tong District Board.

Leung, E.O.E.. & Sihombing, J.E. (1997). The law relating to children. In M.M. Tsoi & N.A. Pryde (Eds.). *Hong Kong's children: Our past, their future.* Hong Kong: Centre of Asia Studies, University of Hong Kong. (In press).

Lui, W.C. (1972). *Confucius: His life and time.* New York: Philosophical Library.

Marx, G.T.(1981). Ironies of social control: Authorities as contributors of deviance through escalation, nonenforcement and covert facilitation. *Social Problems,* 28(3): 221-246.

Michalowski, R.J. (1985). *Order, law and crime: An introduction to criminology.* New York: Random House.

Ng, A. (1975). *Social causes of violent crimes among young offenders in Hong Kong.* Hong Kong: Social Research Centre, The Chinese University of Hong Kong.

Royal Hong Kong Police Force. (1987). *Annual review 1986.* Hong Kong: Government Printer.

___. (1988). *Annual review 1987.* Hong Kong: Government Printer.

Social Welfare Department. (1961). *Annual departmental report, 1960/61.* Hong Kong: Government Printer.

___. (1991). *Annual department report by the director of social welfare for the financial year 1990-91.* Hong Kong: Government Printer.

Sutherland, E.H., & Cressey, D.R. (1966). *Principles of criminology.* New York: J.B. Lippincott Company.

Sutton, J.R. (1988). *Stubborn children: Controlling delinquency in the United States, 1640-1981.* Berkley: University of California Press.

Wilkins, L.T. (1965). *Social deviance.* Englewood Cliffs, NJ: Prentice-Hall.

chapter 6

Juvenile Justice and Young Offenders: An Overview of Canada

John A. Winterdyk
Department of Criminology, Mount Royal College

Facts on Canada

Area: 3,851,792 sq. miles or approx. 10 million sq. km. Canada covers six time zones. **Population**: In excess of 29 million in 1995. Outside of the province of Quebec approximately 80% of Canadians are English speaking, 6% French, with other denominations including Chinese, East Indian, Ukrainian, and German. Seven out of ten citizens are urban dwellers. Approximately 85% crowd into a 200 km wide strip along the United States border. Major cities include Montreal, Toronto, and Vancouver. Ottawa is the nation's capital. Canada's population characteristics are changing rapidly and will continue to do so well into the future. The median age in 1992 was 33.8. For every one hundred new babies added to Canada's population, in 1991, eighty-seven are the result of net immigration (compared to twenty in 1985). In 1994 youth between the ages of twelve to seventeen made up approximately 8% of the population. Since 1970 the percent of newborns males has dropped from 51.5% to 51.3% in 1996. **Climate**: Varies widely by region and latitude. Winters are cool to cold (avg. 0° C to -15° C) while summers can average temperatures from 18° C to mid 20s. **Economy**: Hosts a wide range of natural resources: fishing, pulp and paper; farming; mining (e.g., gold, silver, zinc, coal, asbestos, uranium, hydroelectric, etc.) as well as manufacturing. **Government**: A parliament and ten provincial legislatures and two territories guide the government. In 1997 the Liberal Party was the federal party. Other major parties include: The Reform Party, Social Credit, Parti Québécois, and the Conservative Party. The ruling party has a four year term.

... every juvenile delinquent shall be treated... as a misdirected and misguided child...

Juvenile Delinquency Act, 1908.

... young persons who commit offences should... bear responsibility...

Young Offenders Act, 1984.

By international standards Canada is a fairly young nation. It is also one of the few countries in the world which gained nationhood without a revolution. It was first permanently settled by Europeans in 1608 by Samuel de Champlain of France and then by the English circa 1660s around the Hudson Bay area. Although England and France were interested in colonization, their primary investment in the 'New Land' was fur trading. Within a few years the rivalries over trading routes and territory began to escalate. This culminated in the Seven Year's War (1756-63) in which the French were defeated, but in the Quebec Act of 1774 the French Canadians were granted a certain amount of autonomy in Quebec. However, the Quebec Act said that for criminal law, the law of England would apply.

Since these early times, Canada has been influenced by the different political orientations of its European heritage. And while the Canadian criminal justice system is primarily influenced by England, remnants from the French accusatorial model are still felt. For example, Quebec has retained its French legal heritage by modelling its Civil Code after the 1804 Code of Napoleon, in France. Another legal area of note concerns jurisdictional powers. In accordance with the British North America Act (1867) (replaced by the Constitution Act, 1982, which is generally referred to as the Canadian Charter of Rights and Freedom), Canada adopted a political model in which there is a demarcation between federal jurisdiction and provincial jurisdiction. This division of power has had a profound impact on the administration of juvenile justice in Canada.

I will begin by tracing the historical development of the juvenile justice system in Canada. After presenting an overview of the Juvenile Delinquency Act, an outline of the tumultuous transition which lead to the current legislation for young offenders, the Young Offenders Act in 1984, will be presented. Here the key elements of the act will be covered before describing some of the past and present trends and patterns of youth crime. Next an overview of how young offenders are officially handled by the major elements of the young offenders system will be described. The chapter will conclude with a discussion of some of the major issues currently confronting the handling of young offenders in Canada today.

The Birth of Juvenile Justice in Canada

Creating the Juvenile Delinquency Act (JDA)

During the early pioneer days, Canada's young people were likely granted considerable freedoms given the frontier spirit that prevailed. However, due to economic and physical hardships, life was difficult for families and youth. As

Carrigan (1991) notes, numerous young persons were being either abandoned, abused, or simply neglected. These wayward youth slowly became a growing concern until the mid 1880s when the government found it necessary to intervene. One of the first steps taken in an attempt to control the problem involved making school attendance compulsory in 1871. However, growing urbanization and dramatic increases in the number of "homeless British waifs and street urchins" only helped to fuel the youth problem during the late 1800s (West, 1984:29).

Sutherland (1976) reports that towards the end of the 1890s people felt that more drastic measures were required. The public felt that somehow the State needed to intervene to help ensure that rehabilitation principles could be enforced for the benefit of those involved in delinquent behaviour. And although the state was initially somewhat reluctant to interfere in family matters, the Youthful Offenders Act was passed on July 23, 1894 as a measure to permit the state to intervene when families failed to raise their children 'properly' (Carrigan, 1991). The essence of the legislation was that a juvenile delinquent not be treated as an adult criminal in need of punishment "but as a misdirected and misguided child." This reform and family-centred system led to the development of children's court. The supposition was to keep young persons away from the influence of the adult judicial process. Given the varying sentiments at the time little was done until 1908 when, primarily through the stewardship of J.J. Kelso and W.L. Scott, the JDA was passed.

In addition to setting out the guidelines for juvenile courts, the JDA encompassed a number of key philosophical elements which strongly reflected the treatment philosophy. This treatment philosophy is widely referred to as *parens patriae*.[1] It embodied the essential elements of the positivist school of criminology and is described as representing a **welfare model** (Corrado, Bala, Linden, and LeBlanc, 1992). For example, Section 2 of the JDA defined a juvenile delinquent as:

'juvenile delinquents' means any child who violates any provision of the Criminal Code or any federal or provincial statute, or any by-law or ordinance of any municipality, or who is guilty of sexual immorality

---

[1] A latin expression which means the state has the power to act on behalf of the child and provide care and protection equivalent to that of a parent. The term reflects a paternalistic philosophy which emphasizes treatment and sees delinquent youth as misguided and in need of special consideration and help. (Griffiths and Hatch, 1994)

or any similar form of vice, or who is liable by reason of any other act
to be committed to an industrial school or juvenile reformatory under
any federal or provincial statute...

The general features of the JDA can be summed up as follows:

- Informality of handling (e.g., while the minimum age of delinquency was
  seven the upper limit varied between provinces from seventeen to
  eighteen); individualized sentencing (i.e., provincial responsibility), and
  indeterminate sentencing—based on the rational of *parens patriae*.
- Reliance on childcare experts, social workers, and probation officers.
- Emphasis on diagnosing problems (e.g., social, family, school, personal,
  and physical environment).
- Individualized treatment over punishment. For example, Section 38 of
  the JDA stated: "the care and custody and discipline of a juvenile
  delinquent shall approximate as nearly as may be that which should be
  given by his parents."

And while the act was revised in 1929 and had a number of amendments
made to it in subsequent years, criticism grew over whether the principle of
parens patriae violated basic constitutional rights (Currie, 1986). This issue
drew widespread attention after 1967 when the United States Supreme Court
heard the case of *In Re Gault*, the first juvenile case to be decided on
constitutional grounds. Furthermore, throughout the 1960s and into the early
1970s, there was increasing disillusionment over the rehabilitative philosophy
of the Canadian juvenile system and its programs. This general sentiment was
epitomized in Robert Martinson's classic 1974 paper in which he proclaimed
"nothing works" in the area of community based corrections. Subsequent
support for this view came from Empey (1982), Lundman (1984, 1994), and
Trojanowicz (1978). Also during this time a number of researchers called for
greater accountability of young offenders (e.g., Wilson, 1975). The seeds for
reform had begun to germinate. But, as deMause (1988) has questioned, were
the seeds planted in the interest of the youth in conflict with the law or did the
reforms simply represent a tactic for extending state control (i.e., net widening)
over our youth? This is a pedagogical issue for which there is no clear answer.

The Long Road to Reform

The following synopsis offers a chronological overview of the major legislative
proposals which led to the proclamation of the Young Offenders Act (YOA) in
1984.

- 1965: the Federal Committee on Juvenile Delinquency began to actively campaign to reform the JDA.
- 1970: Bill C-192 introduced a measure to repeal the Juvenile Delinquency Act.
- 1975: "Young Persons in Conflict with the Law" proposals were circulated. Each province was asked to review elements for the new act. Key elements included: title of the act (Young Offences Act vs. Young Offenders Act); ages (twelve to seventeen); jurisdiction of administration; the importance of diversion and use of alternative social and legal measures; detention and general matters pertaining to sentencing and custody; setting the minimum age for transfer to adult court from fourteen to sixteen; legal representation, and federal/provincial financial implications.
- 1977: the Young Offenders Act was first introduced. However, between 1977 and 1981 it was revamped several times.
- February 16, 1981: Young Offenders Bill was tabled in the House of Commons. Seventy-three years after the JDA, then Solicitor General of Canada, Bob Kaplan, tabled the new act declaring the existing act (JDA) "was seriously out of date with contemporary practices and attitudes regarding juvenile justice and inadequate to meet the problems presented today by young people in conflict with the law" (Solicitor General, 1981).
- 1982: the YOA was passed by Parliament with unanimous support from all three major political parties.
- April 1, 1984: the YOA was proclaimed law.

Creating the Young Offenders Act

As noted above, the transition from the JDA to the YOA was a drawn-out process. Political debates for reform began in 1965, and it took nearly twenty years before the JDA was replaced with the YOA. And while the political argument was that delinquency rates had been increasing significantly throughout the 1960s and 1970s, several Canadian researchers suggested that any increase might be largely attributable to more effective police surveillance and a greater determination to bring young people to justice (McDonald, 1969). Furthermore, the period was marked by high unemployment rates and other social problems such as role ambiguity, which in accordance with the General Strain Theory (Agnew, 1992) generates stresses and strains that can leave adolescents feeling lost when they are unable to meet or attain the basic goals common to others in their age group (e.g., owning a television or having stylish clothing—hence the term a "lost generation"). Some youths may feel that the only way to resolve their anger, frustrations, and other adverse emotional states is by resorting to deviant and criminal acts.[2] Agnew (1992) identifies three sources of strain: 1) strain resulting from the failure to achieve positively valued goals (e.g., wealth, fame, and social acceptance); 2) when a youth's positively valued stimuli are removed (e.g., the loss of a friend, moving to a new town, and the divorce or separation of parents) strain can result; and 3) strain arising with the presentation of negative stimuli (e.g., child abuse, criminal victimization, and school failure).

The combination of dramatic social changes, public pressure for accountability of young offenders, the frustration of police with youth courts because they felt the courts interfered with their work, and the political momentum behind the need for reform finally brought the new act to fruition. The new act brought new legal principles and fundamentally different philosophies for handling juvenile offenders into force. The act represented a shift from the positivist school and a welfare model to the neo-classical school and the **modified justice model** (Corrado et al., 1992) which Hagan, Alwin, and Hewitt (1979) generally described as a "loosely coupled system" (see Box 6.1; also see, Hagan, 1983, 1995).

The most important provisions of the YOA may be summarized as follows:

- The YOA (Section 2(1)) defines a "young person" as someone who is twelve to seventeen years of age, inclusive. All jurisdictions are required to comply with this uniform age range in applying the act.
- Those youth under twelve years of age are not to be dealt with by the criminal justice system. Each province maintains its own child welfare legislation to handle any youth requiring special attention. (In most provinces the two bodies work closely together—see Bala, Hornick, and Vogl, 1991 for a sound review).
- Youthful offenders are now referred to as young offenders rather than juvenile delinquents to reflect the change in status and philosophical orientation.

2   This theme was reiterated in a feature article of the "Alberta Report". Dr. Genuis, Executive Director of the National Foundation for Family Research and Education in Edmonton, Alberta, was quoted as saying: "There is also a cultural crisis among teens... Too many of their other anti-social behaviours are on the rise to believe they are not also committing more crimes" (Verburg, 1995: 31).

Box 6.1: Defining the Juvenile Justice System in Canada

Corrado et al. (1992) have described the Canadian young offenders justice system as a *modified justice model*. The general philosophy emphasizes due process balanced by informality in trial proceedings. The former point is intended to recognize that certain transgressions require sanctioning and accountability while the later point is designed to reflect the fact that some youths may suffer from diminished capacity. The system is considered 'modified' in that it resembles a dual handling process. For the less serious offences, youths are typically diverted out of the system into alternative programs or their cases are dismissed. Hence, the overall task of the new young offender system is to strike a balance between diagnosing problem based delinquency and punishment. Therefore, the key agencies within the system include lawyers, child/youthcare workers, and various 'experts' who can attest to the individual's culpability. For the more serious young offender, there is a greater emphasis on accountability and punishment.

While the model might be theoretically described as modified justice model, Hagan (1983) describes its operation as being 'loosely coupled'. Later Hagan (1995) described how the communication and networking between the police, probation officers, crown, and judges, while responsive to one another, still maintain considerable independence—especially when he compared the Canadian model to that of France and Austria (see Hackler, 1996). This, according to Hagan, has resulted in "the type of communication that encourages... greater attention to rituals and procedures..." (p. 405).

- As recommended under Rule 1.3 of the UN Standards (1986), young offenders under the YOA are entitled to due process and ideally the process should be conducted informally.
- Like adult offenders, youth crimes are considered criminal in nature and are handled in a similar manner. Youth found committing less serious offences should be dealt with less punitively (e.g., diversion or community service work) than more serious offenders (e.g., confinement). These principles appear under Rule 25 of the UN Standards (1986).
- Young offenders who are suspected of violating any federal legislation, such as the Criminal Code, the Food and Drugs Act, and the Narcotic Control Act, come under the jurisdiction of youth courts.
- Youth Court may also hear the cases of young persons accused of provincial offences such as traffic violations.
- Sentencing should be determinant with a minimum and maximum range. This principle can also be found under Rule 3.1 of the UN Standards (1986).
- Because of their special status, offending youth should be entitled to childcare/youthcare experts as well as lawyers for counsel.
- Sentencing should reflect a greater level of accountability. Hence, under the YOA there is a greater emphasis on accountability. However, due to

their age, maturity, and history of offending behaviour, delinquent youth are not generally accountable in the same manner as adults. These concepts are also found in the UN Standards (1986) under Rule 13.1 and 19.1.

• The primary purpose of intervention is a balance between sanctioning criminal/deviant behaviour and providing appropriate treatment.
• The primary objective of the act is to provide greater accountability while still respecting the individuals rights and taking into account their 'special needs'.
• In order to address the needs of young offenders, a system of separate and specialized youth courts and correctional programs is maintained.

In essence the shift has been towards due process of law and, as Ted Rubin in 1976 noted (cited in Milner, 1995:67), "The future is clear: law and due process are here to stay in juvenile court... rehabilitation efforts will be pursued in a legal context." However, as indicated above, as controversial as the YOA has been, it does include many of the guidelines put forth by the United Nations (1986).

Having presented an overview of the past and present legislative measures used to address young offenders, we will now examine some of the trends and patterns of youth crime. Thereafter, I will provide an overview on how the key actors of the youth justice system handle young offenders.

The Dimensions of the Delinquency Problem

> Many Canadians, afraid and frustrated, succumb to the temptation of quick fixes served up by ever willing politicians and the media. Lock them up and throw away the key! Send them to boot camp! Bring back the cane! Zero tolerance! Adult time for adult crime! (*Youth Justice*, 1994)

In collaboration with the provinces and territorial departments responsible for youth courts, the Canadian Centre for Justice Statistics (CCJS) currently collects information on young persons in Canada's justice system.[3] Until 1991 Ontario

---

[3]   In 1962 the federal government introduced nationwide the Canadian Uniform Crime Report (UCR) system. This measure helped to minimize many of the

and the Northwest Territories did not submit data. Also because of variations between provincial reporting practices, data are considered suggestive rather than definitive.[4] Notwithstanding these qualifiers it is possible to present a general picture of youth crime in Canada that comes to the attention of the police and how the cases are disposed of. In accordance with Stanton Wheeler's observation in 1967, a "three-way interaction between an offender, victim or citizens, and official agents" will be followed (p. 319). That is, in addition to examining official statistics, where possible, reference will be made to self-report and victimization studies in order to provide a more realistic account of the 'true' juvenile crime picture.

What are the Official Trends?

As illustrated in Table 6.1, official counts of the crime rates for violent and property crimes among young people today appear to have changed little in the past decade. However, this occurred during a time period when most provinces experienced a decrease among adolescent population. Furthermore, in 1981, the federal Ministry of the Solicitor General conducted the first national survey of victims—the Canadian Urban Victimization Survey (CUVS)—which revealed that Canadians are more concerned about youth crime now than they have been in the past.[5]

More recently, based on their extensive analysis of youth crime data, Markwart and Corrado (1995:84) conclude that there is "clear evidence of a real and substantial increase in youth violence in recent years." In particular, Table 6.1 shows that while the incidents of property crime have modestly decreased since 1991, the rate of violent crime among youths steadily increased until 1994-95 when there was a 2% drop over the previous year (Doherty and de Souza, 1996). For example, property offences decreased 11% from 1992-93 to 1993-94 while violent crime increased by 8% between the same time period.

---

limitations of the previous approach. The Canadian UCR was modelled after the American UCR system. In the late 1980s Statistics Canada created the national institute, the Canadian Centre for Justice Statistics, which is now responsible for collecting, aggregating, and disseminating official crime statistics. The first reports were published in 1991. This model is similar to what the Home Office does for England and Wales.

4   While twelve became the minimum age requirement for charges under the YOA in 1984, it was not until April 1984 that the maximum age of seventeen (inclusive) was established across all of Canada. Therefore, reliable comparisons can not be made prior to 1986-87.

5   The results of this massive study have been published in a series of federal publications ranging from 1983 through to 1986.

Nearly 12% of the violent crimes involved minor assault cases (de Souza, 1995).

While the number of violent crime cases decreased between 1993 and 1994 and 1994 and 1995, it was still 125% higher than in 1986 to 1987. This compares to an increase of 41% among adult offenders over the same time period. In spite of the decrease, the largest increase involved the group twelve to thirteen years of age (an increase of 6% over the previous year) (de Souza, 1995). In 1971 the rate was 197 per 100,000, and for 1980 it had risen to 265 per 100,000 (Carrigan, 1991). And while some of the increases over the years have been attributed to expanding police forces, improved crime fighting technology, and increased sensitivity to youth crime, Carrington and Moyer (1994) argue that these explanations for the increase in violent crime cannot account for the entire rate of increase. The most dramatic increase involved drug convictions— up 49% over the previous year.

Overall, rates of youth charged with a criminal code offence as a percent of the youth population declined 6% between 1991 and the end of 1995. Therefore, depending on how one chooses to read official statistics on youth crime in Canada, you can end up with mixed messages. Recognizing the growth in serious crime over property crime prompted Leschield and Jaffe (1995:427) to conclude, "that the deterrence-focused dispositions of the YOA seem not to have the same effect of reducing crime as did the treatment disposition within the JDA."

Table 6.1: Rates of Youths Charged with Violent and Property Crimes 1986-1993

	1986	1987	1988	1989	1990	1991	1992	1993
Violent crimes: per 100 000	408	450	508	614	694	828	806	921
Yr. to Yr. % rate change:		10	13	21	13	19	5	6
Property crimes: per 100 000	3470	3307	3304	3398	3705	4014	3617	3216
Yr. to Yr. % rate change		-5	-0.1	3	9	8	-10	-11

Source: Adapted from Ogrodnik (1994:28).

Types of Crimes Committed

For the fiscal year 1993-94, 115,949 cases were heard in youth court. This is significantly up from 1986-87 when 96,443 cases were heard. Overall, this represented a slight increase over 1992-93. However, for three of the provinces there was a decrease in youth court caseloads (Newfoundland, -17%; British Columbia, -13%; and Alberta, -3%) (de Souza, 1995). This trend was fairly stable throughout the 1980s and early 1990s. For 1994-95 there was a 5% decrease in the number of cases processed in Youth Court (Doherty and de Souza, 1996). The decrease is in-part due to the declining number of youths in their adolescent years (Foot, 1996).

Since 1986-87 the breakdown of offences committed by young offenders has remained comparatively similar. Most of those youth who commit crime in Canada, as in the past, still continue to commit minor offences. For 1994-95 property convictions accounted for 48% of all youth crime cases while violent crime made up 21% (Doherty and de Souza, 1996). However, some recent findings have raised concern about whether official statistics are providing a realistic picture of the extent and nature of youth crime (see Box 6.2). Table 6.2 presents a comparison between 1986-87 and 1993-94 statistics.

Box 6.2 Victimization in the Schools

Although the results are considered largely exploratory, a major victimization survey conducted on 962 (approx. 2%) of the public and Catholic junior and senior high school students in Calgary during 1994 revealed that 28% of the respondents have carried weapons, 2.6% have packed handguns, and 81.5% have been victimized in the past year, often by having something stolen or damaged (Stewart, 1995). A national survey in December of 1996 indicated that "concern about crime" was tied for second as being the most important issue confronting Western Canadians. National unity was ranked first (Walker, 1996).

In summary, since the introduction of the YOA, official counts of youth crime continued to escalate until 1994-95 when there was a small decrease in the absolute number of cases. Furthermore, the nature of youth crime is becoming generally more serious, and the average age at which young persons are becoming involved in delinquent activity is getting lower.

Profile of Young Offenders

For 1994-95 eight out of ten young offenders were male. This has been a typical pattern since the turn of the century in Canada. What has been changing

Table 6.2: Percentage Breakdown of Official Youth Crimes: 1986-87—1993-94

Category	Year	
	1986-87*(a) Percent	1993-94(b) Percent
Theft under $1000	24.7	16.8
Break and enter	24.8	13.5
YOA offences	7.5	9.5
Minor assaults	8.8	9.4
Fail to appear	5.2	9.4
Possession of stolen property	6.1	6.7
Mischief	6.6	5.3
Theft over $1000	4.1	3.7
Aggravated assault/weapon	2.0	3.6
Drug offences/possession	3.0	2.7
Robbery	1.9	2.0
Escape/unlawful at large	N/A	1.8
Frauds	2.2	1.8
Sexual assault	1.3	1.7
Impaired driving	3.5	0.8
Arson	N/A	0.4
Take vehicle without consent	0.003	1.4

*Percentages calculation based on raw data.
Source: (a) *Decision and dispositions in youth court*, Nov., 1990.
        (b) de Souza (1995).

in recent years is the age at which youth are commencing their criminal activities. While, for 1993-94, one-half of youth court caseload involved sixteen and seventeen year olds (20% involved fifteen year olds; 26% twelve to fourteen year olds) there was a 6% increase in caseloads from the previous year for the twelve to thirteen year old age group (Foran, 1995) (see Box 6.3). Sixteen year olds represented the highest crime risk-prone age (approx. 8800 per 100,000 vs. 1000 per 100,000 for twelve year olds) (Doherty and de Souza, 1996).

Female young offenders, until recent years, have been under-represented in the young offender population. In recent years, however, their numbers have been increasing, especially for minor assaults (Reitsma-Street, 1993). Typically young females are charged most frequently with shoplifting offences, mischief, and administrative offences (e.g., failure to comply with decisions of youth court, failure to comply with decisions of the youth justice). These trends are not dissimilar from those expressed in other chapters throughout this book.

A popular explanation for female under-representation in the official statistics draws on three related factors: sex role socialization, differential social control, and variations in opportunity (Hagan, Simpson, and Gillis, 1979).

Box 6.3: A City in Profile

Calgary is a city of nearly 800,000 inhabitants. Being one of Canada's fastest growing cities it has had to come to terms with an apparent increase in youth crime. But a profile of youth crime in the city reveals that the characteristics compare closely to those of the rest of the country. In 1994 there were 6569 youths charged with offences of who 5010 were male (76%). Of these offences 3137 (47.7%) were for theft and 1107 (16.8%) were violence related charges. Over the year the violent crimes included three murders, 641 assaults, and 238 weapons related charges. The other major categories included robber and sex-related crimes (Dempster, 1996).

"Causes" of Delinquency

Why do young people break criminal rules and commit status offences? This is a question not only asked and studied by many Canadian criminologists but by scholars around the world. The range of explanations can often appear overwhelming. In this section I will only focus on studies conducted on Canadian young offenders.

If one can use Canadian textbooks and Canadian journal articles as an indicator of theoretical preference, then it would appear that the sociological/ macro perspectives are the most popular. Factors that have been studied to explain delinquent involvement include:

- Based on the social learning theory (Akers, 1985), peer influence and peer pressure have been studied by some scholars in Canada. Using secondary data Brownfield and Thompson (1991) were able to support the social learning/control theory. They concluded, "measures of peer involvement in delinquency are strongly and positively associated with self-report delinquency" (p. 57).
- The conceptualization of class and family focuses on the power relations in the workplace and the home. Hagan, Simpson, and Gillis (1987) argue that delinquency rates are a function of class differences and economic conditions that in turn influence the structure of family life. Their power-

control theory has been reasonably effective in explaining the relative increase in female delinquency since it recognizes the effects of social changes such as the decline of the patriarchal family and changing sex-roles.

- Drawing on ecological concepts and presuming the rationality of offenders, the routine activity theory, developed by Cohen and Felson in 1979, has attempted to link the increase in delinquency to increased suitability of targets and a decline in the presence of "guardians" (e.g., friends, family, and neighbours). In Canada, Kennedy and Baron (1993) demonstrated that choices, routines, and cultural milieu interact to affect one another to create opportunities for delinquency.

- Gottfredson and Hirschi's recent general theory of crime (earlier version entitled propensity-event theory) has also received recent attention in Canada. This approach represents an attempt to integrate classical and positivist principles into a general model of crime. The theory represents a revision of Hirschi's control theory. The new version suggests that people naturally act in a self-interested fashion. However, our socialization can affect our level of self-control. Delinquency is largely a result of low self-control. However, unlike Hirschi's earlier theory, the new model focuses more on the individual traits than external sources of control. In his study on delinquency and school dropouts, Creechan (1995:238) found the "general theory of crime produced a remarkably accurate prediction of who is normal."

- During the late 1980s and into the 1990s, there appeared to be a return, in some circles, to the positivist/medical model involving factors such as nutrition, chemical imbalances, and neurological problems which may cause a youth to become prone to deviant and violent behaviour (Gibbs, 1995).

- Other factors commonly studied and used to explain Canadian youth crime include, substance abuse (Hendrick and Lachance, 1991), abuse and neglect (Horner, 1993), breakdown in values and norms, and various personality problems (see Romig, Cleland, and Romig, 1989: 28-29 for a summary of causes and related studies).

- One of the most recent studies, which has received considerable press, was headed by Dr. Mark Genuis, Executive Director of the National Foundation for Family Research and Education. Their national survey revealed that parental neglect is the leading cause of youth problems. A number of the other key points discussed in the study relate strongly to Hirschi's control theory. The findings shows that the suicide rate among

Alberta children aged ten to fourteen has risen 146% since 1970 and one-fifth of all adolescents are clinically or emotionally ill (Verburg, 1995).

The cause(s) of youth crime in Canada might best be illustrated in a quote from the Canadian Criminal Justice Association (CCJA), which in 1992 concluded, "causal relationships among these behaviours cannot be determined accurately, nor can we affirm which comes first in time or importance" (CCJA, 1992:3).

Therefore, while the phenomenon of youth crime has been around since Europeans first began to colonize Canada, our legal efforts and theoretical approaches have not had a positive impact on youth crime rates. This has been reflected in our youth crime data as well as our in our recidivism counts.

Repeat Offenders

Until recently, regular statistics were not kept on recidivism rates among young offenders. Resource and methodological problems were the primary culprits. However, due to a growing concern over crime and a general improvement in data collection with the formation of the Canadian Centre for Justice Statistics in 1982, the centre's mandate has been streamlined to better address social, political, and academic concerns (Winterdyk, 1996). Such rates, however, are considered a reasonable measure of how effective the juvenile justice system is deterring and rehabilitating young offenders. As noted earlier, Leschield and Jaffe (1995) suggest that the current emphasis on crime control does not appear to be having a deterrent effect. This observation is also reflected in police data, which reveal that from 1989 to 1993 police reported that incidents involving young persons rose by 24% (Young, 1994). By 1994-95, 42% of all convictions involved repeat offenders of which 25% had three of more prior convictions (Doherty and de Souza, 1995). Collectively, repeat offences represent 12% of all cases brought before the court.

Based on 1990-91 data, Moyer (1992) found that in 19% of youth court cases, the accused had already had five or more previous convictions. It was also revealed that most repeat offenders commit the same types of crimes. That is, about two-thirds were charged with property offences. Based on 1994-95 data, the trend has continued to climb (Doherty and de Souza, 1996). In addition, as reflected in various public opinion polls, repeat offenders tend to commit more serious offences and the seriousness of their crimes escalate during subsequent offences. Still, a majority (54%) of youth court cases involved first-time offenders.

Repeat offenders tend to commit more serious crimes and tend to be somewhat older (50% were seventeen years of age) and they tend to be more criminally active than first-time offenders (Doherty and de Souza, 1995). The study also found that the average elapsed time between offences was eight months unless the young offender had three or more priors, then the interval between offences was less than four months. Given the fact that re-offenders receive harsher penalties than first- or second-time offenders, their continued involvement in delinquent activity raises further doubts about the effectiveness of the YOA and more particularly our modified justice model. Males are more likely (58%) than females (50%) to receive custody dispositions (Doherty and de Souza, 1995).

Although data from five of the twelve jurisdictions were excluded because of low numbers, for those provinces which did report, the mean length of dispositions for repeat offenders was actually less than the mean length of dispositions for first-time offenders. For example, for secure custody dispositions first-time offenders received a mean sentence length of approximately 110 days while those youths with three or more convictions received a mean sentence length of around 120 days (Moyer, 1992). This trend is also reflected in the official 1994-95 data. Contrary to public opinion, with almost half of those youths sentenced to custody for non-violent offences, it does not appear that such punishment represents a mere slap on the wrist. However, the sentence length increase, for repeat offenders, has only slightly increased in the 1990s. Therefore, given the recidivism trends, and as already noted in this section, it is questionable whether the modified justice model is being applied effectively. Using a slightly different orientation, Hackler (1996) arrives at a similar conclusion in his comparative discussion of juvenile justice.

Court Dispositions

According to one article, in 1992-93 Canada's adult inmate incarceration rate ranked seventeenth among fifty-two nations (International data, 1995). With an incarceration rate of around 116 per 100,000 it is well below that of Russia (558) and United States (519). This is in sharp contrast to how many Canadians view our criminal justice system. In fact, based on a smaller international sample (N=14) of the 1993 Edition of Corrections in Canada indicated that Canada ranked third amongst the countries listed.[6]

---

[6]   The following is a listing of the incarceration 1992-93 rates for most of the countries presented in this book. Australia, 91; Belgium, 71; Canada, 116; England/Wales,

With the passing of the YOA, youth court judges have been provided with a wide array of sentencing disposition. These include absolute discharge, fines, restitution, community service orders, probation, and open and closed custody.[7]

Approximately two-thirds of all the cases which appeared before youth courts across Canada for 1994-95 resulted in findings of guilt. Only 28% had their proceedings stayed or withdrawn. For the remainder of cases (4%) not guilty verdicts were reached (Doherty and de Souza, 1996).

Although Canada might be described as being more punitive than many other Western nations (see other contributions), for 1994-95 the bulk (approximately 48%) of case dispositions resulted in probation. This proportion has steadily increased in the 1990s. The medium length of this disposition was one year. Of the remaining cases, 33% resulted in some type of custody (19% open custody and 14% secure custody, 13% of the youths charged received community service orders, and the balance fines (7%). Again, these figures reflect the general pattern of dispositions since the act came into effect.

In Canada it is also possible for offending youths to receive multiple dispositions. While nearly 68% of all cases in 1992-93 involved one disposition, 25% resulted in two dispositions and a small percentage involved three or more. The most frequent combination includes probation and community service (13% in 1992-93) (Leesti, 1994). This type of disposition reflects the principles of the modified justice model described earlier. What has not been determined is the relative effectiveness of these types of dispositions.

Since the enactment of the YOA, there has been considerable debate about whether young offenders are being held more accountable for their offences. Between 1986-87 and 1992-93, Leesti (1994) reported a 41% increase in the number of youth cases receiving custody as the most serious disposition. And while there has been little change in custody proportion, the rates for both closed and open custody increased the same amount—from ten to fourteen per 10,000. However, as will be elaborated upon shortly, while the use

---

[7] 93; Germany, 80; Hong Kong, 179; Hungary, 146; Netherlands, 49; Russia, 558; Sweden, 69; United States, 519. "International data", March-April, 1995:17. According to a *Juristat* report by Foran (1995) on youth custody the following figures for 1993-94 were presented: 18.6% open custody, 14.3% secure custody, 38.9% probation, 6.9% fines, 13.2% community service orders, 3.5% absolute discharge, and 4.7% resulted on other dispositions such as transfers to adult court, restitution, and forfeiture.

of dispositions have gone up the average length of a disposition has decreased in recent years.

Since 1986-87 the proportion of young females receiving a custodial disposition has remained consistent at around 14% while for young males it has increased from 26% in 1986-87 to 31% in 1992-93. Overall the rate of cases receiving custody dispositions as a most serious disposition rose from 17.7 per 10,000 in 1986-87 to 21.1 for 1993-93 (Foran, 1995).

What is interesting to observe, as it reflects different provincial judicial discretionary practices, is that the custody rates vary considerably across the country. For example, open custody is more commonly used in Eastern Canada than in the Western provinces. Young females more commonly have charges laid against them in the Western provinces than those in the Eastern provinces (Reitsma-Street, 1993). This may be due to the fact that the act's enforcement is a provincial responsibility, and due to variations in resources and political agendas uniformity in the administration of juvenile justice is not possible. Hagan (1983) has aptly described this phenomena as a "loosely coupled system" (see Box 6.1). In addition, an issue that has not been adequately addressed but which is reflected in the negative sentiments of the public, is the lack of an efficient and effective model of juvenile justice. As Hackler (1996) has observed, Canadian policy-makers might be suffering from a "smugness about our system."

Since 1986-87, while the use of custodial dispositions have increased slightly, the duration of the dispositions have tended to result in shorter terms. For example, in 1986-87, 56% of the custodial dispositions resulted lasting three months or less. For 1992-93 the proportion had increased to 65%. Furthermore, the proportion of cases receiving six months or more decreased from 1986-87 to 1992-93 (22% vs. 16%) (Leesti, 1994).

This trend would appear to reflect the move towards greater accountability while still attempting to balance 'special needs' of the young offenders. However, between 1986-87 and 1992-93 there has been a 16% increase in the number of youths placed into custodial facilities (Leesti, 1994). Therefore, it can be suggested that in accordance with the mandate of the YOA more youths are being held accountable even though their sentences have become somewhat shorter in duration. This may be viewed as "short sharp shock" intervention, which received considerable attention during the late 1970s "Scared Straight" program. Lundman (1994) reports that this model of intervention did not prove to be an effective mode of treatment. An additional consequence of the increased case load has been the increased processing time in youth court. In 1989-90 the average length of a youth court trial was twenty-three days, up two days from 1986-87 but with considerable variation across the country.

According to Corrado and Markwart (1994), the trend towards greater accountability but shorter sentences may in part be explained by the fact that there is a placement shortage in most provincial containment facilities across the country. Courts must entertain alternative disposition options. Based on various provincial statistics, this observation would appear to be valid. Therefore, the question is whether the Canadian juvenile justice model is one of design or necessity? It is the author's opinion that, based on historical trends of juvenile justice practices in our country (see Carrigan, 1991; Smandych, Dobbs, and Esau, 1991) and the implementation of its legislation, the modified justice model may have evolved out of necessity rather than being founded on sound theoretical and empirical evidence. A number of prominent Canadian criminologists have argued that, to date, Canadian criminology has not faired well in blending criminological ideas with political agendas (Winterdyk, forthcoming). Hence, in addition to Hagan's notion of a "loosely coupled system," our juvenile justice system could also described as a philosophically fragmented model.

Transfers to Adult Court

One of the major changes between the JDA and YOA pertained to the issue of transfers to adult court for youths found committing serious offences. This provision comes under section 16 of the YOA and pertains to youths of fourteen years or older who have committed an indictable offence.[8] Since the introduction of the new act there has been a slight but steady increase each year in the number of youths transferred to adult court. In 1991-92, seventy-one cases were transferred from youth court to adult court while for 1994-95, 123 cases were transferred (Doherty and de Souza, 1996). Of those cases being

---

[8]   Comparatively, Manitoba has a relatively high transfer rate, yet based on 1993-94 data Manitoba had amongst the lowest orders for custody dispositions. In addition to including murder, the province has also used the transfer option for attempted murder and robbery. Ontario, by contrast, has a much more restrictive policy in transferring youth to the adult system. However, it had amongst the highest rate for custody dispositions of all provinces for 1993-94. If a youth between the ages of twelve and thirteen commits a crime and is considered a serious risk to society, section 16(1) of the YOA enables the youth to be transferred to adult court. But, the crown must obtain the consent of the provincial attorney general.

considered for transfer, 50% spend four or more months in Youth Court prior to the decision to transfer.

In recent years there have been a number of sensational violent crimes involving youths which have drawn considerable media and public attention. In 1992 the case of Ryan Garrioch attracted considerable public pressure and eventually resulted in changing the maximum sentence for murders committed by young persons (see Box 7.4).

Box 7.4: Public Pressure Prompts Tougher Laws

On May 11, 1992 in Calgary, Alberta, thirteen year old Ryan Garrioch was stabbed to death while on his way to school. His assailant was a fifteen year old youth. The incident drew national attention as the YOA not only protected the identity of the killer but under the YOA brought a maximum penalty of three years in jail. The Garrioch family started a national petition campaign to have the act toughened. In partial response to this public pressure, Bill C-12 was introduced on May 29, 1994. The bill increased the maximum sentence for murder from three to five years. The bill also addressed some transfer issues. Then in response to additional serious youth crimes and public pressure, Bill C-37 was tabled in government and resulted in a number of amendments to the YOA. The bill raised the maximum sentence for youth convicted of premeditated murder from five to ten years (in contrast to the twenty-five years minimum imposed on adults). However, the Standing Committee of Justice Legal Affairs concluded that "this increase in the penalty structure will not... reduce juvenile violence and will not reduce juvenile recidivism. Moreover, it does not provide resources for programs of delinquency prevention, public education, and community-based rehabilitation programs" (CCJA, 1994:3). Rather, it might be more prudent to have serious offences dealt with seriously in youth court. The April 2, 1995 bludgeoning deaths of a Montreal clergyman and his wife by three teenagers may, nevertheless, apply additional pressure on the YOA.

Even though the number of transfers to adult court currently represent less than 1% of all youths charged with a crime, conditions for transfer are not uniformly applied across Canada. Manitoba, for example, has the highest per capita number of adult transfers. Youths are choosing transfer to "avoid the discipline and structure of a youth custody facility" (Doherty and de Souza, 1996:7). The differences appear to be related to social and political variations that not only reflect a loosely coupled system but also a fragmented philosophical model which places societal interests above those of our youth. Diana Gordon (1990) reflects a similar sentiment in her book.

The Financial Burden of Juvenile Justice

One of the concerns the provinces had throughout the 1970s regarding the proposed changes to the YOA was the increased cost to the provinces to provide the necessary services needed under the new act.

The concerns appear to have been warranted. Between 1988 and 1989 and 1992 and 1993 government spending on the justice system increased 34% to $9.57 billion, which equates to approximately $300 per Canadian per year. The per capita cost had risen to $331 for the fiscal year 1994-94 (CCJA, 1996). After adjusting for inflation, this represents a real growth of 13% or an average annual constant dollar increase of 3.2%. This represents nearly 3% of total government spending. And while politicians point out that the rise is consistent with the rise in other sectors of the government, given the growing concern with fiscal restraint in Canada and more specifically the provinces, some alternatives that have been forwarded suggest that the provinces divert funds from institutional budgets to community alternatives. However, the CCJA notes that realistically this could only be accomplished if both Parliament and the provinces act to enhance YOA funding (CCJA, 1994).

The largest allotment for juvenile justice went to youth corrections, again reflecting the move towards embracing a harsher stand on youth crime in this country. For example, in Ontario about 77% of the $118 million spent on young offenders in 1992-93 was for closed custody/detention—approximately $128,000 per youth under sixteen years of age. These costs rise even more when youth over sixteen are included (CCJA, 1996). From 1988-89 to 1992-93 the increase was 16.2% after adjusting for inflation (Young, 1994). An article on youth justice in Alberta showed that it cost the province between $70-$80 per day to place a youth in custody or just over $25,000 per year (Dempster, 1996).

The area which has been most impacted by the Young Offenders Act has been legal aid. Since young offenders are entitled to legal representation but are often unable to retain their own counsel, they become dependent on legal aid—one of the reasons for its inception. Between 1988 and 1989 and 1992 and 1993, legal aid expenditures went up 70.3%. By 1994 to 1995 expenditures for legal aid were greater than that for young offenders.[9] In fact, the federal government became so concerned that in the early 1990s they placed a ceiling on how much legal aid lawyers could charge per type of case (Hung and

---

[9]   Between 1988 and 1989 and 1992 and 1993 the expenditures for legal aid went from 0.3 billion dollars to 0.6 billion dollars, the fastest growing component of the justice system. For youth corrections, total expenditures declined from 0.36 billion in 1988-89 to 0.49 billion dollars in 1992-93. Not only was youth corrections the only component to experience a decrease in funding, but they continue to receive the least amount of any segment of the criminal justice system (*A graphic overview...*, 1996).

Bowles, 1995). Such trends lend further support to the general observation that the act is not only placing a large burden on taxpayers but reflect its legalistic orientation. It further begs the questions, how much 'justice' can be afford and are these the most appropriate ways of addressing youth crime?

The Youth Justice Process

The Canadian criminal justice system can generally be characterized as lacking coordination (Larsen, 1995). Critics point out that the criminal justice system does not share a common goal, a common philosophy, or a centralized decision-making authority. And while it can be argued that the system does share the generic goal of crime control and protection of society, there is little agreement as to how these goals can be attained. This general lack of coordination is also apparent in the young offender system.

Unlike the adult justice system, in Canada the act (i.e., Young Offenders Act), which was enacted to identify state jurisdictional powers, while being a federal act is provincially administered. Articles appearing in Corrado et al.'s edited book (1992) have identified several of the key problems both within and between provincial and territorial jurisdictions. They range from transfer issues, to appropriate dispositions, and the general effectiveness of the act in having its objectives implemented.

Figure 6.1 provides a graphic illustration of what happens once a youth comes into contact with the young offender system. As noted earlier the history of the juvenile justice system in Canada has undergone a number of dramatic changes in recent years. Today the model reflects a due process model in which an accused youth is entitled not only to legal representation but special consideration, hence the description 'modified justice model' (see Box 6.1).

Initial Contact

The police are usually the first representatives of the formal system youths encounter. Under the YOA, all Criminal Code provisions from the point of arrest to applying for bail apply equally to young persons. The act and Section 10(a) of the Charter of Rights provide that all youths suspected of committing an offence must be informed about their rights by the attending police officer before they are apprehended and/or arrested.

Given that most of the crimes committed by young offenders are minor in nature, discretion is often exercised when handling such cases. Again, the

Figure 6.1: An Abbreviated Model of the Young Offender Legal Process in Canada

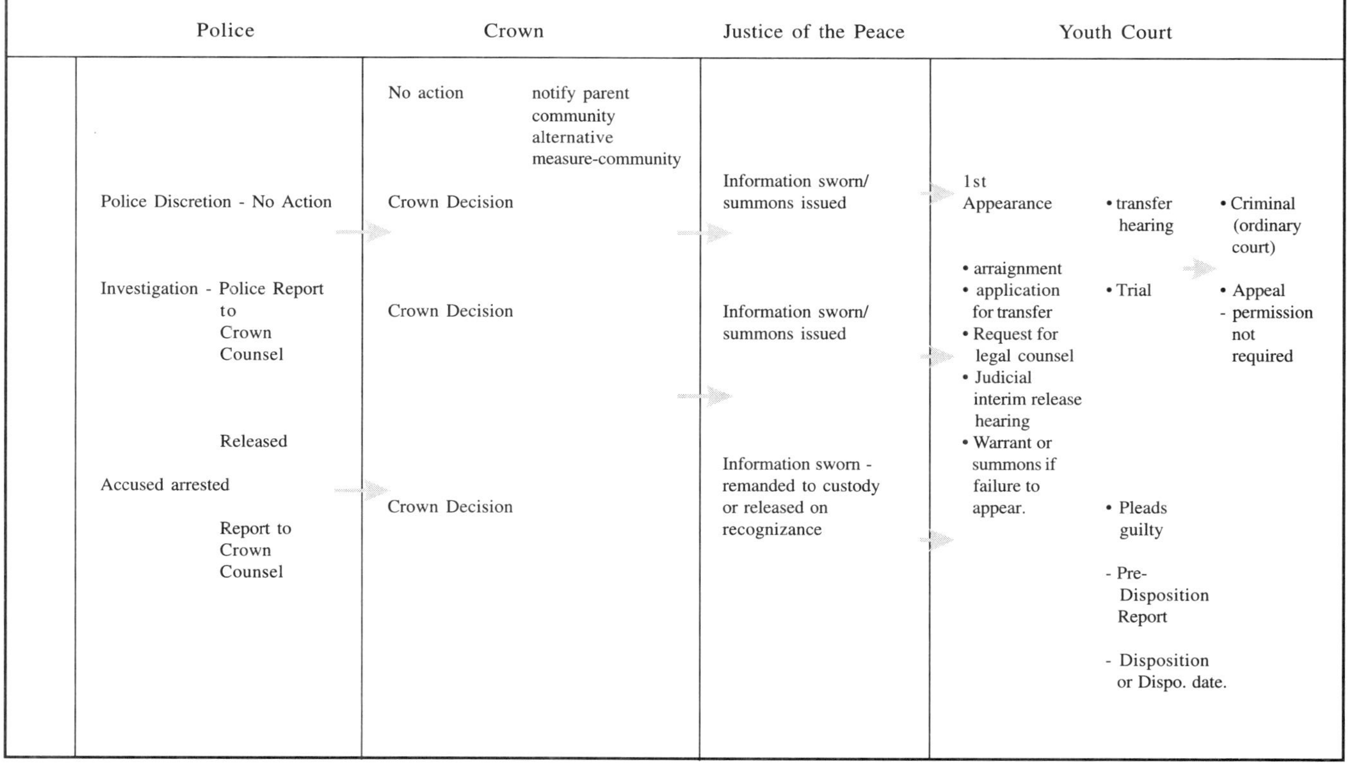

Police	Crown	Justice of the Peace	Youth Court
Police Discretion - No Action	No action / notify parent / community alternative measure-community		
Investigation - Police Report to Crown Counsel	Crown Decision	Information sworn/ summons issued	1st Appearance • arraignment • application for transfer • Request for legal counsel • Judicial interim release hearing • Warrant or summons if failure to appear.
Released	Crown Decision	Information sworn/ summons issued	• transfer hearing • Trial • Pleads guilty - Pre-Disposition Report - Disposition or Dispo. date.
Accused arrested / Report to Crown Counsel	Crown Decision	Information sworn - remanded to custody or released on recognizance	• Criminal (ordinary court) • Appeal - permission not required

notion of *parens patriae*. But, as Doob and Chan (1982) discuss in their article, in whose best interests are discretionary measures taken? In a post JDA study, Carrington and Moyer (1994) found that since the new act police are less likely to divert sixteen and seventeen year old suspects than twelve to fifteen year olds. This discretionary handling appears to be due to police practices rather than a direct consequence of the act. Those youth between ages twelve to fifteen tend to commit less serious crimes and are more likely to receive reprimands, be warned of future consequences should they re-offend, or be returned to their parent(s).

Should the incident warrant formal measures, the police will then use a formal document recommending the laying of a charge. Again, because of provincial jurisdictional authority, the extent to which discretion is exercised varies considerably.

The final decision on the admissibility of statements rests typically with either the police or the Crown. However, other persons in authority and who are involved in the arrestc, detention, examination of a young offender (e.g., probation officers and corrections staff) may also be involved in the decision process. Again, it varies across jurisdictions. What is consistent however is that before giving a statement to the police, Section 56 of the YOA provides the safeguard that a youth is entitled to be advised or has the option of having a lawyer or a parent/guardian present. This special provision is intended to ensure that there is no improper questioning by authorities. Under Section 44(1) of the YOA, a youth charged with a serious (indictable) offence may be photographed and fingerprinted.

While the basic tenets of the criminal law are entrenched into the YOA, sections such as 3(1)(f) have raised considerable debate as to how much discretion—accountability can be exercised. Section 3(1)(f) refers to the young person's "right to the least possible interference with freedom." Hence, given that enforcement of the act rests with each province and police department, the use of informal procedures varies widely between provinces and even between police jurisdictions within provinces. This practice is virtually unchanged from how youth were handled under the JDA.

Youth Court Proceedings

As was the case under the former JDA, legal proceedings under the YOA are conducted in specially designated youth courts. Depending on the jurisdiction, in some provinces it is the Family Court while in others a branch of adult provincial court.

Ontario and Nova Scotia are exceptions to the above scenarios in that they both use a two-tier youth court model. Twelve to fifteen year olds are dealt with in Family Court while sixteen and seventeen year olds are proceeded with in provincial court.

While the YOA (s. 52) stipulates that proceedings in youth court approximate those rules governing summary conviction offences in adult court, the proceedings for indictable offences are less complex and are intended to be more expeditious. For example, unlike in the adult system, there are no preliminary inquiries, and all trials are conducted by a judge alone (there are no jury trials in Family Court/Provincial Court). However, the CCJA (1994) in their review of Bill C-37 strongly endorsed the right to jury trial in murder cases.

Relatively few cases actually end up in youth court. For a majority of those which do end up in youth court, they are the product of a "plea bargain."[10] The youth is "encouraged" to enter a plea of guilty with the understanding that the sentence will be less severe. What kind of message does this send to young offenders? Again, whose best interests are being served?

Should a young offender be required to attend court, Section 11 of the YOA requires that they be advised of their rights and that if they cannot afford to retain counsel one will be provided by the state. And although it is possible to have a guardian or parent attend in place of a lawyer, given the formal legal procedure and potential risk for punishment youths are encouraged to seek legal counsel.

In Canada, even though young offenders are meant to be held accountable for their actions, there are provisions under the act (e.g., s. 38) which do not allow the youths name or identity to be published unless they are considered "dangerous to others". Also, other provisions (s. 45) require that all criminal records be destroyed five years after the completion of an indictable offence and three years after the completion of summary offences. Furthermore, potential employers may not ask whether the potential employee had ever been convicted under the YOA. Such measures reflect the limited accountability young persons are afforded during their adolescent years. In accordance with section 44.1(k), judges may allow for the disclosure of records between the before the non-disclosure period. This option is seldom exercised.

---

[10] Plea bargaining has been described as one of the most controversial, and perhaps least understood, aspects of the Canadian criminal justice system (Griffiths and Verdun-Jones, 1994). Public surveys show that Canadians feel plea bargaining leads to excessively lenient sentences. In essence, plea bargaining in Canada "is concerned with reaching an agreement to secure a concession from the Crown in return for the accused pleading guilty (Griffiths & Verdun-Jones, 1994:318).

Sentencing Options

As noted above, the court is able to draw from a wide variety of disposition options. One of the newest options available to the courts is the use of DNA testing (see Box 6.5). In accordance with Section 20 of the act, available dispositions include:

a) an order for restitution or compensation;
b) an order for up to 240 hours of community service work;
c) an absolute discharge;
d) a fine up to $1000;
e) an order for up to two years' probation;
f) an order for treatment for up to three years; and
g) an order for custody for up to five years.

Although the options may appear straight forward, there is considerable variation between jurisdictions as each province tries to consolidate its disposition philosophy for young offenders. For example, following the enactment of the act there was a significant increase in the number of custodial dispositions, but it varied between provinces (Corrado and Markwart, 1994). A 1991 Gallup poll found that 48% of the respondents supported the notion that young offenders be tried before the same court as adult offenders—in Quebec an overwhelming 71% supported the notion. However, given the number of articles and appeals surrounding the use of this disposition, it is clear that the legal system has not yet found its 'comfort' zone in the use of custodial disposition (Kopyto and Condina, 1986) and the recurring themes of a "loosely coupled system" and "fragmented philosophical model" come to mind.

This controversy is perhaps most evident in the area of transfer to adult court. If a youth is transferred to adult court because of the seriousness of the offence, then he or she will be tried as an adult and all the relevant adult rules of law will apply equally to the youth—including sentencing options. Therefore, while under the YOA a youth having committed murder can only receive a maximum of five years in secure custody, under the adult Criminal Code they

11   Not since 1962 has a Canadian been hung for murder. In 1976 capital punishment was officially abolished. Between 1867 and 1962 Canada hanged 693 men and thirteen women. The 1994 Canadian Police Association Survey revealed that 76.6% of the respondents supported the return of capital punishment for first degree murder.

could receive a maximum of life.[11] Milner (1995:384) has observed that there "has been considerable judicial disagreement about the appropriate interpretation of the YOA's standards for transfer, the interest of society... having regard to the needs of the young person."

Box 6.5: DNA Testing for Young Offenders

With the increasing demand for accountability of serious young offenders and serious adult offences, a June 1995 bill was introduced by the Justice Minister which would enable an amendment to the Criminal Code and Young Offenders Act allowing a judge to issue a warrant authorizing a peace officer to obtain samples of bodily substances through officially prescribed means for forensic DNA analysis. The bill was, in part, fuelled by a public campaign spearheaded by the family whose fifteen-year-old daughter (Tara Manning) was smothered and raped in her Montreal home. Three investigative procedures are identified as acceptable. They include: hair sampling, taking of a buccal swab, and taking of blood by pricking the skin with a sterile lancet. Young offenders, unlike adults, will be entitled to having the samples taken in the presence of counsel or other appropriate adult. The amendment would be added to subsection (2.1) and include a subclause (2). The Minister backed his decision by pointing out that twenty or more American states already have such provisions. DNA testing of young offenders is also available in England, Australia, and New Zealand.

Post Sentencing.... "Corrections"

On any given day 4900 youths are in custody in Canada (Dempster, 1996).

It has hopefully become reasonably clear that the YOA, although intended to ensure due process and accountability of young offenders, has endeavoured through its various provisions to ensure that youths still be granted reasonable discretion in the handling and disposing of cases. Since its enactment the act has drawn considerable attention. In 1994 the July issue of the *Canadian Journal of Criminology* was allocated to articles discussing the pro and cons of the act—ten years after its ascension to law.

As noted above, approximately 30% of cases result in custody dispositions while the balance result in some type of alternative measure—a non-custody disposition.[12] This consistent pattern reflects the desire of the YOA to recognize that young offenders may have special needs and therefore provides provisions which the court can use when deciding a case. Even

---

[12]   Alternative measure programs can include fines; community service orders; compensation by personal service; detention or treatment; restitution; prohibition, seizure, forfeiture, and probation. Historically, probation has been the most commonly used alternative measure—approximately 38% of all dispositions per year since 1986-87.

though alternative measures are popular, Griffiths and Hatch (1994) have observed that, as in adult corrections, there has been no methodologically strong evaluation demonstrating such program's effectiveness. In fact there have been concerns expressed about the net widening tendencies of many community-based programs (see Japan for similar views). One review study found very modest success in the programs they evaluated in Ontario (Hundley, Scapinello, and Stasiak, 1992). The researchers were quick to point out that this does not mean that nothing works. These cautionary observations were largely based on the fact that many of the studies were methodologically weak.

Nevertheless, public sentiment and social policy would appear to suggest that Canada has not recovered from the post "nothing works" syndrome of the 1970s. In fact there seems to have been an increased emphasis on punishment in spite of the fact that both academics and the Canadian Criminal Justice Association point out that there are major limitations to youth justice policies being punishment oriented (see Box 6.6). As Griffiths and Hatch

Box 6.6: Reforming the Juvenile Justice System

In June of 1994 the Canadian Police Association conducted a mail-in survey dealing with reforming our justice system. Their analysis was based on a returned sample of 2651 respondents. Some of the key findings regarding young offenders included: 73.4% were in favour of work-camp-like facilities; 64.8% voted to lower the age for youth court (ten to sixteen years old as compared to the current twelve to seventeen years old). Nearly 60% of the respondents had knowingly been a victim of a crime committed by someone under the age of eighteen; 57.4% generally felt that in most serious cases youths should be treated like adults rather than the more lenient manner of the YOA; and 76.8% felt the publication ban on naming young offenders should be lifted (*Canadian Police Association Year Book* 1994).

In April 1997 the government released the preliminary findings on a national survey on youth crime and youth justice. The survey involved six members of parliament travelling across the country and talking to Canadians in public forum settings.

The report recommended against lowering the maximum and/or minimum age of responsibility. they recommended against lifting the publication ban on naming youths charged under the act and they recommended against youth fourteen years of age and older who commit murder (or other violent crimes) be transferred to adult court. Other draft recommendations include: more education campaigns on youth crime; increased spending for the police, courts, and corrections, and shift resources away from custodial institutions into community-based services (Bindmann, 1997).

The draft recommendation came on the eve of the election call at which point government is dissolved. The Reform Party that subsequently became the opposition party, while the Liberal Party retained leadership, has openly denounced the recommendation as being too soft and have described the report and the YOA as a "joke."

Reforming the Canadian juvenile justice system to meet all Canadian's interests and concerns will not come easily.

(1994:625) observed: "In the coming years, the YOA may come to be viewed as representing less of an enlightened approach to youth crime and young offenders and more of an impediment to addressing the needs of youths, victims, and the community."

Current Issues Facing Canadian Youth Today

It seems that every generation and every country has its issues. Canada is no exception. Today Canadian youth are involved in several forms of behaviour which are either a concern for criminal justice personnel or society as a whole. For example, data from the 1993 General Social Survey suggest a small but measurable increase in the level of fear of crime victimization compared to the 1988 survey results (Hung and Bowles, 1995).

The following summaries are not exhaustive; rather they simply serve to provide an synopsis of some of the key 'problem' areas Canadians are facing in the 1990s regarding young offenders.

Youth Gangs

While street/youth gangs have existed in Canada since the late 1920s, during the late 1980s and into the 1990s we have witnessed a flurry of gang activity, which has been accompanied by a number of articles in an otherwise sparsely covered topic (Gordon, 1995). Recent studies suggest that, not withstanding definitional problems, the problem has escalated and diversified. For example, since the mid-1980s Asian organized crime groups (e.g., triads and tongs) have become a growing concern (Prowse, 1994). Aside from being more violent than 'traditional' youth gangs, they engage in a wide variety of crimes ranging from home invasion robbery to extortion, protection rackets, and distribution of drugs. The primary attraction to gang activity seems to be related to material and psychological rewards, and because of these temptations some youth seem to "drift" (Matza, 1964) into gang-related activities. As a result of their associations, they learn techniques that enable them to neutralize the values and beliefs taught by law-abiding citizens. To date most gang activities seem to be limited to major metropolitan areas, and many metropolitan police forces have established special youth gang units to monitor and counter this growing problem.

168 JUVENILE JUSTICE SYSTEMS

Runaways

Even though being a runaway is not a crime in Canada, the number of youths running away from home has increased significantly throughout the 1980s and into the 1990s (MacLaurin, 1996). The highest risk category are those between the ages of fourteen and fifteen (McDonald, 1994). Due to a lack of employment opportunities, limited social and marketability skills, an increasing number of these youths are turning to youth crimes, prostitution, substance abuse, and militant groups as a means of trying to survive on the streets. Girls are more likely than boys to runaway, and in a substantial number of cases those who run away from home have done so more than once (McDonald, 1994). These chronic runaways become vulnerable to being victimized physically and sexually.

Teenage Suicide

In Alberta alone, suicide among teens (ages ten to fourteen) has risen 146% since 1970 and 695% for youths aged fifteen to nineteen since 1955 (Verburg, 1995). These rates are staggering, and according to some they are a reflection of the turmoil and emotional distress many youth are experiencing. Hence, the 'problem' is seen as a barometer of youth in conflict or at-risk. They may then choose to act out in deviant ways to draw attention (e.g., dropping out of school, teenage pregnancy, alcohol and substance abuse, etc.). Suicide rates may also be linked the number of youth at-risk, those who are vulnerable to the negative consequences of school failure, substance abuse, poor job prospects, early sexuality, and the pressures to assume greater responsibility at earlier ages.

Female Delinquency

In 1895 Cesare Lombroso and William Ferrero wrote the first book on female offenders, *The Female Offender*; however, Gomme (1993) observed that this area has received little attention in Canada. One explanation for the apparent lack of official involvement may be sexism within the Canadian juvenile justice system. Nevertheless, self-report studies reveal the gap between male and female involvement is not as great as reflected in the official data (Hagan, 1985). Reitsma-Street (1993) found that there was a marked increase in the number of charges for noncompliance with the administration of youth justice by females. Reitsma-Street also observed that the rate for minor assaults has also increased noticeably during the early 1990s. Official statistics show that the number of violent crime charges rose from 373 in 1987 to 504 in 1988 and to 1091 in 1991. The rate of increase in violent crime charges for females is higher than that of the males (Fisher, 1993). With increasing role convergence and changing social values, it is anticipated that the numbers for young females offenders will increase.

Youth Violence

As noted earlier, official statistics and self-report studies reveal that while property crime may have declined slightly during the early 1990s, violent crime has increased. These trends have also been reflected in two separate self-report studies, one in Ontario (Youth violence, 1993) and the other in Alberta (Smith, Bertrand, Arnold, and Hornick, 1995). These trends, while imposing, need to be weighed against a multitude of factors in an effort to answer the questions "Why is this happening and what can be done about it?" and "Why does it appear to be an international phenomena?"

Young Offenders Act

As already noted throughout this chapter, the YOA has drawn considerable backlash from all fronts (see Box 6.6). It does not appear that the intended principles of balancing special needs with accountability are being implemented. Instead there has been a shift towards greater protection of society and accountability for deviant behaviour. There exists a major rift between the public outcry for better accountability and the realization that changing the act alone can not prevent youths from committing crimes. Reitsma-Street (1993) has gone so far as to suggest a moratorium on YOA changes. Yet, with the June 1995 amendment to Section 3(1)(a) of the act under Bill C-37, provisions have now been included which emphasize crime prevention and multi-disciplinary approaches. This is an element strongly endorsed by the UN minimum standards (see Introduction) for the administration of juvenile justice.

Summary

Canada is a relatively young nation with an even newer legislative act for the handling of young offenders—formally referred to as juvenile delinquents. This new federal act, the Young Offenders Act, which is administered by the provinces and territories, has been described as a **modified justice model** (see Figure 1—Introduction) that attempts to balance the perceived special needs of young people with a measured degree of accountability. However, unlike the birth of our nation, it was observed that the act's implementation has not gone smoothly. In fact after being in effect for only thirteen years, there is considerable pressure to revise the act, especially as it pertains to the age of responsibility, publication of names, and accountability for serious offences such as murder and aggravated assault. The system has been described as being "loosely coupled" and "fragmented philosophically". For example, Ontario, Manitoba, and Alberta have introduced strict discipline programing (e.g., work or boot camps) for those youth who show a flagrant disregard for the law. What appears to have transpired since the act came into being is that our system is filtering humanity out of the process. This theme was expressed by the former (1994) president of the Canadian Criminal Justice Association, Howard Sapers, at the Association's annual meeting.

In the second section of the chapter it was shown how, since the enactment of the act in 1984, the overall youth crime rate has modestly, but steadily, increased. This is especially evident in the area of violent crimes. While the increases can not be assumed to be directly attributable to the YOA, this socially disturbing trend has raised considerable debate about the effectiveness of the act. For example, headings sampled from local newspapers reflect the sentiment which currently prevails: "Youth law weak, say teen", "Youth court a real nightmare for everybody", "No end seen to spiral teenage crime", and "Young criminals taking a holiday". It seems quite clear that the act has borne the brunt of public discontent. But evidence continues to question whether anyone punishing anyone who hurts another is an effective way to demonstrate that hurting is wrong. This a fundamental issue that all societies must confront.

The third major section of the chapter provided an overview of how youth justice is administered by the major actors in the system. Aside from the cases following a similar format, the key issues pertain to how the act is administered differently throughout between the provinces and territories. As suggested these variations, while understandable to an extent, speak further to the general differing cultural, political, and social views about the objectives of the act as well as the varying financial realities within the provinces and territories.

This overview of the Canadian juvenile justice system has painted a somewhat bleak picture. However, it should be noted that with the amendments through Bill C-37 and various provincial initiatives, there are alternative programs that reflect a more humanitarian/welfare model approach to youth justice. For example, in Ontario there are several communities experimenting with dispute resolution programs that involve pre-trial mediation between the offender and the victim. Manitoba is fairly proactive in using youth justice committees, assist in crime prevention and public education initiatives. A variation of the youth justice committee in Alberta is an experimental community committee that has a mandate to deal with non-violent, first offences. The committee can hand out individual sentences ranging from thirty hours of community service to restitution orders up to $1000. In the Yukon a project is modelled after old Native justice principles. Sentencing circle projects involve a young offender being informally tried in the midst of a circle of individuals consisting of a judge, police, lawyers, and community members, which can include members from both the victim and offender (see the family group conference model employed in Australia—Chapter 2). And in Quebec, Corrado and Markwart (1994) note that their system of service delivery, which involves multi-disciplinary assessment and intervention, may represent the most progressive interpretation of the YOA across Canada. They suggest that other provinces in Canada should look more closely at the Quebec system. However, given the social and political tension that currently exists between Quebec and the rest of Canada, many may be slow follow their suggestion.

And while the majority of Canadians' attitudes seem to be oriented towards due process and accountability, there is a growing movement of individuals and organizations such as the Church Council of Justice and Corrections, the Canadian Criminal Justice Association, and individual research efforts whose findings strongly suggest that we may have gone in the wrong direction. We may need to turn back and trade our conventional concepts of (juvenile) justice of guilt and punishment for models based on prevention, education, diagnosis, and treatment. Like predicting the weather in the Prairie provinces, having all the tools and knowledge may not be enough to control the barometric (public perception) changes which seem to rise and fall with the winds of change. The YOA does encompass many of the minimum standards for the administration of juvenile justice as identified by the United Nations; however, putting them into effect has not gone smoothly. For those of us who experience these extremes, managing life under such conditions can be a constant source of dis-ease.

What lies ahead for the administration of juvenile justice in Canada is not clear, but it might serve us well to look beyond our limited frame of reference to examine what other countries are doing to perhaps provide alternative political and etiological insights. The youth are our future and they deserve our fullest attention and support.

References

Agnew, R. (1992). Foundation for a general strain theory of crime and delinquency. *Criminology*, 30: 47-87.

A graphic overview of crime and the administration of criminal justice in Canada. (1996, May). Ottawa: Canadian Centre for Justice Statistics.

Akers, R. (1985). *Deviant behaviour: A social learning approach*. Belmont, CA: Wadsworth.

Bala, N., Hornick, J.P., & Vogl, R. (Eds.). (1991). *Canadian child welfare law*. Toronto: Thompson Educational Pub.

Bindmann, S. (1997, April 18). Age of criminal responsibility to go down. *Calgary Herald*. (Online).

Brownfield, B. & Thompson, K. (1991). Attachment to peers and delinquent behaviour. *Canadian Journal of Criminology*, 33(1): 45-60.

Canadian Criminal Justice Association. Ottawa, ON. *Bulletin,* Nov. 15, 1992.

___. *Bulletin*, Sept. 15, 1994.

___. *Bulletin*, Jan. 16, 1996.

Canadian Police Association year book 1994. Ottawa, ON: Canadian Police Association, Canadian Badge in Uniform Publication. pp. 27-29.

Carrigan, D.O. (1991). *Crime and punishment in Canada* (Ch. 5). Toronto, ON: McClelland & Stewart Inc.

Carrington, P.J., & Moyer, S. (1994). Trends in youth crime and police response, pre- and post-YOA. *Canadian Journal of Criminology*, 36(1): 1-28.

Cohen, L.E., & Felson, M. (1979). Social change and crime rate trends. *American Sociological Review*, 44: 588-605.

Corrado, R.R., Bala, N., Linden, R., & LeBlanc, M. (Eds.). (1992). *Juvenile justice in Canada*. Toronto, ON: Butterworths.

Corrado, R.R., & Markwart, A. (1994). The need to reform the YOA in response to violent young offenders: Confusion, myth or reality? *Canadian Journal of Criminology*, 36(3): 343-378.

Creechan, J. H. (1995). A test of the general theory of crime: Delinquency and school dropouts. In J.H. Creechan & R. A. Silverman (Eds.). *Canadian delinquency*. Scarborough, ON: Prentice Hall Cdn. Inc.

Currie, D. (1986). The transformation of juvenile justice in Canada: A study of Bill C-61. In B. D. MacLean (Ed.). *The political economy of crime*. Scarborough, ON: Prentice-Hall.

Decisions and Dispositions in Youth Court, 1986-87 to 1989-90. *Juristat,* 10(19). Ottawa, ON: Statistics Canada, Canadian Centre for Justice Statistics.

deMause, L. (Ed.). (1988). *The history of childhood*. New York: Peter Bedrick Books.

Dempster, M. (1996, Jan. 19). Young Offenders Act: Crime and punishment. *Calgary Herald*, B4.

de Souza, P. (1995). Youth Court statistics, 1993-94 highlights. *Juristat,* 15(3). Ottawa, ON: Statistics Canada, Canadian Centre for Justice Statistics.

Doherty, G., & de Souza, P. (1995). Recidivism in Youth Court 1993-94. *Juristat,* 15(16). Ottawa, ON: Statistics Canada, Canadian Centre for Justice Statistics.

Doherty, G., & de Souza, P. (1996). Youth Court Statistics 1994-95. *Juristat,* 16(4). Ottawa, ON: Statistics Canada, Canadian Centre for Justice Statistics.

Doob, A.N., & Chan, J.B. (1982). Factors affecting police decisions to take juveniles to court. *Canadian Journal of Criminology*, 24(1): 25-37.

Empey, L.T. (1982). From optimism to despair: New directions in juvenile justice. In C.A. Murray & L.A. Cox Jr.(Eds.). *Beyond probation: Juvenile corrections and the chronic delinquent.* Beverly Hills, CA: Sage.

Fisher, M. (1993, May 19). Rising crime linked to girls. *The Calgary Sun,* 29.

Foot, D.K. (1996). *Boom, bust and echo.* Toronto: Macfarlane Walter & Ross.

Foran, T. (1995). Youth custody and probation in Canada, 1993-94. *Juristat,* 5(7). Ottawa, ON: Statistics Canada, Canadian Centre for Justice Statistics.

Gibbs, W.W. (1995, March). Seeking the criminal element. *Scientific America,* pp. 100-107.

Gomme, I. (1993). *The shadow line: Deviance and crime in Canada.* Toronto, ON: Harcourt Brace Jovanovich. Ch. 9.

Gordon, D. (1990). *The justice juggernaut: Fighting street crime, controlling citizens.* New Brunswick, NJ: Rutgers University Press.

Gordon, R.M. (1995). Street gangs in Vancouver. In J.H. Creechan & R.A. Silverman (Eds.). *Canadian delinquency.* Scarborough, ON: Prentice-Hall.

Griffiths, C., & Hatch, A. (1994). The Canadian youth justice system. In C. Griffiths & S. Verdun-Jones (Eds.). *Canadian criminal justice* (2nd ed.). Toronto, ON: Harcourt Brace. pp. 595-631.

Griffiths, C., & Verdun-Jones, S. (1994). *Canadian criminal justice* (2nd ed.). Toronto, ON: Harcourt Brace.

Hackler, J. (1996). Anglophone juvenile justice. In J. Winterdyk (Ed). *Issues and perspectives on young offenders in Canada.* Toronto: Harcourt Brace. (Ch. 12).

Hagan, J. (1983). *Victims before the law.* Toronto, ON: Butterworths.

Hagan, J. (1985). *Crime, criminal behaviour, and its control.* NY: McGraw-Hill.

Hagan, J. (1995). Good people, dirty system: The Young Offenders Act and organizational failure. In N. Larsen (Ed.). *The Canadian criminal justice system.* Toronto, ON: Canadian Scholars' Press Inc. pp. 389-418.

Hagan, J., Alwin, D., & Hewitt, J. (1979). Ceremonial justice: Crime and punishment in a loosely coupled society. *Social Forces,* 58: 506-527.

Hagan, J., Simpson, J., & Gillis, A.R. (1987). Class in the household: A power-control theory of gender and delinquency. *American J. of Sociology,* 92: 788-816.

Hagan, J. Simpson, J., & Gillis, A.R. (1979). The sexual stratification of social control: A gender based perspective on crime and delinquency. *British Journal of Criminology,* 30: 25-38.

Hendrick, D. (1991). Processing time in Youth Court, 1986-87 to 1989-90. *Juristat,* 11(4). Ottawa, ON: Statistics Canada, Canadian Centre for Justice Statistics.

Hendrick, D. & Lachance, M. (1991). A profile of the young offender. *Forum on Corrections Research,* 3(3): 17-21.

Horner, B. (M.P. Chairman). (1993, Feb.). *Crime prevention in Canada: Towards a national strategy, 12th report of the standing committee on justice and solicitor general.* Ottawa, ON: Solicitor General of Canada.

Hundley, J.D., Scapinello, K.F., & Stasiak, G.A. (1992). *Thirteen to thirty: A follow-up study of young training school boys.* Ottawa, ON: Corrections Branch, Solicitor General of Canada.

Hung, K., & Bowles, S. (1995). Public perception of Crime. *Juristat*, 15(1). Ottawa, ON: Statistics Canada, Canadian Centre for Justice Statistics.

International data. (1995, March-April). *CJ International*, 11(2): 17.

Kennedy, L. & Baron, S.W. (1993). Routine activities and a subculture of violence: A study of violence on the street. *J. of Research in Crime and Delinquency*, 30(1): 88-112.

Kopyto, H., & Condina, A.M. (1986). Young Offenders Act means more frequent custody terms. *Lawyers Weekly*, 6: 8.

Larsen, N. (Ed.). (1995). *The Canadian criminal justice system: An issues approach to the administration of justice.* Toronto, ON: Canadian Scholars' Press.

Leschield, A.W. & Jaffe, P.G. (1995). Dispositions as indicators of conflicting social purposes under the JDA and YOA. In N. Larsen (Ed.). *The Canadian Criminal Justice System.* Toronto, ON: Canadian Scholars' Press.

Leesti, T. (1994). Youth custody in Canada, 1992-93. *Juristat*, 14(11). Ottawa, ON: Statistics Canada, Canadian Centre for Justice Statistics.

Lundman, R.J. (1984). *Prevention and control of juvenile delinquency.* New York: Oxford University Press.

Lundman, R.J. (1994). *Prevention and control of juvenile delinquency* (2nd ed.). Oxford University Press.

MacLaurin, B. (1996). Runaway and homeless youth in Canada. In J. Winterdyk (Ed.). *Issues and perspectives on young offenders in Canada.* Toronto: Harcourt-Brace.

Markwart, A., & Corrado, R. (1995). A response to Carrington. *Canadian Journal of Criminology*, 37(1): 74-87.

Martinson, R. (1974). What works?—Questions and answers about prison reform. *The Public Interest*, 35: 22-54.

Matza, D. (1964). *Delinquency and drift.* New York: Wiley.

McDonald, L. (1969, Nov.). Crime and punishment in Canada: A statistical test of the 'conventional wisdom'. *Canadian Review of Sociology and Anthropology*, VI: 212-36.

McDonald, R.J. (1994). Missing children. In *Canadian social trends* (Vol. 2). Toronto, ON: Thompson Educational Pub. pp. 213-216 .

Milner, T. (1995). Juvenile legislation. In J.H. Creechan & R.A. Silverman. (Eds.). *Canadian delinquency.* Scarborough, ON: Prentice-Hall Canada.

Moyer, S. (1992). Recidivism in Youth Courts, 1990-91. *Juristat*, 12(2). Ottawa, ON: Statistics Canada, Canadian Centre for Justice Statistics.

Ogrodnik, L. (1994). Canadian crime statistics, 1993. *Juristat*, 14(14). Ottawa, ON: Statistics Canada, Canadian Centre for Justice Statistics.

Prowse, C.E. (1994). *Vietnamese gangs.* Calgary, AB: Calgary Police Services.

Reitsma-Street, M. (1993). Canadian youth court changes and dispositions for females before and after implementation of the Young Offenders Act. *Canadian Journal of Criminology*, 35(4): 437-458.

Romig, D.A., Cleland, C.C., & Romig, L.J. (1989). *Juvenile delinquency: Visionary approaches.* Columbus, OH: Merrill Pub.

Smandych, R., Dobbs, G., & Esau, A. (Eds.). *Dimensions of childhood.* Winnipeg, Man.: Legal Research Institute of the University of Manitoba.

Smith, R.B., Bertrand, L.D., Arnold, B.L. & Hornick, J.P. (1995, March). *A study of the level and nature of youth crime and violence in Calgary.* Report prepared for the Calgary Police Service by the Canadian Research Institute for Law and the Family. University of Calgary. Calgary, Alberta.

Solicitor General of Canada. (1981, Feb. 16). *"News Release. Young Offenders Bill Tabled in House of Commons."* Ottawa, ON: Solicitor General of Canada.

Stewart, M. (1995, May 16). Weapons in schools are a major concern for police. *Calgary Herald.* B1.

Sutherland, N. (1976). *Children in English-Canadian society: Framing the twentieth century consensus.* Toronto, ON: University of Toronto Press.

Trojanowicz, R. (1978). *Juvenile delinquency: Concepts and control.* Englewood Cliffs, NJ: Prentice-Hall.

United Nations (1986). *United Nations standard minimum rules for the administration of juvenile justice.* N.Y.: Dept. of Information.

Verburg, P. (1995, May 1). Rebels without consciences. *Alberta Report,* 30-36.

Walker, R. (1996, Dec. 13). Drop in health concerns seen. *Calgary Herald,* A9.

West, G. (1984). *Young offenders and the state: A Canadian perspective.* Toronto, ON: Butterworths.

Wheeler, S. (1967). Criminal statistics: A reformulation of the problem. *Journal of Criminal Law, Criminology and Police Science,* 58: 317-24.

Wilson, J.Q. (1975). *Thinking about crime.* NY: Vintage Books.

Winterdyk, J. (1996, April/May). The looking glass: Canadian Centre for Justice Statistics. *Law Now,* 14-18.

Winterdyk, J. (forthcoming). *Introduction to Canadian criminology.* Whitby, ON: McGraw-Hill.

Young, G. (1994). Trends in justice spending, 1988-89 to 1992-93. *Juristat,* 14(16). Ottawa, ON: Statistics Canada, Canadian centre for Justice Statistics.

Youth justice: A better direction for our country. (1994, Fall). Ottawa, ON: The Church Council of Justice and Corrections.

Youth violence is on the rise. (1993, March 2). *Calgary Herald,* A8.

chapter 7

Comparative Juvenile Justice: An Overview of Italy

Uberto Gatti
Alfredo Verde
Institute of Criminology and Forensic Psychiatry
University of Genova

Facts on Italy

Area: 301,303 sq. km. **Population**: 57,910,000 in 1995. The capital is Rome (pop. 2.7 million). Other main cities include Milan, Naples, Turin, Genoa, Palermo, Venice, Florence, and Bologna. Population density is 192 per sq. km. **Economy**: Throughout Italy's 130-year history, its various regions have undergone widely differing patterns of development. In very approximate terms, the north of the country is economically and industrially well developed, while the south lags far behind, having fewer industries and a higher rate of unemployment. The post-war period in Italy witnessed a considerable economic boom (60% employed in service industry and 32% in industry), which prompted copious migration from the south to the north and from the rural areas to the cities (71% of the pop.). In recent years the new phenomenon of immigration from non-E.E.C. countries has appeared in Italy, giving rise to a wide range of problems which our society was unprepared to tackle. **Government**: parliamentary republic, with a House of Deputies and a Senate, divided in twenty regions, with a limited autonomy from the central government. A wide constitutional and political reformation is taking place, but it is early to say what will be its results. Main political parties: Forza Italia, Alleanza Nazionale (Polo delle libertà), Partito Democratico della Sinistra and allies (Alleanza dell'Ulivo), Lega Nord, Rifondazione Comunista.

> They were in error who believed that the true measure of crimes is to be found in the intention of the person who commits them.
>
> (Becarria, 1963: 65)

The Birth of the Juvenile Justice System in Italy

Juvenile courts in Italy, unlike many of their Western counterparts, were not established until relatively recently, in 1934. The courts' jurisdiction covers all minors and is divided into three sectors: penal, civil, and the particular sector of "administrative" or rehabilitative jurisdiction.

The juvenile court is made up of four individuals who preside over the cases that come before the court. They include an appeals court judge who presides over the court proceedings, while a court magistrate and two citizens, one man and one woman, act as assistants and consultants in the case. The citizens are chosen from among exponents in the fields of biology, psychiatry, criminal anthropology, education, and psychology. They must have distinguished themselves in community service and be at least thirty years of age (art. 2, R.D. n° 1404/1934).

In accordance with Article 97 of the Italian penal code it states that a person who has not reached the age of fourteen years at the moment when he or she commits a crime must not be punished.[1] Article 98, Sub-section 1 of the penal code states, in turn, that a person who has reached the age of fourteen but not eighteen years at the time of committing a crime and is "capable of understanding and willing" (capace di intendere e di volere—mens rea) must be punished, but the punishment may be reduced. At the age of majority, eighteen years, the person becomes fully responsible for his or her crimes.

Between the ages of fourteen and eighteen the ability to understand and to form mental intent must be clearly ascertained in each case by the sitting judge. Unlike in the adult system, they are not bound by specific technical methods of investigation. The system recognizes that the cognitive inability of a juvenile to understand and to form intent is not necessarily the same as that of an adult. In this respect the courts have established the concept of "immaturity," a condition of inadequate physical, psychological, or even social development.

In practice these guidelines have been interpreted in very different ways, to the extent that some juvenile courts (especially in the north of Italy) have, in the past, frequently acquitted minors on the grounds of immaturity, while others have applied this provision very sparingly. At the present time, acquittal on the grounds of immaturity appears to find limited application. The magistrates prefer to take advantage of the wide range of solutions made available by the new penal procedure for minors.

---

[1]   Minors under fourteen years and minors between fourteen and eighteen years who are not considered "capable of understanding and willing," are usually transferred by the judge to the general welfare system (local authority). There are exceptions such as when the minor is judged as "socially dangerous." They can then be maintained inside the penal system by the adoption of a "secretary measure" of "judicial reformatory," or "control in the community."

Since minors under the age of fourteen are not responsible, they are automatically acquitted. Minors between the ages of fourteen and eighteen may be given a custodial sentence, which is usually reduced to two-thirds of the sentence that would be imposed on an adult offender for the same crime. Usually, however, once having been deemed responsible, they will be offered the benefit of certain leniency measures. The later approach is very representative of the **welfare model** described in Figure 1 in the Introduction.

The Evolution of the Juvenile Justice System in Italy

After the World War II, the first substantial modification of the system was introduced by legislation enacted in 1956. This was oriented towards a rehabilitative approach, and in 1962 a whole range of assistance services was established. These included a social service for minors, which was to work in close coordination with the Juvenile Court and whose task was to provide technical support in the penal field, as well as carrying out a range of interventions to help and support minors in the civil and "administrative" fields.

Before 1956, magistrates in the juvenile courts had mainly made use of penal measures (e.g., crime control and the justice model), though these were tempered with rehabilitative elements. This was in keeping with the thinking of the day, which attributed an important correctional function to the sentence imposed. After 1956, however, juvenile delinquency was tackled from a rehabilitative standpoint by means of a dialectic liaison between the courts and the social services. Thus, the 1956 model combined penal intervention and assistance, punishment, and welfare. The program came under the auspices of the juvenile courts and the centralized social services department of the justice ministry. However, in practice the rehabilitative institutions (which housed minors defined as "wayward in behaviour and character" under the terms of the so-called "administrative" jurisdiction) did not differ greatly in organization or atmosphere from penal detention centres (Senzani, 1970).

According to Betti and Pavarini (1985), the overall effect of this set of provisions was to create a correctional continuum inspired by the need for social control, whether or not the minor had committed any crime. Hence the model was essentially a blend of the crime control and justice model, as described in Figure 1 (see Introduction).

Indeed, the years following 1956 saw a robust expansion in the administrative sector, which became the most commonly used means of dealing with juvenile problems. In spite of the face-lift they had been given by the new rehabilitative ideology, institutions for the rehabilitation of minors remained starkly backward—without trained staff and housed in ancient buildings which were uncomfortable and often lacked adequate sanitation. For example, a number of the institutions included old monasteries, convents, and outdated boarding-schools.

The backwardness of these structures, which distinguished Italy from neighbouring countries such as France, contributed to an upsurge of scathing criticism of the system in the 1960s. The problems related to juvenile justice, which until then had been the exclusive province of specialists, for the first time came in for scrutiny and discussion by protest movements, the mass media, and the general public, as did the psychiatric institutions of the day. In this climate of protest, the authorities went some way to opening up rehabilitative institutions to the outside world. This was nevertheless accompanied by an increased use of penal structures.

In summary, the birth of juvenile justice in Italy did not follow a similar path to that of many Western countries. In fact its genesis was in response to academic, public, and social criticism. For a country which has a rich history in criminological thought and justice reform (e.g., for formulation of a Civil Code, Becarria (1963), and Lombroso (see Martin, Mutchnick, and Austin (1990)), this may seem out of character. However, the situation speaks to the general diversity of juvenile justice around the world and the merits in examining such an issue.

Juvenile Justice after the Decentralization and Reform of the Welfare System

In 1977 a presidential decree (D.P.R. n°616, 24/7/1977) on administrative decentralization brought about a sweeping transformation in the practical workings of the juvenile justice system. The legislation transferred executive authority over decisions taken in the civil and administrative fields from the social services department of the justice ministry to the social services departments of local authorities. Though still imposed by the juvenile courts, rehabilitative measures now took on a completely different meaning. Local authorities, especially in the large cities of northern Italy, fostered the development of alternative social policies, inserting minors from the juvenile justice in the general social welfare processing system for minors and their families. The model deeply transformed justice procedures as there was a shift towards community intervention and small residential structures (such as group homes). This reform, however, gave rise to numerous conflicts between magistrates in the juvenile courts and local authority administrators. In many cases the magistrates demanded greater control over young deviants, including the use of closed, more coercive institutions (Ricciotti, 1982). This was juxtaposed to the local authorities which stressed the roles of assistance and rehabilitation in their intervention. This latter approach was aimed at improving compliance and avoiding the stigmatization and exclusion associated with closed institutions. This was done by placing problem juveniles in non-specialist programs designed for all minors.

A particular area of conflict arose regarding the measures to be imposed on problem juveniles. The new legislation had created the conditions for possible clashes between resources and decisions. Indeed, under the provisions of D.P.R. n°616/1977, the measures to be imposed on deviant minors were to be decided by the juvenile courts. However, the provisions were to be implemented by the local authorities. This meant that the local authorities were, in effect, able to organize alternative forms of intervention that would remove minors from the penal-administrative system and, thus, effect a progressive separation between the justice and welfare systems. This separation, which stemmed from the assignment of jurisdiction to two different bodies (justice ministry and local authorities), led to clashes between magistrates of the juvenile courts and local authority social service departments (Gatti and Verde, 1988). The implementation of the measures imposed by the courts depended on the structures that the local authorities had provided, and magistrates were considerably hampered in their work in that they could only request intervention that was actually available.

Before that time the problem had been less acutely felt, as magistrates and rehabilitation structures both belonged to the same environment (that of the justice ministry). Under this model the values and ideologies were less divergent.

In reply to the criticism levelled at them by the magistrates, the local authorities cited their constitutionally recognized right to autonomy in their intervention. This claim was later given a solid juridical basis by an important pronouncement of the Constitutional Court (n°174/1981). The amendment upheld the local authorities' right to make decisions regarding the means of handling juvenile-related problems. Subsequently, as the new system came to be accepted, conflict diminished even though a few penal social workers and magistrates held on to their familiarity with the justice model and subsequently continued to call for more stringent laws and institutions.

The New Juvenile Penal Procedure

The approval of D.P.R. n°448/1988, which brought in a new juvenile penal procedure, effected further important changes within the broader context of penal procedure code reform. In the shift from an inquisitorial to an accusatory model, a profound change was brought about in the judicial context and penal proceedings concerning juveniles, and it is within this context that the current system is set.

The process is divided into three phases. The first of these, the so-called preliminary investigation, conducted by the Public Prosecutor through the Criminal Investigation Department of the police (under the supervision of the magistrate for preliminary investigations) is not really a judicial phase at all. A preliminary hearing then follows, during which the judge assesses the investigations carried out and, after hearing the arguments put forward by the Public Prosecutor and the defending attorney, decides whether to dismiss the case or order a trial. The third phase concerns the trial itself, during which the evidence is scrutinized and debated.

Within this general context, the norms governing juvenile penal procedure have undergone a series of adjustments in order to apply the new principles to minors in such a way as to protect the minors themselves and to endow the trial with a rehabilitative character while still guaranteeing the individual's rights such as the presumption of innocence and right to legal assistance. In this framework plea-bargaining is not an option for minors, while other provisions are:

- An "abbreviated" trial. This can occur when the accused asks for a preliminary hearing to be regarded as definitive. The accused is then entitled to a one-third reduction in their sentence.
- An "immediate" trial has no preliminary hearing as such. The case goes directly to trial.
- An "accelerated" trial is conducted when the minor has been arrested *in flagrante* or else confesses. For minors a personality assessment must be carried out.

Under the terms of D.P.R. n°449/1988, the preliminary investigation is headed by a magistrate of the Juvenile Court, while the preliminary hearing is carried out by one professional magistrate and two honourary magistrates (one man and one woman). The trial itself takes place in the juvenile court in its ordinary composition. The case is prosecuted by the public prosecutor attached to the juvenile court (see Figure 7.1)

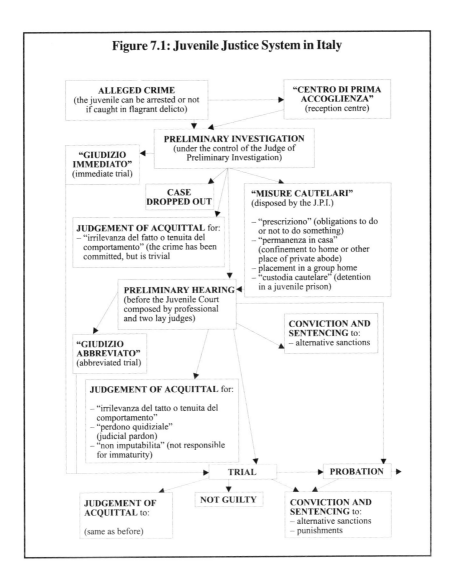

Figure 7.1: Juvenile Justice System in Italy

The magistrate in charge of preliminary investigations is responsible for ensuring that the investigations are carried out in a proper and timely fashion, as well as safeguarding the freedom of the person under investigation. Within the sphere of the preliminary hearing, the magistrate can decide to commit the minor for trial, find "no grounds for prosecution", place the youth on probation, or an alternative sanctions to detention may be applied.

During the trial, which is not usually public, the accused is questioned directly by the presiding magistrate; in order to avoid any trauma, the minor is not cross-examined. A verdict is then reached.

Sentencing Options

We shall now examine the provisions relating to the arrest and detention of minors. A minor can be arrested *in flagrante* if caught in the act of committing a crime eligible for preventive detention (art. 16 sub-section 1 D.P.R. n°448/ 1988). In any case, a minor may be detained if suspected of having committed a non-culpable offence. Such an offence carries a prison sentence of a minimum of two years and a maximum of nine years (art. 17 D.P.R. n°448/1988). In such cases, the minor is housed in a special reception centre (*Centro di prima accoglienza*)—small institutions different from prisons introduced by D.P.R. 448/1988—pending the hearing for the validation of arrest. In the remaining cases of flagrancy (e.g., non-culpable offences carrying a prison sentence of not less than a maximum of five years), the bailiffs or law-enforcement officers may order the minor to be confined to the family home. If the parents are absent or deemed to be unreliable, the Public Prosecutor may order the minor to be taken to a reception centre or to a public or private group home (art. 18bis D.P.R. n°448/1988).

Even though section D.P.R. n°448/1988 sought to limit the use of preventive detention for minors as far as possible, the option for minors has been subsequently extended under section D.P.R. n° 12/1991. The original ruling was deemed not to safeguard the community sufficiently. The measure can now be applied in cases of non-culpable crimes punishable by imprisonment for life or for no less than a maximum of nine years.

Apart from the aforementioned cases, preventive detention may be invoked in cases of aggravated theft, robbery, rape, extortion, weapons or drug-related offences. Detention can only be ordered if there is grave risk of subversion of evidence, the accused attempts to escape, or the nature of the crime is considered to represent a serious risk to society or the individual's safety.

The magistrate can, therefore, impose preventive measures (*misure cautelari*), but only in the case of an offence punishable by imprisonment for life or for a period of no less than a maximum of five years. Such measures (art. 19-22 D.P.R. n°448/1988) are ordered hierarchically within what has been defined as a "correctional continuum" (Gatti and Verde, 1991). The offender can pass from one level to another in the event of non-compliance (the harshest measure being preventive detention in prison for a maximum period of one month). These measures are constituted by *prescrizioni* that involve ordering the minor to carry out study or work activities, "confinement to home or other place of private abode," placement in a group home, and the aforementioned preventive detention.

Concerning the decisions that the court can impose, the penal code states that the orders and sentences applicable to adults may also be applied to minors (e.g., suspended sentence, non-registration of the conviction in criminal records, rehabilitation, alternative sanctions) with considerable latitude and reductions, as well as the particularities specifically designed for minors. These latter are worth examining in detail:

- Judicial pardon: this is a form of depenalization applicable only once. The magistrate deems that a sentence may be imposed which restricts personal liberty for a period of no more than two years. A pardon may be applied when, having assessed the gravity of the offence and the individual's potential for delinquency, the magistrate presumes that the minor will not commit any further offences (art. 169 penal code and art.19 R.D. n°1404/1934). The measure remains on the minor's criminal record until he or she reaches the age of twenty-one years.
- Dismissal on the grounds of inability to understand and to form intent (mens rea) (*incapacità di intendere e di volere*). As mentioned above, this depends on the ascertainment of a condition of immaturity.
- Dismissal on the grounds of the insignificance of the offence (*irrilevanza del fatto*): art. 27 of D.P.R. 448/1988 states that, "if the offence is petty and the behaviour out-of-character, and when to proceed with the case would jeopardise the minor's education," the public prosecutor may ask the magistrate to dismiss the case on the grounds of insignificance of the offence.
- Suspension of the trial and imposition of probation (*sospensione del processo e messa alla prova*): operated by the social services department of the justice ministry, this measure can be adopted either at the

preliminary hearing or during the course of the trial. The probationary period may be as long as three years for a particularly serious crime. The magistrate may also impose *prescrizioni* aimed at making amends for the consequences of the offence and promoting reconciliation with the victim. This latter provision marks a new tentative orientation on the part of the Italian juvenile justice system. It represents a move towards a restorative model of justice that is similar to those countries employing a modified **welfare model**. If the period of probation is successfully completed, the offence is written off and the verdict is not registered in the juvenile criminal records. If, on the other hand, the outcome is negative, and at the same time the offender's behaviour and character development are assessed negatively, the minor is sentenced.

• Custodial sentence: this is usually reduced by one-third and is served in special prisons for minors (*prigioni-scuola*). At any stage of the sentence, the minor may be conditionally released, regardless of the established duration of the sentence.

For young offenders, including those under the age of fourteen years, provision is made for the application of a special security measure (*misura di sicurezza*) involving confinement to a judicial reformatory (*riformatorio giudiziario*). Such measures are applied when the individual is regarded as "socially dangerous". That is, when the youth is deemed likely to commit further crimes, even if he or she has been judged to be non-responsible. The provisions are imposed after the custodial sentence has been served, or, in the case of diminished responsibility, as an alternative to punishment. The new code provides that control in the community (*libertà vigilata*) be applied in conformity with articles 20 and 21, (which refer to *prescrizioni* and confinement to home) while placement in a reformatory is to be effected "in conformity with article 22", which refers to *prescrizioni* and placement in a group home and only in cases concerning crimes punishable by imprisonment for more than twelve years as a maximum term (art. 36, sub-sections 1 and 2). The reformatory is therefore replaced de facto by the group home.

The administrative jurisdiction of the juvenile court tended to be legalistic in orientation and did not readily embrace the notion that young offenders as minors be deemed to be "wayward in behaviour or character"—beyond social control (*irregolarità della condotta o del carattere*) (art. 25 R.D. n°1404/1934, as modified by law n°888/1956). The measures applicable in such cases have progressively fallen into disuse since the new code for penal procedure came into effect and are now rarely applied.

The civil jurisdiction of the juvenile court concerns the various forms of supportive intervention (e.g., adoption, limitation or withdrawal of parental authority, and fostering) invoked in cases of absence of the family, mistreatment, or moral or material abandonment of the minor.

Moreover, with a view to discouraging the exploitation of minors by criminal organizations or by adults in general, the law n°203/1991 has recently reformulated articles 111 and 112 of the penal code. The articles made provisions for increasing punishment for anyone who induces a not responsible or unpunishable person to commit a crime.

Having presented an overview of the juvenile justice administrative scheme, let us now take a look at some of the trends and patterns of youth crime in Italy.

Youth Crime and Its Characteristics

Analysis of the data on juvenile delinquency in Italy is hindered by many problems and limitations. While some of the obstacles are similar to those expressed by other countries covered in this collection, several are unique to the Italian context. First of all, officially based statistical analyses of delinquency often reflect the action of social control agencies rather than the real numbers and features of delinquent behaviour. Secondly, the system for gathering crime figures in Italy works rather poorly, being often unreliable and invariably out of date as reflected in the data presented in the tables below. Furthermore, only recently has Italy begun to employ alternative methods such as self-report studies and victimization surveys (Gatti et al., 1991a; 1991b; 1994). In spite of these drawbacks, it is possible to glean useful information from the statistical analyses of the data available.

The figures for the total number of minors reported to the public prosecutor (see Table 7.1) from 1974 to 1993 are relatively stable between 1974 and 1978, but there is a sharp fall from 1979 onwards. Subsequently, the rates remain steady until 1987, when they again begin to soar. The drop in the number of minors charged after 1979 may be seen in relation to the enactment of D.P.R. n°616/1977. Indeed, the fact that many responsibilities were shifted to the local authorities radically transformed the ideology and the procedures of preventive and rehabilitative intervention. This meant that in practice a great many problem cases were handled by the local authority social services

Table 7.1: Number of Minors under 18 Reported to the Public Prosecutor
(1974-1993, Italy). (*)

Year	Reported to public prosecutor	Total population under 18	Ratio per 100.000	Index (1974=100)
1974	24687	15890882	155	100
1975	23954	15930388	150	97
1976	22352	15933345	140	91
1977	23301	15854629	147	94
1978	25570	15702810	163	104
1979	19034	15503232	123	77
1980	20676	15262215	135	84
1981	17861	15009205	119	72
1982	19350	14937978	130	78
1983	21182	14315804	148	86
1984	19316	13970283	138	78
1985	20126	13639135	148	82
1986	19728	13291279	148	80
1987	21264	12921072	165	86
1988	24523	12597039	195	99
1989	29114	12253159	238	118
1990	39734	11959169	332	161
1991	44977	11481934	391	182
1992	44788	11145532	402	181
1993	43375	10917711 **	406	176

* Data concerning the period 1974-1985 only refer to the total number of minors
   reported to the public prosecutor for whom a criminal trial was initiated.
** Estimated data.

Source: ISTAT (Istituto Nazionale di Statistica)

departments instead of the penal system. It may also be speculated that this
new perspective might have influenced all the other agencies of social control,
thus eliciting literally a new style of intervention, which saw a greater use of
welfare instruments and a consequent reduction in penal proceedings.

After 1988, this new approach ran into trouble. As mentioned above, the
following years saw a striking rise in the number of minors charged. By 1991
the number charged had more than doubles since the 1987 figure. The trend
remained relatively stable in 1992 and 1993. A number of hypotheses can be
put forward in order to explain such a phenomenon. In the first place, the crisis
of the welfare state, which is linked to the more general economic depression,
undermined the quality and functioning of social services. The economic

recession resulted in financial cut-backs, a decline in motivation, enthusiasm, and operational capacity, and a shrinkage in personnel due to policies of non-replacement. From the point of view of criminal phenomena, moreover, we have witnessed an undeniable increase in violent crime in Italy on the part of both adults and minors (see below). This increase is often linked to organised crime, though there has also been a rise in offences connected with the recent phenomenon of non-EC immigration and with the increased presence of gypsies (Viggiani and Tressanti, 1992). The rise in the number of minors charged may also be related to the changes brought about by the new juvenile penal procedure (D.P.R. n°448/1988), which came into effect at the end of 1989. As has already been observed, the new norms modernized and rationalized the system by relegitimizing a whole range of correctionally-oriented penal interventions that had previously been abandoned in favour of social intervention after the introduction of D.P.R. n°616/1977 (Gatti and Verde, 1991).

Analysis of the figures regarding the various categories of offence (see Table 7.2) reveals that the increase in the total number of minors charged is paralleled by an increase in each of the categories considered, including crimes against persons and against property (while the number of thefts reached a peak in 1991 and has since remained rather stable, the number of robberies is continuing to grow). The absolute number of rapes has also been growing. The numbers went from ninety-eight in 1987 to 220 in 1993. Similarly, except for 1993, drug-related offences among minors also rose—both in absolute terms and as a proportion of the total. On the whole this type of offence remains, nevertheless, rather marginal, representing only 6.08% of the total number of minors reported in 1992 and 4.95% in 1993. On a social level, the drug problem in Italy increases strikingly in the young adult age group, though users often admit to having started taking drugs during adolescence (Faccioli, 1990; Pazé, 1991).

The increase and plateau in juvenile crime figures must, therefore, be regarded as a global phenomenon that is not linked to specific types of offence. That the rise in crimes recorded corresponds, at least partially, to a real rise in crimes committed can be deduced on the basis of the concomitant variation in the figures for crimes with a high dark figure (i.e., unreported and/or unrecorded crimes), such as offences against property, and in those for crimes with a very low dark figure, such as murder.

Table 7.3 shows a peculiar aspect of the Italian juvenile justice system, that is, the low percentage of convictions. Only about 15-20% of the cases are tried. Moreover, if we consider the number of cases dismissed in the pre-trial

Table 7.2: Number of Minors under 18 Reported to the Public Prosecutor, by Type of Offence and Age (1986—1993).

Type of offence	Year											
	1986				1987				1988			
	<14	>14	Total	%	<14	>14	Total	%	<14	>14	Total	%
AGAINST THE PERSON	320	2744	3064	15.53	315	2910	3225	15.17	425	3790	4215	17.19
of which:												
– Homicide	3	15	18	0.09	3	36	39	0.18	0	17	17	0.07
– Attempted homicide	3	49	52	0.26	1	58	59	0.20	4	67	71	0.29
– Bodily harm	129	846	975	4.94	159	994	1153	5.42	215	1319	1534	6.26
AGAINST PROPERTY	2201	11519	13720	69.55	2260	11868	14128	66.44	2763	12918	15681	63.94
of which												
– Theft	1813	8713	10526	53.36	1843	8717	10560	49.66	2355	9714	12069	49.22
– Robbery	47	700	747	3.79	60	905	965	4.54	64	802	866	3.53
AGAINST THE FAMILY AND PUBLIC MORALS	39	240	279	1.41	31	281	312	1.47	44	359	403	1.64
of which:												
– Rape	21	108	201	1.02	19	79	98	0.46	13	107	120	0.49

Type of offence	Year											
	1989				1990				1991			
	<14	>14	Total	%	<14	>14	Total	%	<14	>14	Total	%
AGAINST THE ECONOMY AND THE PUBLIC INTEREST	89	1062	1151	5.83	80	1642	1722	8.10	97	2314	2411	9.83
– of which: Drug offences	7	708	715	3.62	9	1279	1288	6.06	29	1814	1843	7.52
OTHER OFFENCES	79	1435	1514	7.67	75	1802	1877	8.83	120	3533	3653	14.89
TOTAL	2728	17000	19728	100.00	2759	18505	21264	100.00	3420	21103	24523	100.00
AGAINST THE PERSON	474	4113	4587	15.76	665	5427	6092	15.33	756	6634	7390	16.43
– of which: Homicide	1	33	34	0.12	1	40	41	0.10	2	54	56	0.12
– Attempted homicide	0	63	63	0.22	2	58	60	0.15	0	73	73	0.16
– Bodily harm	234	1421	1655	5.68	302	1806	2108	5.31	337	2018	2355	5.24

	1989				1990				1991			
	<14	>14	Total	%	<14	>14	Total	%	<14	>14	Total	%
AGAINST PROPERTY	4574	14440	19014	65.31	7269	17190	24459	61.56	8015	21778	29793	66.24
of which:												
– Theft	4060	10801	14861	51.04	6495	14992	21487	54.08	7229	19895	22124	49.19
– Robbery	72	871	943	3.24	127	1112	1239	3.12	133	1253	1386	3.08
AGAINST THE FAMILY AND PUBLIC MORALS	48	230	278	0.95	51	372	423	1.06	38	361	399	0.89
of which:												
– Rape	19	92	111	0.38	16	91	107	0.27	8	100	108	0.24
AGAINST THE ECONOMY AND THE PUBLIC INTEREST	156	2729	2885	9.91	141	2766	2907	7.32	143	3459	3602	8.01
of which:												
– Drug offences	43	2040	2083	7.15	34	2079	2113	5.32	38	2695	2733	6.08
OTHER OFFENCES	146	2156	2302	7.91	222	2631	2853	7.18	243	3550	3793	8.43
TOTAL	5398	23716	29114	100.00	8348	31386	39734	100.00	9195	35782	44977	100.00

Type of offence	Year							
	1992				1993			
	<14	>14	Total	%	<14	>14	Total	%
AGAINST THE PERSON	770	7059	7819	17.4	779	7214	7993	18.4
of which								
– Homicide	1	49	50	.11	1	47	48	.11
– Attempted homicide		8	92	100	.22	0	68	.16
– Bodily harm	339	2258	2597	5.8	342	2391	2733	6.3
AGAINST PROPERTY of which:	7990	21293	29283	65.4	7834	20034	27868	64.2
– Theft	6994	13311	20305	45.3	6937	12358	19295	44.5
– Robbery	122	1314	1436	3.2	140	1282	1422	3.3
AGAINST THE FAMILY AND PUBLIC MORALS of which:	70	514	584	1.3	71	525	596	1.4
– Rape	25	149	174	.39	45	175	220	.5

	1992				1993			
	<14	>14	Total	%	<14	>14	Total	%
AGAINST THE ECONOMY AND THE PUBLIC INTEREST	212	3895	4107	9.2	168	3332	3500	8.0
of which: – Drug offences	61	2967	3028	6.7	49	2099	2148	4.9
OTHER OFFENCES	179	2816	2995	6.7	184	3234	3418	7.9
TOTAL	9211	35577	44788	100	9036	34339	43375	100

Source: ISTAT

phases, we can see that during the 1980s and early 1990s the number of minors convicted has steadily decreased. The reasons for this phenomenon are not completely clear but are probably linked to the increased possibility of dismissing cases before trial, vis-à-vis the 1988 juvenile penal code changes which, as mentioned, introduced many new ways to drop the case before trial.

A more detailed examination of the data relating to the measures imposed reveals that the most common reason for dismissal is "judicial pardon", a measure applied in 40-50% of cases at the beginning of the decade and in 30-40% of cases by the end of the 1980s.

Reception Centres: Pre-conviction

Some important features of the Italian justice system can also be deduced from the data on placements in juvenile penal institutions (see Table 7.4) and in reception centres (Table 7.5). In interpreting the overall figure for juvenile imprisonment, data regarding both of these institutions must be taken into account since reception centres play an important role as filters.

In 1991 about one-third of the minors taken into reception centres subsequently proceeded to preventive detention (De Leo, Patrizi, Donato, and Scali, 1993). The two tables show that the number of minors entering juvenile penitentiaries fell markedly at the end of the 1980s and reached an all-time low in 1990, the year after the new procedural norms came into effect. These norms markedly reduced the option of imposing preventive detention. The following year, however, as mentioned above, these norms were modified to permit a broader use of such measures; subsequently, the rise in the number of admissions to the penitentiary circuit, especially in reception centres. Drug users constituted the largest proportion of detainees. In 1990 they accounted for 25.4% of the juvenile penal population while in 1991 their proportion dropped to 19.4% and 16.8% for 1992 (ISTAT, 1994).

Closer inspection of the data on minors detained in penal institutions reveals an upward trend in the total number of foreigners. Their representation in juvenile penal institutions went from 11.2% in 1983 to 40.9% in 1994. The figures for reception centres are even higher, reaching 47.1% in 1994.

Another clear trend, which is linked to the previous one, is seen in the percentage increase in female offences. the percentage of females in the juvenile penal population rose from 3.6% in 1983 to 16.9% in 1991. For reception centres the percentage of females reached 22.7% in 1994. As has already been said, the two above trends are linked in that foreign females are disproportionately over-represented in the juvenile penal system. In 1994, for example, female

Table 7.3: Number of Minors under 18 Tried by the Juvenile Court: Acquittal (with reasons for decision) or Indictment (1984-1991).

Verdict and reasons for decision	1984	1985	1986	1987
ACQUITTED	9961	10454	10900	13970
Because the *actus reus* did not take place	278	266	351	252
Because the *actus reus* was not committed by the accused	330	408	471	399
Because the victim withdrew the complaint	315	302	340	316
For amnesty	549	326	216	7378
For lack of evidence	745	659	693	484
For limitation of action (*prescrizione*)	112	83	115	122
For leniency (*perdono giudiziale*)	4909	5934	6001	3031
For other reasons	2723	2476	2713	1988
CONVICTED	2972	2534	2497	2022
TOTAL	12933	12988	13397	15992
ratio convicted/tried	22.98%	19.51%	18.64%	12.64%
ratio convicted/reported	15.39%	12.59%	12.65%	9.51%

	1988	1989	1990	1991
ACQUITTED	9974	9105	6917	8611
Because the *actus reus* did not take place	380	327	74	148
Because the *actus reus* was not committed by the accused person	311	361	195	254
Because the vitim withdrew the complaint	340	480	108	145
For amnesty	2903	1049	2546	1189
For lack of evidence	505	379	4	0
For limitation of action (*prescrizione*)	80	54	8	16
For leniency (*perdono giudiziale*)	3843	4473	2714	3461
For other reasons	1612	1982	1268	3398
CONVICTED	1833	2362	1244	2306
TOTAL	11807	11467	8161	10917
ratio convicted/tried	15.52%	20.62%	15.24%	21.12%
ratio convicted/reported	7.47%	8.11%	3.13%	5.13%

Source: ISTAT

Table 7.4: Admissions to Juvenile Prison (*istituti penali minorili*) (1977-1994).

YEAR	n.	% foreigners	% females
1977	7884	—	—
1978	6960	—	—
1979	6877	—	—
1980	7270	—	—
1981	7154	—	—
1982	7645	—	—
1983	7531	11.21	3.65
1984	6847	11.83	4.09
1985	6474	17.98	7.80
1986	5891	15.06	8.20
1987	7402	16.64	9.29
1988	7343	26.23	10.69
1989	5569	33.47	11.71
1990	782	30.69	12.40
1991	1775	38.87	17.24
1992	2289	34.82	16.25
1993	2314	36.69	16.21
1994	2240	40.98	16.96

Source: Ufficio per la Giustizia Minorile, Ministero di Grazia e Giustizia, ISTAT (1995).

foreigners detained in penal institutions constituted 39.3% vs. 5.9% for Italian female detainees. For the most part, these foreign females are nomads charged with property offences.

Imprisonment: Post-conviction

Prison as punishment in the strict sense is inflicted on an extremely limited number of minors. In 1989, for example, only 215 minors were placed in juvenile prisons (*prigione-scuola*). By the end of the same year only thirty-one were in custody in these facilities

Summary

All of the data reported point to a few conclusions regarding the trends which have emerged in recent years. It can be seen that the penal system tends to

Table 7.5: Admissions to Reception Centres—*Centri di prima accoglienza* (1990-1994).

YEAR	Italians				Foreigners				Total admissions			
	boys	girls	total n.	total %	boys	girls	total n.	total %	boys	girls	total n.	total %
1990	623	44	667	(37.1)	664	465	1129	(62.9)	1287	509	1796	(100.0)
1991	2110	70	2180	(53.4)	980	926	1906	(46.6)	3090	996	4086	(100.0)
1992	2512	79	2591	(56.9)	1020	941	1961	(43.1)	3532	1020	4552	(100.0)
1993	2314	62	2376	(57.6)	913	833	1746	(42.4)	3227	895	4122	(100.0)
1994	2089	72	2161	(52.9)	1067	857	1924	(47.1)	3156	929	4085	(100.0)

Source: Ufficio per la Giustizia Minorile, Ministero di Grazia e Giustizia, ISTAT (1995).

avoid incarcerating minors. Detention is used almost exclusively as a preventive measure, one which in some cases represents a sort of anticipation of punishment (De Leo, 1981). In other cases incarceration is used as a sort of emergency response to social situations which are difficult to handle. This is especially true in the case of foreign juveniles.

The statistics regarding foreigners can be seen as the manifestation of a phenomenon already observed in many juvenile justice systems, which has been called **bifurcation**. According to this notion, the modernization and reorganization of the system, implemented through such measures as diversion and alternatives to detention (as in Italy after D.P.R. n°448/1988), generate an undesired spin-off. The result is that the new opportunities are made available to the more fortunate sectors of the target population, while the old methods, which are not abandoned completely in that they are the expression of the intrinsically punitive nature of the system as a whole, end up as a receptacle for those individuals who are less fortunate. Added to this is the fact that foreign juveniles are not eligible for local authority assistance. It should also be noted that the foreign adults whom the minors depend upon often perceive any form of social intervention, even assistance, as a kind of covert control and prefer to handle their problems alone. Finally the statistics also reveal that, in addition to undergoing greater repression than their Italian counterparts, foreign minors are incarcerated for committing comparatively less serious crimes (Verde and Bagnara, 1989). And although the problem of foreign minors in Italy has several unique characteristics, the reader is likely to observe that "minority/foreign" groups in other countries (see, for example, chapters 2 and 6) express similar difficulties. This general trend would appear to deserve both national and international attention, both from an etiological and a political perspective.

Current and Projected Trends

The transformation recently brought about by the new norms of juvenile penal procedure (D.P.R. n°448/1988) was the expression of a process of rationalization and modernization advocated by an authoritative group of juvenile magistrates. The provisions of D.P.R. n°448/1988, which, strictly speaking, should regard only procedural aspects, in reality also introduced substantial modifications.

Basically, the new juvenile justice system represents the result of a compromise among various ideologies. It represents an attempt to pursue a whole range of objectives that are difficult to reconcile: safeguarding the rights of the minor, increasing the minor's responsibility by means of punishment (De Leo, 1985), obtaining rehabilitation through personalized social programs, pursuing depenalization options, and release from imprisonment by reducing the terms of preventive detention. Clearly there are many points of contrast between the correctionally oriented view (e.g., **due process model**—see Figure 1, Introduction), for instance, and the position based on depenalization. The reform introduced a norm which allows for the depenalization of any type of offence on the grounds of insignificance; at the same time, however, it allows a whole range of preventive measures of a therapeutic nature, and some rather harsh (*misure cautelari*), to be imposed on a minor who might be acquitted during the preliminary hearing or trial. This almost suggests a desire to "teach the minor a lesson" even before the trial begins. The format is somewhat analogous to the "scared straight" programs once popular in the United States during the 1980s (see Finchenauer, 1982).

In general the new norms seem to favour extending the intervention of the juvenile justice system by restoring functions that had been transferred over the years to the local authorities. The norms make provision for a range of psycho-social interventions within the penal system, at the same time reintroducing into that system the intervention of the local authority services, albeit in a subordinate position. In this respect article 6 of D.P.R. n°448/1988 constitutes a complete turn-about in the policy of separation of roles established by D.P.R. n°616/1977 on administrative decentralization: "At any stage of the proceedings, the judicial authority may avail itself of the juvenile services of the Justice Department. It may also avail itself of the welfare services instituted by the local authorities." This concept is restated unequivocally in art. 28 sub-section 2 of D.P.R. n°448/1988, which establishes that when probation is imposed, " the magistrate is to entrust the minor to the juvenile services of the Justice Department in order to implement suitable measures for supervision, treatment and support, if necessary enlisting the collaboration of the local authority services."

In other words the new provisions seem to have been aimed at providing a response within the penal system to problems more closely connected with social intervention. This could be seen as an attempt to make up for the inequalities thst had grown at a national level between the north, where social services were beginning to reach European standards, and the south, which remained enmeshed in archaic social policies that held the rights of minors in scant regard. The early results seem to show that the norms have been applied very differently in various geographical areas, not least on account of the varying standards of the local authority social services.

Since the new norms came into effect at the end of 1989, the situation regarding welfare intervention does not seem to have changed greatly. If there has been any turn-about, it concerns the legislative changes relating to the terms of preventive detention, which have given rise, as we have seen, to an increase in the number of minors in preventive detention. Indeed, the modifications introduced in 1991 mark a turning-point in a general trend towards non-incarceration, a process which had reduced the rate of imprisonment of minors in Italy to one of the lowest in Europe. In other words the new policies favour a more **welfare/modified** model of justice, but in practice we still find a strong alliance to the **justice** model.

Current Theoretical "Bias"

The 1991 upturn in crime among minors has been attributed to various recent developments in the phenomenology of juvenile delinquency. The increased presence of foreign immigrants, often illegal, has been implicated, as has the greater involvement of minors in drug-related crime (Ponti and Merzagora, 1991). The progressive and dramatic decline of certain areas of the country, due to the economic recession, has also been cited. In these areas worsening social problems have been accompanied by the further consolidation of criminal fraternities, which offer young people a means of gaining notoriety or of earning a living when legal employment is difficult to obtain (Occhiogrosso, 1992-1993; Viggiani and Tressanti, 1992). This thesis is also sustained by Merzagora and Paolillo (1991), who compared the official statistics for minors involved in crimes of extortion and drug trafficking in the regions of Campania, Sicily, Calabria, and Puglia with the national totals. Their figures showed that a large proportion of such crimes (almost 50% for extortion) are committed in these four regions, which strongly suggests that the minors involved are working for organized crime syndicates. The phenomenon is not new, however, and dates back at least to the middle of the 1980s.

Social alarm over the growing involvement of minors in organized crime has been called into question by the controversial interpretation of those, such as Pavarini (1992-1993), who do not see the repressive shift in juvenile justice as a response to a real increase in juvenile crime. According to this view, the issue of juvenile crime has only very recently come to the fore with the "discovery" of the link between minors and organized crime. In order to test such a hypothesis, it seems important to consider the size of the rise in "real" juvenile crime and how this is measured. The data seem to indicate that there has been a rise in the last few years in some serious crimes committed by minors, such as murder. However, formal and informal agencies of social control, as well as public opinion, also seem to have stepped up the pressure on some categories of minors, such as foreigners, whose deviant behaviour has probably been amplified more than that of native minors.

Summary

Juvenile justice, in Italy, is a comparatively young enterprise and has been slow to evolve. The system can best be characterized as a **justice-oriented** model even though recent legislation would suggest that a **welfare/modified justice** model is being advocated. However, given our social and political history combined with recent economic strains in the country, the system has made limited progress. One of the consequences has been a recent increase in youth crime.

At the present time, the areas of juvenile deviance which are attracting the greatest attention on the part of citizens, the mass media, and public authorities in Italy are those which concern foreign minors, especially gypsies and North Africans, and the involvement of minors in organized criminal activities. The real magnitude of these phenomena, however, appears to be extremely difficult to assess, in that empirical research is still sorely limited.

Public alarm about juvenile crime is a fairly recent phenomenon in Italy, and a clear response on the part of the juvenile justice system has yet to be evinced. Indeed, while the number of minors charged with offences has increased greatly, the number of referrals to reception centres and penal institutions has remained relatively low. Moreover, other types of measure, such as probation, have been adopted to a limited extent, and reparative measures, which under Italian law can only be imposed in connection with probation, have consequently found limited application. This latter option, however, even when available, is very rarely adopted, with the exception of a few juvenile courts which are inclined to make wider use of community service orders.

The world of juvenile justice appears to be hesitating before the complexity of the problems facing it. Moreover, the risk of re-centralization of penal intervention has been perceived as a risk which may be accentuated by the current economic difficulties that are taxing the resources of local authority social services. In addition, problems of financing have hindered programs for prevention, which now seem chiefly oriented towards containing the phenomenon of drug addiction and its related pathologies. The welfare of young offenders of Italy would appear to be caught in-between the chaos. It is time that we recognize the global importance of youth justice.

References

Beccaria, C. (1963). *On crimes and punishments.* (Henry Paolucci, Trans.). New York: Bobbs-Merill.

Betti, M., & Pavarini, M. (1985). Potere giudiziario e governo locale nell'amministrazione della giustizia minorile: il quadro normativo e le ipotesi interpretative. In M. Bergonzini & M. Pavarini (Eds.). *Potere giudiziario, enti locali e giustizia minorile.* Il Mulino, Bologna.

De Leo, G. (1981). *La giustizia dei minori. La delinquenza giovanile e le sue istituzioni.* Einaudi, Torino.

De Leo, G. (1985). Responsabilità: definizioni ed applicazioni nel campo della giustizia minorile. In G. Ponti (Ed.). *Giovani, responsabilità e giustizia.* Giuffré, Milano.

De Leo, G., Patrizi, P., Donato, R., & Scali, M. (1993). L'interazione fra servizi sociali e autorità giudiziaria in alcuni interventi innovativi del processo penale minorile. In De Leo G., Dell'Antonio A. (Eds.). *Nuovi ambiti legislativi e di ricerca per la tutela dei minori.* Giuffré, Milano.

Faccioli, F. (1990). Devianza e controllo istituzionale. In Consiglio Nazionale dei Minori (Ed.). *Il minore in Italia.* Angeli, Milano.

Finchenauer, J.O. (1982). *Scared straight and the panacea phenomenon.* Englewood Cliffs, NJ: Prentice-Hall.

Gatti, U., Fossa, G., Lusetti, E., Marugo, M.I., Russo, G., & Traverso, G.B. (1994). La devianza giovanile in Italia: un'indagine sui comportamenti illeciti autorilevati in un campione di studenti di scuola media superiore. *Rassegna Italiana di Criminologia,* 5.

Gatti, U., Fossa, G., Marugo, M.I., & Materazzi, V. (1991a). Le inchieste di vittimizzazione: problemi metodologici e primi risultati di uno studio-pilota condotto nella città di Genova. *Rassegna Italiana di Criminologia,* 2, 363.

Gatti, U., Malfatti, D., Marugo, M.I., & Tartarini, E. (1991b). La diffusione dei comportamenti devianti fra i giovani: una ricerca sulla popolazione genovese mediante la tecnica dell'autoconfessione. *Rassegna Italiana di Criminologia,* 2, 387.

Gatti, U., & Verde, A. (1988). S'éloigner du système pénal: un approche du problème de la délinquance juvénile en Italie. *Revue internationale de criminologie et de police technique,* 41, 49.

Gatti, U., & Verde, A. (1991). The dividing line between punishment and help: New questions, old answers. In Junger-Tas J., Boendermaker L., & van der Laan P. (Eds.). *The future of the juvenile justice system.* ACCO, Leuven.

ISTAT. (1994). Istituto Nazionale di Statistica. Rome.

Martin, R., Mutchnick, R.J., & Austin, W.T. (1990). *Criminological thought: Pioneers past and present.* NY: Macmillan.

Merzagora, I., & Paolillo, D. (1991). Il coinvolgimento dei minori nella delinquenza organizzata: Un tentativo di indagine quantitativa. *Marginalità e società,* 20, 30.

Occhiogrosso, F. (1992-1993). Introduzione. Anche per i minorenni è necessaria una 'Nuova Resistenza'. *Minori Giustizia* (nuova serie), 4-1, 9 (numero speciale dedicato a "Ragazzi della mafia").

Pavarini, M. (1992-1993). Più o meno carcere. *Minori Giustizia* (nuova serie), 4-1, 357 (numero speciale dedicato a "Ragazzi della mafia").

Pazé, P. (1991). Una legge inadeguata per proteggere i minori dalla droga. *Il bambino incompiuto,* 8, 3, 17.

Ponti, G. & Merzagora, I. (1991). Il minore tra responsabilizzazione, pena rieducativa e delinqunza organizzata. *Marginalità e società,* 20, 14.

Ricciotti, R. (1982). *Il diritto minorile e dei servizi sociali: gli interventi amministrativi e penali.* Maggioli, Rimini.

Senzani, G. (1970). *L'esclusione anticipata. Rapporto da 118 case di rieducazione per minorenni.* Jaca Book, Milano.

Ufficio per la Giustizia Minorile, Ministero di Grazia e Giustizia. ISTAT (1995). Rome.

Verde, A., & Bagnara, F. (1989). L'utilizzazione delle strutture penitenziarie minorili in Italia. *Rassegna di Criminologia,* 20, 317.

Viggiani, L., & Tressanti, S. (1992). Indagine sulla delinquenza minorile. *Esperienze di giustizia minorile,* 39, 1, 35.

chapter 8

Comparative Juvenile Justice:
An Overview of Russia[1]

Dmitry A. Shestakov
Professor of Criminal Law and Criminology
Member of the Russian Academy of Social Sciences
Natalia D. Shestakova
Faculty of Law, St. Petersburg State University

Facts on Russia

Area: Russia occupies an area of 17,075,200 sq. kilometres. It is the largest country in the world. In accordance with territorial-administration there are twenty-one republics, six territories, forty-nine provinces and two cities of federal significance (Moscow—pop. 8.7 million and St. Petersburg—pop. 4.4 million). The country contains ten autonomous regions and one autonomous province. **Population:** At the beginning of 1995 the population was estimated at around 149.9 million (sixth in the world)—growth rate .21% per year. Seventy-three percent of the population resides in urban communities while the balance (27%) are primarily urban dwellers. Representatives of more than one hundred nationalities live in Russia, with the majority (82%) being ethnic Russians, the Tartars account for approx. 3.8%, Ukrainians 3%, and most others constitute no more than 1% each. There are many languages spoken throughout Russia, but the state language is Russian. The most popular religion being Russian Orthodox. As of 1994 the population density was 8.7 persons per square km. **Climate:** In recognizing that Russia reaches covers nearly 150° longitude, the weathers is as diverse as the cultural climate of the country. The climate varies from a continental climate in the south-western regions to extreme cold in Siberia and monsoon in the Far East. Winter temperatures vary in January from -1° to -50° C, and in July from 1° to 30° C. **Government:** Prior to 1987, when Gorbachev initiated major democratic reforms through openness (glasnost) and restructuring (perestroika), Russia was first ruled under a Tsarist regime and then after the 1917 Revolution under a Communist regime until 1985. Today the democratic federal legal state is made up of a republic form of government. State power in the Russian Federation is realized on the basis of power divided into legislative, executive, and judicial jurisdictions. State power in Russia is realized by the President of Russia through federal meetings (parliament, which consists of two chambers: the Soviet of Federation and State Duma) and the supreme courts of Russia. Under the constitution local authorities are recognized and guaranteed autonomy.

[I]t is obvious that a mere knowledge of the rule of law by no means guarantees that it is observed.

A.M. Yakovlev (1988)

---

[1] The editor would like to acknowlege the translation assitance of Irena Luciw, a graduate student at the University of Alberta. The editor was provided with an English and Russian version of the chapter.

> Four years have passed since the Russian federation became a state with a transitional economy. Everyone knows that such countries are characterized by increased criminal activity across practically the entire spectrum of society.
>
> G. Lezhikov, 1995—Ninth United Nations Congress on the Prevention of Crime and the Treatment of Offenders.

The (Turbulent) Evolution of Russia Law

Russia, which is one of the oldest states in the world (see Box 8.1), has a system of legislation that has undergone rapid and dramatic change in recent years. However, the earliest recordings of Russian law date back to the tenth century A.D. Its influence and doctrines can be found in the "*Russkaya Pravda*" which, among other things, describes the essence of Russian criminal law. Other major codes of law were formulated in 1497, 1550, 1649, Military Rules of Peter I in 1716, and "The Order" of his wife Catherine II in 1767—who became known as Catherine the Great.

A characteristic feature of early feudal criminal law was the establishment of concrete *corpus delicti.* The general concern was not so much about establishing guilt but in defining criminal responsibility. Formal responsibility was not codified until 1864 when the first Russian Penal Code was legislated. The laws were based on progressive ideas. Desnitski, Kunitsin, and Solntsev were instrumental in formulating the Penal Code. They wanted to ensure that the law was based on objective criteria in the defining of guilt and that crime had subjective characteristics. They also acknowledged the principle of *mens rea.* Many of their ideas were based on the classical and neo-classical ideas of justice reform taking place in Western Europe at the time.

In his works and lectures, Solntsev's "*Russian Criminal Law*" concentrated on the will and consciousness of the criminals during the time period when they are committing crimes. Solntsev based his opinions upon the rules and orders of Catherine II while he criticized the West-European criminal law literature. For the first time in Russia he provided a deep, scientifically elaborated system of Russian criminal law.

Further legal reform was carried out during the 1860s. The Regulations of the Criminal Legal Procedure of 1864 were supplemented with articles 356.1-356.6. These articles were devoted to the regulation of the execution of minors from ten to seventeen years of age and the Punishment Regulations of 1864

Box 8.1: Russian History in a Box

Russia's historical and legal roots can be traced back to the Greek and Byzantine Empire. Russia's first important battle towards nationhood was in the thirteenth century when Prince Alexander Yaroslavevich beat back the Swedish army near St. Petersburg, on the banks of the Neva. The prince thereafter was referred to as Alexander Nevsky (meaning "of the Neva"). One of Russia's most honoured phrases came from Nevskii who reportedly said: "That who comes to us with a sword, will die from the sword." The phrase can be found on many World War I and World War II memorials. During the Middle Ages territorial Russia grew quickly with hard fought battles against the Rurks and Tartars in the southwest and with the Baltic states in the northwest under Peter the Great in the early eighteenth century. The spoils in the aftermath of Napoleonic war of 1812 and the abolishment of serfdom in 1861 provided the impetus for change. It was during this period that the peasant movement known as "Narodniki" spawned the uprising of the peasant class. And in spite of rapid growth and industrialization, a revolution in 1905 attempted to slow down the changes. In the nineteenth century Russia made a valuable contribution to the development of the world's culture (e.g., Lev Tolstoi and F. Dostoevski), music (e.g., composers Tchaikovski and Musorgski), and science (e.g., Mendeleev and Lobachevski). World War I brought much hardship and loss of lives to the Russian people. Russia became politically very unstable. It led to an overthrow of the monarchy in February 1917. Finally, on October 25 (or Nov. 7 by the new calendar) the RKP (Russian Communist Party), with the help of Germany financial backing, dethroned the tsarist government. This marked the beginning of the seventy years' reign of Soviet Russia under Communism. Private property was abolished and all private land was transferred to the state. Under Joseph Stalin's rule religion was abolished and millions of innocent people were either killed or exiled to Siberia. When Mikhail Gorbachev came to power in 1985 he introduced a number of fundamental reforms known as 'glasnost', or openness, which helped Russia move towards democratizing and a market economy. Combined with 'perestroika', or restructuring , the changes began to stir economic, legal, political, and social reform. Finally, in 1991, the seventy year domination of the Marxist-Leninist-Stalinist totalitarian state collapsed as did the former Soviet Union, the Cold War came to an abrupt end, and the Warsaw Pact disbanded. Boris Yeltsin's social democracy party became Russia's first popularly elected president in June 1991. His sweeping reforms led to the breakup of the Soviet Union into its constituent republics and formed the Commonwealth of Independent States. An controversial election in June 1996 between democracy and a return to communism marked another milestone in Russian history. In a second run-off election in July, Yeltsin's party prevailed.

were adopted. They reflected the following essential features concerning minors (i.e., juvenile offenders):

- Youth under the age of ten can not be charged with misdemeanors.
- Half punishment (the punishment for minors, committing the same crimes as adults is less strict than for adults) is set for minors from the ages of

ten to seventeen. Minors under fourteen can be placed under the custody of parents or guardians or in home correctional facilities.

● Minors must be detained separately from adults (see Box 8.2).

● If the age of a minor is important to the charge(s) or to his or her punishment, then the court appoints a search for birth documents to double-check the age of the offender (art. 413 of the Punishment Regulations).

● The parent, tutor, or relative can 'hand in a recall' (appeal).

● Juveniles under age fourteen are not permitted to testify under oath.

● Corrective shelters instead of imprisonment should be used with minors.

In keeping with the former socialist philosophy, an emphasis is placed on the coordination of home, school, and community. Delinquency was viewed upon as an indicator of the failure to apply basic precepts in the education of Russian youth. Legal rights, unlike in most Western countries, were clearly spelled out by the state rather than presumed to exist naturally. Therefore, in early times, the juvenile justice system could be best described as having represented a **crime control model** (see Figure 1—Introduction).

Box 8.2: Corrective Shelters

According to the "Rules on Corrective Shelters" in 1866, imprisonment of juveniles was to do be dealt with in the same manner as that for adults. They were initially operated by the churches, companies, or in private homes. After the revolution they were placed under the directorship of the Ministry of the Internal Affairs and they have been attached to its department. The purpose of the shelters was to provide (re)education and work projects.

The revised Criminal Code of 1903 stipulated the conditions and requirements for sentencing juveniles. Some of the key criteria include:

● Juveniles between the ages of fourteen and seventeen who committed a serious crime were primarily sent to educational-corrective institutions (see Box 8.2). If there was no such opportunity, then the minor would be sent to specially adapted units attached to the adult prisons or custody houses.

● Female juveniles were sent to nunneries. If it was possible, then they too would be sent to educational-corrective institutions.

Juvenile offenders could be imprisoned for eight to twelve years. However, youths between the ages of ten and fourteen are usually sent to the educational-corrective institution. This is preferred over the use of fines or other corrective measures. With respect to juveniles between seventeen and twenty-one years of age, capital punishment is substituted by 'exile for life'. In Russia this means fifteen years imprisonment, which is subject to possible early release after serving one-third of the sentence.

Before the Russian Revolution there were two types of juvenile justice trends: sociological and classical. The classical model is mostly conservative. In the classical criminological tradition, emphasis is placed on the main process of law and not on circumstantial factors. The sociological perspective (a modified, neo-classical interpretation) still follows the criminal codes of law but at the same time takes the changes of society into consideration. These perspectives have had an enduring impact on how we view juvenile justice and the causes of juvenile crime to this day. Sergievski, Vladimirov, Kistyakovski, Foinitski, and Koni were among the most well-known scientists-criminalists of tsarist Russia.

The question of criminal responsibility for juveniles was raised after the 1917 October Revolution. However, with the dramatic political changes which transpired during the 1920s, criminal legislation underwent repeated revisions—first under the Criminal Code of 1922 and then the General Beginnings of Criminal Legislation of 1924 before the final changes were incorporated in the 1926 Criminal Code. The code placed priority on compulsive education over measures of criminal punishment. This represented a shift from a **strict crime control model** to a **justice model** (see Figure 1—Introduction). This theme was most blatantly expressed in 1935 when Soviet legislation abolished juvenile courts.

Contemporary Russia

Let us now turn to the 1950s and 1960s, which marked the beginning of modern legislation. This period was marked by reign of Joseph Stalin (see Box 8.1) and the Hrushev reforms.

Along with the many political changes, criminal legislation was also amended. In conjunction with the development of democratic principles of law and an emphasis on lawfulness, the Principles of Criminal Legislation of the Soviet Union (SU) and the union's republics were adopted. The age of the criminal responsibility was raised from fourteen to sixteen.

While the underlying principles of the legislation focused on legalistic elements, the philosophy of the legislation reflected the neo-classical ideas of justice with an emphasis on due process and punishment proportionate to the crime. For example, the severity of any punishment was measured against the gravity of the crime. Hence, tolerance for dangerous recidivists was minimal. Judges, however, were required to take into consideration all extenuating circumstances of the offence. If the court found that correction of the juvenile offender could be obtained without criminal punishment, then it could use compulsory measures of an educational character.

The principles of strict crime control were balanced against the possibility of mitigating circumstances. These elements were incorporated in the Principles of 1958 and Criminal Codes of SU's republics. The principles were adopted between 1960 and 1961. They include:

- A reduction in the range of punishable deeds by limiting the number of offences which existed earlier.
- A general reduction of punishment for many crimes.
- The possibility of liberation from the criminal responsibility and use of measures of public influence by holding to bail (art. 52 of the Criminal Code) and by transmission of the case to Comrades Court (art. 52 of the Criminal Code). For example, when one commits an offence that is not considered to be criminal (e.g., a drunk person on the street) he or she would not be taken into custody but placed into the custody of their employer where they would be subject to embarrassment from workers, students, or colleagues.
- An increased emphasis on educational measures which focused on re-education and resocialization rather than stressing criminal responsibility.
- On February 15, 1977, an amendment was introduced allowing for the adjournment of the punishment. (If a person is convicted to not more than three years of imprisonment for the first time, the court may adjourn the decision for one to two years, taking into consideration the character of the committed offence and the personality of the offender and other circumstances. After the period of adjournment is over, the offender can either be sent to serve the punishment or be declared debt free by the court).

Today the 1961 Criminal Code, with its various amendments, defines the current aspects of criminal responsibility and other legal matters as they pertain to juvenile offenders. Matters pertaining to legal procedure and the regulation of the order of criminal proceedings can be found in the Criminal Procedure Code of Russian Soviet Federated Socialist Republic (RSFSR (1960)).

However, at this time, a new juvenile justice project is being conceived. It includes details pertaining to the responsibility for the crime and the appropriate punishment. The project was initiated in response to a growing delinquency problem in Russia. The project envisages the section, "juvenile's responsibility" and the chapter, "peculiarities of criminal responsibility and punishment of juveniles," which contain the:

- general norms which characterize the peculiarities of criminal responsibility;
- main features of punishments to be used with minors;
- possibility of liberation of juveniles from criminal responsibility and application measures of educational influence;
- conditions of liberation of the juvenile from punishment;
- direction for conditions of suspended sentence;
- establishment of a period of time obsoleteness with respect to crimes committed by persons under eighteen years old; and
- a period of clearing off convictions.

The focus of the criteria is directed to youth between the ages of eighteen and twenty.

The principles constitute a refinement of graded responsibility and propose a two-tier model of juvenile justice. The re-emergence of Russian criminology and a more open dialogue with Western countries have played a role in the initiative of the project (see Box 8.3).

Peculiarities of Criminal Responsibility

Russian juvenile law is clear in identifying who can be considered a youth at risk when establishing criminal responsibility. Under Article 10 of the Criminal Code, criminal responsibility is assigned to youths who were at least sixteen years of age before they had committed an offence. The law further notes that upon turning sixteen the youths acquired the cognitive and development ability, as a rule, which allows them to be aware of their actions (i.e., forming *mens rea*). However, the law recognizes that youths between the ages of fourteen and sixteen may be capable of forming intent. Therefore, legislation provides for reduced culpability for youths as young as fourteen (the minimum age of criminal responsibility) with diminished responsibility.

In accordance with Article 10 of the Criminal Code, youths between the ages of fourteen and sixteen are considered criminally responsible for a specific range of offences. They include:

- intentional actions which may provoke a railway accident (art. 86),
- homicide (art.102-106 of CC),
- intentional assault and battery, causing health disorder (art.108-111, 112, part 1),
- rape (art. 117),
- kidnapping (art.125.1),
- theft (art. 144),
- robbery (art. 146),
- burglary (art. 145),
- swindle (art. 147),
- extortion (art. 148),
- possession of the property, especially 'valuables' (art. 147.2),
- illegal possession by means of transport, horse, or another valuable property without a purpose of a repine (art. 148.1),
- intentional destruction or damage of property (art. 149),
- malicious and especially malicious hooliganism (art 206, parts 2 and 3),
- terrorism (art. 213.3),
- deliberately false information about an act of terrorism (art. 213.4),
- possession of a firearm, ammunition, or explosives (art. 218.1), and
- possession of drugs (art. 224.1).

Upon reaching the age of sixteen, all youths are subject to criminal responsibility. However, the gravity of the offence has a bearing on whether the juvenile will receive corrective punishment or sent for re-education. For example, Part 3 of Article 10 reads: "If the court finds that the juveniles' act is not considered a major public harm, then the court can use educational measures. These measures imply diminished criminal responsibility." In accordance with art. 63 of the Criminal Code, juveniles are:

- required to publicly apologize and request a pardon from the victim or provide some other form of restitution as determined by the court;
- subjected to announcement of reproof or strict reproof ;
- given a warning;
- if they are between the ages of fifteen and eighteen required to provide compensation;
- placed under strict supervision of their parent(s) or guardian;
- placed under the supervision of a public organization or a consenting guardian. The court, in accordance with the Statute on Public Educators, may elect to place the youth under the control of a public educator; and
- placed in a special study-educational or medical-educational institution.

If a juvenile is not determined to be criminally responsible in accordance with Part 3 of Article 10, then their file is referred to the Committee on Juvenile Affairs.

Box 8.3: The (Re)emergence of Criminology in Russia

According to research conducted by Louise Shelly (1980), Soviet legal and criminology scholars, prior to the collapse of the Soviet Union in 1991, were incapable of drawing insightful conclusions on crime "because of a combination of ideological and intellectual constraints" (p. 111). These constraints were in part the result of internal population controls. It was not until recently that law schools, where criminology is taught, and scholars were given more liberal access to crime and delinquency data, thus enabling more insightful discussions and evaluations of juvenile crime in Russia.

Committee on Juvenile Affairs (CJA)

Committees on juvenile affairs operate in accordance with the Principles on the Committees on Juvenile Affairs, which were set forth in 1968. However, some of its propositions are invalid because they contradict the legislation currently in force.

In accordance with art. 17 of the Principles on CJA, the committee has a right to consider the following cases of delinquency:

- youths up to the age of fourteen, who have committed a 'dangerous-public' act; and
- youths between the ages of fourteen and sixteen who have committed a 'dangerous-public' act.

Before January 1, 1997, the CJA had a right to consider cases involving the delinquency of youths who were between the ages of sixteen and eighteen who had committed an infraction which contains elements of crime. But there was disagreement within the CJA on how to proceed with such cases. The controversy evolved around the interpretation of articles 8 and 10 of the CPC.

With the enactment of the new Criminal Code of Russian Federation on January 1, 1997 changes were also made to the Criminal Procedure Code, which states that the aforementioned cases are now only considered by court. The new code replaced the code of 1960. Thus the legislation has taken into account that the mandate of the CJA is illegal as it contradicts the Constitution of Russian Federation. In particular CJA jurisdiction operations are in contravention with article 118 of the Constitution of Russia, which states that justice in Russia can only be carried out by a court of law.[2] Furthermore, the CJA violates the UN Convention on the Rights of the Child adopted by the United Nations in 1989. Article 8 of the convention states: a child should not be separated from his or her parents against their will unless deemed necessary by a trained official whose concerns are supported by the court. The court can then deem it to be in the best interests of the youth that such separation is necessary for the well-being of the young person.

Until recently, as the analysis of CJA activity showed, the CJA identified a significant number of its cases as being juvenile delinquents. For instance in 1990, 294,978 cases were considered of which approximately 14% were considered cases involving juvenile delinquents.

---

[2]   The new code retains capital punishment and increases the maximum sentence for banditry and murder from fifteen to twenty years, but it also significantly reduces the number of crimes punishable by death and reduce sentences for non-violent crimes. The new code gives priority to crimes against an individual rather than the state, unlike the old system. Almost one hundred new articles have been added to the new code, and for offences which no longer exist criminals can apply for early release.

During 1991 the CJA handled 30,810 cases that involved offences committed by public gangs. Of this total, 447 cases involved youths under the age of fourteen. Their average age was nine. Seventeen percent of all the cases involved juveniles between the ages of fourteen and sixteen, most of whom had committed criminal acts containing elements of *corpus delicties*. If there is a case where there is not enough evidence to prove the crime, then criminal proceedings are arrested. Approximately 15% (4627) of the CJA judgments resulted in referring the juvenile offender for special education training (see Box 8.4).

According to 1990 data, the CJA handled 94,833 cases in which a fine was levied against the offender's parent(s). Of these dispositions, 20,141 (21.2%) involved juveniles under sixteen who were found guilty of being intoxicated in a public place; 46,875 (49.4%) pertained to cases in which the parent neglected to provide the essential educational needs of their children; 1700 (1.7%) of the cases dealt with drug-related offences, and 1370 incidents included acts of (small) hooliganism by juveniles between fourteen and sixteen years of age. As in most contributions in this book, most juvenile crime in Russia is minor in nature.

An analysis of court activity concerning criminal cases of juvenile as well as civil cases pertaining to the (re)education of the youth under the CJA have produced some interesting findings (Hard Fortunes of the Youth, 1991). The study focused on selective sociological indicators of families with juvenile delinquents. It was generally observed that alcoholism, poor social bonding within the family, and other elements of family disfunction were present.

Box 8.4: A Special teaching and educational institution.

In 1995 a government regulation was introduced which provided for "a special teaching and educational institution for children and juveniles with deviant behavior"— Government of RF 25.04.1995. (Collection of Law. (No 18. 1995)) The special teaching and educational institution areas provide psychological, medical, and social rehabilitation, including correction of behaviour and adaptation in the society, and also provision of the conditions for primary general, fundamental general, middle (complete) general, and primary professional education. The establishment of separate institutions for boys and girls or mixed institutions is also possible. The institution may be of an open type and accomplish preventive functions or of a closed type—for juveniles who have committed public dangerous actions as stipulated by the CC. They are considered in need of special conditions of education and teaching and special pedagogical, individualized treatment. This represents a major ideological break in Russian practices and is more characteristics of the *parens patriae* philosophy found in most Western juvenile justice systems.

Types of Crimes Committed

Before we discuss the types of crimes being committed it should be noted that according to the head of the Institute of the Ministry of Internal Affairs of the Russian Federation, Pavel Ponomarev, for 1994 only about one-third of the total number of crimes actually committed were officially registered. Therefore, the *dark figure* (i.e., amount of unrecorded crime) of crime for juvenile crime, given the findings in many Western countries, is likely to be quite large. The reader should therefore view the data with some caution (Ponomarev, 1996).

In general, juvenile crime in Russia today consists primarily of thefts of personal property, robberies, burglaries, hooliganism, and thefts of state property. The more serious and violent crimes such as rape, intentional assault, and homicides only make up a small percentage of the crime structure (see Table 8.1). These patterns are not unlike those in many Western countries. This current profile did not always officially exist in Russia. Under the socialist system youth crime was reported to be low (Borodin, 1980). But, throughout the 1980s as political and social turmoil within the country spread, Keller (1987:27) reported the "beginning of alienation, disillusionment and rebellion among Soviet youth, including a growing drug problem." Recent public opinion surveys reveal that crime is ranked second behind price increases in terms of public concerns (Lezhikov, 1995). Russia's Interior Ministry drug chief Alexander Sergeyev recently noted that the "number of drug users (among youth) has more than doubled in the past ten years" (Ward, 1996). The drug trade is estimated to top $550 US million a year. This trend is also partially related to a number of social problems such as the increase in AIDS and other related health concerns.

The three main areas of criminal activity are property crimes (more than 60%), hooliganism and vandalism (25%), and crimes against persons (15%). In accordance with the social learning perspective based theories, it is interesting to note that more than 75% of all juvenile offences are committed in group or peer settings. However, unlike what appears to be the case in many Western countries, the groups tend to be small (i.e., two to three persons) and are considered unstable. The group generally exists for less then three months from the time they begin to commit their crimes. In cities like Moscow, youth gangs, along with gypsy hustlers, have become a growing concern. In 1994 Curtis Sliwa of the American Guardian Angels organization visited Moscow and suggested that a "criminal mindset" was beginning to emerge among the youth and that perhaps a Guardian Angel Chapter might be established. On the other hand, the more serious offences are generally recognized as being committed by more stable groups which tend to include adults with criminal experience. Nearly one group out of three is mixed (underage with adults). Almost half of group crimes are committed by such groups.

As indicated in Table 8.1, the proportionate distribution of juvenile crimes varies by the type of crime. Serious crimes only account for around 17% of all youth crime (5 % involve murders and 10% assaults), hooliganism accounts for 13% while the majority of juvenile crime involves robberies of personal property. So while the Western media tend to portray crime in Russia as out of control, the profile is not dissimilar from many Western countries. It should also be remembered that under the old regime crime was seldom acknowledged and official statistics essentially did not exist.

Table 8.1: Types of Crimes Committed by Juveniles

Proportion of crimes committed by Juveniles for 1991

All crimes	16.4%
Serious crimes	17.0
Robberies & burglaries	29.0
Theft of state property	24.0
Theft of personal property	32.2
Hooliganism	13.0
Stolen vehicles/means of transportation	30.5

The number of persons committing crimes between the ages of fourteen and seventeen were: in 1989, 490,995; in 1990, 505,211; in 1991, 525,788; in 1992, 626,227; in 1995, 209,777. Proportion of juveniles in the general number of offenders: in 1989, 17.7%; in 1990, 17.1%; in 1991, 16.7%; in 1992, 16.4%; in 1995, 12.0%. (Data for 1993 and 1994 were not published. Data for 1995 were taken from the statistic certificate of the prosecutor's office.[3]

Since the early 1970s and the collapse of the former Soviet Union in 1991, there has been a constant increase in juvenile delinquency as well as adult crime in Russia. There has also been a marked increase in recidivism rates (see Table 8.2).

While the concept of juvenile crime in Russia is legally prescribed by law as encompassing youth between the ages of fourteen and eighteen, as is the

---

[3]   The governmental system of criminal justice statistics recording is undergoing major changes: it will become an interagency system and will cover all offences (Lezhikov, 1995).

Table 8.2 Growth of Juvenile Crime 1971-1990
(increases are in comparison with 1971)

Rate of juvenile crime per 100000: Youths 14-17

Year	Rate	Percent Change
1971	549	
1975	628	+14
1976	623	+13
1977	615	+12
1981	787	+43
1985	1017	+85
1986	978	+78
1987	965	+76
1990	1320	+140

case in most countries, the nature and extent of delinquency varies by age. Delinquency patterns and trends differ according to social status, emotional maturity, cognitive development, and level of education (see Box 8.5). In the 1970s and 1980s, youths between the ages of fourteen and fifteen constituted not more than 20% of juvenile cases, of which only 5% involved females. However, by 1993 female representation had more than doubled. And by 1995 the rate of juvenile delinquent activity among females was growing 1.5 to 2 times that of delinquency rates for young males. Such trends have been expressed in other contributions to this text. It would appear to suggest that in a few years a general increase in female crime is expected.

Box 8.5: Delinquency and Social Control in Russia

The relative proportion of juvenile crimes between 1989-1995 fluctuated from 17.7 to 12.0%. Rejuvenation of juvenile delinquency by an increase in the share of the younger group of age fourteen to fifteen is to be observed. These changes are connected with dramatic social changes in Russia that have become apparent with the relaxing of social services normally available to minors and a reduction in the social control mechanisms for their behaviour from the family as well as from society in general. Russia's former well-developed educational system has also experienced a breakdown in standards with the fiscal problems of the state. As reflected in the opening quote from Lezhikov (1995: v), the social and economic conditions correspond with a number of the sociologically based theories of crime and delinquency found in American literature.

Explanations of Delinquency

At the turn of the century, explanations for delinquency were based on writings of Marx and Engles. They were developed in Russia by V.L. Lenin. He wrote that criminality was caused by conflicting forces of socio-economic competition. And not withstanding the reliability of official crime statistics of the time, official crime data supported this assertion. Between 1940 and 1975, as Russian Communism became the norm, crime declined 44.1% and 18% between 1958 and 1975 alone (Borodin, 1980).

In Russia the causes of juvenile delinquency would appear to encompass many of the same social-negative phenomena and processes which determine crime in general. Among Russian scholars it is generally felt that the etiological features of juvenile delinquency are connected to general "criminogenic" processes, phenomena, and situations which are primarily related to socialization factors. It is believed these factors play a direct role in the motivation for youth crime. Some of the specific factors which have been studied include:

1. Negative influences in the family. In 30-40% of juvenile cases, problems of alcoholism, abusive family settings, and parents who themselves engaged in illicit activities was present.
2. Difficult financial position in the family.
3. Negative family and/or educational influences.
4. Adult offenders influence the younger population to commit crime. In approximately 30% of criminal cases juveniles are recruited by adults to commit the crimes. The penalty for a juvenile is less serious than that for an adult. Pickpocketing is a common example in which this takes place.
5. Long absence of employment. Between 1989 and 1993 the number of minors who committed legal infractions and who were either not in school or working nearly doubled (see Hungary (Chapter 11) and the problems the new market economy has created).
6. Aggressive feelings, feelings of low self-esteem or suffering from a sense of despair over the uncertainty in their future. These are dangerous symptoms of deterioration of the moral and psychological state of society.

Recent dramatic social and political changes in Russia have created a sense of anomie, Russian society has become marked by a lack of cohesion, cooperation, and consensus as to what is in the best interests of the people and the country. This disparity of goals and means creates strain as described in Robert Merton's work on strain theory (Einstadter and Henry, 1995). In addition, there has been a general decline in moral standards, and an increasing number of children (juveniles) are growing up without morals. Together these conditions may create a disenchanted environment. As can be seen in Table 8.2, juvenile crime has increased at a staggering rate. Amongst the adult population organized crime and black market activity has not only spread throughout Russia but has also spread to foreign countries like the United States or other countries covered in this collection (generally, see Goodwin, 1995; Raine & Cilluffo, 1994).

Although limited, a number of Russian studies have examined the relationship between juvenile crime and socio-environmental factors related to juvenile crime. Some of these include:

1. Neglect and/or absence of proper parental supervision and support;
2. Neglect of future victims, which promotes situation for crimes (in 20-50% of cases negative behaviour, such as drug use, alcohol abuse, and escape from the home, precedes the crime);
3. Lack of constructive employment opportunities;
4. Lack of organized leisure activities;
5. Limited opportunity to educate potential offenders about the law;
6. Lack of accountability for criminal behaviour; and
7. The proportionate increase in the number of youths demonstrating retarded intellectual and cognitive development as a result of disorganization in the family and in the system of education.

A final explanation that has been put forth, from a North American perspective, is that youth crime in Russia is the unfortunate consequence of the rapid emergence of capitalism and democracy (Erlanger, 1996; Goodwin, 1995). Although crime rates in Russia are still significantly lower than those in the United States, certain types of criminal activity have grown significantly since 1991; in particular mafia-style gangs, racketeering, and organized crime. Goodwin describes the current scene as resembling "gangland America of the 1930s." Erlanger (1996) further notes that the Criminal Code had not kept up with the rapid social changes. The 1960 code was a "much revised and patched together document based on a social system that considered private business criminal" and remained full of contradictory or ambiguous laws (p. 6). It is hoped that the new code will enable authorities to better respond to the changing social and criminal scene in Russia.

Recidivism

Prior to 1991 the Soviet state claimed that only a small percentage of juveniles became criminals, and depending on the region, recidivism varied between 3% to 10%. This was considerably lower than the rate for many Western countries. Part of the 'success' was attributed to the ability to enforce communism and supposedly eliminate misery and the indigence of labourers.

While the juvenile problem has increased dramatically in recent years, official statistics indicate that recidivism rates among juveniles are less than that among adults (their share among the general number of recidivists during the period from 1986 to 1993 fluctuated between 5% to 11.8 %). However, it is important to note that since the majority of delinquent acts are committed by older youth, subsequent acts are conducted after the age of eighteen. Hence, they no longer qualify as juveniles. We believe however that the "true" rate of recidivism is in fact quite high. In addition, a number of legal and judicial practices, such as adjournment of sentence, suspended sentence, sentencing without proper explanation, and providing intensive control for behaviour, influence recidivism. However, informed use of the discretionary options has been shown to have a positive impact on reducing the risk of recidivism.

The Youth Justice Process

In the Ministry of the Internal Affairs a special service for predicting juvenile infringement of law exists. This service collects information about the minors who are disposed to deviant behavior and their families. Workers in the service are generally persons with a teaching background or training in psychology. They carry out contacts with registered juveniles and juveniles without a dwelling (i.e., homeless) and then attempt to provide education and housing for them.

As noted earlier the administrative procedures for handling juvenile offenders are defined by the general rules spelled out in the Criminal Legal Procedure Code (CLPC) of Russia; in particular, Chapter 32 of CLPC which defines the legal rights and responsibilities of minors (i.e., ages fourteen to eighteen). There are also special rules for procedure on crimes committed by persons under eighteen. These are found in articles 391 through 402 of the CLPC.

The formal order of procedure is influenced by the age and social-psychological peculiarities of the youth. The procedures are intended to provide due consideration for the rights of a youth. These peculiarities help to promote a greater sense of fairness and due process when determining criminal responsibility.

Until recently in Russia, the accused did not have a right to legal counsel. Under the old system, defence council only became involved after the preliminary investigation was complete. And while this has changed, neither the police nor the Crown is required to inform the young offender of a right to counsel. Such a practice reflects the accusatorial process of Russian justice, and the model has been subject to abuse and corruption throughout the justice system (see Figure 8.1).

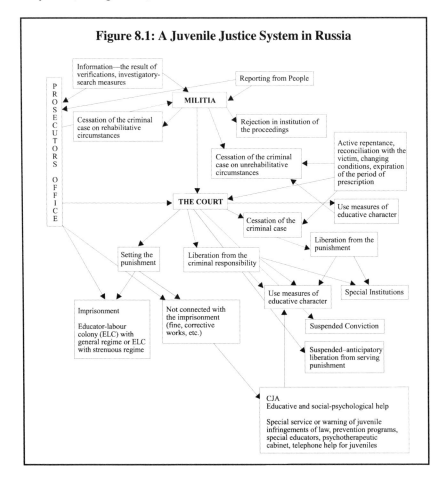

Figure 8.1: A Juvenile Justice System in Russia

Initial Contact

As noted earlier the Russian model of juvenile justice is based on the **justice model**. Once a youth has been referred to court a preliminary hearing is conducted in order to ascertain jurisdiction and procedural arrangements (see Figure 8.1). These procedures are strictly formal. With changes in 1991, judges were no longer nominated by local Party officials but may be appointed after serving at least five years in the legal profession and must be at least twenty-five years of age (Constitution Art. 119). Unlike most Western countries, appointments can be extended for up to ten years.[4] The objective of the initial contact is to establish the facts about the offender in order to assess whether there is a case for criminal responsibility. In order to do so, three specific procedures must be followed.

First, the exact age of the minor must be established. This is necessary in order to determine which legal procedures can be applied under article 5 of the CLPC. Age must be verified through official documentation such as a birth certificate or passport.

After the youth's age has been determined, a second set of elements which must be considered pertain to the youth's "state of being". For example, the following issues have to be assessed:

- emotional maturity;
- the youth's cognitive, intellectual, and moral character;
- living and educational conditions.

The final set of considerations pertain to the facts of the case. Following the criteria defined under Article 392 of the CLPC, the court must determine whether the youth can be held accountable for his or her offence.

Preliminary Hearing

Preliminary procedures (see Figure 8.1) can only begin after initial contact has determined that the youth meets the required criteria identified in the previous

---

4   Interestingly, there has been no move to remove judges appointed under the old regime.

section. While all cases are investigated by investigators associated with the Ministry of Internal Affairs, the proceedings are similar to those of adult offenders.

The Supreme Court of Russian Federation in its resolutions is very clear on the legal conditions which must be met and followed in determining criminal responsibility—the social and educational circumstances surrounding the youth and whether the youth acted under his or her own accord or with the assistance or encouragement of an adult.

If the basic criteria can not be adequately addressed during the preliminary investigation, the case is handed back to the investigator for additional investigation. Only after the court is satisfied that it has sufficient evidence upon which to assess the implications of the alleged crime will the case be allowed to come before the court. In order to ensure that the essential court conditions can be met, inquiry agencies (the local militia office for preventing of juvenile's infringements of law) are used. The investigators for the agencies are qualified professionals (see Box 8.6). Besides inspectors of the local militia office for preventing juvenile's infringements of law, preventive pedagogues (teachers) working in the system of the Ministry of Education, social workers of the Ministry of Social Defence and volunteers from the CJA may all participate in the preliminary inquiry.

Box 8.6: The Role of the Juvenile Investigator

Investigators have a particular specialization. The investigator conducts inquiries into the circumstances surrounding the case of a juvenile (usually the client's family and social environment) to develop a better understanding of their client's behaviour in order to decide whether to send the case to the court or to the CJA. Then, in consultation with the prosecutor, a decision is made as to how to proceed with the case. In Western countries, the role of the investogator is comparable to that of a probation officer preparing a pre-sentence report. The overriding purpose is to determine how best to create a protocol that promotes a condition for re-education.

In accordance with Article 393 of the CLPC, the investigator can recommend that the young offender be detained while awaiting trial. This option can only be applied to serious offences. However, if the investigator pronounces such a judgment, the presiding judge or crown prosecutor must question the minor to ensure that the decision to detain the minor is in the best interests of the youth and society at large. Should the recommendation to detain the youth be supported by the court, the minor is entitled to appeal the decision. The appeal must be done in accordance with Article 220 of CLPC. This can take place at any time during the preliminary inquiry or during the court examination.

Because of the special status of juvenile delinquents, there are special provisions (i.e., Article 394 of the CLPC) that allow the minor to be placed under the guardianship of his or her parent(s), or a relative or suitable guardian as recognized by the court. Article 158 provides for the right to a defence and representation. The guardian must state in writing (in arbitrary form) that they recognize their responsibility to supervise the minor and to bring the youth to court as required. The conditions are formally defined in a subpoena provided by the investigator or a senior administrator where the youth attends work or school. While formal in nature, the process does provide for the least restrictive alternative to be used—hence acknowledging the special status afforded young offenders.

If the act involved the participation of an adult, then the case receives special attention during the primarily investigation. In an effort to reduce any further influence by the offending adult, the case is processed as quickly as possible. If there is enough evidence to prove that the minor is guilty, then they do not charge the adult and minor separately but together.

Since most minors attend school, a teacher may be asked by the crown and/or defence to participate in questioning a minor who is still under the age of sixteen. However, as stipulated under Article 397 of the CLPC, a teacher can also be involved during the preliminary inquiry of youth older than sixteen, but only if the minor is considered to suffer from a disorder that causes distress or a psychological disability—mentally deficient. The teacher has a right, with permission of the investigator, to not only question the youth but to also comment on the observations made by the investigator. The process of enabling one of the minors' teachers to be involved in the preliminary examination not only helps to ensure continuity but also ensures that all relevant facts are weighed fairly by the crown and defence. The intent is to recognize the special needs of the youth. In this fashion our system reflects elements of the **participatory model** (see Figure 1—Introduction).

Unlike most Western countries, the Russia juvenile justice system does not look favourably upon including the expert testimonies of psychologists or psychiatrists during the preliminary stage. This dates back to the strong classical influences which existed prior to the Revolution. However, the presence of legal representation is necessary if there is sufficient evidence to show that the minor is mentally deficient but not necessarily mentally ill.

One of the inherent legal rights juveniles are entitled to (Article 399 of the CLPC) is to have their parent(s) involved in their legal representation. In addition, the investigator may either request the involvement of the parent or deny their participation if there are reasonable grounds to believe that it is necessary for the interests of the minor.

In summary, in keeping with its justice model, the preliminary hearing is a critical element of the legal process. In order to fully establish the facts of the cases, it may be necessary to detain the youth while the facts of the case are being determined. The CLPC focuses on the fact that the juvenile's rights are in need of a particular defence. Therefore, there is a special provision in Chapter 32 of the CLPC which regulates procedures on crimes committed by juveniles and includes additional guarantee of their rights and interests.

Trial Process

All juvenile cases are heard in a general court of law and require the participation of the youth and his or her lawyer. Unless it is felt that the case could have a negative impact on the youth, **all juvenile cases are heard in open court**. In addition the court has a right to remove the minor from court when evidence, which according to the defence or crown, could have a negative effect on the minor. For example, the question of whether the parents need to be subpoenaed for legal representation or the minor's educational and emotional status is being discussed. Therefore, while resembling a justice model, the trial process allows for mitigating circumstances—somewhat analogous to the *parens patriae* philosophy found in many Western juvenile justice systems.

As of December 26, 1996, the Russia Federation Council approved the constitutional law that stipulates that judges will be appointed by the Russian president and that all courts must be funded entirely by the federal budget.

Trial Provisions

The law use to make provisions for the possible liberation from criminal responsibility and punishment by referring adult and juvenile cases to the **comrade court**. But since 1985 this measure has not been used because it no longer fits the changing social structure. The public has grown apathetic as it tries to find its way under the new mantle of capitalism and democracy. This has not helped the plight of the Russian youth.

As a possible alternative, current laws do provide for the possibility of deferring a convicted juvenile to a public educator who is trained to provide specialized educative support. This is similar to a child-care worker or probation officer found in many other countries. The law also provides the option for juvenile cases to be tried either in common court or by judge and jury. Specific conditions apply.

Before the trial can commence, the court must meet certain criteria. The court must inform the institution or organization where the minor studies or works. They must also inform the CJA regarding the time and the place where the case will be tried, and, if not already addressed, ensure that the minor will have representation in court. Once these conditions are in place, then in accordance with the legalistic model of justice, the trial is conducted in an **adversarial** manner (CPC Art. 49).

If the minor has no parents, lives alone, or lives with a person who does not qualify as a legal tutor or guardian, the court must appoint a representative from the Guardianship and Trusteeship Agency to legally represent the minor. Such representation is considered necessary in order to protect the needs and rights of the minor. However, if such representation can be thought to have a negative bearing on the case, Article 399 of the CPC provides conditions that can exclude such participation. The law foresees such a provision in case of abuse his position, but in practice such cases are virtually unknown.

After hearing all the evidence (interrogation of the accused, estimation of written and material evidence, experts' resolutions, pleadings, hearing of the last word of the accused, withdrawing to the consultative room to pass the sentence), the court can then makes its legal decision and passes sentence.

Selection of Punishment

Sentencing practices are defined by law as having a range of dispositional discretion. The range of dispositions can be found in the relevant sections of the Criminal Code (CC). Before passing sentence the presiding judge takes into consideration the minor's character and the extent of public danger which resulted from the crime. The judge weighs these facts in determining the severity of punishment deemed necessary to ensure the offender recognizes his or her responsibility. The general procedural guidelines for sentencing are defined under Article 37 of the CC.

The sentencing of minors is further affected by the general provision of Article 38 of the CC, which requires that the youth's personality and character be considered in the sentencing process (see Box 8.6, above). The actual list of punishments, excluding the conditions and dimensions of its fixing, can be found in articles 21 through 23 of the CC. The range of punishments include: imprisonment, correctional work without imprisonment (e.g., community service work), fine, absolute discharge, entrusting a duty to redress committed harm (e.g., victim reconciliation), confiscation of personal property thought to interfere with the rehabilitation process, deprivation of the ranks, and—as an exclusive punishment—capital punishment. However, the disposition must fit both the crime and individual's character. Therefore, in some circumstances certain punishments can not be applied, for example, discharge from office or deprivation of the ranks. Furthermore, in accordance with the principles of "due process" and recognizing the special status of minors, Russian law recognizes that some measures should not be considered justifiable forms of punishment for minors. For example, under Article 23 Part 2 of the Criminal Code, capital punishment can not be used against persons under the age of eighteen, and Article 24 stipulates that a minor can not be incarcerated for more than ten years [the same rule applies in Norway—editor's note]. There are no exceptions to this stipulation.

Labour Colonies

The practice of alternative sanctions is gaining acceptance among Russian judges. The court has the legal right to place the young offender in a correctional institution as an alternative to prison (see Box 8.2) where they are educated and taught about the workforce. Other administrative measures could include community hours or fine payments. Article 63 of the CC provides for the use of such sanctions as long as the minor is not considered a serious public risk and if it is believed that the youth could be re-educated. These measures are not punishment, they do not involve convictions, and they are sizably milder than conventional measures of punishment. Essentially, these measures are the same as those which are used by the CJA. However, if the court feels that correction through re-education is not viable, then incarceration may be used to protect society. In such cases the youth is considered not only a risk to society but he or she has not expressed any sense of remorse.

As is the case in many Western countries, juvenile offenders serve their sentences separately from adults. They are sent to educational-labour colonies specifically intended for minors under Article 24 of the CC. Males charged for the first time are regularly incarcerated while first-time female offenders are generally sent to re-educational colonies. Repeat male offenders are kept in a higher security prison than are first-time offenders (See Box 8.7).

For first-time offenders incurring a sentence of less than three years, the court is obliged under Article 401(2) of the CPC to examine the possibility of substituting incarceration with an alternative sanction. In accordance with Article 46(1) of the CC, the court is obliged to consider the minor's personality

---

Box 8.7: Educational-Labour Colonies

Educational-labour colonies an alternative to imprisonment for juveniles. There are two basic kinds of such provisions:1) educational-labour colonies with a general regime similar to the work camps found in North America and recently introduced in Western Australia (see Ch. 2) and 2) the educational-labour colonies with their intensive regimes—similar to the 'boot' camps more commonly found in the United States (see Ch. 10). The educational-labour colonies are for juvenile males who are sentenced for an offence, that is considered minor for the first-time offenders. All convicted juvenile females are sent to educational-labour colonies. The second type of labour programs are used only for convicted males who either were imprisoned before or who had been sent to the former type of educational-labour colony and had violated the requirements of the regime.

---

and ability to benefit from re-education before resorting to incarceration. Should the court decide that imprisonment or correctional work is the appropriate sanction, under Article 44 of the CC the court may substitute probation as a form of a suspended sentence.

Even though the Russian model of juvenile justice is largely based on the justice model, the agents of the court recognize the importance providing alternative preventative sanctions whenever possible. Considerable emphasis is placed on understanding the causes and conditions which prompted the crime in the first place. Formal sanctions are used as a last resort after the range of alternatives can be argued to not be in the best interests of society. Hence, the prosecutorial and sentencing processes are very individualized for minors and, as stated earlier, the primary objective is to focus on crime prevention through re-educative dispositions.

The Future: A Need for Reform

Since the dramatic political, social, and economic changes in Russia after 1991, the problem of juvenile delinquency has become more evident. The shift from old Russian traditions is still taking place as many of the legal and political directions remain undefined. But the toll of the changes has been reflected in a general increase in the delinquency rates. The pattern and trends of delinquency are similar to those being experienced by Hungary (see Chapter 11). This is in spite of the fact that there has been an increased acceptance of Western ideas on how to address delinquency both socially and politically.

Over the past few years, Russia has experienced:

- A steady increase in the rate delinquency. For example, in 1993 there were 224,000 officially recorded juvenile crimes. This represented 8% of all known crimes. The numbers represent a 36% increase since 1990;
- An increase in the number of violent crimes committed by minors;
- An increase in the number of minors reoffending;
- An increase in group-related juvenile activity as well as in increase in juvenile crimes involving so called "mixed" groups (i.e., adults and minors) as well as organized criminal groups—especially in the area of the drug trade;
- An increase in the number of minor crimes involving the use of alcohol and drugs.
- The establishment of more juvenile courts in a number of states.

Given the recent trends in juvenile crime in Russia, it appears that the previous system of social prevention under the former Soviet Union has fallen into decay. It is necessary to address this growing problem. The old punitive prevention policies must be replaced with programs and legislation that can strike a balance between accountability while addressing the needs of the minor and the family. These measures should be based on interdisciplinary and interagency approaches that are able to address the social and economic factors that contribute to the delinquency problem. In accordance with the UN Beijing Rules (see Box 1—Introduction), our juvenile justice system needs to find a balance between a strict legalistic justice model and a welfare model that recognizes the special needs of young persons and has been recommended as the 'universal' model for all countries. In partial response to this need, a special inquiry into the relationship between family problems and delinquency was initiated in 1995.

During the mid 1970s in Russia, the scientific trend of "Family Criminology" began to emerge. The perspective considers in detail the connection between family problems and crime, and beginning in 1995 the State Duma has initiated a project known as, "On Prevention of Family Violence". This legal reform project also includes a project concerning the so-called "family courts" where cases of juvenile delinquency are supposed to be considered. The purpose of the project is to help identify and address the needs children at risk as well as protect their rights and interests. However, in light of the fact that a significant number of delinquent offences are related to negative social conditions within the family, consideration must be given to the establishment of special "family" courts. These courts could focus on the greater social issues while balancing legal concerns of criminal, civil, and family matters. It is anticipated that such courts will be established after the final results of the "On Prevention of Family Violence" project.

In summary, the future of juvenile justice in Russia is likely to undergo major changes as the face of Russian society continues to evolve. What may appear to be positive reform policies to outsiders have been met with mixed reactions in the Soviet Union. The newfound freedoms (e.g., speech, assembly, and multicandidate elections) are in sharp contrast to Russia's long history of authoritarian structures. The transition has not gone smoothly due to long suppressed inter-ethnic fights, labour turmoils, and soaring crime rates. In such a climate it hardly appears likely that progressive social reform for juvenile justice will be quick in coming. However, we are optimistic, and any such changes must be based on a sound examination of the facts and trends. The changes should also emphasize the importance of prevention rather than relying on our past antiquated punitive practices of crime control. In order to accomplish some of these broad goals, there is a need for more reliable data such as self-report and victimization data. And now that we are able to share information more freely with other countries, it would be beneficial to examine and compare our needs and goals with those of other countries—especially those whose history may have followed a comparable path to that of Russia.

References

Borodin, S.V. (1980). Soviet Union. In V.L. Stewart (Ed.). *Justice and troubled children.* NY: New York University Press.

Einstadter, W., & Henry, S. (1995). *Criminology theory.* Orlando, FL: Harcourt Brace.

Erlanger, S. (1996, March/April). Images of lawlessness distorts Moscow's reality. *CJ Europe,* 6(2): 5-6.

Gaverov, G. (1985). Problems of legislation and judicial practice improving in the field of the application of the measures of educational character to the juveniles. *Problems of Prevenrive Crimes Improving.* Irkutsk.

Goodwin, T. (1995, winter). Crime in Russia: Bitter fruit of capitalism and democracy. *Synapse,* 34: 1-5.

Hard fortunes of the youth—Who is guilty? (1991). Moscow, Russia.*

Juvenile delinquencies and their prevention. (Kazanski University. 1983).

Keller, B. (1987, July 26). Russia's restless youth. *The New York Times Magazine.* (pp. 14-53).

Lezhikov, G.L. (1995, May). Russia: Statistical information on crime and its use of crime control. *CJ International* (Online).

Legal problems of preventing delinquency. (1990). Tomsk, Russia.

Miheev, R. (1985). The age: Criminal-law and criminology problems. *Problems of Preventive Crimes Improving*, pp. 3-17.

Peculiarities of the delinquency in different regions and problems of effective preventing of it. 1985. (N/A).

Ponomareu, P.G. (1996). Legal measures against legalization of criminal arrests as means of combating organized crime in Russia. *AJCS Today*, (14)4:1, 3.

Popular Science Journal " The Youth" (N 2. 1992). St. Petersburg, Russia.

Primachenok, A. (1990). Improving of the criminal-law system of measures to prevent juvenile delinquency. Minsk, Russia.

Raine, L.P., & Cilluffo, F.I. (Eds.). (1994). *Global organized crime: The new empire of evil*. Washington: The Center for Strategic and International Studies.

Russian legislature of X-XX centuries. (1987). Moscow, Russia.

Shelly, L. (1980). Policing soviet society: The evolution of state control. *Law and Social Inquiry*, 15(3): 479-520.

Shestakov, D. (1996). *Family criminology*. St. Petersburg, Russia.

Sibiryakov, S. (1993). *The children—Delinquency-trouble*. Volgograd, Russia.

Sidorova, V. (1981). Practice of the cumpulsory measures of an educational character use. *Soviet Justice,* N 7, pp. 9-10.

Some questions of an application of the legislation on juvenile delinquency: An oveview of the judicial practice." (1983). *Bulletin of the Supreme Court of the USSR,* N 6, pp. 35-40.

Velchev, A., & Moshak, G. (1990). The minor and delinquency. Kishinev, Russia.

Ward, O. (1996, Oct. 2). Use of hard drugs soaring with young rich Russians. *Toronto Star* (Online).

---

*   Russian titles were translated into English for this contribution.

chapter 9

Juvenile Crime and Juvenile Law in the Federal Republic of Germany

Hans-Jörg Albrecht
Faculty of Law, University of Technology Dresden
Director-elect of the Max-Planck-Institute of Foreign
    and International Criminal Law in Freiburg

Facts about Germany

Area: 356,733 sq. km. **Population:** As of 1995, 81,264,000 or 228 per sq. km. Eighty-six percent live in urban areas. After German re-unification in 1990, the size of the population now (1996) is at approximately 80 million, including some 7 million foreigners (8.7%). **Climate:** A mild continental climate. Average lows in winter hover around -1° C to summer average of approximately 19° C. **Economy:** A highly industrialized country—56% service industry and 40% industry. **Government:** The political system of Germany is federal in nature, with sixteen states (Bundesländer). The division of legislative and administrative powers between the federal level and the state level is laid down in the German Constitution which gives the federal parliament a strong position in legislation (in fact, the major fields of almost exclusive competence of state parliaments concern police and education while most other legislation—e.g., adult criminal law, juvenile criminal law, juvenile welfare law—falls within the competence of the federal parliament). On the other hand, implementation of laws or administration is entrusted (with some exceptions, e.g., defence) to the "Länder". With respect to criminal justice (i.e., basic criminal law and procedural criminal law) virtually all statutes are federal statutes, while the single states are empowered to implement justice administration (including public prosecution, criminal courts and corrections).

> The adolescence that occurs without stress and strain is too unusual to be called normal.
>
> Reuter, The Sociology of Adolescence,
> *American Journal of Sociology*, 1937, 43, p.414.

The History of Juvenile Criminal Law

In 1923 the Youth Court Law (*Jugendgerichtsgesetz*) entered into force in Germany. The Youth Court Law signalled a profound change in dealing with young offenders. It provided for a different legal framework for criminal cases committed by juveniles (fourteen to seventeen years old). Until then juvenile offenders (twelve to seventeen years) fell under the jurisdiction of the adult system, although being of minor age led to mitigated penalties (Eisenberg 1995).

The Youth Court Law was the first significant result of rehabilitative thinking in modern German criminal legislation. The idea of rehabilitation was expressed by the so-called "modern school of criminal law" which was opposed to the classical doctrine of punishment and the use punitive sanctions in favour of behaviour-modifying rehabilitative measures. The leading figure of the "modern school of criminal law", Franz von Liszt, put it this way: "If a juvenile commits a criminal offence and we let him get away with it, then the risk of relapse in crime is lower than the risk we face after having him punished" (Liszt 1905:346). The development of the "modern school of criminal law" coincided partially with the emergence of the "youth court movement," which also stressed the impact of rehabilitating juvenile offenders. In addition the movement stressed the need for a completely different system of justice for juvenile offenders, which then was conceived as a system of education. The "youth court movement" relied heavily on the thinking of the North American child-saver movement as well as on North American experiences with juvenile courts. In 1908 Frankfurt became the first German city to establish a special department for juvenile offenders. The first juvenile prison opened in 1911.

One year before the enactment of the Youth Court Law, another youth law, namely the Youth Welfare Law (*Jugendwohlfahrtsgesetz*, 1922), became effective. The Youth Welfare Law was aimed at youth (under the age of civil responsibility, which then commenced at the age of twenty-one (today eighteen), in need of care and education. The development of German youth laws has been based on those basic beliefs that have characterized the emergence of youth laws in virtually all Western juvenile justice systems (Empey 1982; Klein 1984). These basic beliefs are embedded in the positivistic based perception that juveniles are different from adults in terms of psychological and physiological properties as well as the existence of a particular social status creating particular sources of stress and conflicts during a limited developmental period between childhood and adulthood. A belief prevailed that juvenile criminal behaviour indicates the need for mediated legal intervention because of the juveniles' particular social and psychological status.

Juvenile criminal law and juvenile welfare law are part of a bipartite approach to youth problems by separating the juvenile criminal offender from otherwise endangered children and juveniles. Although both of these approaches were based upon the idea that the failure of parents in raising their offspring and in providing adequate education must have the consequence of public education, organized either by youth departments or (in case of criminal behaviour of the juvenile) by the juvenile criminal court, the basic difference lies in the input requirements. Admission to the criminal justice system and to the juvenile criminal court requires suspicion and indictment because of a criminal offence. Admission to the juvenile welfare system requires establishing the need for care and education with no minimum age requirements. The Youth Court Law amendments of the twentieth century (1943, 1953 and 1990; see Kerner 1990) adhered to the principle of education, although in 1943, under the influence of German fascism (Kerner and Weitekamp, 1984), a special amendment concerning juvenile felons introduced the possibility of the transfer of juvenile offenders sixteen years and older to adult criminal courts with adult criminal penalties (including the death penalty). Furthermore, the age of criminal responsibility was lowered and set at twelve years for juveniles having committed serious crimes. This law was abolished immediately after World War II. The amendment of 1953 brought important changes in terms of the opportunity to sentence young adults as juveniles and the possibility to place juvenile offenders under probation supervision in the case of a suspended sentence of youth prison (see Box 9.1). With the latest Youth Court Law amendment of 1990, among other changes, the indeterminate sentence of youth imprisonment was abolished; diversion and victim-offender mediation have been widened; and important restrictions on placing juveniles in pretrial detention have been introduced.

Box 9.1: Member of Parliament Demands Decreasing the Age of Responsibility to Twelve

In the 1990s the media and police have drawn considerable attention to a group of young people (ages eleven to thirteen) who have been heavily involved in delinquent and criminal activity. They drew specific attention since German juvenile criminal law does not deal with youths under the age of thirteen. They are dealt with by the juvenile welfare system, which since the early 1970s no longer provides for closed and secure juvenile custody. The police in particular have argued that nothing can be done to stop this group of delinquent children from committing serious crimes. Responding to this a member of the federal parliament declared on September 12, 1995 that the age of responsibility should be lowered to twelve years. It was argued that from the age of twelve most youths are cognitively enough developed to understand the wrongfulness of any criminal actions. The plea failed to receive any support from either the federal parliament or the federal government.

Juvenile Criminal Law between Adult Criminal Law and Youth Welfare Laws

The creation of the Youth Court Law focused on the educational and rehabilitative needs thought to be indicated by the criminal offence of juvenile offenders. But German juvenile justice was never dominated by a social welfare model; the idea prevailed that both punishment and education should be reconciled within the framework of juvenile justice. Strict separation between the juvenile offender on the one hand and children and juveniles who are in need of care and education can be observed throughout the (short) history of juvenile laws. Throughout this century voices have been raised in favour of a "unified" welfare approach to "delinquent" children and juveniles. But juvenile criminal law never deviated far from general criminal law. It remained bound to the rule of law with respect to the "triggers" of public intervention and to a compromise between punishment and education. Hence, it remains a subsystem in the general criminal justice system.

The criminal justice system in Germany classifies individuals into four categories according to age. Under the age of fourteen no criminal culpability exists. The onset of criminal responsibility is now at fourteen years (sec. 19 German Criminal Code). But as criminal law is based on the assumption that full criminal responsibility is the product of a fully completed process of socialization and moral development, a particular system of juvenile criminal justice shall respond to criminal offences committed by juveniles (Kaiser 1993). Furthermore, sec. 3 of the Youth Court Law demands full proof that a juvenile offender was mature enough to be aware of the wrongfullness of an illegal act and was capable of behaving according to such an awareness. However, criminological research shows that juvenile court practice does not comply fully with sec. 3, but rather pays lip service through routinely assuming criminal responsibility of juvenile offenders. Full criminal responsibility commences at the age of eighteen. Young adult offenders (eighteen to twenty years old) are presumed to be adults and therefore they are presumed to be fully responsible in the case of criminal offending; however, under certain conditions (sec. 105 Youth Court Law) young adults may be prosecuted as if they had been juveniles when committing the crime. With sec. 3 and 105 it was acknowledged that the concept of adolescence requires flexibility in assuming criminal culpability because of considerable variation in the process of maturation, social and moral development as well as integration into the world of adults.

Children (up to the age of thirteen) and juveniles (fourteen to seventeen years old) who are defined to be in need of care and education are handled by youth welfare departments set up under the Youth Welfare Law (now *Kinder- und Jugendhilfegesetz*). Although general youth problem behaviour does not justify juvenile court proceedings, a criminal offence committed by a child may be used as an indicator of the need for care and education. In general, public youth welfare is understood as a last resort with private youth welfare having priority over public interventions.

The links between the Youth Court Law and the Juvenile Welfare Law are visible in a certain overlapping of measures that may be initiated on the basis of mere welfare considerations and educational measures, which may be imposed as a consequence of a criminal offence committed by a juvenile. Furthermore, the Youth Court Law requires specialization of the juvenile criminal court insofar as judges should have special (psychological and sociological) knowledge of youth and finally, as a general rule, judges in juvenile criminal courts should at the same time be appointed as a family judge (*Vormundschaftsrichter*) responsible for applying juvenile welfare law in the family court.

The Definition of Juvenile Crime

The definition of juvenile crime does not differ from that of adult crime. Juvenile criminal procedures may be initiated only if there is sufficient reason to assume that a juvenile has committed a criminal offence. The same standards as in adult criminal procedures apply. Decisive for the definition of juvenile crime is the age of the perpetrator at the time of the offence. So criminal offences as defined in the German Criminal Code apply to juveniles as well as to adults; as do the basic rules which must be followed when establishing criminal responsibility. The differences between juveniles and adults lie in the type and the range of penalties that can be imposed. Procedural rules referring to the organization of juvenile criminal prosecution and juvenile criminal courts as well as to juvenile criminal trials also differ.

Contrary to other justice systems, especially North American systems of juvenile justice, German youth laws do not provide for so-called "status offences," nor does the Youth Court Law provide for waivers of juvenile rights and the possibility of transferring juvenile offenders to adult criminal courts. On the contrary, as has been pointed out above, young adults (eighteen to twenty years) may be transferred to the juvenile justice system instead of being tried in an ordinary criminal court. On the other hand, a specific set of youth protection laws includes criminal offences in cases of adult violations of these laws. Although there are no youth-specific types of behaviour which could serve as a trigger for juvenile criminal justice measures, a debate goes on about the question of whether offences laid down in the basic criminal statutes for juveniles and adults should be adapted in some respects to the particulars of the world and lifestyles of young people. Here it is argued that criminal offence statutes like fraud or forgery as well as certain aggravating circumstances are perhaps well suited for judgments on adult behaviour, but are perhaps too complicated to be fully understood by a fourteen or fifteen year old juvenile (Ostendorf, 1992). Furthermore, certain juvenile behaviour patterns, such as forcefully taking items belonging to opposing soccer fans, are assumed to be triggered by expressive motivations and do not reflect the instrumental reasons at the centre of legal considerations in framing offence statutes like robbery or theft.

The Principle of Education
The major difference between juvenile criminal law and juvenile justice on the one hand and adult criminal law can be found in the general orientation of the two systems. While the offence itself is the centre of adult criminal law, youth criminal law emphasizes the offender. Youth criminal law is bound to the goal of education and rehabilitation of the young offender. Although a juvenile is held legally responsible for a crime (*mens rea* must be proven), the primary goal of juvenile criminal justice concerns education and rehabilitation. Juvenile criminal law does not emphasize the criminal offence or the seriousness of the offence but the offender and his or her rehabilitative needs. This orientation has led to an ongoing conflict about the relationship between punishment and education. The debate began shortly after the enactment of the Youth Court Law and the general discussion around the lack of uniformity in its wording. While the "modern school of criminal law" pushed for a rehabilitation oriented system, partisans of the punishment approach expressed the fear that the principle of education could serve as a "Trojan Horse", ultimately undermining criminal law in general (Heinz, 1992:123). The wording of the Youth Court Law is not uniform. With respect to the sanctions provided in the Youth Court Law the term "educational measure" is used in conjunction with the term "punishment" (*Jugendstrafe*). This allows for several interpretations; the reading depends on whether the criminal offence or the educational needs of the juvenile offender are emphasized.

However, the adoption of the principle of education as well as the disregard for general prevention, general deterrence, and seriousness of the offence as a guiding rule in sentencing does not mean that the general principle of proportionality is never applied. The principle of proportionality (*Verhältnismäßigkeit*) is derived from the German constitution and requires that the state must comply with the legal requirements that the "educational. measure" chosen must be: (1) sufficient to reach the goal which is pursued by the intervention, (2) the least severe measure among several which equally are suited to attain the goal envisaged, and (3) proportional to the goal to be achieved. This principle also serves to set an upper limit to legal intervention in juvenile criminal cases. Therefore, while any disposition has to be proportional to the offence committed, it is also guided by the goal of education. The meaning of education has also been involved in an ongoing debate. Streng (1994), among others, suggests that the meaning of education in the context of juvenile criminal law should not go beyond the prevention of individual relapse into crime. Any meaning of education extending to the manipulation of the motivation of norm compliance, attitudes, and general behaviour patterns is moreover likely to violate constitutional rights (of the juvenile offender and his or her parents) and, in practical terms, overestimates the capabilities of any justice system.

Extent, Structure, and Development of Youth Crime

General Trends in Youth Crime

Analyses of the development of youth crime in the Federal Republic of Germany can be based on police crime statistics as well as on criminal court statistics. In German criminal procedure the finding of guilt and sentencing are not split into two decisions. The finding of guilt and the sentence are produced in a single decision. Unlike the situation in a number of other countries, German police statistics count "suspects", they do not refer to arrested offenders. Suspicion of a criminal offence does not necessarily lead to a formal arrest. Police may arrest a suspect under the conditions that proper identification is not possible on the spot or that police will initiate placement in pre-trial detention, which then must be applied for by the public prosecutor and ordered by the court. But in most criminal cases a formal arrest is not made.

Longitudinal self-report studies and victimization surveys are not available for the Federal Republic of Germany. Reliance upon police-based statistics in the analyses of youth crime means that analysis extends to the legal response to the youthful offender. Since crime statistics reflect the investigative work done by police and the general mechanisms of social control, such as the victims decision to report a crime, we have to take into account that official accounts on crime are dependent on the public's willingness to report crimes.

As Graph 9.1 demonstrates a considerable increase in the relative figures of juvenile suspects took place during the 1960s and 1970s. Throughout the mid 1980s these figures stabilized, but by the end of the decade and the beginning of the 1990s there was a marked increase in juvenile crime. Parallel movements in the figures of juvenile crime can be observed in virtually all countries of Western Europe (Kaiser, 1989). On the other hand demographic changes lead to a considerable decrease in the proportions of child, juvenile, and young adult suspects in the population of suspects at large. While juveniles accounted for approximately 15% of all suspects in 1980, their share dropped to 9.5% in 1991. Children accounted for 6.3% of all suspects in 1980 and 4.4% in 1991. During the same period the proportion of young adult suspects (eighteen to twenty years) decreased from 13.5% to 10.2%. However, the increase in juvenile offender rates can to a large extent be explained by an enormous increase in the rates of petty theft.

Crime data for the east of Germany are available, but as police information systems have to be reorganized these data are not yet very reliable. In general we find that there is an increase in crime at large as well as in juvenile crime. As it was expected the trend in the east moves towards convergence with crime rates in the west. Most recently, with data from the 1993 and 1994 police crime statistics, it has been argued that young people in the east of Germany are far more exposed to those risks thought to contribute to crime and therefore far more involved in committing crime—in particular auto theft (Frehsee, 1995). It might also be that police and the public in the east of Germany are still differing from the west in terms of control styles and crime reporting patterns vis-à-vis young people.

Serious crimes, especially serious violent crimes, represent rare events in younger age groups. Graphs 9.2 to 9.4 show the trends in murder, robbery, and aggravated assault figures during the last fifteen years. For murder and robbery it is obvious that clear distinctions can be made between children and juveniles on the one hand and young adults on the other hand. Young adults are more heavily involved in serious crimes than are children and juveniles where theft accounts for a large proportion of crime involvement.

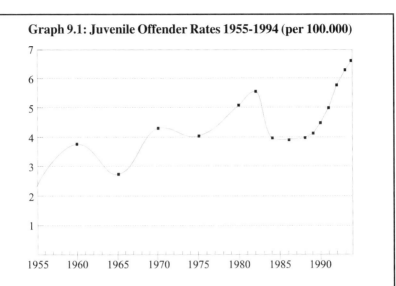

Graph 9.1: Juvenile Offender Rates 1955-1994 (per 100.000)

In 1963 traffic offences were omitted from police statistics; since 1983 multiple offenders were counted only once.

Source: Federal Police Statistics (Bundeskriminalamt, Wiesbaden)

Graph 9.2: Child, juvenile and young adult homicide suspects 1977-1994 (per 100.000)

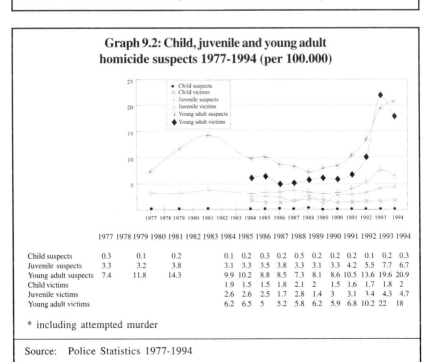

	1977	1978	1979	1980	1981	1982	1983	1984	1985	1986	1987	1988	1989	1990	1991	1992	1993	1994
Child suspects	0.3	0.1	0.2					0.1	0.2	0.3	0.2	0.5	0.2	0.2	0.2	0.1	0.2	0.3
Juvenile suspects	3.3	3.2	3.8					3.1	3.3	3.5	3.8	3.3	3.1	3.3	4.2	5.5	7.7	6.7
Young adult suspects	7.4	11.8	14.3					9.9	10.2	8.8	8.5	7.3	8.1	8.6	10.5	13.6	19.6	20.9
Child victims								1.9	1.5	1.5	1.8	2.1	2	1.5	1.6	1.7	1.8	2
Juvenile victims								2.6	2.6	2.5	1.7	2.8	1.4	3	3.1	3.4	4.3	4.7
Young adult victims								6.2	6.5	5	5.2	5.8	6.2	5.9	6.8	10.2	22	18

* including attempted murder

Source: Police Statistics 1977-1994

Graph 9.3: Child, juvenile and young adult suspects of robbery/victims of robbery 1977-1994 (per 100,000 of the age group)

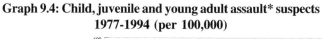

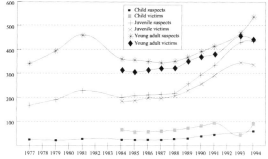

	1977	1978	1979	1980	1981	1982	1983	1984	1985	1986	1987	1988	1989	1990	1991	1992	1993	1994
Child suspects	27	29	31			20	18	15	15	15	18	27	29	20	24	32		
Juvenile suspects	82	91	121		88	95	96	91	93	103	142	165	177	187	244			
Young adult suspects	120	130	155			125	121	113	113	105	111	133	157	200	214	224		
Child victims						26	24	22	21	24	30	48	69	64	63	73		
Juvenile victims						37	40	41	41	47	61	406	141	164	166	226		
Young adult victims						65	67	67	66	69	77	99	125	159	156	196		

Source: Police Statistics 1977-1994

Graph 9.4: Child, juvenile and young adult assault* suspects 1977-1994 (per 100,000)

	1977	1978	1979	1980	1981	1982	1983	1984	1985	1986	1987	1988	1989	1990	1991	1992	1993	1994
Child suspects	30	27	32			29	27	26	27	29	33	41	48		55	62		
Juvenile suspects	171	196	231			207	212	216	216	222	260	297	336		432	437		
Young adult suspects	346	397	463			363	357	353	348	352	371	395	414		472	538		
Child victims						69	58	60	62	65	73	84	95		48	93		
Juvenile victims						196	190	200	199	210	229	259	294		346	338		
Young adult victims						315	308	316	324	323	353	372	381		456	441		

* aggravated assault only

Source: Police Statistics 1977-1994

Trends in the rates of child, juvenile, and young adult victims of violent crime parallel very closely those of the offender rates in these age groups, which suggests a considerable degree of overlapping in offender and victim roles. Research on self-reported crimes and victimization has indeed revealed that those juveniles and young adults ranking very high on scales of self-reported crime are those with the highest risk of being victimized (Villmow and Stephan, 1983).

Graphs 9.5 and 9.6 give some insight into crimes committed by juveniles and young adults. Property and non-violent crimes such as petty theft and fraud outweigh other offence types in the population of female offenders. Female juveniles' share of police recorded crime was 21% in 1994 while for female young adults it was 18%. And while there has been no qualitative change in the size of female crime, the proportion of female crime has increased somewhat during the last decades (see Albrecht, 1987).

In general the structure of criminal offences committed by male juveniles is determined through theft and criminal damage. Serious violent offences and drug offences play a minor role. Drug offences become more important in the group of young adults (and even more so in the adult population). Although Graph 9.5 points to considerable proportions of aggravated theft (which includes burglary), robbery and other violent offences for male juveniles are significantly lower in seriousness compared to young adult and adult crimes of the same category (Dölling, 1992).

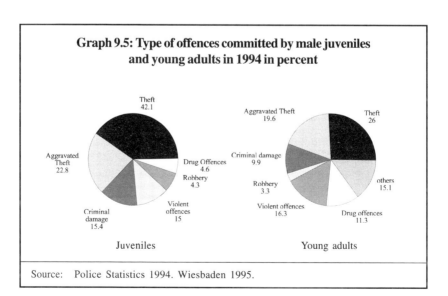

Graph 9.5: Type of offences committed by male juveniles and young adults in 1994 in percent

Theft
42.1

Aggravated Theft
19.6

Theft
26

Aggravated Theft
22.8

Drug Offences
4.6

Criminal damage
9.9

Robbery
4.3

Robbery
3.3

others
15.1

Criminal damage
15.4

Violent offences
15

Violent offences
16.3

Drug offences
11.3

Juveniles

Young adults

Source: Police Statistics 1994. Wiesbaden 1995.

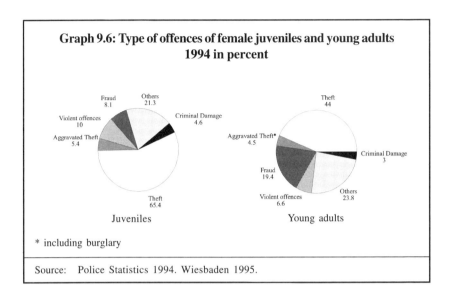

Graph 9.6: Type of offences of female juveniles and young adults 1994 in percent

Juveniles   Young adults

* including burglary

Source: Police Statistics 1994. Wiesbaden 1995.

Furthermore, the picture of youth crime emerging from the analysis of official crime data indicates that criminal behaviour may represent rather normal behaviour, even in terms of police recorded crime and court dispositions. Estimates of prevalence of criminal convictions amount to as much as one-third of members of male birth cohorts having a criminal record before reaching the age of twenty-four (Kaiser 1988). Cohort studies recently came up with the finding that when reaching the age of fourteen approximately 6% of male children have been suspected at least once of having committed a crime (Karger and Sutterer, 1988). Prevalence rates of police recorded crimes are even more elevated among the population of ethnic minority youth. By the age of fourteen approximately 14% of ethnic minority youth (compared to approximately 5% of German youth) have been suspected at least once of having committed a crime (see Box 9.2).

Conflicting Explanations

The various increases in officially recorded crime has received much attention in criminology and criminal politics. The assessment of these trends in the development of youth crime remains a controversial issue. Three conflicting positions may be identified:

1. It is argued that rising crime rates among children and juveniles point to a growing menace to society and require strong preventive and (partially) repressive action (Stümper, 1973).

Box 9.2: Public Pressure Demands Getting Tougher on Young Adults

From the 18th to 20th of September 1991, Hoyerswerda (a small town in Saxony, Germany) became a place where a group of several hundred young people, most of them skinheads, attacked a centre for asylum-seekers. The outburst of violence against ethnic minorities orginated from an attack on Vietnamese people selling cigarettes and other items on the street of this small town by a group of skinheads. The Vietnamese people retreated to their home, a centre for asylum-seekers. Within the next few days a group of young people gathered in front of the home and began attacking the building. In the ensuing violence, several people were seriously injured.

In the city of Rostock a similar incident occurred in August of 1992. Subsequently another incident occurred in the small northern German town of Moelln. Here three Turkish people were killed when their home was set ablaze by a group of young people. These incidents triggered a debate on juvenile violence, in particular violent acts committed by young adults (eighteen to twenty years of age) who in practice are sentenced to juvenile court. Demands were voiced to change this provision. Recently the state of Bavaria (in southern Germany) introduced the first draft bill which aims at reforming section 105 of the Youth Court Law. If passed the amendment would place young adults found committing a serious offence to fall under the jurisidiction of adult criminal court. And while there is consderable public support for the amendment, little support can be found among those responsible for administering the juvenile justice law.

2. The increase in youth crime is exaggerated by police and politicians. The increase should be regarded as an artificial product resulting from an increase in police attention paid to children and juveniles as well as reflecting a net widening effect and particularly an increase in the efficiency of police crime investigation (Albrecht, P.A. and Lamnek, 1979; Albrecht, P.A., 1993).

3. There was actually an increase in youth crime, but this increase was mainly due to an increase in crime of a non-serious nature, which should not be overdramatized (Steffen, 1979).

Research on the "causes" of juvenile crime carried out in the 1950s and 1960s pointed to the relevance of the broken family, bad parenting, school problems, and unemployment (Villmow and Kaiser, 1974). Since the mid 1960s, results from self-report surveys on delinquency and crime indicate a shift from etiological concepts in explaining crime to labelling theory, which leads to new perspectives on juvenile delinquency and delinquency prevention. The finding that delinquent behaviour is ubiquitous in youth populations, while official criminal law-based interventions concentrate on a rather small proportion of those who could be the target of legal interventions, gave rise to the assumptions that:

- juvenile crime represents "normal" behaviour, and
- juvenile criminal behaviour alone is not sufficient to justify public intervention in terms of education and/or punishment pursuing the goal of rehabilitation.

From these perspectives, prevention serves to discriminate against marginal and deprived youths with considerable risks to deepen disintegrative processes. Although in-depth studies on the relationship between undetected and known crime among youths revealed that the assumption of ubiquity of crime holds true only for petty or trivial offences, while serious crimes and repeated criminal offences are restricted to a rather small group of juveniles, the argument became decisive in designing youth criminal policy in the 1970s and 1980s.

Conclusions drawn from these studies supported the view that a juvenile offence is not a signal demanding official intervention and public education. Longitudinal research on offence patterns shows that as many as 70% of juvenile offenders are one-time offenders (Krüger, 1983). These findings lead to the conclusion that prevention of juvenile delinquency should rely heavily on non-prosecution and diversion rather than the use of youth prison and other punitive measures. Decision-makers should refrain from using social deprivation as guiding criteria in juvenile court decision-making. The 1980s therefore saw an increasing use of diversion and community-based measures such as community service, social training courses and most recently restitution, conflict mediation, and reconciliation schemes. Informal sanctions and informal systems of control as represented by the family, peer groups, and schools currently outweigh formal systems of control. In turn we observe a renewed criminological interest in family, school, religion, and employment as decisive elements in the prevention of juvenile delinquency (Albrecht, H.-J., 1991). This renewed interest also corresponds to a shift in theoretical thinking about juvenile delinquency and its prevention from stress and labelling theories to control theories of juvenile crime (Kaiser, 1993).

On the macro level, research turned to the question of how large-scale changes in the roles and functions of the family, school, and religion in post-industrial societies could be related to changing patterns of juvenile crime. It is argued that the potential of the family, the school, and the neighbourhood in providing bonds between juveniles and society has diminished steadily. However, it is also argued that probably nothing has changed in terms of behaviour patterns of juveniles; rather systems of informal control have broken down thus exposing children and juveniles to formal control systems with respect to behaviour that would have been handled informally in the past. Both explanations point to a common perspective for prevention: strengthening the role of the community, the neighbourhood, family, and school in handling problem behaviour. Based on the research findings, it is obvious that formal interventions do not make a difference with respect to exiting from criminal lifestyles, but, on the contrary, formal interventions seem to add to the juvenile offender's problems in adjusting to societal demands. The focus of current research is on the feasibility of replacing formal juvenile court responses to juvenile delinquency through restitution and victim-offender reconciliation schemes. Restitution and victim-offender mediation receive strong support outside and inside the criminal justice system (Schöch, 1992). Survey research seems to confirm the acceptance of restitution by the public and by the victims of juvenile crime (Sessar, 1992).

Particular Problem Groups and Particular Risks

In the 1980s two subgroups of juvenile delinquents attracted considerable attention from German criminological research. These subgroups comprise ethnic (or foreign) minority youth and chronic juvenile offenders. Research has pointed out that substantial proportions of police-recorded crime and self-reported delinquent acts can be linked to a disproportionally small group of juveniles (Krüger, 1983; Karger and Sutterer, 1988). This observation has led to a growing interest in identifying early signs of chronic offending, but G. Albrecht (1990) concludes that it will not be possible to convert the retrospective finding of high-rate juvenile offenders into ethically and economically feasible prospective prevention strategies.

Ethnic and foreign minority juveniles are also targeted for preventive reasons. The most important group of foreign youth in quantitative terms are the Turks. Official statistics suggest that crime rates among certain ethnic and foreign minority groups are two to four times greater than rates observed in the majority group (Albrecht, H.-J., 1987a; Karger and Sutterer, 1990). Time-series data for foreign offender rates and foreign population rates demonstrate clear trends that might be interpreted as the result of changes in behaviour patterns of second and third generations and of changes in migration patterns. Disproportionate involvement of foreign minority members in police recorded crimes can be observed especially in the age-bracket of eighteen to twenty year old suspects. In 1993 almost half of the suspects (46.5%) were traced to foreign minority members (34% of all juvenile offenders and 30.7% of children (*Bundeskriminalamt*, 1994). Walter (1995) suggests demographic characteristics may account for the increase in crime participation among foreign populations. For example, in the state of Northrhine-Westfalia between 1984 and 1993 the crime rate among young foreigners more than doubled (from 6651 to 13,614) while the increase among young Germans was from 4075 to 5038. Conversely, between 1984 and 1993 the crime rate among "guest-workers" (e.g., transient workers) and immigrant workers did not change much (*Bundeskriminalamt*, 1995). A tentative explanation could be that first generation immigrants experience improved conditions of living, housing, medical care, etc., which outweigh existing differences between minority and majority groups (Kunz, 1989).

Most self-report surveys do not include ethnic or foreign minorities, but samples are regularly drawn from the German resident youth population (Albrecht, 1988). However, evidence derived from those surveys is not conclusive. At the beginning of the 1980s research based on self-reports from the city of Bremen concluded that not only did a larger involvement in delinquency on the part of foreign juveniles not occur but that those foreign juveniles interviewed seemed to be remarkably conformist (Schumann, Berlitz, Guth, & Kanlitzki, 1987).

As we observe segmentation in society along ethnic lines, we may assume that the lowest segments of society are increasingly filling up with immigrant groups that are most likely to be affected by unemployment, bad housing, poverty, insufficient education and vocational training. The research questions, which in the 1960s and 1970s highlighted class, crime, and justice issues (as well as class solidarity and class conflicts), will in the 1990s and in the decades to come be replaced by ethnicity and crime (in addition to ethnic solidarity and ethnic conflicts). Therefore, in general, crime and delinquency among minority youth should be explained by the same theories which are applied to the majority group (Kube and Koch, 1990). Although bonding theories fit the sensitive situation of second and third generation immigrants who actually live between two rather distinct cultures (e.g., Turkish juveniles), this position creates particular problems in terms of conflicts between traditional norms valued by parents and those values and norms of the peer group (Mansel and Hurrelmann, 1993).

Economic recession in the 1970s, exposing the young to unemployment, created at the beginning of the next decade renewed interest in the possible links between youth unemployment and youth crime (Münder, Sack, Albrecht,

H.-J., and Plewig, 1987; Kaiser, 1993b). Despite considerable increases in unemployment rates among juveniles and young adults, the proportion of those unemployed and suspected of having committed a criminal offence decreased. These diverging trends do not suggest a causal relationship between these variables on the micro level, but point to a re-enforcing impact of unemployment. Youth gangs attracted scientific attention in the late 1970s with soccer hooliganism (Heitmeyer and Peter, 1988; Kersten, 1993). In the 1990s, after German re-unification, the problem of right-wing extremist violence towards immigrants committed by groups of juveniles and young adults arose (Viehmann, 1993). Most of these bias-motivated violent offences were committed by juveniles or young adults: 70% of offenders fall into the age bracket of fourteen to twenty years, 3% of the offenders are thirty years or older (*Verfassungsschutzbericht*, 1991). However, the proportion of bias-motivated violence of all violent crimes committed by youth is rather small; furthermore, most inter-ethnic violence is not linked to racism or hate but to conventional triggers of violent behaviour (Solon, 1994).

In recent years youth violence has been targeted as an eminent social and policy problem. A dilemma arises as demands for "get tough" approaches to right-wing juveniles conflict with educational demands put forward by the Youth Court Law. The answer to the dilemma seems to lie in the conception of youth violence. Youth violence may be conceived as indicative of anomie and social disintegration (following rapid social and economic changes produced by German unification), youth violence may also be understood as being part of a much broader violence-prone political radicalism. Finally, youth violence may be explained as a specific transitional phenomenon of male youth associating in gangs (Kersten, 1993). Dependent on these conceptions, youth violence against foreign and ethnic minorities may be the product of social turmoils, representing "hate-crimes," and therefore deserving of repressive action or indicative of mere changes at the surface of ordinary violent gang activities. However, the prevalent approach in explaining youth violence towards minorities refers to the traditional hypothesis of frustration-aggression (Rommelspacher, 1993; Bliesener, 1992).

Furthermore, the mass media, especially video, have been singled out recently for particular attention in this respect. It is assumed that the presentation of violence on video and television (facilitated by easy access to video and television) contributes considerably to youth violence (Glogauer, 1991; Jung, 1993) such assumptions have not been, until now, supported by scientific evidence.

Juvenile Criminal Law and
Juvenile Criminal Proceedings

Processing the Juvenile Offender

Although the basic principles of criminal law apply to juvenile offenders, Youth Court Law's basic orientation extends towards educating the young offender. No special juvenile offences exit in German criminal law. Criminal prosecution in Germany commences regularly with investigation of the crime by police (see Figure 9.1). Police have no discretionary power to dismiss criminal cases (e.g., after cautioning the juvenile) but have to refer every suspect (be it an adult or a juvenile) to the public prosecutor's office where a decision is made whether a charge should be filed or not. Without a formal indictment of the public prosecutor's office no juvenile case can be brought to the juvenile criminal court.

After criminal proceedings have been initiated, investigators will begin to gather information on personal and social circumstances relevant for evaluating the personality of the juvenile offender and for the choice of sanction (sec. 43 Youth Court Law). Immediately after initiation of criminal proceedings against a juvenile offender the Juvenile Court Aid (*Jugendgerichtshilfe*) has to be notified. From here a social worker investigates the personal and social circumstances of the juvenile offender for the Crown in order to provide information relevant to which sanction seems appropriate for the juvenile offender. The court aid has the right to be present during trial. The juvenile court has no discretion in admitting the social inquiry report prepared by the aid. The court must hear the report in order to comply with the general procedural rule that any evidence relevant for the finding of guilt and the appropriate sentence must be heard in trial (for a summary see Laubenthal, 1993). Other than the parents of the juvenile offender, court hearings are not open to the public (including the media).

In recent years the position of the victim has been strengthened beyond those rights. Today, the victim has the right not only to be present during the trial but to act as a "prosecutor" (*Nebenklage*—"side-prosecution"). Finally, in a major criminal law reform in 1987, a series of victim's rights were added to the Code of Criminal Procedure (among them the right to have access to the court files, the right to be informed about the outcomes of the criminal trial, etc.). All these options available for the victim of an adult offender are not valid in juvenile court proceedings according to the leading doctrines (see

Schaal and Eisenberg, 1988). As the victim's rights are still highly valued, the debate is now on whether the particular goal of juvenile justice, that is education, actually may justify restricting the victim's rights.

The right to appeal against a verdict of guilt is restricted for juvenile offenders. Juvenile offenders must choose between two options. They have the right of a full re-trial or the right to have their case reviewed on legal grounds.

The use of pre-trial detention is also restricted in juvenile proceedings. For juvenile suspects aged fourteen to fifteen escape risks may only be assumed on the grounds that the juvenile has made an attempt to escape or that the juvenile has no permanent place of residence in order to justify pre-trial detention (§72 II Juvenile Court Law). None of the reasons valid for adult offenders may be introduced as valid legal grounds to justify pretrial detention. In addition, when deciding on pre-trial detention in a juvenile case, the court has to consider whether it is sufficient to place the juvenile offender in a foster home. In the case of an order to place the juvenile offender in pretrial detention, the court aid has to be informed (§72a Juvenile Court Law) in order to assure that all information relevant for the decision on pretrial detention, including information on possible alternatives such as foster care, can be made available. Contrary to handling adult detainees, juvenile pre-trial detention must be organized in a way which favours education. As a consequence a juvenile offender placed in a pre-trial detention centre is obliged to work.

Criminal Penalties

Each offence in the German Penal Code carries its own penalty with a minimum and a maximum range. The penalty ranges provided in the criminal penal code, however, do not apply to juvenile offenders. The Youth Court Law contains a specific system of sanctions or measures that are divided into three categories.

a. Educational Measures

Educational measures cover a range of orders that can be imposed in a juvenile court. Educational measures shall, according to Section 10 of the Youth Court Act, have a positive impact on the behaviour patterns of juvenile offenders in terms of securing and enhancing conditions of socialization. A catalogue of specific orders is annexed to sec. 10. Among the orders listed there we find community service, participation in social training courses, participation in victim-offender mediation, participation in traffic education, supervision by a

Figure 9.1: An Abbreviated Model of the Young Offenders Legal Process

Input	→	Crime Investigation	→	Indictment/Dismissal	→	Trial Corrections	→	Juvenile
victims complaint (ca. 90% of cases) proactive policing (eg. drug offences, ca. 10% of the cases)		**Police: No discretionary powers.** Investigation of juvenile crimes Information of juvenile court aid Transfer of case files and evidence to the public prosecutors office		Public Prosecutors Office (juvenile branch): Decision-making on whether to dismissal/divert or indict criminal cases; Monopoly in bringing cases to juvenile criminal courts; Principle of legality applies (with certain exemptions) **Discretionary powers**: §45. Dismissal of case without any further action (petty crimes); Dismissal of case if sufficient reactions to the juvenile offender have been taken by others (eg. family, school); Dismissal of case if the juvenile public prosecutor thinks that imposition of eg. mediation, restitution, community service by the juvenile judge is sufficient (and if the juvenile offender complies		**Criminal courts (juvenile branch):** Basic Functions: Adjucation and Sentencing, Supervision of Juvenile Corrections **Procedural options of the juvenile court** 1. Dismissal of the case (§47) 2. Simplified trial 3. Full trial **Sentencing Options** Educational measures Disciplinary measures - Restitution, Fine, etc. - short-term detention -Youth imprisonment min/max: 6 months to 5 years - Suspended		Supervision of Juvenile Corrections at large through the **Juvenile Judge** Basic functions Decision-making on parole and appeals against orders/action of youth prison administration ↑ Juvenile Court Aide ↑ Juvenile Court Aide ↑ Juvenile Judge ↑ Probation Services

Director of the Youth Prison

↑

- Unsuspended

with the order imposed.
Indictment to:
- juvenile judge (single judge); if only educational or disciplinary measures are expected to be the outcome.
- juvenile court; (Schöffengericht);
- juvenile court (district court); in case of murder/homicide

Juvenile Court Aid:
Presenting a pre-sentencing report in the trial (including proposals for disposition and sentencing)

Juvenile Court Aid:
Investigation of the juvenile offenders' personality and social environment; Providing information for the public prosecutors' decision on diversion/indictment as well as on pretrial detention.

social worker, attendance at vocational training, etc. The assistance provided by the children and youth welfare law may include also placement in a home or a foster family. Table 9.1 gives some insight into the use of short-term detention. It is obvious that very rare use is made of this type of enforcement. The power to enforce educational measures through short-term deprivation has provoked a debate on whether the order to do community service then violates the German constitution (which prohibits forced labour outside the prison system). But the procedure was recently upheld based on the argument that it was the educational nature of community service imposed on juvenile offenders under the Youth Court Law (*Bundesverfassungsgericht* (Constitutional court) 1991).

b. Disciplinary Measures
The second category of juvenile sanctions concerns **disciplinary measures** (*Zuchtmittel*, sec. 13 Youth Court Law). Disciplinary measures are classified in three subcategories:

- Cautioning by the juvenile judge. This is a formal verdict which is entered into the criminal record.
- Fulfilling certain conditions (e.g., paying a fine), doing community service (the maximum number of hours of community service is not prescribed by law but is limited by the general principle of proportionality), compensating the victim of the offence and making a formal apology to the victim.
- The most severe disciplinary measure concerns short-term detention (*Jugendarrest*) which may last for up to four weeks or may be imposed during weekends or during spare time. Short-term detention means placement in a special unit (separated from youth prison) for juvenile offenders.

c. Youth Imprisonment:
As defined in sec. 17, Youth Court Law, youth imprisonment is the only juvenile criminal penalty in the strict sense of the word. Although official records provide for two separate court information systems, one for juvenile sanctions and the other for adult penalties, a verdict of youth imprisonment is entered into the adult criminal record when the juvenile offender has reached the age of eighteen. All other juvenile measures are exclusively kept in juvenile records. The minimum sentence for youth imprisonment is six months, the maximum is five years. With respect to those offences for which the criminal code provides

a maximum term of imprisonment of more than ten years, the maximum youth imprisonment may be ten years. The reason to set the minimum term of imprisonment at six months (in adult criminal law the minimum is one month) lies in the belief that treatment and education of a youthful offender is only efficient if a certain minimum term of secure placement is available. As is the case in adult criminal law, a sentence of youth imprisonment may be suspended if the juvenile offender is regarded to be a low risk and if the sentence does not exceed one year. A juvenile offender serving youth imprisonment may be paroled after having served one-third of the sentence (sec. 88, Youth Court Law) while in adult criminal law the minimum term which has to be served before being eligible for parole is half of the prison sentence.

The Choice among Different Sanctions
With respect to the choice between these different types of measures the focus is on educational needs. Section 5 of the Youth Court Law says that disciplinary measures may be applied only if educational measures are not sufficient in responding to the educative needs displayed by the juvenile offender. Moreover, sec. 17 II of the Youth Court Law states that juvenile imprisonment may be imposed only if educational or disciplinary measures are not sufficient to educate the juvenile offender or if the crime requires criminal punishment.

Young Adults and Juvenile Justice
Young adults (eighteen to twenty years old) are basically presumed to be adults and thus may be tried and sentenced according to adult criminal law. But as a general rule, sec. 105 of the Youth Court Law requires that a young adult be adjudicated and sentenced as a juvenile:

- if a psychological evaluation reveals that the young adult offender shows a typical youthful personality in terms of intellectual and emotional maturity, or
- if the offence in question concerns typical juvenile misbehaviour according to the type, the circumstances, or the motives of the offence.

With regard to the treatment of adolescent offenders, virtually all adolescents adjudicated on the basis of the most serious offences are sentenced according to the Youth Court Law. An exception involves traffic offences. A substantial proportion of adolescent offenders are processed

Table 9.1: The use of educational and other measures as well as enforcement through short term detention in the Hamburg Juvenile Justice System

	1991	1992	1993	1994
Total of juvenile court orders/verdicts	3086	2795	2939	2534
Thereof:				
Community service	417	397	476	388
Fine	454	312	458	424
Placement under the supervision of a social worker	187	158	231	226
Restitution	86	124	105	123
Combinations of educational measures	214	170	47	26
Total educational measures eligible for enforcement	1358	1161	1317	1187
No. failed educational measures enforced by short term detention	7	8	10	12
Enforced by short term detention percent	0.5	0.7	0.8	1.0

Source: Hinrichs, K.: Weisungen und Auflagen brauchen keinen Zwang durch Jugendarrest. *DVJJ-Journal* 1/1996, pp. 59.

through the adult criminal justice system.

The proportion of young adult offenders tried and sentenced as juveniles has increased steadily during the last decades. Graph 9.7 shows the proportions of young adults sentenced as juveniles broken down by offence categories. On average slightly more than 60% of all young adults are sentenced as juveniles. Virtually all young adults are sentenced as juveniles in the case of robbery. An explanation of the considerable variation in referring young adults to juvenile criminal courts may be found in the rather high minimum penalties. The minimum penalties are one year for robbery, five years for aggrevated robbery, two years for rape, and five years to life for murder. The minimum penalty for murder is dictated by the circumstances surrounding the homicide.

The system of juvenile justice and the practice of treating young adults as if they were juveniles recently came under pressure with the enormous increase of bias-motivated violent crimes committed almost exclusively by juveniles and young adults. The debate on how to develop juvenile criminal law in the future centres today around two suggestions:

- The abortion of the choice available today in the Youth Court Law with respect to handling young adults and the legal difference between juveniles and young adults. Young adults of eighteen to twenty years should, according to this opinion, fall under the category of juveniles.
- Keep young adults completely in the adult system but cut by half the minimum and maximum penalties available for adult offenders (such a system has been adopted in Austrian juvenile criminal law).

What can be learned by the experiences of the German criminal justice system with respect to young adult offenders is that there exists a youth-specific system of justice, which is located between a juvenile welfare system and adult criminal justice. Secondly, besides a welfare approach to juvenile delinquency or juvenile problem behaviour, a justice approach to juvenile crime is feasible that can be extended to young adults. Since the transitional periods have been prolonged and the entrance to the adult world has been made more difficult for certain subgroups of juveniles, if the differences between young adults and adults are not respected, then an instrumental character of criminal law prevails that precludes justice for young offenders.

Decision-making in the System

Contrary to common law systems where the public prosecutor has full discretion in deciding whether a formal indictment should be filed or not, the German system of prosecution in the field of juvenile criminal justice is based on the principle of "legality." This means that as a general rule the public prosecutor is obliged to file a charge in every case where there is reasonable evidence that the offender has committed a crime. Nevertheless, there are important exceptions from the general rule of legality laid down in the Code of Criminal Procedure that permit the dismissal of cases in the field of petty offences on opportunity grounds (sections 153 and 153a of the Code of Criminal Procedure). Even more important are those exceptions made in Youth Court Law.

In criminal proceedings against a juvenile offender a public prosecutor is allowed to dismiss the case on those grounds which justify case dismissal in adult criminal proceedings, that is, the offence was a misdemeanor of a minor or trivial nature and the personal guilt of the offender was negligible. In addition, Section 45 of the Juvenile Court Law empowers the public prosecutor to dismiss any case if an adequate educational measure has been carried through by some other institution or by individuals such as teachers, parents, or other

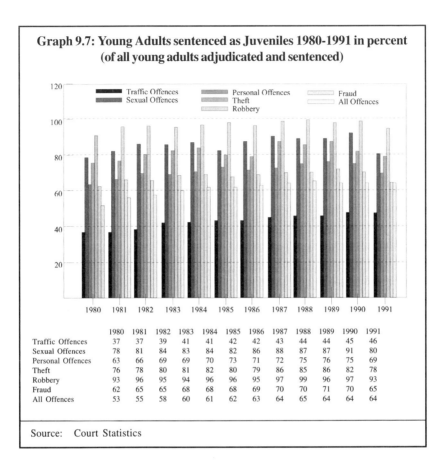

Graph 9.7: Young Adults sentenced as Juveniles 1980-1991 in percent (of all young adults adjudicated and sentenced)

	1980	1981	1982	1983	1984	1985	1986	1987	1988	1989	1990	1991
Traffic Offences	37	37	39	41	41	42	42	43	44	44	45	46
Sexual Offences	78	81	84	83	84	82	86	88	87	87	91	80
Personal Offences	63	66	69	69	70	73	71	72	75	76	75	69
Theft	76	78	80	81	82	80	79	86	85	86	82	78
Robbery	93	96	95	94	96	96	95	97	99	96	97	93
Fraud	62	65	65	68	68	68	69	70	70	71	70	65
All Offences	53	55	58	60	61	62	63	64	65	64	64	64

Source: Court Statistics

relatives. If the public prosecutor has filed a formal charge, then the juvenile judge may dismiss the case (with the concurrence of the juvenile public prosecutor) on the same reasons mentioned above (sec. 47 Youth Court Law). This type of diversion has been considerably extended during the 1980s based upon the idea that the average juvenile offender does not need education and the attention of the juvenile court but will grow out of crime and stay out of crime when diverted by the public prosecutor. The German legislature in the Youth Court Law amendment of 1990 has explicitly adopted this position and thus supported the idea that juvenile court procedures should be a "last resort" (see Box 9.3).

The System in Action

Adjudication and Sentencing

Despite the increases in the number of offenders during the 1960s and 1970s, there was only a slight increase in the adjudication and sentencing rates. But during the 1980s the conviction and sentencing rates declined from approximately 1500 juvenile offenders per 100,000 youth per year at the end of the 1970s to slightly more than 1000 in 1990 (Heinz, 1990). Research on public prosecutors, decision-making patterns revealed that dismissals of criminal juvenile cases are rather frequent and that every second juvenile offender has his or her case dismissed through the juvenile public prosecutor (Heinz, 1989; Heinz 1990). In fact, diversion by the juvenile public prosecutor has become a major dispositional alternative to formal measures according to juvenile court law in the last decade. In recent years strong voices have been raised to set as a prerequisite for dismissals victim-offender mediation. A considerable number of victim-offender mediation schemes have been established which have been evaluated positively although proper evaluation designs are observed rarely and obviously minor offenders are the dominant target (Albrecht, H.-J., 1990).

The proportion of the most severe dispositions (i.e., youth imprisonment) has remained fairly stable in the 1970s—approx. 1.2 per 100,000 even though the number of juvenile suspects has increased steadily since 1986 from 4 to 6.5 per 100,00 in 1994 and the average length of incarceration has increased slightly. Conversely, there has been a marked increase in the number of educational measures requiring community service and social training by the juvenile offender. This trend reflects a growing concern within the juvenile justice system for community-based responses to juvenile offenders while short-term detention (*Jugendarrest*) continues to be on the decline (from 24% in 1976 to 16% in 1990). Approximately two-thirds of sentences for juvenile imprisonment fall into the range of up to one year.

Correctional Supervision

The rate of juvenile and adolescent incarceration, or pre-trial detention, since the late 1960s have been steadily declining (approximately 40 per 100,000 in 1961 to 10 per 100,00 by 1989). A corresponding decline can be observed in prisoner rates for young adults (eighteen to twenty years) as well as for the age group of twenty-one to twenty-five years. Prison rates for adults twenty-six years and older have remained fairly stable. Very few females are detained in youth prisons.

Box 9.3: The Actors in the Juvenile Justice System

The Juvenile Criminal Court

The Federal Republic of Germany has three criminal courts of original jurisdiction. Two of these criminal courts fall under the term *Amtsgericht* (an equivalent to magistrate courts). One of these criminal courts, a single judge, consists of one professional judge who hears cases involving a potential penalty of up to one year imprisonment. The other court (*Schöffengericht*) consists of one professional judge and two lay judges. The third court of original jurisdiction, the district court (*Strafkammer*), hears cases involving a potential penalty of more than three years. The latter court consists of three professional judges and two lay judges. Within this concept of criminal courts, two subsystems deal with adult offenders and juvenile offenders. In principle the structure of juvenile courts parallels that of adult courts. That means two of the juvenile criminal courts also fall under the term *Amtsgericht*. As is the case in the adult subsystem, the single professional juvenile judge hears cases involving juvenile court measures such as educational and disciplinary measures. But the juvenile single judge may also resort to youth imprisonment of up to one year. The other juvenile criminal court on the level of the *Amtsgericht* also consists of one professional juvenile judge and two lay judges (who should have experience in social and youth welfare work). This court is competent to hear all other juvenile criminal cases with the exception of the most serious offences listed in a catalogue (e.g., crimes involving the death of the victim). For those offences the district court (*Jugendstrafkammer*, three professional judges and two lay judges) has been assigned exclusive competence.

Research on how the juvenile judge is perceived by juvenile offenders came up with discouraging results. Juvenile offenders perceive juvenile judges as punitive and authoritarian not as supportive and a father-like figure (Hauser, 1980). Furthermore, research on disposition in the juvenile justice system demonstrates that individualization of treatment or juvenile sanctions (which should be guided by the individual needs of the juvenile offender) does not take place. As such strategies may be regarded to reinforce marginalization of disadvantaged youth, a debate arose around the question of whether there should be changes from the traditional but idealistic conception of juvenile judges and, moreover, juvenile criminal law (Heinz, 1990b; Balbier, 1990).

The Juvenile Public Prosecutor

The role and function of the juvenile public prosecutor as defined within the juvenile court law parallel those of the juvenile judge. Their decision-making should be guided by the aim of meeting juvenile offenders' needs in terms of education and rehabilitation. But obviously these basic legal demands are in conflict with bureaucratic and workload problems. A survey carried through in the 1980s on juvenile public prosecutors showed that the average case load of a juvenile public prosecutor approximates 1400 juvenile cases per year (Adam, Albrecht, H.-J, and Pfeiffer, 1986). Furthermore, juvenile public prosecutors have no special educational background to deal with young offenders.

The Juvenile Court Aid

The Juvenile Court Aid plays a key role in providing the juvenile public prosecutor and the juvenile court with systematic information on social and personal characteristics of the juvenile offender. This information should enable the public prosecutor as well as the juvenile judge to make the appropriate decisions. But it is the bipartite function of the Juvenile Court Aid which actually leads to role conflicts and problems with respect to procedural safeguards. As part of the juvenile welfare system the aid is used to provide support to children and juveniles, as part of the juvenile criminal justice system the aid is supposed to support the public prosecutor and the criminal court. Problems can arise over whether the juvenile suspect should be entitled to a formal warning that anything he or she tells the aid can be used against him or her and that the suspect is not obliged to provide information. It is evident from the perspective of the right to have a fair trial and the rule of law that every juvenile suspect should be entitled to such formal warnings.

The Defence Counsel

All juvenile suspects have the same right to have a defence counsel as the adult suspect. German procedural law differentiates between so-called cases of "necessary defense" (where a defence counsel has to be present and the court is obliged to assign a defence counsel) and cases of "voluntary defence" (where the defendant is free to have a defence counsel). The case of necessary defence is regulated by law and refers, e.g., to cases where the defendant is charged with felonies (sec. 140 Criminal Procedural Law). In juvenile cases the necessary presence of a defence counsel is extended (sec. 68 Youth Court Law). Beyond those cases which are presumed to be cases of necessary defence, juveniles are entitled to a defence counsel if the juvenile suspect is held in pre-trial detention and if parental rights have been removed (e.g., in cases of serious neglect). Unlike the adult system, the role of the defence counsel is somewhat ambiguous in juvenile cases. In juvenile cases the goal of education interferes. It has even been argued that a defence counsel is completely unnecessary in juvenile proceedings as the juvenile public prosecutor and juvenile judge are supposed to decide in the best interests of the juvenile offender (Walter, 1987). But in recent years changes can be observed which encompass a shift from emphasizing the role of the defence counsel in the process of rehabilitating the juvenile offender to an emphasis on specialization of defence counsels in the particular legal and statutory problems in juvenile criminal proceedings (Albrecht, P.A., 1993; Bundesministerium der Justiz, 1987).

Comparing the rates demonstrates that throughout the 1980s, the ratio of juvenile pre-trial detainees and juvenile prisoners is 1:1, the corresponding ratio for young adults is 1:2 and for adults 1:4. This occurs despite the statutory requirement that pre-trial detention be used only in those cases where there is reason to believe that the juvenile offender will either not attend court hearings or will receive a long youth prison sentence. The disproportional use of pre-trial detention in cases of juvenile offenders may be understood as a strategy of the juvenile justice system using pre-trial detention as a "short, sharp shock" immediately after the offence has been committed or as a means of crisis intervention (Gebauer, 1987; Heinz, 1987; Heinz ,1990a).

Despite the decrease in the use of youth imprisonment, the proportion of juveniles placed under some type of judicial control increased considerably since the 1960s. The rate climbed from 200 per 100,000 in 1965 to 400 per 100,000 in 1989. With establishing and expanding intermediate sanctions such as probation and parole, the significance of imprisonment changes from immediate physical control to a last resort, strengthening the deterrent impact of sanctions based on supervision and control outside the prison but nevertheless backed up by the threat of imprisonment. The assumption of greater elasticity of probation and parole as well as the restriction of the use of prison to a symbolic level is supported by changes in criteria for revoking probation. In the 1960s the offender population put on probation was characterized by low risk (as measured by prior record) and a limited need for control (no prior record and a stable work record had been major pre-conditions for granting probation). However, since the mid 1970s the target group for probation parallels a group which formerly had been sent to prison.

In juvenile pre-trial detention, the proportion of foreigners is rather pronounced. Depending on the region, foreign youth in correctional facilities comprise up to 57% of the youth inmate population. Enormous differences in rates of young prisoners may be observed in Western Europe. The rate of imprisoned young offenders (up to twenty-one years) varies between approximately thirty per 100,000 (Italy, Netherlands, and Greece) and approximately 300 (England and Wales) in the 1980s.

Problems in Sentencing Juvenile Offenders
As has been pointed out earlier, reliance on the principle of education in the juvenile justice system is accompanied by discriminative decision-making in that disadvantaged youth are more likely to be sentenced to intensive types of sanctions. Beside discriminative practices within the juvenile criminal justice system, further problems are currently being discussed which refer to differential treatment compared to the adult criminal justice system and to enormous regional variations in the type of dispositions used in juvenile cases.

Criminological studies revealed that juvenile judges make considerably more use of sanctions involving deprivation of liberty than do their counterparts in the adult system (Heinz, 1990). While unconditional prison sentences amount to approximately 5% of all adult offenders sentenced, the rate of juvenile offenders sentenced either to an unconditional term of youth prison or to short-term detention is approximately 25%. Despite the fact that average seriousness of juvenile crimes is well below that of adult crimes. Juvenile offenders are thus treated more harshly than their adult counterparts (which is explained by the prevailing belief that placement in secure detention will lead to favourable rehabilitative outcomes (Heinz, 1992). Differential treatment can be observed with respect to the length of prison sentences. The average juvenile prison sentence is longer than adult prison sentences in comparable offence categories (Pfeiffer, 1991).

Moreover, studies on decision-making have shown that considerable regional variation exists with respect to the disposition of juvenile offenders, which cannot be explained by differences in characteristics of offences or offenders (Heinz, 1990b). Obviously, these extremely different styles of implementing educational policies reflect differing court traditions which ultimately provoke the problem of equal treatment. Equal treatment seems to be rather difficult to attain when basing decision-making on the principle of education.

Does the Youth Prison Meet the Promise of Education and Rehabilitation?

In summing up research on treatment in juvenile correctional institutions, pessimistic assessments prevail. Although studies based upon proper designs are scarce, there is no reason to belief that efforts focusing on the offenders' vocational skills or other treatment options are accompanied by lower recidivism rates. If differences in rates of recidivism between differentially treated groups are observed, these are usually rather small and may reflect a priori differences between the groups treated differently (Geissler, 1991). In general we may assume that the possibly positive effects of treatment or support offered in youth prisons are outweighed by negative influences of prisonization and the prison subculture. Comparing dispositional alternatives in the juvenile justice system such as short-term detention, suspension of prison sentence, community service, cautioning and imprisonment evaluation has to be based on research using natural variation in decision-making between different juvenile court districts. The results of such research lend support to the conclusion that different types of juvenile court measures have similar effects in terms of rates of recidivism as well as the general toll of juvenile crime in those court districts relying on different dispositional strategies (Heinz, 1990b). Variation in the intensity of intervention is not associated with juvenile criminal behaviour nor with juvenile crime. And even though other Western European countries rely on rather different policies vis-à-vis juvenile crime and juvenile offenders, they face similar crime and delinquency problems (Kaiser, 1989).

Summary

Juvenile criminal policy in Germany underwent some important changes in the last decades. These changes may be described in terms of a shift from institutionalization to de-institutionalization and community-based as well as intermediate responses to youth crime, from formal proceedings to diversion and from a **welfare based model** to a **justice model**.

As far as the future development of the juvenile justice system is concerned, it may be pointed out that, contrary to the recommendations of the UN Beijing Rules (see Box 1—Introduction), there has been a shift from advocating a unified juvenile welfare law to keeping a separate criminal law for juvenile and young adult offenders. This coincides with the growth of distrust of rehabilitation and education as major goals of juvenile welfare and juvenile criminal justice. While in the 1970s and until the beginning of the 1980s, the focus of juvenile law reform was on rehabilitation and treatment—a youth welfare approach to juvenile crime, the 1980s and 1990s are characterized as emphasizing the need to grant juvenile offenders the same rights in terms of due process and fair trial as adult offenders in the adult criminal procedural law. The latest juvenile court law amendment (1990) brought some important changes in this respect, although some critical issues in Youth Court Law were not touched at all. The indeterminate youth prison sentence was abolished and the position of intermediate sanctions was strengthened. Moreover, with victim-offender mediation, a new perspective was introduced which places less weight on the offender's person but puts the focus on the impact the offence had on the victim and on society. On the other hand, parliament did not follow suggestions to abolish short-term detention and to amend the conditions for imposing youth imprisonment. As recent proposals for youth law amendments suggest, decriminalization and diversion will continue to be among the prominent topics of reform (DVJJ-Kommission zur Reform des Jugendstrafrechts, 1992).

As a consequence of German reunification in 1990, the criminal justice system, including juvenile justice, actually had to be established according to West German standards in the east of Germany. As all parts of the justice system have to be either reorganized or completely built up (as the socialist system did not provide the required social services), the burden of cost weighs heavily. As in Russia and Hungary, Germany is experiencing some transition. Recent social and political trends have tended to be conservative as we continue to embrace the justice model in an effort to respond to the increases in youth crime patterns. This in turn may lead to shortages and budget cutting in the east as well as in the west for a certain period of time.

Just as the initial formation of our juvenile justice system was influenced by the developments in North America it may be timely to examine other foreign trends. The challenge for the remainder of this century is to address the issues associated with chronic offenders, ethnic groups, re-unification, and how we might accommodate the UN recommendations. As noted in the Australian contribution, these issues can not be studied "solely with the narrow framework of juvenile justice system reforms."

References

Adam, H., Albrecht, H.-J., Pfeiffer, Ch. (1986). *Jugendrichter und Jugendstaatsanwälte in der Bundesrepublik Deutschland*. Max-Planck-Institut für Strafrecht: Freiburg.

Albrecht, G. (1990). Möglichkeiten und Grenzen der Prognose "krimineller Karrieren". In Deutsche Vereinigung für Jugendgerichte und Jugendgerichtshilfen (Ed.). *Mehrfach Auffällige—Mehrfach.*

Betroffene. Erlebnisweisen und Reaktionsformen. Forum Verlag: Godesberg, pp. 99-116.

Albrecht, H.-J. (1987). Die sanfte Minderheit. Mädchen und Frauen als Straftäterinnen. *Bewährungshilfe* 34, pp.341-359.

Albrecht, H.-J. (1987a). Foreign minorities and the criminal justice system in the Federal Republic of Germany. *The Howard Journal*, 26: 272-286.

Albrecht, H.-J. (1990). Kriminologische Perspektiven der Wiedergutmachung. In A. Eser et al. (Eds.). *Neue Wege der Wiedergutmachung im Strafrecht*. Max-Planck-Institut für Strafrecht: Freiburg, pp. 43-72.

Albrecht, H.-J. (1991). Bilan des connaissances en Republique Federale d'Allemagne. In Ph. Robert (Ed.). *Les politiques de prevention de la delinquance*. A l'Aune de la Recherche. L'Harmattan: Paris, pp. 43-56.

Albrecht, H.-J. (1993). Ethnic minorities: Crime and criminal justice in Europe. In F. Heidensohn, M. Farrell, M. (Eds.). *Crime in Europe*. Routledge: London, New York, pp.84-102.

Albrecht, H-J. (1988). Ausländerkriminalität. In H. Jung (Ed.). *Fälle zum Wahlfach Kriminologie, Jugendstrafrecht, Strafvollzug* (2nd ed.). München: Beck, pp.183-204.

Albrecht, P.A.(1993). *Jugendstrafrecht* (2nd Ed.). C.H. Beck: München.

Albrecht, P.A., & Lamnek, S.(1979). Jugendkriminalität im Zerrbild der Statistik. Juventa: München.

Arbeiterwohlfahrt Bundesverband e.V. (Ed.). (1970). Vorschläge für ein erweitertes Jugendhilferecht. Denkschrift der Arbeiterwohlfahrt zur Reform und Vereinheitlichung von Jugendwohlfahrtsgesetz und Jugendstrafgesetz. Schriften der Arbeiterwohlfahrt, No. 22: (3rd ed). Bonn.

Balbier, R.-W. (1990). Brauchen wir ein neues Jugendstrafrecht? *DVJJ-Journal*, pp.48-51.

Bliesener, Th. Psychologische Hintergründe der Gewalt gegen Ausländer. In DVJJ-Regionalgruppe Nordbayern (Ed.). *Ausländer im Jugendstrafrecht. Neue Dimensionen*. Erlangen 1992, pp.15-32.

Bundeskriminalamt. (1994). Polizeiliche Kriminalstatistik 1993. Bundeskriminalamt, Wiesbaden.

Bundeskriminalamt. (1995). *Polizeiliche Kriminalstatistik 1994*. Bundeskriminalamt, Wiesbaden.

Bundesministerium der Justiz (Ed.). (1987). *Verteidigung in Jugendstrafsachen*. Burg Verlag: Bonn.

Bundesverfassungsgericht (Constitutional court) Neue Juristische Wochenschrift 1991, pp.1043.

Dölling, D.(1992). Die Bedeutung der Jugendkriminalität im Verhältnis zur Erwachsenenkriminalität. In Bundesministerium der Justiz (Ed.). *Grundfragen des Jugendkriminalrechts und seiner Neuregelung*. Forum Verlag: Godesberg, pp. 38-59.

Dünkel, F. (1990). Freiheitsentzug für junge Rechtsbrecher. Situation und Reform von Jugendstrafe, Jugendstrafvollzug, Jugendarrest und Untersuchungshaft in der Bundesrepublik Deutschland und im internationalen Vergleich. Forum Verlag: Bonn.

DVJJ-Kommission zur Reform des Jugendkriminalrechts. (1992). Für ein neues Jugendgerichtsgesetz. *DVJJ-Journal*, 1-2, pp.4-39.

Eisenberg, U. (1995). *Jugendgerichtsgesetz mit Erläuterungen* (6th ed). Beck: München.

Empey, L.T. (1982). *American delinquency. Its meaning and construction* (2nd ed.). The Dorsey Press: Homewood.

Frehsee, D. (1995). Sozialer Wandel und Jugendkriminalität. *DVJJ-Journal* 3-4: 269-278

Gebauer, M. (1987). *Die Rechtswirklichkeit der Untersuchungshaft in der Bundesrepublik Deutschland*. Schwartz: Göttingen.

Geissler, I. (1991). Ausbildung und Arbeit im Jugendstrafvollzug. Haftverlaufs- und Rückfallanalyse. Max-Planck-Institut für Strafrecht: Freiburg.

Glogauer, W. (1991). *Kriminalisierung von Kindern und Jugendlichen durch die Medien* (2nd ed.). Nomos: Baden-Baden.

Hauser, H. (1980). Der Jugendrichter—Idee und Wirklichkeit. Schwartz: Göttingen.

Headey, B., Krause, P., & Habich, R. (1990). *The duration and extent of poverty—Is Germany a two-thirds-society?* Arbeitsgruppe Sozialberichterstattung. WBZ, Berlin.

Heinz, W. (1987). Recht und Praxis der Untersuchungshaft in der Bundesrepublik Deutschland. Zur Disfunktionalität der Untersuchungshaft gegenüber dem Reformprogramm im materiellen Strafrecht. Bewährungshilfe 34, pp.5-31.

Heinz, W. (1989). Jugendstrafrechtsreform durch die Praxis—Eine Bestandsaufnahme. In Bundesministerium der Justiz (Ed.). *Jugendstrafrechtsreform durch die Praxis*. Burg Verlag: Bonn, pp.13-44.

Heinz, W. (1990). Gleichheit vor dem Gesetz in der Sanktionspraxis? Empirische Befunde der Sanktionsforschung im Jugendstrafrecht in der Bundesrepublik Deutschland. In Göppinger, H. (Ed.). Kriminologie und Strafrechtspraxis. Tagungsberichte des kriminologischen Arbeitskreises. Vol.7. Aktuelle Probleme der Kriminologie. Tübingen, pp. 171-209.

Heinz, W. (1990a). Die Jugendstrafrechtspflege im Spiegel der Rechtspflegestatistiken. Ausgewählte Daten für den Zeitraum 1955—1988. Monatsschrift für Kriminologie und Strafrechtsreform 73, pp. 210-276.

Heinz, W. (1990b). Mehrfach Auffällige—Mehrfach Betroffene. Erlebnisweisen und Reaktionsformen. In Deutsche Vereinigung für Jugendgerichte und Jugendgerichtshilfen (Ed.). Mehrfach Auffällige—Mehrfach Betroffene. Forum Verlag: Bonn, pp.30-73.

Heinz, W. (1990c). Diversion im Jugendstrafverfahren. Aktuelle kriminalpolitische Bestrebungen im Spiegel empirischer Untersuchungen. Zeitschrift für Rechtspolitik 23, pp. 7-11.

Heinz, W. (1992). Abschied von der "Erziehungsideologie" im Jugendstrafrecht? Zur Diskussion über Erziehung und Strafe. Recht der Jugend und des Bildungswesens 40, pp.123-143.

Heitmeyer, W., & Peter, J.I. (Eds). (1988). Jugendliche Fußballfans. Soziale und politische Orientierungen, Gesellungsformen, Gewalt. Juventa: Weinheim, München.

Heitmeyer, W. (1995). Gewalt. Schattenseiten der Individualisierung Jugendlicher aus unterschiedlichen Milieus. Juventa, Weinheim, München.

Hermann, D., & Wild, P. (1989). Die Bedeutung der Tat bei der jugendrichterlichen Sanktionsbestimmung. Monatsschrift für Kriminologie und Strafrechtsreform 72, pp.13-33.

Hermanns, J. (1983). Sozialisationsbiographie und jugendrichterliche Sanktionspraxis. Max-Planck Institut: Freiburg.

Hupfeld, J. (1993). Zur Bedeutung des Erziehungsgedankens und des richterlichen Spezialisierungsgrades in der Jugendstrafrechtspraxis. DVJJ-Journal, 1: 11-17.

Jung, H. (1993). Massenmedien und Kriminalität. In Kaiser, G. et al. (Eds.). Kleines Kriminologisches Wörterbuch. (3rd Ed.). C.F. Müller: Heidelberg, pp.345-350.

Jung, H. (1993a). Täter-Opfer-Ausgleich. Anmerkungen zu seiner Bedeutung für das Rechtssystem. Monatsschrift für Kriminologie und Strafrechtsreform, 76, pp.50-56.

Kaiser, G. (1993). Jugendstrafrecht. In G. Kaiser et al. (Eds.). Kleines Kriminologisches Wörterbuch. C.F. Müller: Karlsruhe, pp.199-204, p.199.

Kaiser, G. (1988). Kriminologie (2nd ed.). C.F. Müller: Heidelberg.

Kaiser, G. (1989). Jugenddelinquenz im internationalen Vergleich. In Innenministerium Baden-Württemberg (Ed.). Jugend und Kriminalität. Innenministerium Baden-Württemberg: Stuttgart, pp. 13-48.

Kaiser, G. (1993b). Kriminologie. (9th ed.). C.F. Müller: Heidelberg.

Karger, Th., & Sutterer, P. (1988). Cohort study on the development of police-recorded criminality and criminal sanctioning. In Kaiser, G. & Geissler, I. (Eds.). Crime and criminal justice. Max-Planck-Institut für Strafrecht: Freiburg, pp.89-114.

Karger, Th., & Sutterer, P. (1990). Polizeilich registrierte Gewaltdelinquenz bei jungen Ausländern. Monatsschrift für Kriminologie und Strafrechtsreform 73, pp. 369-383.

Kerner, H.J., & Weitekamp, E. (1984). The Federal Republic of Germany. In Klein, M.W. (Ed.). *Western systems of juvenile justice*. Beverly Hills, CA: Sage. pp.147-170.

Kerner, H.J. (1990). Jugendkriminalrecht als "Vorreiter" der Strafrechtsreform? Überlegungen zu 40 Jahren Rechtsentwicklung in Rechtsprechung, Lehre und Kriminalpolitik. *DVJJ-Journal*, No. 133: 68-81.

Kersten, J. (1993). Das Thema Gewaltkriminalität in kulturvergleichender Sicht. *DVJJ-Journal*, 1: 18-26.

Klein, M.W. (Ed.). (1984). *Western systems of juvenile justice*. Beverly Hills, CA: Sage.

Krüger, H. (1983). Rückfallquote: rund 30%. *Kriminalistik*, 37: 326-329.

Kube, E., & Koch, K.-F. (1990). Zur Kriminalität jugendlicher Ausländer aus polizeilicher Sicht. Monatsschrift für Kriminologie und Strafrechtsreform 73, pp.14-24.

Kunz, K.-L. (1989). Ausländerkriminalität in der Schweiz—Umfang, Struktur und Erklärungsversuch. *Schweizerische Zeitschrift für Strafrecht*, 106: 373-392.

Lajios, K. (1993). *Die psychosoziale Situation von Ausländern in der Bundesrepublik Deutschland. Integrationsprobleme und seelische Folgen*. Leske + Budrich, Opladen.

Laubenthal, F. (1993). *Jugendgerichtshilfe im Strafverfahren*. Köln.

Liszt, F.v. (1905). Die Kriminalität der Jugendlichen. In Liszt, F.v.. Strafrechtliche Aufsätze und Vorträge. Vol.2. Berlin. pp.331-355.

Mansel, J., & Hurelmann, K. (1993). Psychosoziale Befindlichkeit junger Ausländer in der Bundesrepublik Deutschland. Soziale Probleme 4. S. 167-192.

Münder, J., Sack, F., Albrecht, H.J., & Plewig, H.-J. (1987). Jugendarbeitslosigkeit und Jugendkriminalität. Luchterhand: Neuwied.

Ostendorf, H. (1992). Ansatzpunkte für materiell-rechtliche Entkriminalisierungen von Verhaltensweisen junger Menschen. In Bundesministerium der Justiz (Ed.) *Grundfragen des Jugendkriminalrechts und seiner Neuregelung*. Forum Verlag Godesberg: Bonn, pp.194-204.

Pfeiffer, Ch. (1991). Wird nach Jugendstrafrecht härter bestraft? *Strafverteidiger* 11, pp. 363-370.

Rommelspacher, B. (1993). Männliche Jugendliche als Projektionsfiguren gesellschaftlicher Gewaltphantasien. Rassismus im Selbstverständnis der Mehrheitskultur. In Breyvogel, W. (Ed.). *Lust auf Randale. Jugendliche Gewalt gegen Fremde*. Verlag Dietz, Bonn. pp. 65-82.

Schaal, H.-J., & Eisenberg, U. (1988). Rechte und Befugnisse von Verletzten im Strafverfahren gegen Jugendliche. Neue Zeitschrift für Strafrecht 8: 49-53.

Schöch, H. (1992). Empfehlen sich Änderungen und Ergänzungen bei den strafrechtlichen Sanktionen ohne Freiheitsentzug? C.H. Beck: München.

Schumann, K.F., Berlitz, C., Guth, H.-W., & Kanlitzki, R. (1987). Jugendkriminalität und die Grenzen der Generalprävention. Luchterhand: Neuwied, Darmstadt.

Seifert, W. (1991). *Ausländer in der Bundesrepublik—Soziale und ökonomische Mobilität*. Arbeitsgruppe Sozialberichterstattung, WBZ, Berlin.

Sessar, K. (1992). Wiedergutmachen oder strafen. Einstellungen in der Bevölkerung und der Justiz. Centaurus: Pfaffenweiler.

Solon, J. (1994). Jugendgewalt in München—Ausdruck deutscher Fremdenfeindlichkeit oder unvermeidbare ethnische Konflikte. *der Kriminalist*, 26: 73-79.

Steffen, W. (1976). Die Effizienz polizeilicher Ermittlungen aus der Sicht des späteren Strafverfahrens. Bundeskriminalamt: Wiesbaden.

Steffen, W.(1979). *Kinder- und Jugendkriminalität in Bayern*. Landeskriminalamt: München.

Streng, F. (1994). Der Erziehungsgedanke im Jugendstrafrecht. Zeitschrift für die Gesamte Strafrechtswissenschaft 106, S. 60-92.

Stümper, A.(1973). Die kriminalpolitische Bewertung der Jugendkriminalität. Kriminalistik, pp. 49.

Sutterer, P., & Karger, Th. (1994). Self-reported juvenile delinquency in Mannheim, Germany. In Junger-Tas, J., Terlouw, G.-J., Klein, M.W. (Eds.). *Delinquent behavior among young people in the Western world. First results of the International Self-Report Delinquency Study*. Kugler Publications: New York. pp. 156-185.

Verfassungsschntzbericht 1991. Bonn. 1992.

Viehmann, H. (1993). Was machen wir mit unseren jugendlichen Gewalttätern? *DVJJ-Journal*, 1, pp.26-29.

Villmow, B., & Kaiser, G. (1974). Empirisch gesicherte Erkenntnisse über Ursachen der Kriminalität. In Der Regierende Bürgermeister von Berlin (Ed.). *Verhütung und Bekämpfung der Kriminalität*. Berlin.

Villmow, B., & Stephan, E. (1983). Jugendkriminalität in einer Gemeinde. Eine Analyse erfragter Delinquenz und Viktimisierung sowie amtlicher Registrierung. Max-Planck-Institut für Strafrecht: Freiburg.

Walter, M. (1987). Der Strafverteidiger im Jugendkriminalrecht. In Bundesministerium der Justiz (Ed.). *Verteidigung in Jugendstrafsachen*. Burg Verlag: Bonn, pp.11-28.

Walter, M. (1993). Jugendrecht, Jugendhilfe, Jugendschutz. In Kaiser, G. et al. (Eds.). Kleines inologisches Wörterbuch (3rd ed.). C.F. Müller: Heidelberg, pp.191-199.

Walter, M. (1995). *Jugendkriminalität*. Stuttgart, München, Hannover: Boorberg.

chapter 10

Delinquency and Juvenile Justice in the United States

Marla C. Craig and Mark C. Stafford
Department of Sociology, University of Texas at Austin

Facts About the United States

Area and Density: Almost 4 million square miles, with seventy-four people per square mile. There are fifty states in the United States (U.S.), including the island of Hawaii in the Pacific Ocean and Alaska in northwest North America, which is separated from the rest of the continental states by Canada. **Population**: Over 260 million people in 1994. Males make up 49% and females 51% of the population. The 1994 median age was thirty-four. Approximately 83% of the population is white; 13% is black; and 4% is either American Indian, Alaskan Native, or Asian/Pacific Islander. About 76% of the U.S. population ages five and over speak only English; of those who speak another language, most speak Spanish. The most populated states are California, Texas, New York, Florida, and Pennsylvania. The most populated cities are New York, Los Angeles, Chicago, Houston, and Philadelphia. Washington, D.C. is the nation's capital. **Climate**: Varies considerably by region and state. The midwestern city of Chicago, Illinois has an average daily temperature of 49° F (17° C), and the southwestern city of Dallas, Texas has an average daily temperature of 65° F (33° C). Juneau, Alaska, which is in the most northern state, has an average daily temperature of 41° F (9° C); and the average is 77° F (45° C) in Honolulu, Hawaii, the most southern state. **Economy**: The U.S. economy involves agriculture, forestry, and manufacturing (e.g., manufacture of industrial machinery and electronic equipment). Finance, insurance, and real estate also make up a substantial part of the economy. Wheat and feed grains were the major agricultural exports in 1993. The leading trade partners are Japan and the European Union. Corn, beef, and soybeans are major U.S. exports to Japan, while soybeans, animal feeds, and nuts are major exports to the European Union. **Government**: A federalism (federal republic) comprised of a national government, fifty state governments, and many local governments, including those for counties, cities and towns, school districts, and special districts. There are two major political parties: Republican (conservative) and Democrat (liberal).

Brief History

Vikings discovered America as early as 1000; however, European expansion did not begin until the late 1400s and early 1500s (Degler, 1973:8-12). The earliest European settlers were Spaniards who encountered native Indians. The English settled America in the early 1600s by establishing colonies; those colonies declared independence from England in 1776, and achieved it through means of the American Revolution.

Colonial law at the time of the Declaration of Independence "was English law and the system of courts and justice thoroughly British" (Degler, 1973:124). Although independence did not end English legal influence, the American legal system was organized differently than the English system. For example, "American courts tended to simplify the complexities of British legal machinery, which was largely uncodified, and to organize constitutional and statute law into written codes" (Degler, 1973:124).

Eighteenth-century American criminal law did not distinguish between juvenile delinquency and adult crime. Instead, Americans relied on common law, which specified that children under the age of seven could not be guilty of a serious crime (Bremner, *I*, 1970:307). Children under age fourteen also could not be guilty unless it was shown that they could distinguish right from wrong. If so, they were to be judged as adults, along with anyone age fourteen or over, although some colonies made exceptions by establishing older age limits. If found guilty, juveniles could receive the same punishments as adults, including the death penalty (Streib, 1987:56). However, judges and juries usually were more lenient toward juveniles (Platt, 1969:183).

Nineteenth-century reformers believed that increasing industrialization, urbanization, and immigration in the U.S. had caused moral decline, and they feared that any child "not carefully and diligently trained to cope with the open, free-wheeling, and disordered life of the community would fall victim to vice and crime" (Rothman, 1971:210). Those were fears especially strong for orphaned, poor, and vagrant children whose families may have been unable to protect and nurture them. Reformers reasoned that if families were not up to such tasks, child-saving institutions should intervene. Houses of refuge and, later, reformatories were institutions created as substitute families to be used when necessary for raising children.

The first houses of refuge were built in the 1820s in large cities, such as New York, Boston, and Philadelphia, and their goal was to rehabilitate (reform) not just young law-violators but all children with problems (Bremner, *I*, 1970:671). Reformers did not worry that they might be violating the rights of children; on the contrary, they believed that "a good dose of institutionalization could only work to the child's benefit" (Rothman, 1971:209). State courts affirmed that belief by rejecting complaints by parents of institutionalized children. An important case involved Mary Ann Crouse whose father objected that her institutionalization was unconstitutional on the grounds that there had been no jury trial. In a landmark decision in 1838, the Pennsylvania Supreme Court supported the state's power to institutionalize children: "May not the natural parents, when unequal to the task of education, or unworthy of it, be superseded by the *parens patriae*, or common guardian of the community?" (*Ex parte Crouse* 4 Wharton [Pa.] 9 [1838] in Bremner, *I*, 1970:692). The court concluded that houses of refuge were more like schools than prisons; thus, children did not need the same procedural safeguards accorded adults in criminal trials.

In contrast to the court's conclusion in the *Crouse* case, there was increasing evidence that houses of refuge "had become [little more than] prisonlike warehouses for ... larger numbers of children from the margins of society" (Empey and Stafford, 1991:54). Perhaps more important, critics claimed that houses of refuge had failed in rehabilitating problem children (Bremner, *I*, 1970:696-697). It was believed that at least part of the problem was that houses of refuge were located in large cities; if child-saving institutions were to be successful substitute families, they needed to be in rural areas, away from urban depravity. During the second half of the nineteenth century, then, reformatories and state industrial schools were created in rural areas in many regions of the U.S. Their goal was the same as houses of refuge—to rehabilitate all problem children (Bremner, *II*, 1970:439). However, they were no more successful in achieving that goal.

By the end of the nineteenth century, reformatories were criticized for being little more than prisons that did not rehabilitate (Bremner, *II*, 1970:439-440). Reformers could have abandoned the rehabilitative ideal entirely, but instead they created the juvenile court as another possible means for rehabilitating problem children. In 1899 Illinois created the first statewide juvenile court system to handle such problems as child abuse, neglect, dependency, and juvenile delinquency. To maintain the state's *parens patriae* power, the juvenile court was "designated a ... non-criminal court ... which ... assumed that disposition of juvenile cases would be in the best interests of the child and need not be overly concerned with the child's rights" (Bremner, *II*, 1970:440). Court sessions were informal with few procedural safeguards to protect juveniles; and the law that created the court was to "be liberally construed to the end that ... the care, custody and discipline of a child shall approximate ... that which should be given by its parents" (*Revised Statutes of the State of Illinois*, 1899, Sec. 21, in Bremner, *II*, 1970:511). By the mid-1900s, all states had established juvenile courts, as had many other nations (Caldwell, 1961:496).

Reforms in U.S. Juvenile Justice

In the 1960s the juvenile court and its rehabilitative ideal were seriously challenged. That challenge stemmed, in part, from a series of Supreme Court cases. In the 1966 *Kent* case (383 U.S. 541 [1966]), the Court pointed to a gap between the rehabilitative ideal and the reality of juvenile-court processing: "The child receives the worst of both worlds: ... he gets neither the protections accorded to adults nor the solicitous care and regenerative treatment postulated for children." The next year in the *Gault* case (387 U.S. 1 [1967]) the Court continued to point to that gap and, contrary to the conclusion in the 1838 *Crouse* case, ruled that several procedural safeguards should be provided to juveniles facing the possibility of institutional confinement: notice of charges, assistance of counsel, opportunity to confront and cross-examine witnesses, and a privilege against self-incrimination.

The Supreme Court's assessment of the juvenile court in the 1960s was accompanied by increasing arrest rates of young people (Empey and Stafford, 1991:81-84). Moreover, substantial increases in the number of sixteen to twenty-four year olds (the age group most likely to violate the law) led to increased fears of juveniles and calls for control of their behaviour.

At about the same time, evidence began to accumulate about the ineffectiveness of rehabilitation programs. The most influential evidence was provided by Robert Martinson and his colleagues (Martinson, 1974:25; Lipton, Martinson, and Wilks, 1975) who concluded from an extensive evaluation of rehabilitation programs that "with few and isolated exceptions, the rehabilitative efforts that have been reported so far have had no appreciable effect on recidivism." That conclusion was a shocking blow to supporters of the rehabilitative ideal, and it was only made worse by subsequent evaluations that reached similar conclusions (e.g., Sechrest, White, and Brown, 1979).

All of these factors—the Supreme Court's assessment of the juvenile court, increasing arrest rates of young people, and evidence about the ineffectiveness of rehabilitation programs—have led to recent calls to rethink the juvenile justice system, and even to abolish it (Dawson, 1990; Feld, 1990, 1993). Throughout the 1980s and 1990s, there has been increasing public pressure to "crack down" on juvenile offenders—to "get tough" on kids.

Since *Gault* many states have changed their juvenile codes to deemphasize rehabilitation and more strongly emphasize public protection, punishment, justice, deterrence, and accountability (Feld, 1993:245-246; Snyder and Sikmund,

1995:71). For example, the purpose of the 1996 Texas Juvenile Justice Code (Ch. 51.01) is mainly to "provide for the protection of the public and public safety." Consistent with that purpose, the code is to, first, "promote the concept of punishment for criminal acts" and then, second, to rehabilitate. Although identifying rehabilitation as a purpose (albeit a secondary one), the code reveals only a partial commitment to the rehabilitative ideal by linking it to accountability: "to provide treatment, training, and rehabilitation that emphasizes the accountability and responsibility of both the parent and the child for the child's conduct." That partial commitment is at odds with judicial interpretations of earlier (pre-1960) Texas juvenile justice codes, which said that the purpose of the juvenile justice system was "not one of punishment, but ... protection of the child for its own good, ... not ... to convict and punish juveniles but to guide and direct them."

Related legislative changes in various states in the 1980s and 1990s have included a shift from indeterminate to determinate and mandatory sentencing such that fixed and specified sentences are given to juvenile offenders, with the terms set by legislators (Feld, 1993:219). Moreover, laws have been changed so that juveniles can be tried more easily in adult criminal courts rather than in juvenile courts.

There is more evidence of a "crackdown" on juvenile offenders. There has been an increase in the institutionalization of juvenile offenders since the 1980s (Krisberg et al., 1986), and some states permit the execution of persons who were teenagers at the time they committed their offences (*Thompson v. Oklahoma* 487 U.S. 815 [1988]; *Stanford v. Kentucky* 109 S.Ct. 2969 [1989]).

Public Beliefs about Crime/ Delinquency and Juvenile Justice

Many Americans believe that crime and delinquency are serious social problems. A 1995 Gallup poll found that 27% of Americans identified crime and violence as the most important problems in the U.S., and 6% identified drugs and drug abuse (Maguire and Pastore, 1995:140). Moreover, those percentages have increased considerably since the early 1980s; in 1981 only about 5% of Americans identified crime, violence, drugs, or drug abuse as the most important problems in the country.

Juveniles in the U.S. are especially likely to express concern about crime and delinquency. When asked to consider a list of social problems about which they might worry, 93% of a sample of 1994 high school seniors said they "often" or "sometimes" worried about crime and violence, and 77% said they worried about drug abuse (Maguire and Pastore, 1995:203). Those percentages were higher than percentages for high school seniors in the early 1980s; for example, 86% of 1982 high school seniors said they were worried about crime and violence, and 70% worried about drug abuse.

The U.S. has relatively high crime and delinquency rates compared to other industrialized nations; hence, it is scarcely surprising that many Americans fear crime. Forty seven percent of respondents in a 1994 Roper survey indicated that they were afraid to walk alone at night in their own neighbourhood (Maguire and Pastore, 1995:168-169). The demographic groups most likely to express fear of crime are females, whites, upper-income people, and older people, but these groups do not necessarily have the highest victimization rates. For example, while young males express less fear of crime than other groups, they have the highest victimization rates (Stafford and Galle, 1984). However, many people may respond to their fear by reducing their risk of victimization (e.g., by refraining from relatively high-risk behaviours, such as going out alone at night); otherwise their victimization risks might be higher.

When asked what should be done about crime and delinquency, Americans tend to point to punishment rather than rehabilitation. In a 1993 survey by the *Los Angeles Times*, a national sample of adults was asked "where does government need to make a greater effort these days: in trying to rehabilitate criminals who commit violent crimes or in trying to punish and put away criminals who commit violent crimes?" Only 25% of respondents indicated that a greater effort ought to be made to rehabilitate criminals; in contrast, 61% said there was a need to punish criminals (Maguire and Pastore, 1995:177). For most demographic groups, punishment was favoured by almost twice as many as favoured rehabilitation (e.g., 57% of females said "punish criminals" and only 26% said "rehabilitate" them). The only exception was that blacks were just as likely to favour rehabilitation (44%) as punishment (46%).

The shift away from the rehabilitative ideal in U.S. juvenile justice over the past several decades is consistent with public beliefs. Seventy two percent of respondents to a 1994 Gallup poll said "programs that treat juveniles differently than adults who commit the same crimes ... [and] emphasize protecting and rehabilitating juveniles rather than punishing them" had not been successful at all, or at least not very successful, in controlling delinquency (Maguire and Pastore, 1995:179). Only 1% said that such programs had been very successful, and only 24% said that they had been even moderately successful.

In contrast to the philosophy of the original juvenile court in the late 1800s and early 1900s, many Americans today believe that juveniles who commit delinquent offences ought to be treated the same as adults, although some consideration is given to whether or not the juvenile is a first-time offender. Seventy-eight percent of respondents in a 1994 *Los Angeles Times* poll said that juveniles who commit violent crimes ought to be treated the same as adults instead of receiving more lenient treatment in a juvenile court (Maguire and Pastore, 1995:179). Fifty percent of respondents in a 1994 Gallup poll said that juveniles convicted of their first offence should be given the same punishment as adults convicted of their first offence, and 83% said that juveniles convicted of their second or third offences should be treated the same as adults convicted of the same number of offences (Maguire and Pastore, 1995:180).

Americans' beliefs about the death penalty perhaps best reveal their disagreement with the rehabilitative ideal and the philosophy of the original juvenile court. Respondents in a 1994 Gallup poll were asked: "when a teenager commits a murder and is found guilty by a jury, do you think he should get the death penalty or should he be spared because of his youth?" Sixty percent responded that the teenager should get the death penalty; indeed, for no demographic group did less than 50% respond that way (Maguire and Pastore, 1995:184).

What accounts for Americans' increasing punitiveness towards juvenile offenders? It is probably too simplistic to point merely to fear of crime because Americans' beliefs about crime and punishment are "a complex mix of perception, reason, emotion, and social ideals of justice" (Warr, 1995:302). Grasmick and McGill (1994:39) found relationships among white Americans between "conservative Christian beliefs, causes attributed to crime, and punitiveness toward offenders." Specifically, a literal interpretation of the Bible is related to a tendency to attribute juvenile delinquency to the offender's character rather than to social causes (e.g., poverty, peer pressure), and such attributions make adherents more punitive. Increasing punitiveness towards juvenile offenders may be due to a revitalization of conservative Christianity in the U.S. Warr (1995:301) also indicated that increasing public support for the death penalty may stem from an increasing politicization of crime that began in the late 1960s when politicians used crime and criminal justice issues to excite and unite voters.

Delinquency in the U.S. and Trends

Recent media reports suggest an epidemic of juvenile delinquency in the U.S. For example, consider this recent report of violence in schools:

> In the last month alone, a teenager was shot to death on a school bus in St. Louis ..., a teacher in Los Angeles was critically wounded in the head by a stray bullet [from a gang dispute] ..., and a teacher and two students were shot and killed ... in a junior-high classroom in Moses Lake, Wash., by a student with a high-powered rifle. (*New York Times*, March 3, 1996, p. 8)

There are increasing reports of killings over athletic jackets and shoes, and teenage drug use. However, how accurate are recent media reports of delinquency in the U.S.? Are juveniles more likely than adults to violate the law? Has the amount of delinquency been increasing?

Different sources of information can be used to answer such questions. First, there are official data compiled by the police and other legal officials. Second, there are unofficial data: (1) self-report surveys that ask juveniles about their commission of delinquent offences and (2) victimization surveys that ask about experiences as victims of crime and delinquency. Third, there are homicide victimization data compiled by the National Center for Health Statistics.

Official Arrest Data

The most widely used source of official data on U.S. delinquency is the *Uniform Crime Reports* (*UCR*), which provides data on arrests of juveniles (defined in *UCR* as persons under eighteen years of age) for many offences. Juveniles accounted for approximately 20% of all the 1994 U.S. arrests for serious violent offenses—murder, rape, robbery, and aggravated assault—and they accounted for about 35% of arrests for serious property offences—burglary, larceny/ theft, motor vehicle theft, and arson (F.B.I. 1995:221). Juveniles comprised about 26% of the U.S. population in 1994 (Day, 1993:14); hence, proportionately speaking, juveniles were less likely than adults to be arrested for violent offences, and they were more likely than adults to be arrested for property offences.

The same pattern holds when particular types of serious violent and property offences are considered. Juveniles were involved in less than 20% of the 1994 arrests for murder, rape, and aggravated assault; hence, they were under-represented in arrests for those offences. Among serious violent offences, juveniles were over-represented only for robbery, with 32% of the arrests involving juveniles. In contrast, juveniles were over-represented in arrests for all serious property offences. They accounted for approximately 35% of the arrests for burglary and larceny/theft, 44% of the arrests for motor vehicle theft, and a whopping 55% of the arrests for arson.

The *UCR* also provides data on arrests for less serious offences (F.B.I., 1995:221). Juveniles were over-represented in arrests (accounted for more than 26% of arrests) for vandalism, stolen property (buying, receiving, possessing), curfew/loitering, and running away. The last two offences are "status offences," which are illegal only for juveniles (i.e., they are unique to the status of being a juvenile).

Proportionately speaking, juveniles were less likely than adults to be arrested for prostitution, fraud, embezzlement, forgery, gambling, nonaggravated (simple) assault, vagrancy, disorderly conduct, and weapons violations (carrying, possessing, etc). Alcohol and drug abuse are commonly portrayed in U.S. media reports as juvenile rather than adult problems. However, contrary to those reports, juveniles were under-represented in arrests for driving under the influence, drunkenness, liquor law violations, and drug abuse.

Have there been recent increases in juvenile arrests, especially for serious offences? Figure 10.1 plots the number of juvenile arrests per 100,000 juveniles ages ten to seventeen for murder, rape, robbery, aggravated assault, burglary, larceny/theft, and motor vehicle theft for 1975 to 1994 (arson is not plotted because *UCR* did not report arson arrests over the entire period). Arrest rates are plotted rather than the number of arrests because the number of juveniles in the U.S. (and their percent of the total population) has varied over time.

For each of the offences except burglary, the arrest rate for juveniles increased from 1975 to 1994. For example, the rate at which juveniles were arrested for murder increased 132%—from 5.7 juvenile arrests per 100,000 population ages ten to seventeen in 1975 to 13.2 in 1994. Similarly, the juvenile arrest rate for aggravated assault increased 134% over the twenty-year period. There were smaller increases for rape (58%), motor vehicle theft (33%), robbery (26%), and larceny/theft (13%). The exception: the juvenile arrest rate for burglary decreased 42%.

Recent media reports of an epidemic of juvenile delinquency in the U.S. are justified most by the arrest rates for murder and aggravated assault, with the largest increases occurring after the mid-1980s (see Figure 10.1). Indeed, the juvenile arrest rate for both offences has at least doubled since that time. (See Box 10.1)

Figure 10.1: Juvenile Arrest Rates per 100,000 Population, Ages 10-17, U.S., 1975-1994

Year	Arrest Rate
1975	5.7
1976	4.9
1977	5.7
1978	5.9
1979	6
1980	6.2
1981	6.6
1982	6.6
1983	5.4
1984	4.6
1985	5.5
1986	6.1
1987	6.9
1988	9
1989	10.1
1990	12.1
1991	12.6
1992	11.9
1993	13.7
1994	13.2

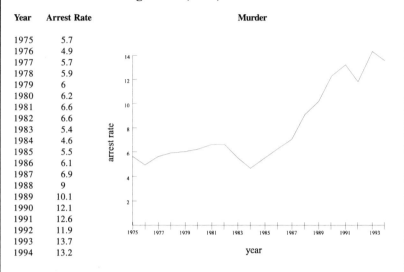

Murder

Year	Arrest Rate
1975	13.1
1976	14.1
1977	14.6
1978	15.3
1979	16.4
1980	15.5
1981	15.8
1982	17.4
1983	17.6
1984	20.2
1985	20.2
1986	20.9
1987	21.4
1988	20.6
1989	21.5
1990	22
1991	22.9
1992	22.7
1993	22.1
1994	20.7

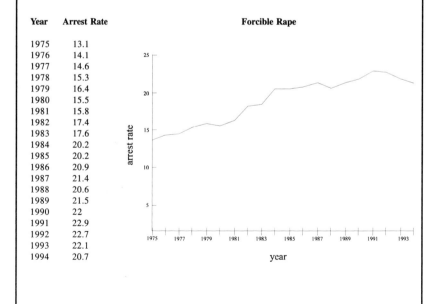

Forcible Rape

Figure 10.1: Juvenile Arrest Rates per 100,000 Population, Ages 10-17, U.S., 1975-1994

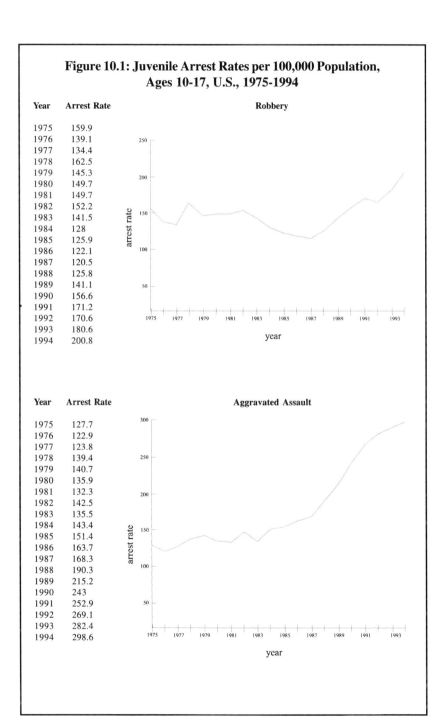

Year	Arrest Rate
1975	159.9
1976	139.1
1977	134.4
1978	162.5
1979	145.3
1980	149.7
1981	149.7
1982	152.2
1983	141.5
1984	128
1985	125.9
1986	122.1
1987	120.5
1988	125.8
1989	141.1
1990	156.6
1991	171.2
1992	170.6
1993	180.6
1994	200.8

Robbery

Year	Arrest Rate
1975	127.7
1976	122.9
1977	123.8
1978	139.4
1979	140.7
1980	135.9
1981	132.3
1982	142.5
1983	135.5
1984	143.4
1985	151.4
1986	163.7
1987	168.3
1988	190.3
1989	215.2
1990	243
1991	252.9
1992	269.1
1993	282.4
1994	298.6

Aggravated Assault

Figure 10.1: Juvenile Arrest Rates per 100,000 Population, Ages 10-17, U.S., 1975-1994

Year	Arrest Rate
1975	849.1
1976	787.5
1977	800.5
1978	847.1
1979	803.6
1980	767.6
1981	739.7
1982	721.1
1983	639.7
1984	587.9
1985	606.7
1986	588
1987	575.4
1988	535
1989	520.8
1990	533.9
1991	528.3
1992	517.2
1993	483.6
1994	493.2

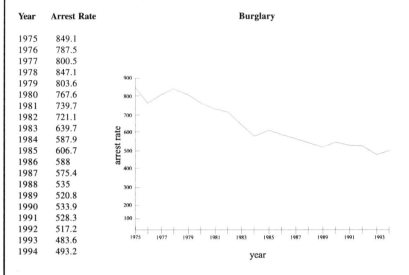

Burglary

Year	Arrest Rate
1975	1553
1976	1501.5
1977	1477.5
1978	1537.7
1979	1567.2
1980	1500.6
1981	1479.5
1982	1549.1
1983	1516.7
1984	1559.5
1985	1613.1
1986	1649.8
1987	1692.8
1988	1690.4
1989	1646.9
1990	1767.1
1991	1773.7
1992	1696.5
1993	1633.7
1994	1758

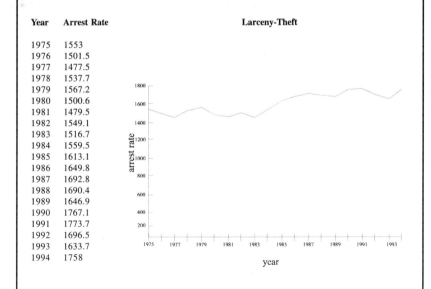

Larceny-Theft

Figure 10.1: Juvenile Arrest Rates per 100,000 Population, Ages 10-17, U.S., 1975-1994

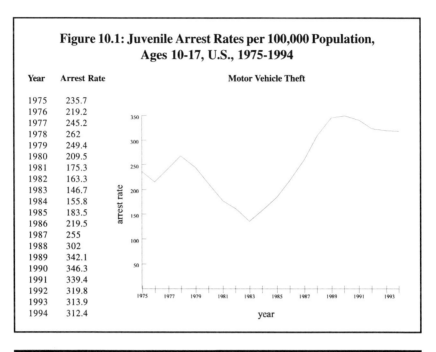

Year	Arrest Rate
1975	235.7
1976	219.2
1977	245.2
1978	262
1979	249.4
1980	209.5
1981	175.3
1982	163.3
1983	146.7
1984	155.8
1985	183.5
1986	219.5
1987	255
1988	302
1989	342.1
1990	346.3
1991	339.4
1992	319.8
1993	313.9
1994	312.4

Motor Vehicle Theft

Box 10.1: Juvenile Murders, Drugs, and Guns in the U.S.

There is disagreement about the causes of recent increases in the murder rate among young Americans. Blumstein (1995:6) argues that the cause is the "rapid growth of the crack market [beginning] in the mid-1980s" and the diffusion of guns. According to Blumstein, juveniles have been recruited into the drug industry and armed with guns for self-protection. As more guns have appeared in a community of tightly "networked" juveniles, there has been an incentive for other juveniles to arm themselves for self-protection and status-seeking (Blumstein, 1995:6). Since juveniles tend to be reckless and unskilled at dispute resolution, the diffusion of guns has increased the chances that disputes will result in murders. As support for his argument, Blumstein (1995:6) points to a doubling of the murder arrest rate for juveniles since 1985, a doubling of the arrest rate for nonwhite juveniles for drug offences, and a doubling of the number of juvenile murders committed by guns.

In contrast, Klein (1995:112-126) argues that, at least as far as gang murders are concerned, recent increases in the U.S. have not been caused by gang members' involvement in crack sales and distribution. Klein (1995:116) agrees with Blumstein that the increase in gang murders can be "attributed to the greater lethality of weapons now in the hands of the offending gangs." However, Klein (1995:40) claims that the connection between gangs and crack has been exaggerated by the American media, law enforcement officials, and politicians. While drug use is common among gang members, drug sales and distribution are not (Klein, 1995:36). Moreover, while there is a crack (and other drug) connection to some American gang murders, most of them pertain to non-drug gang rivalries (Klein, 1995:125-126).

Problems with Official Arrest Data

Most juvenile offenders are never arrested; hence arrest data tend to underestimate delinquency. Moreover, arrest data may reflect biases of law enforcement officials. For example, there may be racial/ethnic and gender biases such that racial/ethnic minorities and females are more (or less) likely than other juveniles to be arrested for the same offence, at least in some jurisdictions (e.g., in some jurisdictions, girls may be more likely than boys to be arrested for status offences—see Teilmann and Landry, 1981). Law enforcement officials also may change their behaviour over time, "cracking down" at some points by arresting more offenders and "letting up" at other points by arresting fewer offenders. Hence, there could be increases or decreases in arrests over time without changes in actual delinquent behaviour.

Unofficial Data

Self-report Data

Because of problems with arrest data, researchers have turned to unofficial data on delinquency, the most common being self-report data. These data are unofficial in the sense that they are not collected by legal officials. Instead, researchers conduct surveys, either by interviews or self-administered questionnaires, asking questions like this: "During the last twelve months [or some other designated period, such as the last six months], how often have you ... [a description of some offence, such as 'used marijuana']?" Survey respondents may be national samples of youths, or they may be more limited samples such as high school students in a particular city or state. Regardless, the principal advantage of self-report over arrest data is that they are not limited to offenders who have been caught by law enforcement officials.

Column 1 of Table 10.1 shows the results of a recent self-report survey of a national sample of high school seniors conducted by researchers at the University of Michigan. Whereas a low percentage of juveniles are arrested in a particular year, a high percentage report committing delinquent offences. For example, 90% of 1994 high school seniors reported arguing with one or both parents (a status offence) at least once during the last twelve months; 30% reported theft under $50 and taking something from a store; 25% reported unlawful entry of a house or other building; and 19% reported taking part of in a group fight (including, but not limited to, a gang fight).

The University of Michigan survey has been conducted annually since 1975; hence it is possible to examine changes in self-reported delinquency over time. The last column in Table 10.1 reveals substantial increases from

Table 10.1: Percentage of High School Seniors Reporting Involvement in Delinquent Offenses During the Last 12 Months

Offences	*1994	1975-80	1981-85	1986-90	1991-94	1975-94
			% Change			
Argue with parents	89.9	-1.9	3.0	2.0	-0.1	2.3
Theft under $50	30.7	2.2	-2.9	0.9	-3.8	-5.2
Take something from a store	30.3	-12.2	-7.3	14.3	-2.6	-13.7
Unlawful entry of a house/building	24.8	-10.7	14.4	4.5	2.1	-11.7
Take part in a group fight	19.3	1.1	22.6	8.7	-5.4	10.9
Fight in school/work	16.2	8.2	18.2	9.9	-9.5	11.0
Damaged school property on purpose	13.8	3.1	3.8	1.5	7.8	7.8
Hurt someone badly	13.4	23.2	19.8	16.2	3.9	41.0
Theft over $50	11.0	17.9	-1.4	53.0	8.9	96.4
Auto theft	5.9	23.1	43.6	29.4	-4.8	51.3
Theft of a car part	5.7	26.8	26.4	23.2	-9.5	1.8
Damaged work property on purpose	5.6	37.2	-15.4	26.9	-15.1	9.8
Use weapon to rob someone	4.8	7.4	40.0	2.9	41.2	77.8
Arson	3.2	-11.8	11.7	10.0	52.4	88.2
Hit teacher	3.0	3.2	3.3	-16.1	0.0	-3.2

* Not a percentage change but the actual percentage of 1994 high school seniors reporting involvement in delinquent offenses at least one time during the previous year

Sources: Kathleen Maguire and Ann L. Pastore, eds. *Sourcebook of Criminal Justice Statistics, 1994.* Washington, D.C.: U.S. Government Printing Office, 1995. Edmund F. McGarrell and Timothy J. Flanagan, eds., *Sourcebook of Criminal Justice Statistics, 1984.* Washington, D.C.: U.S. Government Printing Office, 1985.

1975 to 1994 in the percentage of high school seniors who committed theft over $50 (96% increase), arson (88% increase), using a weapon to rob someone (78% increase), and auto theft (51% increase). Those increases are consistent with recent media reports of a growing epidemic of delinquency in the U.S.

However, the increases pertain to offences with relatively low percentages of students who committed them. For example, only 11% of the 1994 high school seniors (column 1) reportedly committed theft over $50 during the twelve months preceding the survey. In 1975 only 5.6% of the high school seniors reportedly committed that offence, so a 96% increase from 1975 to 1994 corresponds to an absolute increase of only 5.4%. The absolute increase for arson was 1.5%; for using a weapon to rob someone, it was 2.1%; and for auto theft, it was 2.0%. The small base rate for these offences (i.e., the small percent who committed the offence at the beginning of the period) means that any increase at all will result in very large percentage increases.

Except for the offences with small base rates, there were no huge increases from 1975 to 1994 in the percentage of high school seniors who committed property offences, and there actually were percentage decreases for some offences (see figures for taking something from a store, unlawful entry of a house or building, and theft under $50 in the last column of Table 10.1).

The same was true of violent offences. The largest percentage increase was for using a weapon to rob someone (78% increase). For most of the other violent offences—hitting teachers, fighting in school or work, and group fighting—the percentage increases or decreases tended to be small. The exception was hurting someone badly; there was a 41% increase from 1975 to 1994 in the percentage of high school seniors who reported committing that offence. However, most of that increase occurred during the late 1970s (compare columns 2-5 of Table 10.1) or prior to recent media reports of youth violence.

In addition to property and violent offences, the University of Michigan survey also asks questions about drug use (results not shown here). The illegal drugs most widely used by American high school seniors are alcohol and marijuana (reportedly used by 73% and 31% of 1994 high school seniors during the last twelve months (Maguire and Pastore, 1995:279) and cigarettes (used by 31% of 1994 high school seniors during the last month) (Maguire and Pastore, 1995:280).

There have been regular decreases in reported drug use for many types of drugs since peaks in the late 1970s (Johnston, O'Malley, and Bachman, 1994:78-79; Maguire and Pastore, 1995:279-280). Between 1975 and 1979, alcohol use during the last twelve months increased but has decreased since then. Similarly, reported marijuana use during the last twelve months peaked in 1979, but there were decreases from 1980 to 1992, after which there were small increases. Cigarette use during the last twelve months peaked in 1976, decreased until the early 1980s and then levelled off, with increases for 1993 and 1994 high school seniors. The peak year for cocaine use during the last twelve months was 1985, but it decreased after that, except for increases in 1993 and 1994. Contrary to many media reports of increasing teenage drug use in the U.S., the overall picture shows a decrease in teenage drug use, although there have been small increases in the last few years. See Box 10.2.

Box 10.2: U.S. Media's Distortion of Juvenile Drug Use

People from all over the world have formed a view from the American media that there is a serious drug problem among young Americans and that the problem has become worse over time. However, can American media accounts be believed? Orcutt and Turner (1993) cast doubts on such accounts by showing how *Newsweek* and other U.S. print media in the mid-1980s transformed results from annual surveys of student drug use into misleading reports of a "coke plague."

Since 1975 the University of Michigan Institute for Social Research (ISR) has conducted annual surveys of drug use among samples of high school seniors in the U.S. Prevalence estimates for most illegal drugs—percent having used a particular drug in the last thirty days (thirty-day prevalence), in the last twelve months (annual prevalence), and ever used (lifetime prevalence)— decreased from the late 1970s to the mid-1980s. However, the staff of *Newsweek* saw a potential "plague" in the thirty-day and annual prevalence estimates for cocaine use for 1985, which were significantly higher than the 1984 estimates (Orcutt and Turner, 1993:192-194). Even though there had been *no* significant change in lifetime prevalence (percent having ever used cocaine), *Newsweek* workers used it as the focus of a series of articles about a "coke plague," seemingly because it involved larger percentages (lifetime prevalence for cocaine use was about 17% in 1985 compared to thirty-day prevalence of about 7%). Graphic artists at *Newsweek* "transformed statistically nonsignificant fluctuations in the ISR estimates of lifetime prevalence from 1980 to 1985 into [a graph with] striking [and apparently significant] peaks and valleys," with the highest peak for 1985 (Orcutt and Turner, 1993:194). An accompanying article forecast even higher peaks (percentages) in the near future.

Other news magazines and newspapers rushed to report the "coke plague" and sometimes with even greater distortion of ISR findings. For example, the *New York Times* transformed a ISR finding that nearly 40% of U.S. high school seniors had used cocaine by age twenty-six or twenty-seven into a statement claiming that 40% of 1985 graduating seniors had used the drug (Orcutt and Turner, 1993:198). Only after the prevalence of cocaine use by high school seniors decreased in the late 1980s did *Newsweek* and other print media retreat from reports of a "plague," and even then not in feature stories (Orcutt and Turner, 1993:200-201).

Victimization Data

Victimization surveys provide another kind of unofficial data on delinquency. The most comprehensive victimization survey in the U.S. is the *National Crime Victimization Survey*, which has been conducted by the Bureau of the Census since 1972. Every person age twelve or over in a selected household (approximately 56,000 households in 1994) is interviewed and reinterviewed at six-month intervals for three years (Maguire and Pastore, 1995:642; Perkins and Klaus, 1996:8). The questions are worded something like this: "During the last six months, did anyone beat you up?"

Victimization rates for both violent crimes (rape, robbery, and assault) and theft are higher for juveniles (ages twelve to nineteen) than adults (ages twenty and over) (Perkins and Klaus, 1996:4). While juveniles ages twelve to nineteen made up about 14% of the U.S. population in 1994, a third of all victims of violent crimes were juveniles (Perkins and Klaus, 1996:6). Moreover, the victimization rates were higher for older juveniles (ages sixteen to nineteen) than younger juveniles (ages twelve to fifteen) (Perkins and Klaus, 1996:4).

The *National Crime Victimization Survey* was redesigned in 1993, and the data before and after the redesign are not comparable. However, it is possible to examine trends in victimization rates prior to 1993. While victimization rates for violent crimes decreased or remained relatively stable for most age groups from 1973 to 1992, the rate for juveniles (ages twelve to nineteen) increased (Zawitz et al., 1993:21). However, the theft victimization rate for both juveniles and adults decreased over that period.

The *National Crime Victimization Survey* gathers information on victims' perceptions of the age, sex, and race of the person(s) who victimized them in violent crimes. Violent crime victims perceive their offenders as disproportionately young, black, and male, which is important because these are also the demographic groups with the highest victimization rates (Zawitz et al., 1993:18, 23). There are two explanations for the similarity between victims of violence and violent offenders. First, people are more likely to be victimized when they associate frequently in groups disproportionately made up of offenders. Thus, "younger persons are more likely to be victims of violent crime than older persons because the former are more likely to associate with other youth who are, themselves, disproportionately involved in violence" (Sampson and Lauritsen, 1990:111). Second, it may be that violence victims and offenders are the same people. In this connection one of the best predictors of victimization is self-reported offending (Sampson and Lauritsen, 1990:113).

Homicide Victimization Data

The *National Crime Victimization Survey* does not include questions about homicide. However, data on homicide victims are compiled each year by the National Center for Health Statistics (NCHS) from records of all deaths occurring in the U.S. Information on cause of death is collected by each state and provided to NCHS or is coded by NCHS from copies of original death statistics.

According to NCHS, in the early 1990s homicide was second only to motor vehicle accidents as the leading cause of fatal injury for young people below age twenty (Snyder and Sikmund, 1995:24). Unlike many other offences, homicide victimization rates tend to be higher among young adults than teenagers (Empey and Stafford, 1991:136). In virtually every age group, black males have the highest homicide victimization rate and white females have the lowest (with black females ranking second and white males ranking third).

Figure 10.2 shows juvenile homicide victimization rates per 100,000 population ages ten to nineteen for the years 1975 to 1990 (National Center for Health Statistics, 1979-1994). The risk of being murdered increased for both juvenile white males and juvenile black males over the twenty-six-year period, but black males experienced the largest increase. The black male homicide victimization rate remained relatively stable (actually decreased slightly) from 1975 to 1984, but it almost tripled from 1984 to 1990. By contrast the white female victimization rate remained virtually unchanged from 1975 to 1990; and while black females experienced an increasing risk of murder from 1985, the increase (a 67% increase from 6.1 to 10.2) was much smaller than the increase for black males.

Causes of Juvenile Delinquency

What are the causes of delinquency? Many sociological theories and studies have addressed that question, with emphases on such predictors as peers, family, school, and juveniles' demographic characteristics.

Peers: One of the strongest predictors of delinquency is association with delinquent peers. According to Sutherland's (1947) differential association theory, delinquent behaviour is learned through intimate social relations, including peer relations. Juveniles who associate with delinquent peers are likely to violate the law because they learn attitudes that condone it. Akers' (1985) social learning theory extends differential association theory by claiming that delinquency results not only from learned attitudes but also from reinforcements (rewards and punishments) for delinquency and modelling (or imitation) of others' behaviour.

Consistent with the logic of both theories, Warr and Stafford (1991:857) have found that "the behavior of friends affects adolescents' [delinquent] behavior through their attitudes about delinquency." However, more consistent

Figure 10.2: Juvenile Homicide Victimization Rates
per 100,000 Population, Ages 10-19, U.S., 1975-1990

Year	Homicide Rate
1975	4.5
1976	4.3
1977	4.7
1978	5.1
1979	6.1
1980	6.3
1981	5.7
1982	5.2
1983	4.4
1984	4.4
1985	4.4
1986	5.1
1987	4.3
1988	4.8
1989	5.5
1990	7.1

White Males

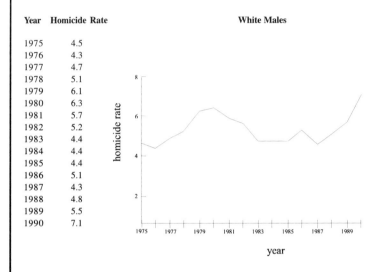

Year	Homicide Rate
1975	27.2
1976	24.7
1977	23.4
1978	21.8
1979	26.3
1980	26.9
1981	27.5
1982	25.9
1983	23.5
1984	21.6
1985	25.2
1986	28.4
1987	34.1
1988	42.3
1989	50
1990	63.4

Black Males

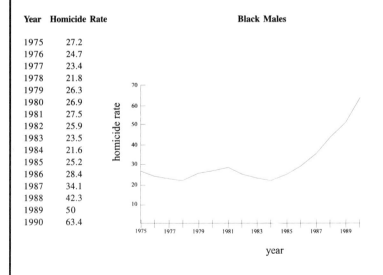

Figure 10.2: Juvenile Homicide Victimization Rates per 100,000 Population, Ages 10-19, U.S., 1975-1990

Year	Homicide Rate
1975	2
1976	2
1977	2.1
1978	2.3
1979	2.3
1980	2.6
1981	2.4
1982	2.4
1983	1.8
1984	2.2
1985	1.9
1986	2.3
1987	2
1988	2
1989	2.2
1990	2.3

White Females

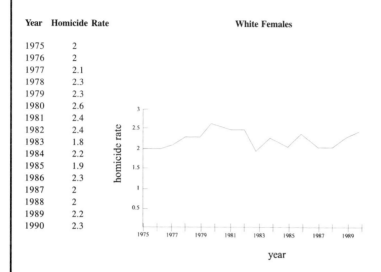

Year	Homicide Rate
1975	8.9
1976	10.4
1977	8.2
1978	7.2
1979	7.5
1980	7
1981	7
1982	6.8
1983	6.1
1984	6.8
1985	6.1
1986	7.3
1987	7.4
1988	8.1
1989	7.7
1990	10.2

Black Females

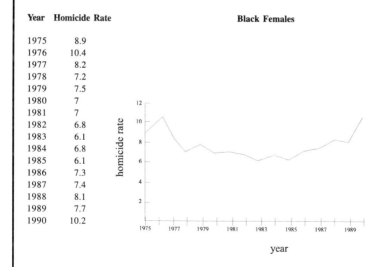

with social learning theory than differential association theory, regardless of "their own attitudes toward delinquency ... adolescents are strongly influenced by the behavior of friends."

Family: Weak attachment to parents is also a strong predictor of delinquency (Loeber and Stouthamer-Loeber, 1986). According to Hirschi (1969), attachment involves affectional ties between juveniles and parents. If juveniles are strongly attached to parents (i.e., they admire their parents and care what their parents think about them), they will be less likely to commit delinquency. If attachment to parents is weak, juveniles will not internalize conventional norms or develop respect for authority, and consequently will be more likely to commit delinquency.

Can parents do anything to reduce the effects of delinquent peer associations? Research by Warr (1993:251) shows that time spent with family, especially on weekends, has such an effect. Among juveniles who spend "a great deal of time" or "quite a bit of time" with their parents on weekends, there is little or no relationship between association with delinquent peers and delinquency. Time spent with parents may restrict juveniles' opportunities to commit delinquency; for example, it may prevent attendance at weekend parties involving alcohol and drug use.

School: Cohen (1955) has argued that lower-class boys are evaluated against a "middle-class measuring rod" in schools, but that they are destined to fail because they lack ambition, thrift, and courtesy. School failure is said to lead to a collective frustration among lower-class boys, which leads to delinquency. Many studies have found that students who do the worst in school are the most likely to commit delinquent offences (e.g., Rankin, 1980; Wiatrowski, Griswold, and Roberts, 1981). However, that likelihood is not limited to lower-class boys; school failure is related to delinquency among juveniles in all social classes, and among girls as well as boys.

Age, Gender, Social Class, and Race: Researchers have examined the extent to which delinquency is correlated with demographic variables, such as age, gender, social class, and race. U.S. arrest rates increase rapidly during the teenage years, peak at about age eighteen, and then decrease (Empey and Stafford, 1991:72-73), although the peak age is higher for violent offences than property offences (Jensen and Rojek, 1992:96). The age pattern in self-report data is similar to that in arrest data, with self-reported delinquency tending to increase through the teenage years and the peak age varying by offence (Elliott et al., 1983).

Males accounted for approximately 75% of all arrests of juveniles in 1994 (F.B.I., 1995:226); indeed, females accounted for a majority of juvenile arrests only for running away. Even for prostitution most (51%) of the arrests of juveniles in 1994 involved males rather than females. However, the ratio of the male to female arrest rate has been decreasing since 1960 (Jensen and Rojek, 1992:94). Like arrest data, self-reported delinquency is higher for males than females, and the ratio of male to female self-reported delinquency has been decreasing over time (Jensen and Rojek, 1992:144-145).

Public conceptions and media accounts in the U.S. often depict delinquency as committed mainly by economically disadvantaged (lower-class) juveniles. The *Uniform Crime Reports* do not include data on the social class of arrested juveniles, but there are many studies that examine the relationship between social class and officially recorded delinquency (for reviews, see Tittle, Villemez, and Smith, 1978 and Tittle and Meier, 1990). The evidence is mixed, with some studies showing that lower-class juveniles are over-represented in official data and other studies indicating little or no over-representation. The best conclusion to be drawn from these studies is that there is a slight tendency for lower-class juveniles to be over-represented in official data, but the differences by social class are not nearly as large as differences by age and gender. The same conclusion can be drawn from studies of the relationship between social class and self-reported delinquency, although there is some evidence of more serious, repetitive delinquency among lower-class juveniles (Tittle and Meier, 1990:280-286; Farnworth et al., 1994).

As for race, black juveniles tend to have higher arrest rates than white juveniles, particularly for violent offences (Empey and Stafford, 1991:77-78). However, self-report data paint a different picture; there are much smaller black-white differences in self-reported delinquency than in arrest data (Hindelang, Hirschi, and Weis, 1981:35, 169-170; Elliott, 1994).

U.S. Juvenile Court Procedures

As Feld (1993:209) has observed: "Juvenile courts' procedures are structured by an amalgam of United States Supreme Court constitutional decisions such as *Gault*, state statutes, judicial opinions, and court rules of procedure." One consequence is that there is considerable variation in juvenile court procedures from one jurisdiction to the next. Thus the following description of juvenile court procedures represents only a very broad outline (see Figure 10.3).

The typical delinquency or status offence case begins with a referral to juvenile court by police, parents, school officials, probation officers, social service agencies, or victims (Snyder and Sikmund, 1995:125).[1] Although there was variation by type of offence, about 85% of all 1993 delinquency cases were referred to juvenile courts by the police (Butts, 1996:4-5). In contrast, other referral sources accounted for most of the formally processed status offence cases in 1993 (Butts, 1996:8), with school officials and parents being a common referral source for such status offences as truancy and ungovernability (Snyder and Sikmund, 1995:125).

Soon after a case is referred to juvenile court, a decision is made by an intake officer, judge, or prosecutor to either process the case formally or informally. In 1993 more than half of all delinquency cases were processed informally (Butts, 1996:5). Most of these were dismissed (Snyder and Sikmund, 1995:77), but many resulted in voluntary probation, restitution, or community service (Snyder and Sikmund, 1995:131). Even a higher percentage of status offence cases were processed informally (roughly 80% that came to the attention of juvenile courts or child welfare agencies, according to Snyder and Sikmund, 1995:138).

Compared to informally processed cases, formally processed cases tend to involve more serious offences and/or offenders who are older or have more extensive juvenile court records. Although the number of formally processed delinquency cases has increased in the 1990s, there has been little change during this period in the percentage of delinquency cases that have been handled formally (Snyder and Sikmund, 1995:132).

Juveniles may be held in secure detention while their cases are being processed formally. Detention is used when there is reason to believe that a juvenile is a threat to the community or is at risk of physical harm if returned to the community. Moreover, many juveniles are detained to ensure their appearance at formal hearings or to allow for diagnostic evaluations (Butts, 1996:4).

---

[1]   In this section, "delinquency" is distinguished from "status offences." While status offences typically are considered "delinquency" in the U.S. (in the sense that all law-violating behaviour by juveniles is "delinquency"), reports of U.S. juvenile court data use special terminology; and that terminology is adopted here. Whereas "delinquency" in this section refers to an act that would be a "crime" if committed by an adult, a "status offence" denotes an act that is illegal only for juveniles.

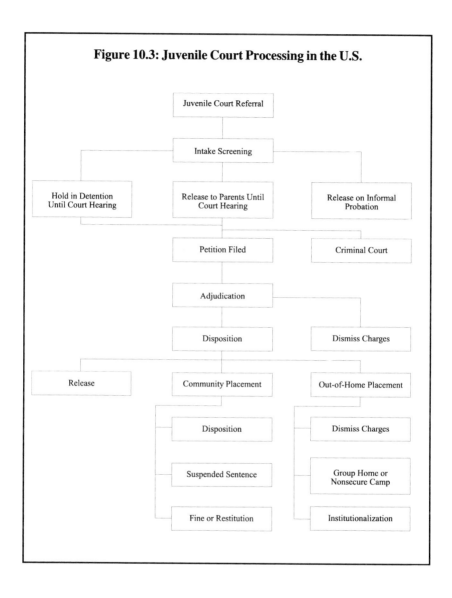

Figure 10.3: Juvenile Court Processing in the U.S.

The decision to hold a juvenile in secure detention typically is made by probation officers or detention workers (Snyder and Sikmund, 1995:78). In 1993 juveniles were detained in about 20% of all formally processed delinquency cases (Butts, 1996:4); and this was true of about 8% of all formally processed status offence cases, with most involving running away, liquor law violations, and ungovernability (Butts, 1996:8-9).

One of the first decisions that must be made during intake screening is whether a case will be processed in adult criminal court rather than in juvenile court (Feld, 1993:233). In some states a juvenile court judge must authorize all transfers to criminal court by waiving the juvenile court's jurisdiction to the case ("judicial waiver"). In other states prosecutors have the discretion to file certain types of cases in either juvenile or criminal court ("prosecutorial waiver" involving "concurrent jurisdiction between juvenile and criminal courts over certain offenses") (Feld, 1993:233). In still other states, prosecutors are required to file certain serious cases involving juvenile offenders in criminal court ("legislative offence exclusion"). While judicial waivers focus on the offender and "individualized clinical assessments of the offender's amenability to treatment" (Feld, 1993:234), prosecutorial waivers and legislative exclusions focus on the offence and the appropriate punishment. Increasingly, juvenile cases are being transferred into criminal courts by prosecutorial or legislative actions rather than by judicial waivers (Snyder and Sikmund, 1995:154), which reflects the general shift away from the rehabilitative ideal in U.S. juvenile justice.

Although transfers to criminal court by judicial waiver accounted for less than 2% of all formally processed delinquency cases in 1993, that percentage is higher than it was only a few years earlier (Butts, 1996:5, 7). The highest percentage of transfer cases involved offences against persons (42% of all cases transferred by judicial waiver in 1993), followed by property offences (38% of all cases), drug offences (10%), and public order offences (9%) (Butts, 1996:6, 8).

If a case is handled in juvenile court, a delinquency petition is filed, which states the charges and requests the court to adjudicate the juvenile as a delinquent. Petitions for adjudicatory hearings almost always are granted. At the adjudicatory hearing (trial), the facts of the case are presented and witnesses are called (Snyder and Sikmund, 1995:78). "A youth referred to juvenile court for a delinquency offense may be adjudicated ... a delinquent after admitting to the charges in the case, or after the court finds sufficient evidence to prove ... that the youth committed the facts alleged in the petition" (Snyder and Sikmund, 1995:133).

Juveniles were adjudicated as delinquents in about 60% of all petitioned delinquency cases and as status offenders in about 55% of all petitioned status cases in 1993 (Butts, 1996:6, 8-9). When this occurs a disposition plan is developed by the probation staff, sometimes along with the prosecutor, recommending to the judge what should done to the juvenile. There are many options, including fines, restitution, probation, institutionalization, community service, and referral to a community-based treatment program, such as a drug counselling program.

More than half (about 60%) of all adjudicated cases (both delinquency and status offence cases) resulted in probation in 1993 (Butts, 1996:6, 8-9). Juveniles on probation remain in their communities and continue their normal activities, such as school and work. However, probation usually entails certain conditions, such as meeting regularly with a probation officer, adhering to a curfew, and refraining from further delinquency. There also may be provisions for the revocation of probation if the conditions are violated; and when probation is revoked, the court may impose a more severe disposition, including institutionalization (Snyder and Sikmund, 1995:135).

Three out of ten adjudicated delinquency cases and two of ten adjudicated status offence cases resulted in out-of-home placement of juveniles in 1993, including placement in a training school, camp, ranch, privately operated facility, foster home, and group home (Snyder and Sikmund, 1995:133; Butts, 1996:6, 8-9). Delinquency cases involving public-order offences and offences against persons were most likely to result in out-of-home placement in 1993 (Butts, 1996:7). The relatively high likelihood of out-of-home placement for public-order offences is at least partially because escapes from institutions and probation violations are counted in this offence category (Snyder and Sikmund, 1995:133). As for adjudicated status offence cases, running away and ungovernability were most likely to result in out-of-home placement (Snyder and Sikmund, 1995:140).

Many cases that are processed formally do not result in adjudication of a juvenile as a delinquent or status offender (40% of all petitioned delinquency cases and 45% of petitioned status offence cases in 1993) (Butts, 1996:6, 9). However, many such "nonadjudicated" cases still result in juveniles agreeing to voluntary (informal) dispositions, including probation and out-of home placement. About 60% of all nonadjudicated delinquency cases in 1993 were dismissed by the court, and this was true of 66% of nonadjudicated status offence cases (Butts, 1996:6, 9). However, in 23% of nonadjudicated delinquency cases, the juvenile agreed to informal probation and 2% agreed voluntarily to out-of-home placement. In 17% of nonadjudicated status offence cases, the juvenile agreed to informal probation and 1% agreed to out-of-home placement.

Discussion and Conclusions

Many juvenile justice reforms in the U.S. today, including recent reforms, are linked to a shift in the legal rights of juveniles (Stafford, 1995). The *parens patriae* doctrine, which justified the creation of the juvenile court in the late 1800s and guided juvenile justice policies for the first two-thirds of this century, gave legal officials the power to protect juveniles. Concomitantly, juveniles were granted protective rights out of a belief that they lacked the capacity to care for themselves and make effective choices. "Protection and rehabilitation [were] the keystone [of the juvenile court through mid-twentieth century], giving judges almost unlimited discretion" (Horowitz, 1984:4). However, in the last third of this century, juveniles have been granted fewer protective rights and more liberating rights. The shift has stemmed from a growing belief that juveniles can make choices that are just as effective as those made by adults. Hence, increasingly it is believed that juveniles do not need protective rights as much as they need liberating rights, including the right to due process in juvenile court, free expression in school, and abortion rights, to name just a few. However, the extension of protective rights to juveniles has led to an expectation of greater responsibility among juveniles and a demand that they be held accountable for their actions.

The shift from protective to liberating rights has not been complete. Some juvenile justice policies continue to grant protective rights to juveniles. For example, reliance on probation as the most common disposition for adjudicated juvenile court cases continues to reflect a longstanding belief that juveniles deserve a second chance when they violate the law and that they can be rehabilitated by proper guidance. Other, more recent juvenile justice polices tend to grant liberating rights to juveniles. For example, the Supreme Court ruled in the *Gault* case that although juveniles do not need all the protections accorded to adults in criminal trials, they should at least have "the essentials of due process and fair treatment" (quoting from *Kent*, p. 562).

There is inevitable tension from granting both protective and liberating rights to juveniles, which is illustrated by a recent disagreement in the American Civil Liberties Union—(A.C.L.U.) (Rosenbaum, 1989). In a draft of a brief for the Supreme Court in the late 1980s, A.C.L.U. attorneys argued that teenagers are ineligible for the death penalty because they lack the capacity to make effective choices about committing capital offences. However, at the same time, other A.C.L.U. lawyers were arguing before the Court in abortion cases that teenage girls do have the capacity to make effective choices about having abortions. The tension centred on whether to argue for a protective right or a liberating right for juveniles. Recognizing the impossibility of arguing before the same Court that both types of rights should be granted to juveniles, the A.C.L.U. resolved the problem by declining to file a brief in the death penalty case.

The shift in U.S. juvenile justice over the past several decades away from the rehabilitative ideal towards punishment and accountability has created similar tensions. Indeed, U.S. juvenile justice policy has been characterized as "schizophrenic" as a consequence of its older (although continuing) focus on the need to protect juveniles and its newer focus on the need to hold them accountable for their wrongdoings and punish them (Empey and Stafford, 1991:ch. 20). The tension increasingly is being resolved in favour of punishment and accountability over protection and rehabilitation. However, an important question has largely been ignored: has there been improvement in the physical, psychological, and social well-being of juveniles as a consequence of the shift from protective rights and the rehabilitative ideal to liberating rights and an emphasis on punishment and accountablity? There is considerable need for more research on the impact of juvenile justice reforms in the U.S. For example, there have been few systematic studies of the impact of transferring juvenile offenders to the adult criminal justice system (Snyder and Sikmund, 1995:156). Indeed, there is little evidence, after decades of debate, that institutionalization of juvenile offenders is more effective than probation in reducing recidivism among released offenders. Those and similar issues cry out to be studied; until then, U.S. officials will be operating in the dark about the consequences of many juvenile justice policies.

References

Akers, Ronald L. (1985). *Deviant behavior: A social learning approach* (third edition). Belmont, California: Wadsworth.

Blumstein, Alfred. (1995). Violence by young people: Why the deadly nexus? *National Institute of Justice Journal* 229:2-9. Washington, D.C.: National Institute of Justice.

Bremner, Robert H. (Ed.). (1970). *Children and youth in America: A documentary history*. 3 Vols. Cambridge, Massachusetts: Harvard University Press.

Butts, Jeffrey A. (1996). Offenders in juvenile jourt, 1993. *Juvenile Justice Bulletin*. Washington, D.C.: U.S. Department of Justice.

Caldwell, Robert G. (1961). The juvenile court: Its development and some major problems. *Journal of Criminal Law, Criminology and Police Science* 51:493-511.

Cohen, Albert K. (1955). *Delinquent boys: The culture of the gang.* New York: Free Press.

Dawson, Robert O. (1990). The future of juvenile justice: Is it time to abolish the system? *Journal of Criminal Law and Criminology* 81:136-155.

Day, Jennifer Cheeseman. (1993). *Population projections of the United States by age, sex, race, and Hispanic origin in 1993-2050.* Current Population Reports. Series P-25, no. 1104. Washington, D.C.: U.S. Government Printing Office.

Degler, Carl N. (1973). *The democratic experience: A short american history* (third edition). Glenview, Illinois: Scott, Foresman and Company.

Elliott, Delbert S. (1994). Serious violent offenders: Onset, developmental course, and termination. *Criminology* 32:1-21.

Elliott, Delbert S., Suzanne S. Ageton, David Huizinga, Brian A. Knowles, and Rachelle J. Canter. (1983). *The prevalence and incidence of delinquent behavior: 1976-1980. National estimates of delinquent behavior by sex, race, social class and other selected variables. A report of the National Youth Survey (Project Report No. 26).* Boulder, Colorado: C/A Publications.

Empey, LaMar T. and Mark C. Stafford. (1991). *American delinquency: Its meaning and construction* (third edition). Belmont, California: Wadsworth.

Farnworth, Margaret, Terence P. Thornberry, Marvin D. Krohn, and Alan J. Lizotte. (1994). Measurement in the study of class and delinquency: Integrating theory and research. *Journal of Research in Crime and Delinquency* 31:32-61.

Federal Bureau of Investigation. (1995). *Crime in the United States: Uniform crime reports, 1994.* Washington, D.C.: U.S. Government Printing Office.

Feld, Barry C. (1993). Criminalizing the American juvenile court. Pp. 197-280 in *Crime and justice: An annual review of research,* Vol. 17, edited by Michael Tonry. Chicago: University of Chicago Press.

Feld, Barry C. (1990). The punitive juvenile court and the quality of procedural justice: Disjunctions between rhetoric and reality. *Crime and Delinquency* 36:443-466.

Grasmick , Harold G. and Anne L. McGill. (1994). Religion, attribution style, and punitiveness toward juvenile offenders. *Criminology* 32:23-46.

Hindelang, Michael J., Travis Hirschi, and Joseph G. Weis. (1981). *Measuring delinquency.* Berverly Hills, California: Sage.

Hirschi, Travis. (1969). *Causes of delinquency.* Berkeley, California: University of California Press.

Horowitz, Robert M. (1984). Children's rights: A look backward and a glance ahead. Pp. 1-9 in *Legal rights of children,* edited by Robert M. Horowitz and Howard A. Davidson. New York: McGraw-Hill.

Jensen, Gary F. and Dean G. Rojek. (1992). *Delinquency and youth crime* (second edition). Prospect Heights, Illinois: Waveland Press.

Johnston, Lloyd D., Patrick M. O'Malley, and Jerald G. Bachman. (1994). *National survey results on drug use from the monitoring the future study, 1975-1993. Vol. I: Secondary school students.* Rockville, Maryland: National Institute on Drug Abuse.

Klein, Malcolm W. (1995). *The American gang: Its nature, prevalence, and control.* New York: Oxford University Press.

Krisberg, Barry, Ira M. Schwartz, Paul Litsky, and James Austin. (1986). The watershed of juvenile justice reform. *Crime and Delinquency* 32:5-38.

Lipton, Douglas, Robert Martinson, and Judith Wilks. (1975). *The effectiveness of correctional treatment: A survey of treatment evaluation studies.* New York: Praeger Publishers.

Loeber, Rolf and Magda Stouthamer-Loeber. (1986). Family factors as correlates and predictors of juvenile conduct problems and delinquency. Pp. 29-149 in *Crime and justice: An annual review of research,* Vol. 7, edited by Michael Tonry and Norval Morris. Chicago: University of Chicago Press.

Maguire, Kathleen and Ann L. Pastore. (Eds.). (1995). *Sourcebook of criminal justice statistics, 1994.* U.S. Department of Justice. Washington, D.C.: U.S. Government Printing Office.

Martinson, Robert. (1974). What works? Questions and answers about prison reform. *The Public Interest* 35:22-54.

McGarrell, Edmund F. and Timothy J. Flanagan. (Eds.). (1985). *Sourcebook of criminal justice statistics, 1984.* U.S. Department of Justice. Washington, D.C.: U.S. Government Printing Office.

National Center for Health Statistics. (1979-1994). *Vital statistics of the United States (1975-1990).* Vol. II, Part A. Hyattsville, Maryland: Public Health Service.

Orcutt, James D. and J. Blake Turner. (1993). Shocking numbers and graphic accounts: Quantified images of drug problems in the print media. *Social Problems* 40:190-206.

Perkins, Craig and Patsy Klaus. (1996). *Criminal victimization 1994.* Bureau of Justice Statistics Bulletin. Washington, D.C.: U.S. Government Printing Office.

Platt, Anthony M. (1969). *The child savers: The invention of delinquency.* Chicago: University of Chicago Press.

Rankin, Joseph H. (1980). School factors and delinquency: Interactions by age and sex. *Sociology and Social Research* 64:420-434.

Rosenbaum, Ron. (1989). A tangled web for the supreme court. *The New York Times Magazine,* March 12, 60.

Rothman, David J. (1971). *The discovery of the asylum.* Boston: Little, Brown.

Sampson, Robert J. and Janet L. Lauritsen. (1990). Deviant lifestyles, proximity to crime, and the offender-victim link in personal violence. *Journal of Research in Crime and Delinquency* 27:110-139.

Sechrest, Lee, Susan O. White, and Elizabeth D. Brown. (Eds.). (1979). *The rehabilitation of criminal offenders: Problems and prospects.* Washington, D.C.: National Academy of Sciences.

Snyder, Howard N. and Melissa Sickmund. (1995). *Juvenile offenders and victims: A national report.* Washington, D.C.: Office of Juvenile Justice and Delinquency Prevention.

Stafford, Mark C. (1995). Children's legal rights in the U.S. *Marriage and Family Review* 21:121-139.

Stafford, Mark C. and Omer R. Galle. (1984). Victimization rates, exposure to risk, and fear of crime. *Criminology* 22:173-185.

Streib, Victor L. (1987). *Death penalty for juveniles*. Bloomington, Indiana: Indiana University Press.

Sutherland, Edwin H. (1947). *Principles of criminology* (fourth edition). Philadelphia: J. B. Lippincott Co.

Teilmann, Katherine S. and Pierre H. Landry, Jr. (1981). Gender bias in juvenile justice. *Journal of Research in Crime and Delinquency* 18:47-80.

Tittle, Charles R. and Robert F. Meier. (1990). Specifying the SES/delinquency relationship. *Criminology* 28:271-299.

Tittle, Charles R., Wayne J. Villemez, and Douglas A. Smith. (1978). The myth of social class and criminality: An empirical assessment of the empirical evidence. *American Sociological Review* 43:643-656.

Warr, Mark. (1995). The polls - poll trends: Public opinion on crime and punishment. *Public Opinion Quarterly* 59:296-310.

Warr, Mark. (1993). Parents, peers, and delinquency. *Social Forces* 72:247-264.

Warr, Mark and Mark Stafford. (1991). The influence of delinquent peers: What they think or what they do? *Criminology* 29:851-866.

Wiatrowski, Michael D., David B. Griswold, and Mary K. Roberts. (1981). Social control theory and delinquency. *American Sociological Review* 46:525-541.

Zawitz, Marianne W., Patsy A. Klaus, Ronet Bachman, Lisa D. Bastian, Marshall M. DeBerry Jr., Michael R. Rand, and Bruce M. Taylor. (1993). *Highlights from 20 years of surveying crime victims. The national crime victimization survey, 1973-92.* U.S. Department of Justice. Washington, D.C.: U.S. Government Printing Office.

CASES

In re Gault, 387 U.S. 1 (1967)
Kent v. United States, 383 U.S. 541 (1966)
Stanford v. Kentucky, 109 S. Ct. 2969 (1989)
Thompson v. Oklahoma, 487 U.S. 815 (1988)

chapter 11

Comparative Juvenile Justice: An Overview of Hungary

Mária Herczog
Dept. for Family Affairs and Child Protection
Ferenc Irk
National Institute of Criminology and Criminalistics
Budapest, Hungary

Facts about Hungary

Area: Located in the centre of Europe, in its eastern part. The country covers 93,030 sq. km. The area is referred to as the Carpathian Basin. The capital is Budapest (pop. 2 million). **Population**: Hungary is a republic with 10,470,000 inhabitants—1995 (110 persons per sq. km). The age breakdown of the population shows 1,911,000 people aged one to fourteen, 1,619,000 aged fifteen to twenty-four, 4,771,000 aged twenty-five to fifty-nine, and 1,896,000 in the age group sixty and older. Hungary is experiencing a rapidly aging population and a decline in child births. Population growth rate is -0.1. In the academic year of 1994-95, about 1,926,900 children aged six to fourteen were in primary education (basically an eighth-grade elementary school system); and 609,900 participated in secondary education, of whom 418,500 studied in secondary schools, the rest attended vocational schools. This figure is very low by international standards—even by East European standards. The majority of the population is atheist. While most of the religious population is Roman Catholic, with large numbers belonging to the Protestant and Jewish churches, there are no precise figures available as the census does not contain reference to religious conviction. The number of people belonging to ethnic minorities is also estimated. Such minorities are Croat, German, Greek, Romanian, Serb, Slovak, and Slovenian ethnic groups. The largest minority group is the Romany population. The Hungarian language can trace its origin back to the Finnougric tribes of languages. **Climate**: Hungary has a continental climate with Mediterranean and Atlantic influences. Average temperature in January is -2° C and 23° C in July. **Government**: In 1990 the former single-party, Soviet-type communist system termed People's Republic was replaced by a freely elected multi-party parliament which consists of six political parties. A socialist-liberal democrat coalition government emerged in the 1994 elections. The parliament has a single chamber with a powerful government and a less dominant President of the Republic. The Constitutional Court has a major role in ensuring checks and balances of the branches of power.

In Hungary the tendencies of delinquency have been turning unfavourably over the past decade. This can be illustrated with the following:

— In the last twenty-five years the number of criminal offences has increased fourfold and between 1988-91 the number of offences doubled.
— Offences against property represented two-thirds of all cases in 1988 and three-quarter of all offences in 1995.

— The most significant change occurred between 1989-92 but
there is a growing fear that because of the rapid and not readily
'absorbed' changes, another crime wave can come within ten
years.

— In 1980 34% of all offenders were adolescents or young adults.
In 1995 this number had increased to 41.6%.

— Since 1987 the means of investigating cases have not kept
abreast with the increase in crime. In 1995 less than 60% of all
reported cases were investigated.

(The National Crime Prevention Program, 1996).

The State of Juvenile
Delinquency in Hungary

The general public in Hungary does not generally believe juvenile delinquency
is related to the youths' social and cultural background, their lack of family
care, or their academic ability. Even professional public opinion is highly divided.
These facts combined with a lack of research, programs, and policy evaluation
tend to promote emotionally based debates. However, such debates are not
common in Hungary. Media attention is limited primarily to crimes which have
a news value rather than to possible solutions, prevention, or professional
responsibility.

This apparent lack of concern for juvenile crime and its correlates is
reflected in the statistics. In 1994, 17,297 young individuals were accused of
having committed offences. Of those, 34.1% (5902) had their cases dismissed
for various reasons. Due more to a lack of adequate resources than being
based on a rational model of juvenile justice, an overwhelming majority of
juvenile delinquents (4445 or 58.9%) are released on probation. In 1994, 198
(2.6%) of young offenders were sentenced for a term to a reformatory institute
while 2279 (30.2%), those who had committed more serious crimes, were given
juvenile prison terms. But, due to the lack of resources, 1493 had their sentence
suspended. The majority of juvenile crimes, however, are property-related
offences (75.8% in 1994). The rest are crimes against public order (11.1% in
1994), against individuals (6.3% in 1994) and traffic crimes (4.1% in 1994). And
although representing a comparatively small percentage, there has been a
growing number of serious crimes, gang related crimes, and crimes involving
adults contributing to the delinquency of a juvenile.

Since the political changeover in 1990, there has been a sharp increase in the number of juvenile delinquents. This appears to be due to a number of factors. One important factor being the hiatuses of a structurally and professionally outdated child and juvenile protection system. Juvenile and adult crime rates have increased in general since 1989 (see Table 11.1). Much of this can be explained by the opening up of borders, an unexpected gap between living standards and potentials, in addition to increasing deprivation and unemployment. Another important reason is a lower level of efficiency of police detection and apprehension resulting from fiscal restraints which have arisen amidst the transformation called for by the political changes.

Table 11.1: Adult and Youth Crime: 1975-1995

Year	Total No. of Adult Crimes	Total No. of Juvenile Crimes
1975	72,049	7,268
1980	72,881	6,535
1985	85,766	9,449
1990	112,254	12,848
1991	122,835	14,307
1992	132,644	15,476
1993	122,621	15,001
1994	119,494	14,479
1995	121,121	14,321

Source: Statistical yearbook. (1995).

As a result of the growing number crimes committed by children and young juveniles, a growing number of people have demanded that the age limit of culpability (i.e., fourteen) should be decreased (see Box 11.1). Fortunately however, their voice is not very strong. As for the administration of juvenile justice, because of limited resources, qualified manpower, and no concrete objectives, there has been little effort put forth to either lower the age limit, let alone adequately address the growing delinquency problem.

Contrary to point 1.1 in the 1984 Beijing Rules (see Box 1—Introduction), there has been no special attention paid to the juvenile delinquency problem. In fact no major development has taken place since the problem management of the beginning of this century, which at the time was highly progressive even by international standards. Very few of the rules laid down in international and United Nations agreements and adopted mandatorily have actually been observed.

Box 11.1: Age of Responsibility

In 1995, presumably children and teenagers who were never found, were throwing stones at a passing train. Two of the passengers where seriously injured, one of them, a six year old boy, died later. In addition to the injuries and death, numerous windows were broken. There was an immediate public and media outcry for the apprehension of the offenders and a call for the lowering of the age of responsibility just in case children were involved in the crime. Comparisons were drawn with the Jamie Bulger case in England when two English boys killed a young infant (see Ch. 4).

Prevention, probation, and follow-up care are in a critical situation. The number of the so-called social patrons has dropped drastically while that of the official patrons has not increased to the desirable extent. And even though relevant professional training was started in 1994 within the framework of full-time and postgraduate training for social workers the results of these programs may take some time before they are felt in the juvenile justice system.

In essence, the history of juvenile justice in Hungary has not been a promising one. Along with the major social and political changes, as well as the lack of attention given prevention and social work with the families of problem youth, the youth have become victims of the changes (see Box 11.2).

Box 11.2: Delinquents' as Victims of Change

A group of teenagers in Gyor, a Hungarian city near the Austrian border, regularly blackmailed and robbed school aged children, took their money, stole their jackets and sport shoes, and even took lunch boxes. These incidents occurred over several months. The children had to pay "protection money". If they failed to do so, the youngsters were often beaten. The victimized children were too afraid to come forward and tell their parents or teachers. The team leader of the youth 'gang' was less than fourteen years of age and all other members of the group were between fifteen and seventeen years of age. After finally being detected, all the youths were apprehended and placed into custody.

Social and Legal Definition of Delinquency

The Hungarian Penal Code currently in force was adopted by parliament in 1978 (Act IV of 1978). It was amended several times, particularly after the political changeover in 1989-1990. According to the Penal Code, "a crime is a voluntary or involuntary act (in case the latter is penalized by law) which is dangerous for society and which involve a punishment by law" (Paragraph 1 of Article 10). An act is dangerous for society if it endangers the state, the social or economic order of the Republic of Hungary, and threatens, or infringes upon, the rights of citizens (Paragraph 2 of Article 10).

Unlike many Western countries, Hungary does not have a separate act for juvenile offenders. Instead, special provisions for juveniles are described in Chapter VII of the Penal Code. Having a separate act for juvenile delinquents would mean a sharp distinction between adults and youngsters. To do so would involve all the legal obligations stipulated and acknowledged under the international regulations (e.g., Beijing Rules, In Declaration Rijadh Directions— See Box 1, Introduction). To undertake such changes would at least help to clarify how to handle youths under the age of fourteen, what kinds of preventive and care activities should be taken and by whom and how. In addition, guidelines for the handling of young adults (ages eighteen to twenty-one) could be more clearly defined. Alternatively, handling the problems of adults and juveniles together could also help with the reforms and the growing role of alternative sanctions. A notable lack of separation means that in Hungary both adults and juveniles are treated to same under our Penal Code even though young offenders need a 'milder' approach.

In accordance with the relevant provisions in force, a juvenile is a delinquent who has passed fourteen years of age but has not reached eighteen years when committing the crime (Article 107). A juvenile delinquent may be subject to punishment or legal measures as defined within the Penal Code. The primary intent of both punitive forms is correction. Prison sentences should be imposed only in cases where the intent of the punishment or measures cannot be realized in another way (Article 108 partially amended in 1995). Public work and confiscation of property can not be enforced. A term in a correctional institution can be imposed (Article 109 partially amended in 1995).

Penal substantive law contains a number of other alleviating provisions in the case of juvenile delinquents. For instance:

- The longest term of confinement for a juvenile who has passed sixteen when committing a delinquency is fifteen years in the case of crimes that can involve life imprisonment; and ten years in the case of crimes that involve imprisonment longer than ten years (Article 110).
- A juvenile who has not yet passed sixteen years of age when committing the delinquency can be sentenced to a maximum of ten years in the case of a crime that can involve life imprisonment.
- All juvenile sentences must be served in a juvenile penitentiary institution (Article 111).

- A juvenile delinquent may be sentenced to pay a fine only if he or she has an income of his or her own or possesses appropriate assets (Article 114).
- In connection with banishment, a provision prescribes that a juvenile who lives in an appropriate family can not be banned from the town/ village in which his or her family resides (Article 116).
- Limiting provisions of probation do not apply to juvenile delinquents. Probation is possible irrespective of the delinquency committed (Article 117).
- The court may rule that the juvenile delinquent be sent to a reformatory institution when it is believed necessary in the interests of the juvenile's corrective education. Such a ruling may prescribe a term of one to three years. In cases where the term is longer than one year, it is possible for the court to temporarily release the juvenile delinquent (Article 118).
- Juvenile delinquents who receive a suspended sentence can be placed on either probation, parole, or temporarily released from a reformatory institution (Article 119).
- The entire duration of the pre-trial confinement should count towards the term in the reformatory institution. Consequently, one day of pre-trial confinement equals one day in the reformatory (Article 120/B).
- A juvenile delinquent will be exempt from the disadvantages attached to a criminal record earlier than an adult. Such a disadvantage should be ruled only if the sentence is more serious than in the case of an adult (Article 121).

The provisions are grounded in the neo-classical school of criminological thought, which provides for judicial discretion, minimum and maximum sentences, as well as the principle of extenuating circumstances. The model of justice, in accordance with Figure 1 of the Introduction, could best be described as a **crime control model**. These are only assumptions as there has not been any research or surveys conducted on the subject. However, based on media coverage and as reflected in public opinion polls, both the media and public would like to see more serious punishment and prison sentences administered against juveniles. They do not appear interested in whether these severe measures are actually effective.

The prevention versus punishment dilemma is a very difficult one as prevention seems to represent an "insecure investment" without knowing its exact costs and effectiveness. In 1996 the Institute for Criminology and Criminalistics began an evaluation project designed to assess the cost and effectiveness of prevention and punishment programs for juvenile delinquents in Hungary.

Evolution of Juvenile Justice in Hungary

The two most significant documents of nineteenth century Hungarian penal law were the 1843 penal bills and the so-called Csemegi Code of 1878, the first Hungarian Penal Code. Neither, however, provided for the criminal liability of juvenile delinquents as they both belonged to the "classical school". At the same time there are records showing that the necessity of different regulations for juvenile delinquents was raised in the committee preparing the 1843 Bill on prisons and a provision was put forth to introduce the institution of reformatory school.

Following the German pattern, the Csemegi Code regarded juvenile delinquents as "little adults" and did not provide for criminal liability differently. However, it still contained formulations which could be the basis of less severe sentences in cases of twelve to sixteen year old delinquents.

Legislative Act No. XXXVI, known as the First Penal Novel (1908), was enacted in the wake of criticism—a change of attitude as a result of increased juvenile delinquent activities. For the first time the criminal liability of juvenile delinquents was handled differently. This was also the first law to introduce the institution of suspended sentence. According to the preamble of the legislative act showing Dutch, Belgian, and American influence, "...it is not restoration but protection and education that should be the guiding principle when facing child and juvenile delinquents" (Lévai, 1994).

The age of juvenile status was determined as between twelve and eighteen years. No procedure could be initiated against delinquents younger than twelve, although "house discipline" (e.g., incarceration at school) was permitted. The "ability of discretion" was replaced by "intellectual and moral development". Although its content remained undefined, the opportunity to exercise some discretion in sentencing helped the judge. Instead of relying only on short term imprisonment measures that are most expedient and suit the character of the young delinquent, judges are now able to make judgments in accordance with the principle of individualization. The maximum term of reformatory confinement was not specified, but it could not exceed the delinquent's twenty-first year of age.

Juvenile delinquents' courts were set-up and regulated by Legislative Act No. VII of 1913. The spirit of this act, which was essentially an amendment to the Penal Novel, already reflected the awareness of the relationship between child protection and criminality. In this way juvenile delinquents' courts did more than perform mere judicial tasks, and by involving patrons and patronage associations they preceded all European states. On the other hand, the spirit of the law could not always be realized due to the lack of institutional systems for the handling and protection of young offenders.

During the short-lived, 133-day Commune in 1919, the communist power regarded juvenile delinquency as a product of capitalism (see Ch. 8 on Russia) and did not consider it justified to penalize young delinquents. Active child protection was proposed based on school protection and topped by the system of judicial child protection, which aimed at solving problems through juvenile education. According to Decree No. LXXII, "...after the necessary temporary measures, children and young people should be passed on to the general health care and educational child protection institutions...."

A fundamental change during the period between the two world wars was the restitution of the First Penal Novel in force prior to the Commune. It remained in force through 1948 with only minor amendments. Then after a few basic changes in 1950 and 1951, the 1952 Law Decree No. 34 provided for penal law and penal procedures pertaining to juvenile delinquents. It is based on the principle that although education is in the focus of juvenile penal law, it is still essentially penal law. The age of juvenile status remained (twelve to eighteen) while the old term of "intellectual and moral development" was replaced by the following provision: if owing to an underdeveloped intellect, the juvenile could not fully recognize the fact that his or her act was dangerous for society, investigation could be refused, procedure terminated, and exemption could ensue.

Legislative Act No. 23 of 1953 divided juveniles into two groups: those aged twelve to fourteen and those aged fourteen to eighteen. The only forms of punishment applicable with the younger age group were admonishment, probation, reformatory education, and special education—a **welfare** approach (see Figure 1—Introduction). Special education as a sanction was a new feature and was applied to mentally handicapped individuals who were unfit for correctional education. As for those aged fourteen to eighteen, the main rule stipulated penalization—a crime control approach. Educational measures could be applied only as a supplement. The shortest term of imprisonment was thirty days and the maximum length five years. In exceptional cases a longer sentence was allowed and even capital punishment was possible. Juvenile courts fell within the structure of the judiciary. Special judges and the courts themselves were appointed by the minister of justice. The two lay assessors in the juvenile court included a member from the women's movement and a member from the teacher's trade union.

Legislative Act No.38 of 1957 relegated social policy decisions to the authorities of local administration. To date this has settled the distribution of tasks: child and juvenile protection and prevention is the duty of the local system while subsequent intervention and ruling is held by the judiciary.

Act V of 1961, the so-called first socialist Penal Code, did away with the relative autonomy of juvenile delinquents' criminal liability. Provisions that had formerly been codified in a separate decree were included in Chapter VI of the new act. This chapter dealt with juvenile delinquency. The act abolished capital punishment and put correctional education in the focus—a principle set forth under the Beijing Rules. It set the maximum term of confinement at ten years and created better chances for re-integration into society by the institution of exemption. The act represented a shift away from crime control to a more **participatory/welfare** model (see Figure 1—Introduction).

In response to the inefficiency of juvenile protection inspectors, the minister of education enacted a decree in 1970 on professional probation officers. And while the use of social patrons has not disappeared completely over the past twenty years, the number of probation officers has slowly been increasing. While there were 219 probation officers in 1994, there are no nationwide statistics as to the number of social patrons. But in 1994 there were 13,393 young people on probation compared to 2056 under the care of social patrons.

Preparation of Bill VI of 1978, the Penal Code, commenced in the early 1970s. By then a mass of new research information had accumulated and criminology as an area of study had emerged in Hungary. Heads of the justice administration, however, did not intend to change the concept or details of earlier regulations and all codifying committees were of the opinion that the criminal liability of juvenile delinquents should be considered as criminal liability in the strictest sense. Consequently, the new act contained only minor changes, the most important being the abolishment of remedial education as a separate category of measures. For example, Article 37 of the Penal Code stipulates the objective of penalization for all delinquents is "...with a view of protecting society, prevention of the perpetrator or other persons from committing another offence."

In spite of repeated 'tinkering' with the legislation, it did not provide the solution to countering the ravages of the economic and political chaos that dominated Hungary during the late 1980s and into the 1990s. For example, in 1994 there were 910 personal offences committed by juvenile delinquents. Of these, thirty-three (3.6%) involved manslaughter and 701 (77%) bodily harm or assault. In addition, there were 1069 instances of fighting and rioting and 535 robberies. With the exception of public disorder offences, the number of these offences has been roughly the same since 1988 (see Table 11.2). In 1995 spiralling juvenile delinquency rates combined with the failures of a cumbersome judiciary helped to bring about changes through the passing of Act XLI. The act also represents an attempt to align Hungarian standards of juvenile justice with those of its European neighbours. Some of the key elements include:

- Imprisonment of a delinquent child is only allowed if the objective of punishment cannot be reached in any other way.
- The term of confinement to a reformatory institution is no longer indefinite, and the duration of pre-trial confinement should be considered as part thereof.
- Pre-trial confinement beyond the basic conditions stipulated by law can only be justified by the extreme severity of the offence.
- Juvenile delinquents should preferably be confined to a reformatory institution prior to their trial.
- In cases involving imprisonment of less than five years the prosecutor may suspend prosecution for a probation period of one to two years in order to give the juvenile delinquent the chance to develop in the right direction.

These measures represent another (legal) step towards embracing a more **paternal/welfare model** of juvenile justice in Hungary. In practice however, as we will see in the next section, the intent of the provisions has not been actualized.

Role of the Key Actors in the Administration of Juvenile Justice

Although there is a broad social safety net for juvenile offenders in Hungary ranging from social workers to community work and alternatives to punishment, it plays a marginal role. This is largely due to the former ideological and political

Table 11.2: the Number of Young Delinquents and Percentages According to Criminal Actions

Juvenile Delinquents' Number and Rates

	1990		1991		1992		1993		1994	
	number	%	number	%	number	%	number	%	number	%
Total	12,848	100.0	13,509	100.0	15,476	100.0	15,001	100.0	14,479	100.0
Against Persons	849	6.6	711	6.3	884	5.7	854	5.7	910	6.3
Manslaughter	31	0.2	21	0.2	23	0.2	27	0.2	33	0.2
Bodily Harm	613	4.8	532	4.1	701	4.5	678	4.5	701	4.8
Traffic Crime	713	5.6	577	4.3	665	4.3	663	4.4	598	4.1
Against Moral	145	1.1	86	0.6	143	0.9	160	1.1	149	1.0
Sexual Abuse	55	0.4	43	0.3	64	0.4	62	0.4	64	0.4
Fighting and Rioting	862	6.7	843	6.2	1,213	7.8	1,403	9.4	1,606	11.1
From this: Rioting	643	5.0	662	4.9	887	5.7	1,026	6.8	1,069	7.4
Against Property	9,955	77.5	11,055	81.8	12,219	79.0	11,618	77.4	10,980	75.8
From this: Stealing	5,160	40.2	5,332	39.5	5,704	36.9	5,182	34.5	5,182	35.8
Break in	2,690	20.9	3,686	27.3	3,881	25.1	3,856	25.7	3,814	26.3
Robbery	409	3.2	552	4.1	628	4.1	556	3.7	535	3.4
Other	324	2.5	239	1.8	352	2.3	303	2.0	236	1.6

practice, the lack of professional debates, a weak sense of advocacy on the part of the delinquents and their helpers, and the lack of research and evaluation on juvenile delinquency. In fact foreign trends and practices are known only by a very limited circle in Hungary. The entire field is not a prime subject of research and publication.

When a young offender comes to the attention of the police their actions are regulated by the Penal Code. Criminal and procedural matters were discussed above. Criminal procedure is provided for by the much-amended Act I of 1973. The most important differences are described in Chapter XIII. Some of the key aspects include:

- The rules of criminal procedure against juvenile delinquents are applicable for a person of juvenile age who has acquired adult status by marriage or has passed age eighteen after committing a delinquency.
- Provisions of Chapter XIII do not apply for those who committed the offence partly before and partly after passing eighteen years of age (Article 292).
- A juvenile delinquent can not be ruled to pay a fine without a trial.
- Prosecution should be undertaken by a juvenile prosecutor appointed by the supervisory prosecutor. The juvenile prosecutor is obliged to be involved in all the phases of the trial. A juvenile delinquent can not be subject to (private) accusation (Article 295).
- In the first and second instance trials (with the exception of trial by the Supreme Court) the court is appointed by the minister of justice and acts as a juvenile court. One of the lay assessors of the first instance procedure should be a teacher (Article 296).
- A defence attorney should mandatorily participate in procedures against juvenile delinquents (Article 298).
- The juvenile delinquent's guardian should be summoned as a witness so that the character, the level of intellectual development, and general background of the juvenile be better revealed (Article 301).
- Pre-trial confinement of a juvenile delinquent is justified only in exceptional cases. Juvenile delinquents should be separated from adults during such confinement (Article 302). This is an open process, the media and the public are allowed to attend juvenile proceedings unless the court (i.e., judge) rules otherwise.
- The court passes a sentence to confine the juvenile delinquent to a reformatory institution. The sentence, however, does not stipulate that the delinquent is guilty (Article 305).

For criminal procedures the interior minister's precept regarding investigation (Precept No. 40 of 1987 of the Interior Minister) is followed. Some of the key procedural elements include:

- In Hungary culpability, a status milder than criminal liability, is from fourteen to eighteen years of age.
- Penal law considers those under fourteen to be children. The status of child excludes criminal liability; therefore in such instances investigation should be denied or stopped and the local guardianship authority should be notified so that it can initiate protective measures.
- Rules pertaining to juvenile delinquents are applicable for suspects who have married or passed eighteen years of age after committing a delinquency.
- If the juvenile delinquent has no defence attorney the police are obliged to call in one and ensure that the defence attorney be present at the first hearing.
- During the procedure the juvenile's legal representative (usually the parent) has the right to speak on behalf of the youth. In case the legal representative is impeached or excluded, the investigative authority should appoint a case guardian through the local guardianship authority.
- In juvenile criminal procedures the suspect's age, character, intellectual development, and living conditions are significant subjects of evidence. To this end:
  - the child's custodian should testify as to the conditions of the child's upbringing. No such testimony can be refused.
  - a case survey should be prepared which provides a truthful picture of the juvenile's character and living conditions.
  - reports should be requested from the school and the employer.
  - in case there is an indication or antecedence of mental disorder, the expert opinion of a psychologist or special education teacher should be obtained.
- The legal representative of the juvenile delinquent and, if needed, a psychologist or another expert, may be present at the hearing.
- In case the juvenile suspect is seriously endangered, if he or she left his or her environment or if he or she would be homeless once released from the pre-trial confinement, the juvenile should be taken temporarily to a state child and juvenile protection institution.

- In the event of confinement, the family or legal representative should be notified without delay and the juvenile delinquent should be separated from adult criminals.
- A child or juvenile person who is found loitering should be taken to the nearest police station if their home is not closer or if they can not be handed over to their legal guardian.
- In case the criminal procedure against a juvenile delinquent reveals an infringement in connection with the youth's education, employment, or other relevant activity, the relevant authority should be notified in accordance with Article 117 of the relevant Decree of the Interior Minister.
- Upon release from a prison or reformatory institute, it is decreed that an effort should be made to provide support. Needless to say, such attempts face tremendous difficulties.

Collectively, the above points embrace some of the fundamental corporatist views, especially with reference to their general features, tasks, and objectives. This is partially due to financial constraints as evidenced by the lack of sufficient staff, automobiles, and time to address the caseloads. In addition, the rules are not taken seriously and the delinquents and their families are seldom aware of their rights. Therefore, only in a few cases are the regulations followed. This is possible since there is no monitoring system or regular supervision. Even in the known and reported cases the general response is: "theoretically it is alright, but the circumstances are inadequate to meet the standards." Subsequently, our system functions perhaps more as a crime control model out of necessity than by design.

The Actors

As can be seen from the above description, the intent of the interior ministry is to not only hold juveniles accountable for their action but to provide special support. To this end there are literally hundreds of associations and foundations lawfully registered to address these needs. Unfortunately, these intentions remain unfulfilled. Nevertheless, it can be argued that the Hungarian judiciary system essentially conforms with the minimum standards stipulated by the Beijing Rules. In particular, the relevant laws in force provide for the special treatment of juvenile delinquents in terms of material, procedural, and punitive respects. However, on the basis of Hungarian legal material, legal application and correctional practices, it can be said that the Hungarian penal judiciary system is an attenuated variation of the same system relating to adult offenders. In practice the juvenile system does not a represent a separate system as is characterized by other modern social states (Lévai, 1994).

As noted above, the law provides provisions stating that juveniles be treated differently when being investigated by the police. Unfortunately, police investigations very often do not observe the rules relating to the notification and presence of the legal representative or the guardian or the involvement of a defence attorney. In fact there is often no real connection between the social protection system and the investigators and procedure officers during the investigation and the criminal procedure. Therefore, contrary to the stated objectives, juveniles seldom have a chance to obtain professional help. Even the probation officer, who should be notified immediately after a youth has been charged, usually does not find out about the case until after the charge has been laid. In this way the probation officer is in no position to provide early assistance to either the released suspect or to the suspect during pre-trial confinement.

So, contrary to Beijing Rule 1.3, the Hungarian model of juvenile justice does not provide adequate support for juvenile offenders. In fact some schools expel the student even at the slightest suspicion and stigmatization almost automatically occurs. At the same time, due to the underdeveloped local supply system, real family assistance stands no chance against this, or indeed, at any later stage. Overburdened probation officers and patrons, the lack of professional standards, and the scarcity of assistance reduce the efficiency of protective efforts.

Although no data prevail, on the basis of the social and cultural background of the perpetrators, we can say that the defence attorney plays only a marginal role in protecting the rights of suspected juvenile offenders. A defence attorney is called in only when the family cannot provide their own attorney. As for the police, their efficiency is indicated by the number of cases detected. The police have no vested interest in giving the juvenile suspect any opportunity to prove their innocence.

Before youths even get to court their basic rights are often dramatically compromised. The situation is further undermined by the juvenile court judges. Judges receive no special initial or in-service training; nor do they consider it their duty to explore areas beyond the scope of general law. Finally, specially trained probation officers, patrons, and social workers are few and far between; therefore, the preparation of cases and the exploration of circumstances is highly arbitrary.

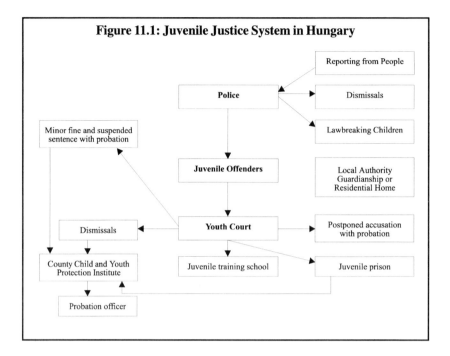

Figure 11.1: Juvenile Justice System in Hungary

Pre-trial

Pre-trial confinement takes place with only a few of the delinquents, in 1994 4.8% of the juvenile suspects (N=822) were subject to inadequate confinement. This is contrary to the international agreements signed by Hungary. Act XLI of 1995 stipulates that after July 1, 1996, wings and units suitable for pre-trial confinement of juvenile delinquents should be set-up in three reformatory institutions and a special children's home. This is an important issue because pre-trial confinement is very often prolonged, there are many juvenile suspects spending six to twelve months in confinement and they have no access to a meaningful occupation or education during this period. Given the lack of constructive outlets and otherwise poor conditions, pre-trial detention can produce more problems for the youth than before they entered the system.

In accordance with the Beijing Rules promulgated in Hungary by Act LXIV of 1991, the signatory states should make every effort to "... take steps towards the handling of the suspect or guilty child's case without a judiciary procedure, while maintaining full observance of human rights and legal guarantees" (Paragraph 3 of Article 40 of UN Resolution 40/33/1985). Accordingly, young delinquents should be treated in accordance with their situation and the crime they committed—"the principle of proportionality".

The intent is to focus on the needs of the youth as opposed to exacting "just dessert". This, unfortunately, is by no means fully implemented in Hungary. It is particularly true for the lack of protection, guardianship, control, counselling, release on parole, family care, general professional educational programs, and non-institutional solutions. It is not only the lack of institutions, professional experts, and financial resources that prevails; professional conviction and attitude are likewise non-existent.

Juvenile (In)justice

Owing to the excessive burdens on the police and courts, the investigation and trial of cases are highly prolonged. It is not infrequent for two or three years to elapse between the delinquency and the court ruling; therefore, any educational impact involved in the ruling is dissipated. Moreover, the juvenile delinquent who has passed eighteen years of age can no longer be confined in a reformatory institution.

The practice of adjudication is influenced by the fact that the duration of pre-trial confinement does not count towards the term of reformatory confinement. On July 1, 1996 the rule was changed. Until then judges generally felt that juveniles were at a disadvantage and therefore often passed sentences that allowed for immediate release. A direct consequence of this attitude was the extremely low number of delinquents referred to reformatory institutions.

Probation and patronage of young adults extend beyond the time when they reach adulthood. This is partly justified by the relevant provisions in force (the Penal Code increased the age of probation and patronage from eighteen to twenty-four years). The best example is the fact that young adults in state care can remain in the relevant institution until they are twenty-four years old. This, unfortunately, marked the low level of efficiency of the system and a lack of professional insight. And even though point 3.3 of the Beijing Rules stipulates that provisions pertaining to juvenile delinquents should be expanded to so-called young adult perpetrators, Lévai (1994:343) notes: "the psychological traits and social position of a young person around 20 is closer to those of a 17-18 year old than to those of an adult if only a few years older." Nevertheless, it would be inexpedient to increase the top age limit from the point of view of criminal policy, as the institutional system that serves for re-socialization would thereby be extended to incorporate a criminally active and sociologically and criminologically heterogeneous group. If twenty-one years of age were the threshold of adulthood in Hungary, the authorities would have to "deal with 15,000 more juvenile delinquents per year" (Lévai, 1994).

Another major area confronting the proper handling of juvenile cases concerns probation, suspension of confinement, parole, and the provisional release from a correctional institution, which involves a probation officer commissioned by the court. Aside from a general lack of proper training, there has been much debate about the role of probation within the judiciary profession. Foreign models of probation differ and there are several different approaches in Hungary. The major weakness and difference of the present system are that the employer of the probation officer is a county institution (i.e., Child and Juvenile Protection Institute), but the officer is called in by the local government or the court. In this way, although the probation officers work in the same institution as family social workers and foster parent supervisors, they have no formal contact with them, even if the family is the same. In addition, there is no cooperation between the school, educational advisory centres, and family assistance centres, even though the latter are equally maintained by the local government. Even if one of the parties was in favour of a cooperation, this cannot be forced, so the problem tends to go unaddressed.

Participation in education, finding a job and a place to live are objectives which are difficult to achieve under the current social and political environment in Hungary. This has been particularly so since the late 1980s. Earlier being unemployed was in itself punishable ("penal idleness", Article 266 of the Penal Code, punishable with thirty days imprisonment until 1989). Another handicap of efficient probation is the inadequate number of social service agencies, their limited scope of activity, and the lack of cooperation and complex problem management. Consequently, probation is arbitrary and dependent on the persons involved. Family assistance is generally not part of the probation activity and is extended only in a limited way even if other problems (e.g., social and child safety) prevail.

Correctional education takes place in one of the three reformatory institutions. Two of these centres are for boys while the third is an old educational institute used for female offenders. The reformatories all come under the auspices of the ministry of welfare, but they perform their tasks in relative isolation. For example, court documents are often supplied months after the arrival of the young offender. Therefore, it is no surprise that they are able to provide only marginal re-socialization services.

By international standards the average length of incarceration could be considered severe. With confinements averaging one-and-a-half years, their educational value is questionable. Contacts with the local social system are arbitrary and lack professional protocol. Juvenile delinquents in state custody are often "forgotten" by the earlier protection institution and the county Child and Juvenile Protection Institute. For them rehabilitation is almost hopeless, as most of them have nowhere to go and their family ties are uncertain or non-existent. Escapes are frequent and many of them commit delinquencies while deserting. They escape in order to prolong the confinement, for once out, they have no home, no job, and no food. The number of those who would like to live there has been increasing while fewer of them are capable of leaving. And while the centres have a beneficial correctional educational impact on the youth, many experts question their location. Two of the facilities are located in Budapest and the third on the outskirts of the city. In general the lack of national distribution means that family contact and other opportunities for rehabilitation are very difficult. For those juveniles who are held at one of the three centres, a lack of resources makes it difficult to allow weekend leave.

From an organizational perspective it has been questioned whether these correctional institutions should belong to the ministry of justice, the ministry of education, or the ministry of welfare. The argument revolves around who should be responsible for the welfare of juvenile delinquents whose problems are professionally considered to be social problems that are similar to those of children.

In addition to a large number of juveniles being classified as mentally challenged, the number underprivileged and under-socialized young person are also over-represented among the juvenile offender population. Gypsies (see Box 11.3) are also over-represented. But for political reasons it has remained a delicate issue since they have not been officially recognized for the past forty years. And while there is no official data describing the size of the Gypsy (referred to as Romany) population, it is a well-known fact that 60% of the Gypsy population live below the poverty line and as most of them are unskilled, they were the first to lose their jobs as a consequence of the industrial crisis. The number of juveniles who drop out of school is higher than the national average while less continue studying in secondary and higher educational institutions. The proportion of Gypsy children in child protection institutions is 25-80%; this rate varies significantly from county to county. One reason for the great variation is that as a result of forced assimilation, identity and culture were never emphasized and masses of children come from families where everyday customs and education differ from "the good Hungarian practice". The risks for criminalization in these instances are very high. The children have lost their point of reference and their beloved ones, and find themselves in an environment where they have no chance to succeed. As a result they become marginalized and lose the protection of a community. Furthermore, because of social and cultural isolation, many young Gypsies lack proper family socialization. In fact many Gypsy delinquents are considered by psychologists to be mentally handicapped. Their problem is not solved by probation or correctional education; quite the contrary. Prejudices are tangible and almost impossible to prove; on the other hand, special care and assistance does not prevail. Nor is there any affirmative action in theory or in practice. Equity before the law inevitably recreates inequalities.

Box 11.3 Gypsies in Hungary

Based on the work of a German philologist in 1780, Gypsies appear to have originated from India around 1000 A.D. They were driven out of India by the Tamerlane and moved westward. Earliest records of their presence in Europe (Mount Athos—Greece) was around 1100 A.D. By the late 1400s most Europeans knew them as vagabonds, fortune-tellers, singers, dancers, beggars, and charming tricksters. Unlike many other countries, Gypsies were never ostracized in Hungary. They were tolerated and generally embraced. In fact they served Hungary in times of war and espoused hatred toward Hungarian neighbours—even the Romanian Gypsies. They can be found in both rural and urban settings throughout Hungary (Bercovivi, 1983).

Recent Demographic Trends

The number of delinquencies committed during the age of culpability (i.e., in childhood rather than at juvenile age from the point of view of penal law) is an indication of the future trend of juvenile delinquency.

In Hungary, the number of delinquencies involving public indictment was 120,880 in 1975. In 1993 this number increased to 400,935 (an increase of 231.7%). In 1975 the number of known perpetrators of delinquencies involving public indictment was 72,049, while in 1993 the same figure was 122,621 (an increase of 70.2%). There are two possible explanations for the delinquency rate changes from 1975 to 1993. First, the number of those who committed multiple delinquencies has increased, and secondly the efficiency of detection may have decreased thereby enabling youth to commit multiple delinquencies.

Meanwhile, Gonczol (1995) suggests that the increase in delinquency may be a by-product of the new market economy of the early 1990s and all the social problems it created (e.g., unemployment and loosening of social bonds as both parents entered the work force).

Child Delinquency
The number of child delinquents increased from 2557 in 1975 to 4128 in 1993 (an increase of 61.4%). The increase was 13.2% in 1990-1991 and peaked in 1992 with 4492 delinquents. Most of the young offenders did not commit the offence on their own. As with juveniles, the most common offences committed by children were property-related offences. There was a 138.8% increase from 1975 to 1995. Since 1990 property-related offences have constituted approximately 90% of all offences committed by child delinquents. The period since the late 1970s was marked by spiralling motorization in Hungary. Consequently, the number of delinquents involved in traffic crimes grew from 301 to 663 in 1993. And while there have been more personal crimes committed by child delinquents and juvenile delinquents, the numbers have not changed significantly. The other major delinquent activity areas include theft and burglary involving theft. In recent years, sixty to seventy young persons have been charged with assault-related offences.

Juvenile Delinquency
The number of juvenile delinquencies increased from 7258 in 1975 to 14,321 in 1995 (doubling in twenty years—see Table 11.3). This is a higher increase than that of the number of adult perpetrators (from 72,049 to 122,621, an increase of 70.2%). And while the proportionate rate of increase when compared to the delinquent population was not as extreme (i.e., from 10.1% in 1975 to 12.2% in 1993), the actual figures can be significantly higher, as the rate of detection of juvenile delinquents dropped significantly between 1975 and 1993 (see Table 11.1).

The number of juvenile delinquents per 10,000 juvenile inhabitants was 161 in 1985 and increased to 217.4 by 1994. The differing rate of increase is due, in part, to the fact that the increase followed the general demographic upswing, which peaked as a result of two successive demographic interventions (in 1950-54, then in 1972-76). Consequently, the juvenile population peaked at the turn of the 1980s and the early 1990s. This demographic asymmetry has its primary impact in the high number of young adult delinquents.

The number of crimes against public order has increased (1098 in 1975 to 1593 in 1995). While not appearing to be significant, this figure is even more remarkable when one takes into account that after the political changeover, the category of forbidden crossing of the border, a former offence, ceased to be punishable.

Table 11.3: The Number of Children Delinquents and Percentages According to Criminal Actions

Number and Rates of Children Delinquents

	1990		1991		1992		1993		1994	
	number	%	number	%	number	%	number	%	number	%
Total	3,744	100.0	4,240	100.0	4,488	100.0	4,128	100.0	4,168	100.0
Against Persons	76	2.0	89	2.1	108	2.4	96	2.3	128	3.1
Manslaughter	2	0.1	1	0.0	1	0.0	1	0.0	3	0.1
Bodily Harm	52	1.4	63	1.5	76	1.7	62	1.5	94	2.3
Traffic Crime	75	2.0	54	1.3	50	1.1	66	1.6	94	2.3
Against Moral	34	0.9	22	0.5	34	0.8	30	0.7	55	1.3
Sexual Abuse	6	0.2	9	0.2	14	0.3	4	0.1	12	0.3
Fighting and Rioting	97	2.6	132	3.1	148	3.3	161	3.9	249	6.0
From this: Rioting	46	1.2	51	1.2	73	1.6	80	1.9	130	3.1
Against Property	3,457	92.3	3,938	92.9	4,147	92.4	3,764	91.2	3,640	87.3
From this: Stealing	1,835	49.0	2,079	49.0	2,265	60.5	2,006	48.6	1,904	45.7
Break in	1,026	27.4	1,120	26.4	1,086	24.2	1,117	27.1	1,062	25.5
Robbery	100	2.7	157	3.7	174	3.9	168	4.1	151	3.6
Other	5	0.1	5	0.1	2	0.0	11	0.3	2	0.0

Table 11.4: Juvenile Delinquency 1985-1994

Year	All known delinquents	If 1985= 100.0%	Number of Delinquents/ 10,000 inhabitants	Juvenile Delinquents number	rates	If 1985= 100.0%	Delinquents/ 10,000 juvenile inhabitants	Number of child delinquents	If 1985= 100.0%
1985	85,766	100.0	80.5	9,449	11.0	100.0	161.0	3,745	100.0
1986	93,176	108.6	87.6	10,554	11.3	179.5	4,064	108.5	
1987	92,643	108.0	87.2	9,887	10.7	104.6	168.0	3,302	88.2
1988	82,329	96.0	77.6	8,667	10.5	146.4	146.4	3,652	97.5
1989	88,932	103.7	84.0	9,661	10.9	102.2	154.8	3,723	99.4
1990	112,254	130.9	108.2	12,848	11.4	136.0	191.6	3,744	100.0
1991	112,835	143.2	118.6	13,508	11.0	143.0	192.5	4,240	113.2
1992	132,644	154.7	128.3	15,476	11.7	163.8	214.5	4,488	119.8
1993	122,621	143.0	118.9	15,001	12.2	158.8	213.9	4,128	110.2
1994	119,494	139.3	116.3	14,479	12.1	153.2	217.4	4,168	111.3

As is the case in most other parts of the world, youth crime in Hungary has been increasing at an uncomfortable rate. And while the specific indicators may vary somewhat, the primary causes reflect a lack of social control, lack of conformity and uniformity, as well as a general condition of social upheaval— a state of anomie. Furthermore, it would appear that little progress has been made to adopt a social welfare model of juvenile justice. This has been reflected in the police data that indicate an increase in more violent behavior.

Child and Juvenile Victims of Crime
In Hungary victimization data on juvenile crime has only been collected since 1988. In that year, 105,532 offended parties were registered, of whom 2000 were children, and 3876 were of juvenile age. The number of offended parties increased to 230,915 by 1993 (an increase of 118.8%), of whom 2626 (30.8%) were children and 7160 (84.7%) of juvenile age. While the total number of offended parties was highest in 1991, the number of offended children was highest in 1990 and the number of offended juvenile parties has increased steadily since the beginning of the period under examination.

Examining the victims of particular delinquencies, it can be stated that:

- The number of offended parties involved in crimes against sexual morals was 445 in 1988 and 412 in 1993. In 1988, 16.9%, and in 1993, 14.3% of the offended parties of such delinquencies were children, while the same figures for offended juvenile parties were 20.7% in 1988 and 28.8% in 1993.
- Offended parties involved in manslaughter or attempted manslaughter were 398 in 1988 and 464 in 1993. The rate of offended children was 11.6% in 1988 and 5.8% in 1993, while the same figures for offended juvenile parties were 1.8% and 1.3% respectively.
- The number of parties offended in intended bodily harm cases was 5580 in 1988 and 8181 in 1993. Children offended constituted 2.4% in 1988 and 1.7% in 1993, while the same figures for offended juvenile parties were 4.5% and 5.5% respectively.

Examination of the relationship between juvenile perpetrators and offended parties reveals that most of them are not acquainted with each other. Those who are acquainted are predominantly schoolmates or related as parent and child.

Current and Projected Trends

Future Directions

There are three major factors that influence the image of delinquency in Hungary:

1. The proportion of the population consisting of youth from the ages of fourteen to eighteen.
2. The legal definition of a juvenile offender. While the current lower age limit is fourteen years of age there has been discussion about lowering it to twelve years.
3. The response of society and the state. How will the state choose to respond to the growing delinquency problem?

The first item pertains to demographic issues, which can not be affected by criminal policy or by general crime prevention. The second factor is subject to debates on codification, which are greatly influenced by the attitude taken towards the third point.

In our opinion delinquencies should be separated as their causes are basically different. Aggressive and brutal crimes, which undermine the system of values of society and the stability of the legal system, should be handled entirely differently. Here the principal task is to protect legal security and values.

Within the sphere of those delinquent acts that do not harm or endanger life or involve theft not motivated by financial gain, these acts should be treated separately. These are crimes that can and are dealt with by society. The third classification of delinquent acts should involve crimes that result in public harm or are motivated by financial gain. For these types of crimes, individuals should be held criminally responsible. Each reflects a different causal relationship and provides alternative options that are in conformity with the legal norms.

Developments and changes currently being perused by Hungary are measured against the country's efforts to be a member of the Council of Europe and a full member of the European Union. As a signatory of a number of international agreements, Hungary has undertaken adherence to, and promulgation of, all of the contracts and conventions adopted by the developed world (Beijing Rules, Riyadh Guidelines, UN Rules regarding the support of juvenile delinquents in confinement, Convention on the Rights of Children—see Introduction). However, there is still a significant discrepancy between the provisions of these agreements and the Hungarian legal practice. On the whole, however, the most up-to-date and widely accepted trend is to decrease the necessity of legal intervention and develop a sensitivity to human dignity and values and the basic liberties of the individual. This points towards the adoption of special laws and procedures, the establishment of special authorities and institutions and favours problem management that excludes court procedure. Should Hungary be able to embrace these, its model of juvenile justice would be more in keeping with the UN recommendation that all countries adopt a social welfare model.

It is encouraging to see that criminal accountability is shifting towards providing education and re-socialization. Similarly, prevention has become more emphatic, as have the use of alternative programs to incarceration. Some of these include: a renewed probation system, cooperation with the supply system (school, local government, family assistance, and other service providers), and the modernization and differentiation of juvenile confinement institutions.

Unfortunately, because of the economic recession and transformation in the wake of the political changeover, many of the above objectives remain conceptual dreams. Our "prematurely born welfare sate" is currently beyond the Hungarian economic development and load-bearing ability. Furthermore, since the media tend to focus on shaping public opinion by offering biased coverage that concentrates primarily on the scandalous aspectof youth's behaviour, the public is not likely to be sympathetic to the plight of young people. These circumstances are further undermined by the social problems that have emerged after the introduction of the market economy. Overall, it is questionable when and to what extent the justice administration and the parliament will be prepared to implement full-fledged reform. For example, the bill on child protection has been a proverbial political "ping-pong" for the past ten years and alternative punishment for young offenders has not received widespread public support. And given that there is no money to sponsor pilot projects, it appears that change will be slow in coming. However, given the international agreements mentioned above, there is an obligation for legislators to move towards honouring the UN conditions. The need to embrace the agreements is perhaps best conveyed in the following quote:

> The penal system of juvenile delinquency in itself is incapable of offsetting the unfavorable social and economic processes, the disturbances of the child protection system and the lack of social

policy measures and institutions to prevent juvenile delinquency (Lévai, 1994: 345).

Summary

Hungary, while a small country, has a long history of being a tenacious survivor. It has survived attacks from the Tartars, Turks, Habsburgs, and Russians. Hungarian history and character are best exemplified in our national anthem, which describes Hungarians as "people torn by fate".

After the Soviet army liberated Hungary in 1945, the Communists quickly gaine dpower and eliminated free elections and subjected Hungarians to various atrocities. Then in 1956 there was a revolution against Stalinism. Although the uprising was defeated by Soviet troops, Yanos Kadar promised democratic socialism. However, it was not until 1990 that the Communist party voluntarily gave up its autocracy. One of the many by-products of the struggle appears to be the steady growth in crime and delinquency rates. An increasing number of Hungarian scholars also believe that the crime and delinquency problem by the breakdown of society and the inability of state to respond in any concrete way.

As the realities of the economic, political, and social transition in Hungary play a major role in the everyday operation of juvenile justice administration, it should be noted that point 1.5 of the Beijing Rules acknowledges that international agreements can only be implemented within such a context. For example, a bill on child protection has been in the pipeline for ten years and to date it has not been tabled by parliament. And even though Hungary has agreed to move towards a social welfare model, the vanguards of the law do not take the move toward a social welfare model seriously. Since there is no strong advocacy, research and evaluation are non-existent, scandals are investigated only in an extremely limited circle and are considered as isolated instances. In this way there is little chance for influencing public opinion and decision-makers. Therefore, the plight of young offenders, like many social issues in Hungary, will receive only token attention for the near future.

It was also shown in this chapter that delinquency in Hungary is closely linked to social and cultural status (e.g., education, housing, income, and lifestyle). This is particularly evident with the Gypsy population, but it has also been found to be true of most poverty stricken areas throughout the country. Since 1988 delinquency rates have increased and the incidence of violent crime has grown most dramatically. Gonczol (1995:13) reports that when compared to a half-dozen westernized countries, Hungary offered "the least to the young in terms of long-term prospects." We have noted that educational training is very poor, and (elementary) school dropout rates are high. For example, in 1990, 29% had failed to complete elementary school. For a country trying to become an extension of the market economy, a population of marginally educated youth can hardly help the cause.

The contributing factors to delinquency in Hungary fit some of the classical sociological indicators found in most textbooks on the subject. The breakdown in social bonds and a sense of anomie are well recognized by most criminology scholars in our country. These are issues not commonly known in Hungary prior to independence. The social, cultural, and political price has been great. But we believe that we can not return to the former punitive and oppressive regime of the past. Rather, Hungarians must recognize they have endured many "storms" and this is but one more challenge that we must rise above. Through bringing into effect the agreements signed and through discussion with other countries we can, and must, begin to systematically introduce comprehensive social policy to meet the general aim of promoting juvenile welfare.

References

Bercovici, K. (1983). *Gypsies*. NY: Greenwich House.

Criminal statistics. (1994). Budapest, Hungary.

Gonczol, K. (1995). Anxiety over crime increase. *CJ Europe*, 5(1), 9-16.

Lévai, M. (1994). *A fiatalkorú bûnelkövetôkkel szemben kiszabható büntetô szankciók reformja*. Reform of sanctions applicable for juvenile delinquents/ Magyar Jog No.6: 341.

National crime prevention program. (1996). Draft manuscript. National Institute for Criminology and Criminalistics. Budapest, Hungary.

Paragraph 3 of Article 40 of UN Resolution 40/33/1985.

Statistical yearbook. (1995). Budapest, Hungary.

United Nations Resolution. 44/33/1985.